D1621145

ECONOMY AND SOCIETY
IN ANCIENT GREECE

ECONOMY AND SOCIETY IN ANCIENT GREECE

by M. I. FINLEY

EDITED WITH AN INTRODUCTION BY
BRENT D. SHAW
AND RICHARD P. SALLER

1981
CHATTO & WINDUS
LONDON

Published by Chatto & Windus Ltd
40 William IV Street
London WC2N 4DF

Clarke, Irwin & Co. Ltd
Toronto

BRITISH LIBRARY CATALOGUING IN PUBLICATION DATA
Finley, M. I.
Economy and society in Ancient Greece.
1. Social structure
I. Title   II. Shaw, Brent D.   III. Saller, Richard P.
305'.0938'5   HD650.5S6

ISBN 0 7011 2549 7

Printed in Great Britain by
Redwood Burn Limited
Trowbridge

CONTENTS

EDITORS' PREFACE

The work of Sir Moses Finley on the social and economic history of the ancient world, and particularly the world of the Greeks, has now become so well known that it needs little introduction. General readers and college students are probably most familiar with the books he has written or edited since the publication of his pathbreaking *World of Odysseus* in 1954: *The Ancient Greeks, Aspects of Antiquity, The Ancient Economy*, and *Democracy Ancient and Modern*, to name a few. However, readers may not be acquainted with the special studies of Greek social and economic institutions that have laid the groundwork for the books themselves. Sometimes, because of the use of Greek and Latin sources, they are not easily understood by the general reader, and often they have appeared in journals not ordinarily consulted by the student of the classics. Also, the simple fact that they are widely dispersed in time and through a large number of journals makes access to them difficult, even for the professional historian.

With these ideas in mind we decided to present the general reader, the student, and the scholar with a representative collection of what we believe to be Sir Moses Finley's most important papers in three areas of his research: the community of the Greek city or *polis*, the problem of slavery and dependent labour in the ancient world, and the Mycenaean and Homeric worlds of early Greece. As with most selections, this one has been somewhat arbitrary, but generally we were guided by considerations of relevance to current student interests and the degree of accessibility of the original publications.

In an attempt to demystify the world of academic literature for the general reader, we have tried, as far as possible, to avoid the obscurantism of abbreviations, foreign terms, and difficult annotation. In as many cases as seemed reasonable, we have translated passages and terms that Sir Moses originally cited in languages other than English. Titles and cross-references have been reduced to an easy-to-use note and reference format, uniform for all chapters. Minor corrections, additions and deletions have been made by the author in all chapters. Note should be taken of one major change: the chapter entitled 'Debt-bondage and the problem of slavery', originally published in French as 'La servitude pour dettes', now appears for the first time in its full English text.

Our introductory essay attempts both to trace the formative steps in the development of Finley's thinking as an historian and to relate this development to the articles collected in this book. We have also included, as part of this aim, a comprehensive bibliography of Professor Finley's writings. The section on books and articles is complete (except that the numerous translations into foreign-language editions have been omitted), but the section on his reviews and essays could only be selective in view of their considerable number; in the latter case we have tried to include representative works from all his fields of interest from the early 1930s to the present. It is hoped that this bibliography will assist the reader, and perhaps provoke further interest in pursuing Finley's work beyond the limits of this volume. Finally, especially to help the student, we have appended at the end of the notes to most chapters a list of important works by other scholars that have appeared on the subject since the publication of the original article, and have attempted to indicate their general relevance to the approaches taken by Finley.

Preparing a volume of fourteen articles covering three decades of Finley's most important work from the early 1950s to the later 1970s has been work of the most pleasurable sort, in which we received valuable assistance from several quarters. Not least was that offered by Sir Moses himself, who graciously acceded to our request to undertake what we perceived to be a most valuable and much needed project. Throughout he not only has offered his help in matters of detail, but, more broadly, has insisted on the complete independence and freedom of action of the editors. The task of writing the bibliographical addenda was made easier by the suggestions of Dr J. T. Killen (Jesus College, Cambridge) and Mr Paul Millett (University of Leicester). Professor David Cohen (Berkeley) kindly read the Introduction and suggested many improvements. We also wish to thank Professors Meyer Reinhold (Missouri-Columbia) and Martin Ostwald (Swarthmore College), who offered valuable information in conversation about the study of ancient history at Columbia in the 1930s and later.

Brent D. Shaw *University of Lethbridge*
Richard P. Saller *Swarthmore College*

September 1980

EDITORS' INTRODUCTION

Arnaldo Momigliano, in assessing a group of books published by M. I. Finley in the early 1970s, opened his review with the comment that when Finley moved to Great Britain from the United States in 1954 he was already 'the best living social historian of Greece and the one most prepared to face the methodological problems which social history implies'.[1] One of the most important characteristics distinguishing Finley's work is indeed the sophistication of method displayed in his analysis of ancient societies. And yet, as Momigliano also points out, he 'seldom raises questions of method as such'.[2] Thus it is our purpose in this introduction to draw out and isolate some of his methodological practices, and to trace the intellectual roots of his peculiar analytical approach that lie in the less well known, early part of his career in the United States. This aim presents difficulties, in part because Finley does not fit neatly into any single intellectual tradition, and also because he did not publish extensively during the formative years of his career.

Having received his B.A. *magna cum laude* from Syracuse University in 1927 at the age of fifteen, Finley moved to New York to begin studies at Columbia University, where he received an M.A. in Public Law in 1929. Following his graduation he took up a research post with a then current project, the *Encyclopaedia of the Social Sciences*.[3] After a three-year stint in the project, he became a research assistant to Professor A. A. Schiller in Roman Law at Columbia (1933–4) and in the following year was awarded a Research Fellowship in the Department of History (1934–5). From the same date he also held a part-time teaching post in history at the City College of New York which he was not to relinquish until 1942. It was Schiller, according to Finley, who gave him his 'first realisation of the proper place of legal studies in the field of history'.[4] The first item in Finley's bibliography is an article concerning Roman law and administration, a study of the legal status of 'orders' issued by the Roman emperor (*mandata principum*). The legal training is also evident in the sophistication and sureness with which he later treated Greek legal material (as in *Studies in Land and Credit in Ancient Athens, 500–200 B.C.* and the review of Pringheim's book on *The Greek Law of Sale*, arguably one of the most important articles published on Greek law in recent decades). That his teacher in ancient history at the graduate level at Columbia was W. L. Westermann is also significant, since Westermann already had a long-established interest in the specialised study of slavery and other forms of dependent labour in the ancient world, especially in Ptolemaic Egypt. No less important is the fact that his graduate education took place not in a Classics Faculty but in History, where the standards and approaches proper to that discipline were stressed:

As a graduate student at Columbia University in the early 1930s, I was brought up on Weber and Marx, on Gierke and Maitland in legal history, on Charles Beard and Pirenne and Marc Bloch. The explanation is simply that I was trained in the faculty of history, and these were among the writers whose ideas and methods were in the atmosphere of historical study, partly in lectures but even more in endless conversation with other students.[5]

This description of the early steps in Finley's academic career gives little idea of the formative atmosphere in which his fundamental interests were developed. A variety of factors in the 1930s produced an intellectual and emotional intensity in some New York academic circles that has not been matched since, except perhaps during the Vietnam War. The economic collapse at home and the spread of fascism in Europe seemed urgently to demand both intellectual analysis and political action. The traditional structure of higher learning seemed to offer neither:

As I think back to this period, I have the firm impression that lectures and seminars were pretty securely locked in an ivory tower. By this I do not refer to the political views of the professors of history, which varied considerably, but to the irrelevance of their professional work as historians. The same lectures and seminars could have been given – and no doubt were – in an earlier generation, before the First World War. . . . There was the same pervasive impression that the study of history was an end in itself. Whereas we, who were growing up in a difficult world with problems we believed to be urgent and to demand solutions, sought explanation and understanding of the present in our study of the past.[6]

The recourse, then as now, was to a process of self-education amongst the students themselves, a process of dialectical learning often more fecund than the formal instruction of the classroom. In the milieu of the early 1930s it is quite understandable that this dialogue demanded a debate with Marx:

And so we went off on our own to seek in books what we thought we were not getting in lectures and seminars. We read and argued about Marc Bloch and Henri Pirenne, Max Weber, Veblen and the Freudians, such analysts on the right as Mosca (on political parties) and Pareto (though I must confess I found him unrewarding and quickly gave up). And we studied Marx and the Marxists: not just *Das Kapital*, not even primarily *Das Kapital*, but also Marxist historical and theoretical works.

Marxism is therefore built into my intellectual experience, what the Greeks would have called my *paideia*. Marx, like the other thinkers I have mentioned, put an end to any idea that the study of history is an autonomous activity and to the corollary that the various aspects of human behaviour – economic, political, intellectual, religious – can be seriously treated in isolation.[7]

The context in which Finley and his fellow students absorbed Marxist thought is to be noted: even to the critical contemporary student and certainly to those who later reflected on the matter, much of the 'left-oriented' thought of the times was part of an unsophisticated and not well-thought-out (even, one might say, simplistic) reaction to the perceived threat of fascist power and ideology.[8]

Adding to the general intellectual ferment in New York during this same period, and bringing an air of direct action to concerns over the economic and political crises of the time, was the emigration of many of the best minds from fascist Germany. Particularly important from our point of view is the move of the *Institut für Sozialforschung* (The Institute for Social Research) under the guidance of Max Horkheimer, who had been its director since 1930, from Frankfurt to New York in 1934.[9] The Institute became affiliated with Columbia University, and Finley became involved in various Institute activities, participating in seminars and writing reviews for the Institute's journal, the *Zeitschrift für Sozialforschung*.[10] From 1937 to 1939 the Institute employed him as a factotum, a job which included the translation of works into English that it wished to present to an American audience.

Horkheimer and his colleagues understood their mission in New York to be the continuation of the German intellectual tradition of the left which was being destroyed in Hitler's Germany. The tradition of philo-sophical, historical and social thought which it represented derived from three distinct post-Hegelian developments in German thought: Kantian epistemology, the rise of phenomenology (especially that of Dilthey), and the materialist critique of Hegel, notably that by Marx. To be part of this tradition entailed participation in a highly sophisticated series of critiques concerning the philosophy of history and methodology –

critiques of much greater depth than those normally engaged in by working historians.[11] Of course, it would be impossible to summarise in a few pages the complex of ideas generated by members of the Institute for Social Research, which were never, in any case, uniform, or their positions in various *combats*. Nevertheless, it might be possible to suggest a few general characteristics central to their analyses that are also reflected in Finley's writing.

The thinking of the Institute was basically Marxist, although it tended to avoid current doctrines of dogmatic orthodox Marxism in favour of extending the dialectic present in the works of Marx himself through a critique both of his writings and of the more philosophically oriented post-Marxian tradition. However, one of Marx's basic demands – that society be viewed as an interrelated whole – was accepted as a common fundamental principle. The members' works constituted attempts to explain the ways in which different elements of society interacted with each other and how these interactions produced change – in short, an examination of historical dialectic. In particular there was a continuation of Marx's interest in the connection between forms of economic and social relationships and the ideological and cultural expressions of a society. But in contrast with the orthodox Marxism of the day, Horkheimer and his colleagues refused either to accept a simplistic relationship between material base and ideological superstructure or to assume the primacy of economic forms (the so-called 'base'), and instead called for an interdisciplinary approach to a holistic analysis of society.[12]

At least in its early days, the Institute was in the mainstream of the west European Marxist tradition also in its expectation of radical social change, including the imminent collapse of the capitalist system. It was argued that the intellectual, whatever he thought to the contrary, could not be a detached observer: he must engage in *praxis*, action that would bring about change.[13] The Institute's members, for the most part, refused to speculate about what would come after the revolutions; or rather, they saw their job to be the application of critical theory to reveal the contradictions in capitalist society that would of themselves produce the major changes. Of special interest for our purposes are Horkheimer's comments about freedom. In his view, the nineteenth-century liberal idea of 'freedom from' (interference, prohibition, domination, exploitation) was to be replaced by the more positive ideal of 'freedom to' (i.e. participate in a rational society). As an illustration of what he had in mind, Horkheimer pointed to the ideal of the Greek *polis*, but without slaves.[14]

Brief and inadequate as this summary of Institute thinking is, it is nevertheless suggestive of the general intellectual context in which some of Finley's basic ideas took shape. It has overtones of and connections with phenomenology, though clearly not with the uncritical emotional-empathetic variety of which Finley himself is unsparingly and devastatingly critical.[15]

These influences can be discerned in a marked shift in the form and content of his earliest published works. Finley's first articles, published in 1934–5, display the traditional interests and approaches of the classical scholar. 'Mandata Principum' (1934) sought to provide 'a thorough examination of all the available references . . . to mandata' on the grounds that 'such a study would throw considerable light on the still clouded problems of the general classification of imperial constitutions and their validity as sources of law'.[16] In his second article, 'Emporos, naukleros, and kapelos' (1935), some of Finley's enduring interests begin to appear: Weber and Hasebroek are cited along with Oertel and Pöhlmann on the problem of the relevancy of 'capitalistic' as a category for analysing the ancient Greek economy, and the argument begins with a lament about the inappropriate imposition of 'modern channels of thought . . . and terminology'. Yet it is fair to say that the approach of the article, written under Westermann's aegis, is more or less traditional: all the uses of the Greek words for 'trader' in its title are examined in order to test possible distinctions among them – predominantly a philological exercise.

Finley's next full article did not appear until almost two decades later (1953), but the development of his ideas and specifically the influences of his early study of Marx and the fathers of sociology, and his association with the Institute can be traced in several reviews published between 1935 and 1941. In the first, published in the Zeitschrift für Sozialforschung (1935), Finley praised the first ten volumes of the Cambridge Ancient History, but pointed to a major shortcoming:

Although the avowed purpose was to create a complete synthesis of ancient history in its manifold phases, much of the work is devoted to political and military minutiae. Art, literature, philosophy, and above all social and economic history are treated as separate details, never as co-ordinated parts of the whole story of the ancient world.[17]

Finley, in short, was calling for a holistic approach. Indeed, in nearly all of his early reviews he criticised the authors' treatment of various facets of life (e.g., religion or labour) as autonomous and isolated, rather than integral and interrelated. The sort of approach for which Finley was asking is exemplified in his own 'Sparta' essay, written thirty years later and reprinted in this volume (Chapter 2). There, peculiar Spartan institutions are treated not in terms of their origins, but in terms of how they functioned together to promote stability or change in the society as a whole.

In this paper and in all his other work Finley has consistently sought to provide the very type of *explanations* for social change that he called for in his early reviews. In a biting critique, the authors of the eleventh volume of the *Cambridge Ancient History* (A D 70–192) are condemned on the grounds that for them 'phenomena like the Roman Empire are so transcendental that man cannot really explain them'.[18] Consequently, the thousand-page volume supplies no answer to the key question: 'How does one reconcile the "peace and prosperity" of the years A D 70–192, proclaimed with such apparent unanimity by contemporary writers, with the rapidity, violence and finality of the ensuing "collapse"?'[19] What Finley was searching for in the book and failed to find was the sort of dialectical explanation that sought to expose the 'negative seeds of change' within the *status quo*. The corollary of the requirement of explanation was a dismissal of simple fact-collecting ('vulgar' positivism) as inadequate: historical knowledge should not be likened to a picture that consists of the accumulation of particular colours at specific points. This theme runs throughout Finley's work and is perhaps expressed most strongly in his essay on the ancient city, published in 1977 (Chapter 1 below).

Another tenet of the Hegel-Marx-Institute tradition adopted by Finley was an insistence on the *historical* nature of human existence and thought. In his 1941 assessment of Will Durant's *The Life of Greece* (part of what was to become the epitome of popular history, 'The Story of Civilisation'), Finley firmly rejected the ahistorical, popular notion of 'an essential sameness of institutions and problems throughout the ages'.[20] The need to distinguish the historical development of ideas, and hence the quite different nature of the institutions forged by ideological and economic forces at different times, is reiterated later in his attack on the reductionism of certain political theories that emphasise structural similarities. As he remarked on the development of ahistorical anthropological analyses, 'I must confess a total inability to appreciate the value of removing all the differences between Bushmen, Pygmies or Eskimos and the United States or the Soviet Union in the search for some notional homologous residue.'[21] Hence Finley frequently stresses the clear differences between archaic and modern societies and thought, especially in his books on democracy and economy.

In his final review of this period, centred on Farrington's study of science and politics in the ancient world, we can see a coalescing of all his concerns over the relations between the material and ideological worlds of antiquity, now with the noticeable influence both of Weber and of Marcuse, whose first English study, *Reason and Revolution*, had just been published in New York (1941). These concerns can be seen perhaps most clearly in Finley's rejection of a purely religious explanation for the importance of the Delphic oracle:

The strength and prestige of the oracle was the work not of the Delphians but of the rulers all over Greece. . . . Their ideologists spread its fame in drama and story, inventing oracles where none existed, explaining away where the priests had guessed badly or had maintained a damaging silence. It would be naive to assume – if we did not have ample evidence to the contrary – that they went to Delphi for advice. They went because it was important, in the long-run interests of their form of social organisation, that the hand of the gods be ever visible on the right side; and because, once having elevated Delphi as they had, they could not safely neglect so powerful an instrument.[22]

The question of the deliberate manipulation of ideological forms is again a central concern of the Frankfurt School, as seen for example in the studies by Walter Benjamin on the media of cultural expression. These forms of control, Finley contends, are particularly open to scrutiny in antiquity:

The literature of antiquity, and especially its prose, requires careful correction in all matters of belief and ideology. Not only was this literature a monopoly in production of the members and proteges of the aristocracy but, with the notable exception of drama, its audience was restricted to the same narrow circle. . . . It thus becomes easy to understand the frank and almost naive cynicism with which ancient writers – confident in the solidarity and discretion of the aristocratic intellectuals – revealed the motives and mechanisms of the manipulation of symbols and superstition.[23]

Finley pursued this theme in a much later study on ideological control, that of censorship, with much the same type of approach.[24] His interest in ideology also drew him to examine the deliberate creation of idealised historical characters and types that could be manipulated in the interest of the dominant social groups. One of these is what Finley calls 'the cult of the peasant', who, though an 'object of contempt' to aristocratic ideologues, could be glorified as 'the true bulwark of society' when it suited their purposes.[25] When choosing a subject for his inaugural lecture at Cambridge University in 1970, Finley again turned to the issue of the manipulation of images, offering a subtle study of the use and distortion of venerated historical figures and institutions, such as Solon or Thomas Jefferson, to justify contemporary ideologies.[26]

True to the Hegel-Marx-Institute tradition, Finley is far more interested than most historians in how contemporary thought about the ancient world fits into the broader intellectual tradition of the West. The essay on the ancient city, for example, sets the stage for further study by a review of the issues as developed by the great sociologists and historians of the late nineteenth and early twentieth centuries. This perspective is necessary because, in Finley's view, the historian takes his direction not only from the ancient sources, but also from his contemporary world – the past is always seen in the context of present categories and debates.[27] As Horkheimer argued, the researcher cannot be a disinterested observer; the intellectual should be engaged in the process of bringing about social change himself. Finley, more than any other ancient historian of his generation in the English-speaking world, has accepted that task imposed by his profession. The practical experience of his early involvement with special teaching projects, and his five-year stint of service in the administrative side of American war relief agencies in 1942–7 no doubt affirmed his attitudes about the critical importance of the practical communication of ideas. On the other hand, it was Finley's participation in politics (in the wider sense of the word) that led to his confrontation with established authority and, ultimately, to his departure from the United States.

The commitment of the professional historian should, in short, extend far beyond the classroom. In both his communication of the historian's ideas to a non-professional audience and his more general critique of ideology, Finley has been tireless, contributing to a wide range of media other than formal academic journals and bluntly attacking popular misconceptions about the ancient world and about the abuse of ancient ideas and institutions in modern ideologies. In reviews written in the 1930s and 1940s, Finley sought to strip away the facade of objectivity by pointing out the connection between current 'politics' and the fundamental premises of the works under review. Durant's treatment of ancient Athens, for example, he identified as part of a more general attempt of 'dabblers in history and historical fiction . . . to tear down the landmarks on the road to Western political democracy'.[28] Finley concluded his review with a call for accurate and intelligent popularisation to take the place of Durant's bestseller. In writing accessible books on the same subject, such as *The Ancient Greeks*, Finley has attempted to illustrate what is needed and actually to put into practice this part of his 'programme'. Many of his writings in popular journals, newspapers, reviews, schooltexts, and magazines, as well as his participation in radio and television, have also been directed to this end.[29] So, too, his long-standing concern with education has advanced beyond the simple recognition of the problems to proscriptive analyses, from the 'crisis' in classical studies generally, to the proper type of training required of ancient historians, and to matters of *curricula* and teaching in secondary schools.[30] Despite these efforts, Finley recently voiced the pessimistic conclusion that there has been 'more retrogression than progress' in historiography since the days of Grote and Mommsen because the gap between professional historians and the intelligent reading public has widened in the twentieth century.[31]

With regard to Finley's post-war career before his move to Britain, we might note finally a few other fundamental influences on his thinking. Prime amongst these is Weberian sociology, discernible in both his social analysis and his methodological theory. In the sphere of social analysis, we see that Finley has throughout all his work clearly rejected the Marxist conception of 'class' as the only, or even the most profitable, way of analysing social relations in ancient society.[32] He has preferred to give primacy to the Weberian concepts of 'order' and 'status', especially the latter, which he considers 'an admirably vague word with a considerable psychological element'.[33] Several of the essays collected in this volume, notably those dealing with slavery and categories of dependent labour, achieve their success by recourse to the metaphor of a 'spectrum of statuses' (see especially Chapters 7-9), along which various social groups can be located in accordance with the rights and duties which they possessed or lacked. This emphasis on a system of social analysis 'with a considerable psychological element' may be connected with the Frankfurt School's stress on the use of social psychology as a bridge between the means of production and the actions of the individual; its analytical value is apparent in his essay on technology (Chapter 11). Here, the lack of technological progress in antiquity is traced back, ultimately, to the use of dependent labour; but the real focus of the article is on the 'non-productive *mentality*' of the wealthy landowners, which provides the causal connection between the widespread recourse to the use of dependent labour on the one hand, and the phenomenon of technological stagnation in the ancient world on the other.[34]

The other element of Weberian influence is in methodology, especially the use of the 'ideal type'. In Finley's writings, however, the 'ideal type' does not appear as a mode of analysis that is distinctly Weberian, but rather has been considerably tempered by and melded with Horkheimer's ideas about induction based on delving into the significant particular. Rather than accumulating masses of atomistic facts, the historian should concentrate on the *typical* experience of concrete facts that elicit a wider general whole. In this 'impressionistic' approach: 'The historian . . . narrates, moving from one concrete datum of experience to the next. The importance of the experiences, together with their mass and their interconnections, evokes the general ideas.'[35]

Finley's readers may at times find this style of argumentation unconventional, puzzling, and even disconcerting. How many ancient historians proceed in their arguments with comments like 'and now I have another story . . .' (p. 192)? Finley does not intend to be frivolous in making such remarks, and on other occasions he offers a more conventional systematic presentation of all the evidence, from which he then generalises (most notably in his study of the *horoi* in *Studies in Land and Credit*). But the occasions on which ancient historians have a reliable and useful sample of data to answer a sociological or economic question about antiquity are rare. Rather than resorting to traditional induction on the basis of a hopelessly inadequate sample, Finley prefers to employ the tactic of delving into the particular to discover the universal. So he presents 'another story' or example, and analyses it to discover general attitudes embedded in it. Needless to say, such a method runs the risk of basing generalisations on unusual examples, but, as Momigliano has observed, Finley is 'a sharp interpreter of ancient texts'.[36] What this means, in part, is that he is extremely sensitive to the context of the story or example and, hence, its probable general field of meaning. This sensitivity allows him to avoid examples whose circumstances would make them atypical. Of course, the method has provoked complaints that it overlooks complexity on the one hand and neglects the unique on the other. The answer to such criticisms can be found in the essay on the ancient city, where Finley defends the use of Weberian 'ideal types' for analytical purposes (Chapter 1). Often, effect is achieved by a polarisation or juxtaposition of opposite types. This sort of elaboration even moves to the extremes of paradox, where the internal opposition of types of behaviour, institutions, or thought within a society compels the analyst to think about the implications of such conflict. So, the discussion of Sparta (Chapter 2) concludes with the comment: 'the final paradox is that her greatest military success destroyed the model military state'.

At the same time, as he was engaged in teaching history at Rutgers University, from 1948 until 1952, Finley maintained his close connections with Columbia, where he was completing his doctoral dissertation on 'Land and Credit in Ancient Athens'. This continuing association brought him into contact with a group of scholars whose views were also to have a substantive effect on his analysis of ancient society. At the centre of the group was the Hungarian exile Karl Polanyi, who had taken up a professorship in economic history at Columbia in 1946, a post he held until his retirement in 1953. Even after that date Polanyi remained at Columbia to become joint director with Conrad Arensberg of an interdisciplinary research project on the 'economic aspects of institutional growth', which continued in operation until 1957–8. The Columbia circle became a centre for the discussion and propagation of Polanyi's 'substantivist' theories on the economy. The project included a wide range of active participants both from Columbia and from other institutions.

Finley's participation in seminars, discussions, and conferences organised by the group left its imprint on his ideas, clearly visible in his interpretation of the society of the 'Dark Age' in *The World of Odysseus*, published at the end of this period (1954). Not only are Polanyi's theories on exchange to be found in that book, but also the first signs of a thorough questioning of the category of 'economic'. Furthermore, some of the fundamental tenets of Finley's *The Ancient Economy* (1973) – e.g. the 'embeddedness' of the economy and the sphere of non-market exchanges – are already apparent in his 1953 study on land, debt and property in ancient Athens (Chapter 4 in this collection). Polanyi was also drawing his attention to comparative materials on non-classical economic regimes of antiquity, such as Koschaker's work on the distribution systems of the Near Eastern palace kingdoms (used extensively in Chapter 12 below). The influence of this group, however, should not be exaggerated: clearly Polanyi made a deep impression, but Finley has been careful on more than one occasion to stress the *suggestive* nature of Polanyi's work, while at the same time distancing himself from all of Polanyi's formal conclusions.[37]

History, as Marc Bloch wrote, is to a certain extent a craft, and each historian develops his own skills which cannot be easily traced to any broad intellectual tradition. Since Finley shows himself to be a skilled practitioner of the craft in the following essays, it is worthwhile to consider some of his positions concerning the practice of ancient history as revealed there.[38]

The methodological issue that has occupied Finley most has been that of how the ancient historian should generalise – a question dealt with explicitly in one of his few methodological essays and implicitly in many reproduced in this volume. In 'Generalisations in Ancient History' (1963) he argued that, whether one admits it or not, the ancient historian does (and must) make use of generalisations. One of the factors that has made Finley such a devastating critic of the works of others is his capacity to identify the (often unstated and unnoticed) underlying generalisations in them, which frequently collapse when exposed and put to the test. The test can be as simple as an appeal to contemporary experience. Note, for example, the response in Chapter 12 to the argument that the language of Linear B could not be Greek because certain symbols could be read as more than one Greek syllable, thus producing ambiguity and confusion. Finley identifies the underlying generalisation – that all systems of writing must be unambiguous – and asks whether it holds for a system used repeatedly by trained scribes in certain narrowly defined contexts. Finley's answer: 'Greek poetry is inconceivable in Linear B, continuous prose is possible though unlikely, but inventories and the like would be perfectly intelligible to the initiates (much like any code)' (p. 277 n.18). To confirm the point, he turns to modern experience and asks: 'how many literate persons today, outside a narrow professional circle, can read a corporate balance sheet?'

Of course, modern experience may have little bearing on some types of generalisations about pre-modern societies, in which case evidence from other pre-modern societies can be of use. One such case is the nature of oral epic. Having noted that no hint of feudal institutions is to be found in the *Iliad* and the *Odyssey*, Finley asks whether it is true, as a rule, that oral epic poets like Homer completely ignore such basic social institutions. 'Even a quick reading of *Beowulf* or the *Song of Roland* or the *Nibelungenlied* leaves one fully aware that *Gefolgschaft* and vassalage were key institutions, although there, too, the details and the rules are scarcely touched upon' (p. 222). It appears to be generally true, then, that oral epic poets supply hints of basic social institutions such as those found in feudalism; therefore, the absence of feudal institutions in the Homeric epics indicates the probable absence of such institutions in the world Homer described.

This last example introduces the issue of arguments from silence. Since ancient historians always face a dearth of data, there is a frequent temptation to justify conclusions by the silence of our sources. (Such conclusions are often prefaced with an apology to the effect that 'arguments from silence are weak, but . . .'.) Finley uses the *argumentum e silentio* for important issues and usually without apologetic qualification (e.g., the absence of words meaning 'to buy' or 'to sell' in the Linear B tablets, p. 206, or the absence in the Homeric poems of much of the terminology of social status and tenure found in the tablets, p. 215). As with the use of 'typical examples', his sensitivity to context meets the usual objections levelled against arguments of this kind. Thus, having drawn an important conclusion from the fact that no Greek 'king' receives a *temenos* in the *Iliad* or *Odyssey*, Finley adds in a footnote: 'In particular, there is neither the word itself nor the idea in the one passage in which *one would most expect to find both*, *Odyssey* 6.9–10 on the founding of Scheria' (Chapter 13, note 60, our italics). Here and elsewhere attention to what would be expected in certain contexts lends force to generalisations drawn from its absence.

Those who wish to avoid generalisations in writing ancient history point to occasions when an issue has been confused by overgeneralisation. Much of Finley's work is devoted to remedying this problem, and one of his favourite techniques for adding precision to a debate is to develop a typology, a method employed often in the papers collected in this book. When exploring the issue of whether the Athenian empire was popular among its subjects or a hated, exploitative political structure, Finley abandons the question in this form as too general to be meaningful, and instead breaks it down into more specific questions by the use of 'a crude typology of the various ways in which one state may exercise its power over others for its own benefit' (p. 45).

The methodological problem most frequently addressed in the last three papers of this volume concerns the use of philological arguments. We need only look at the world around us to see that the relationship between words and things or institutions is very complex. In the Greek language the variety of words for 'slave' illustrates the complexity: 'Such a profusion of words is likely to mirror historical reality' (p. 134); but when we ask 'in what way' the words reflect reality it is clear that the possibilities are numerous.

There may have been an original diversity in the institutions, paralleling the diversity in terminology; and these differences may have continued, or they may have been gradually eliminated by a process of convergence while the multiple terminology remained. Or different words may have been coined, at the start, to describe essentially the same status or institution in different localities . . . Finally, there is always the possibility of a word remaining unchanged while the institution diverges in one region or another. I do not believe that there are any rules in this matter; examples are available of each of these possibilities in the area of technical social terminology (p. 134).

Awareness of the various possibilities has several consequences. The possibility of evolution of meaning provokes doubt about etymological arguments: 'The meaning of a word in a given text, whether tablet or poem, *can never be discovered from its etymology*' (Chapter 13, note 20, our italics). Similarly, 'the relative constancy and uniformity of the texts' of the Linear B tablets over space and time may suggest little change from fifteenth-century BC Knossos to thirteenth-century Pylos, but the rigidity of form and jargon could also mask significant differences' (p. 203). Indeed, in some instances the apparent meaning of a word can be entirely misleading: the ancients were just as capable of legal fictions, for example, as men are today (p. 208). Do these difficulties mean that all linguistic arguments should be abandoned? Not at all. Finley, in fact, bases his conclusions in Chapter 13 on a word study, but with pre-cautions taken to overcome these problems. The meanings of words are not determined etymologically but are controlled by the context. The conclusion that society underwent major changes between Mycenaean times and the world described in the Homeric epics is based on the change in the vocabulary of land tenure and social status right across the spectrum of those social institutions, and the scale of the change gives the argument weight. A careful examination of language can be illumi-nating for the ancient historian, but it is Finley's concern that assump-tions about the relationships between words and things be made explicit and openly evaluated before accepting any argument based on them.

This linguistic argument leads, quite naturally, to the analogue of social institutions as 'morphemes' of a social whole which can only acquire 'meaning' when placed in context. The emphasis on the *whole* has the methodological implication that no historical datum has meaning in isolation; it must always be seen and interpreted in context (p. 232). Context eliminates that multiplicity of possible meanings, so it is the specific context in which the term, institution or event is embedded that gives it its proper meaning (p. 211). And, just as context is necessary for the individual words of a language to be understood as part of a whole discourse, so too social institutions take their interpretive meaning from context. That is the whole point of the last chapter of this volume: 'to fix *the place* of marriage within Homeric society' – that is, to put the insti-tution within its total social context. A similar approach accounts for the success of the analysis in Chapter 6, 'Was Greek civilisation based on slave labour?', where Finley avoids the pitfalls of quantification (sheer guesswork, as he points out (p. 102), in order to concentrate on the *location* of slavery in the social system of the Greek *polis* (p. 112). The insistence on locating a social institution in its whole context in order to discover part of its meaning is repeated not only with slaves and marriage, but also with religious institutions (p. 129) and the ancient city (p. 20).

The papers in this collection also offer the reader some of Finley's most explicit and extended uses of comparative analysis. More than a few ancient historians have expressed doubts about the value of comparative evidence on the grounds that since no two societies are identical, evidence from other societies cannot fill in missing facts of Greek history. It is an objection founded on the assumed incommensurability of two human societies; but objections of this sort presume that the study of history amounts to little more than the accumulation of facts. Finley would be the first to admit that comparative evidence cannot be used with assurance to extrapolate data that we do not possess in our Greek sources (though he is sometimes willing to use such evidence to make informed *guesses*, acknowledged as such, see p. 121). History, however, is more than an assembly of isolated data, and so comparative analysis has valid uses as the historian attempts to interpret his evidence. For Finley comparison is not just a mode of analysis or the juxtaposition of two sets of facts – it is the essence of history itself, in so far as 'it is the historian's duty to find connections of all types', including the ways in which human societies are commensurable (p. 113). A knowledge of other societies can suggest the limits of the possible and how particular kinds of evidence should be interpreted in relation to society as a whole. Babylonian documents are used in the discussion of the Linear B tablets in order to illustrate how far legal fictions can be carried in palace records (p. 208), and, more generally, knowledge of the Near East is drawn upon to suggest what the tablets can tell us about the Mycenaean world. Care must be taken in the selection of the proper points of comparison: in this case, the central feature of a palace-directed economy makes Egypt, Syria, Asia Minor and Mesopotamia more appropriate as choices than Homeric society (p. 232). After the proper societies for comparison have been chosen, the next step is to identify, perhaps with the aid of a typology, the precise level of comparability (in the above case, between all those Near Eastern economies characterised as 'Big Organisations' and the particular economy under analysis, that of Mycenaean Greece). Thus, once comparison is undertaken, differences between societies should not be overlooked. Rather, they should be taken into account in a systematic fashion that avoids 'the bits-and-pieces method of comparative analysis [which] is both limited and, ultimately, misleading' (p. 211). The 'bits-and-pieces method' can be dangerous because superficial similarities in markedly different contexts are likely to be meaningless.

So, what is the overarching paradigm within which ancient historians might operate successfully? Where are the broad frontiers of the 'type' of society they are studying? In his discussion of 'Anthropology and the Classics' (1975) Finley recommends that the ancient historian should avoid, for the most part, comparisons with both modern and industrial societies as analysed by sociologists and the 'primitive', non-literate communities studied by anthropologists. The gap between these 'type' societies and the ancient ones is simply too great to ensure a general validity of comparison.

Ideally, we should create a *third discipline*, the comparative study of literate, post-primitive (if I may), pre-industrial historical societies . . . For most of the concerns of the classicist . . ., pre-Maoist China, pre-colonial India, medieval Europe, pre-revolutionary Russia, and medieval Islam offer a more appropriate field for the systematic investigation of uniformities and differences, and therefore for an increased understanding of the society and culture of his own discipline.[39]

This understanding – what has been called 'a comparative perspective' – is one of the most valuable assets that Finley, with the enormous range of his reading, brings to his work. But it must be stressed again that we are not just speaking of a comparative method, but of a more general commensurability of types of society that permits the exposition of general uniformities between them – uniformities, because history, as a human research, cannot find its paradigm in the 'laws' of physics, but must strive for an *understanding* of human phenomena.[40]

In Finley's view, the precise use of comparative method is superior to its alternative, 'common sense', and this brings us to a paradox of his method. Reviewers and others have consistently noted Finley's 'uncommon common sense', and yet Finley himself has described this quality as 'the most dangerous of all tools of analysis, since it is only a cover for the author's own (modern) values and images, in the absence of, or in disregard of, evidence' (Chapter 12, note 46). The paradox may be merely apparent, arising from different notions of what 'common sense' is. In one form, it serves as a 'cover' for unconsciously assumed laws:

The relationship between trade and politics in classical Greece still seems to be treated most of the time as if there were no conceptual problems, as if, in Rostovtzeff's language, it is only a question of facts. And that means, necessarily that the concepts and generalisations which are constantly brought to bear, expressly or tacitly, are modern ones, even though they hide beneath the mask of common sense.[41]

But if by 'common sense' we mean the ability to cut through meaningless abstractions and to imagine a historical situation in concrete terms, then Finley undoubtedly possesses it and puts it to good use. To take one obvious instance from the following papers, in his discussion of how Athens profited from her empire Finley takes into account the fact that ' "Athens" is of course an abstraction'. To proceed further it must be asked, 'Concretely, who in Athens benefited (or suffered) from the empire, how and to what extent?' (p. 57). This sort of instinct for the concrete, it may be observed, is one sign that for all his affinity to the continental and especially German intellectual tradition, Finley has by no means abandoned his Anglo-American roots with their element of pragmatic empiricism.

There is one other element in Finley's historical writing that deserves consideration – the central role of confrontation or polemic. This aspect of his writing has been noted by many who have reviewed his work, but often they fail to note the conscious role assigned to polemicism, that of drawing the distinctions between various historical viewpoints with sufficient clarity that a choice is forced upon the reader:

All that is required is a recognition that the study of history either has significance or is nothing, that it is imperative to get clean away from the succession of megalomanic names and imposing battles . . .[42]

It is necessary, because such compilations of facts do not force any decisions; 'for all its technical competence (such history) has no meaning. How can it? It asks no questions to begin with.' Hence Finley's appreciation of the careful but controversial portrait of ancient Mesopotamian society evoked by Oppenheim, and the anti-traditionalist analysis of ancient India by Kosambi:

Some of Oppenheim's views have already evoked a counter-attack. Kosambi's book will enrage many readers, at home and abroad. Precisely.[43]

It is one of the historian's duties to take sides – the myth of 'unbiased reportage' in this sense is something that every historian ought to eschew in favour of an interpretation of the past. So, in his praise of Sir Ronald Syme's *Roman Revolution* (1939) Finley finds that element which separates it from other historians' work on the same subject:

He is not writing for *homo ludens*, but for *homo politicus*. His views are strongly held, stated 'quite nakedly, without hedging', and the keystone is 'a deliberately critical attitude towards Augustus.' It is a partisan work; so is every good piece of historical writing.[44]

Thus, all the historical work of Moses Finley has been directed towards the same end, though with two separate objects. For his fellow practising historians, the purpose has been put most plainly by Andrewes in his evaluation of the contributions of Momigliano and Finley to their profession: 'Both have worked powerfully all their lives to compel ancient historians to think hard about what they are doing, and why they are doing it'.[45] The other object is you, the reader. And here the aim is the same; in Finley's words:

History is 'unfixable' (Geyl's word) because its data and their combinations are infinite and repeatable. It is also concrete. The raw materials are what the professional historian can fix (within limits of probability) and then, in reflecting upon them out loud, he and the reader engage in a discourse, and inquiry. That is precisely what the word *history* meant in its original sense.[46]

Finally, there is the historian's involvement with the present – something which he cannot exorcise by the critical evaluation of the past. In the context of present problems, we can learn from the past (interpreted correctly), but the knowledge is of little value unless we *act* upon it. So, in his sensitive assessment of the question of 'The Jews and the Death of Christ' the historian acknowledges the limitation of his craft and his duty to the present:

Far be it from me to suggest, no matter how faintly, that it is ever unimportant to get the historical record right. But the feeling will not go away that there is an Alice-in-Wonderland quality about it all . . . The dead past never buries the dead. The world will have to be changed, not the past.[47]

PART ONE

THE ANCIENT CITY

THE ANCIENT CITY:
FROM FUSTEL DE COULANGES TO
MAX WEBER AND BEYOND

The Graeco-Roman world, with which I am concerned to the exclusion of the pre-Greek Near East, was a world of cities. Even the agrarian population, always a majority, most often lived in communities of some kind, hamlets, villages, towns, not in isolated farm homesteads.[1] It is a reasonable and defensible guess that, for the better part of a thousand years, more and more of the inhabitants of Europe, northern Africa and western Asia lived in towns, in a proportion that was not matched in the United States, for example, until the Civil War. (Admittedly only a guess is possible, since statistics are lacking for antiquity.) The ancients themselves were firm in their view that civilised life was thinkable only in and because of cities. Hence the growth of towns as the regular and relentless accompaniment of the spread of Graeco-Roman civilisation; eastward after the conquests of Alexander as far as the Hindu Kush, to the west from Africa to Britain with the Roman conquests, until the number of towns rose to the thousands.

So self-evident did the urban underpinning of civilisation seem to the ancients that they scarcely engaged in a serious analysis of the city. They did not even attempt a formal definition (apart from administrative 'definitions', to which I shall return briefly). Writing a glorified guidebook of Greece late in the second century A D, Pausanias dismissed the claim of a little town in central Greece to city status: 'no government buildings, no theatre, no town square, no water conducted to a fountain, and . . . the people live in hovels like mountain cabins on the edge of a ravine' (10.4.1). That at least points to a definition: a city must be more than a mere conglomeration of people; there are necessary conditions of architecture and amenity, which in turn express certain social, cultural and political conditions. Many centuries before, Aristotle had pointed in the same direction. The siting and planning of a town, he wrote in the

Originally published in *Comparative Studies in Society and History* XIX (1977) 305–27, and reprinted by permission of the journal.

Politics (1330a34ff), involves four considerations: health, defence, suitability for political activity, and beauty.

Pausanias, it will have been noticed, did not object to the pretentious little town on the grounds of its small size. And Aristotle saw in smallness a virtue, even a necessary condition: Babylon, about which he must have known very little, was for him an epithet, a symbol of elephantiasis, hence a negation of the true city (*Politics*, 1265a10ff). In his day, in fact, there was probably no town in the Graeco-Roman world with a population greater than 125,000 or 150,000, probably not half a dozen exceeding 40,000 or 50,000 (figures that one may double if the inhabitants of the city's agricultural hinterland are included). The trend after Aristotle was for a substantial growth in urban population, but if Rome and possibly Carthage finally reached perhaps half a million, the norm was even closer to Pompeii, with some 20,000 inhabitants at the time of its destruction in AD 79.

It will also have been noticed that neither Aristotle nor Pausanias was concerned with the 'administrative definition' of a city, though the former was writing about the autonomous city-state, the *polis* in Greek, the latter about a tiny town in one of the provinces of the Roman empire. Any territorial state which has a number of conglomerations within its borders must necessarily define and distinguish among those conglomerations, for purposes of police, taxation, road maintenance and all the other demands and services that social life entails. A survey of such definitions and distinctions today alone would reveal a bewildering variety, because these are technical matters marginal to a study of the city, and I shall largely ignore them.

The phrase 'city-state' which I just used with reference to Aristotle is an English convention in rendering the Greek word *polis*. This convention, like its German equivalent, *Stadtstaat*, was designed (I do not know when or by whom) to get around a terminological confusion in ancient Greek: the word *polis* was employed in antiquity for both 'town' in the narrow sense and 'city-state' in a political sense. When Aristotle examined the right conditions for siting a town, he wrote *polis*, the word he used hundreds of times in the *Politics* for his main subject, which was the city-state, not the town. He had no reason to fear that his readers would be led astray, as modern historians allow themselves to be.

For Aristotle, as for Plato before him, the *polis* arose because of the incapacity of the two prior forms of human association, the household and the larger kinship grouping, to satisfy all the legitimate needs of their members. Self-sufficiency, *autarky*, was the objective, and a properly structured and constituted *polis* should be able to attain that goal, save for the unavoidable lack of essential natural resources, for which (and which alone) foreign trade was admissible.[2] It is self-evident that *autarky* is a nonsensical idea for a town. Plato and Aristotle did not write nonsense: they took city and hinterland, town and country, together as a unit, not as distinct variables in competition or conflict, actual or potential. Even those farmers who lived outside the town were integrally *in* the *polis*. What we commonly call 'class conflict' is invariably between 'rich' and 'poor,' not between landowners and manufacturers, or between labour and capital, or between masters and slaves. Discussions of property and property ownership are only about land. Although they distinguished between gentlemen-farmers, living in the town, and working farmers in the countryside, that was a distinction between men of leisure, who were alone capable of the good life, and men who worked for their livelihood, again not a town-country distinction. The working farmer ranked higher on the scale than the artisan, but that was a matter of morality.

The ancient city was soon to lose its autonomy. The process began soon after Aristotle died, with the creation of the Hellenistic monarchies, and it was completed when the Romans embraced the Hellenistic world, and much else, within their empire. Yet even then, and to the end of antiquity, each city normally included a rural hinterland of some extent, often of very considerable extent, within its recognised territory. The city without a territory was a rare phenomenon, largely restricted to coastal communities of a peculiar kind. What is more important for our purposes, the traditional unity of town and hinterland – political, juridical and residential – went on unchallenged. Both Hellenistic and Roman emperors, for example, acknowledged that the hinterland was an integral part of the city for tax purposes. The same held true in the definition of municipal citizenship, which retained genuine value, juridically, politically and psychologically, after the disappearance of city autonomy.

It will not have escaped notice that I have so far avoided defining what I mean by a city. Neither geographers nor sociologists nor historians have succeeded in agreeing on a definition. Yet we all know sufficiently what we mean by the label, in general terms; no one will dispute that there was a city of Athens which was both physically and conceptually distinct from the city-state of Athens. The block in definition arises from the difficulties, apparently insuperable, of incorporating all the essential variables without excluding whole periods of history in which we all know cities existed, and on the other hand, of settling for a least common denominator without lodging on a level of generality that serves no useful purpose. The more sophisticated factor analyses in contemporary urban geography and sociology, with as many as one hundred variables,[3] most of which were absent from the ancient city (and the medieval and Renaissance cities as well), neatly reflect the unbridgeable divide in the history of cities created by the Industrial Revolution.[4]

That is indeed the conclusion (or the assumption) of historians and sociologists specialising in the modern city, and I accept that they are right to ignore the ancient city. The reader must then be wary of global titles: the classic volume of the Chicago urban school, published in 1925 under the title, *The City*, is a good example. One can only wish, and plead, that they have the courage of their convictions and not feel impelled to make a cultural gesture to the distant past with a sentence or two, or perhaps a paragraph, more often erroneous than not. When Handlin writes in introducing the volume called *The Historian and the City* (a title promising, even more than *The City*, something that is not there), 'The ancient world had been a world of cities, but each had been a world unto itself', he is wrong in fact and he also confuses a Weberian ideal type (he cites Weber at this point) with a statement of fact.[5] Or when Thernstrom suggests that it 'may some day be possible to develop a model of the process of urbanisation which applies equally well to ancient Athens and contemporary Chicago,' he presupposes a savage reductionism, stripping urban history down to demography and social and geographical mobility. His qualification, that it would be unrewarding to 'search for such regularities today', is merely a bow to difficulties in method and in the availability of information, not a recognition of the irreducible structural difference between pre-industrial and industrial cities.[6]

In my view, the starting-point for the historian of the ancient city must be the attachment between hinterland and city. The geographer Strabo, writing at the beginning of the Christian era, promised (4.1.5 and elsewhere) that the newly conquered western and northern barbarians would become civilised as soon as they settled down to agriculture and therefore to urban life. That combination is illuminating. No ancient author considered the relationship between the urban and rural sector in terms of the acquisition, production and exchange of goods. That theme is not only absent from the literature that has survived from antiquity, apart from the moral and cultural concerns I have already noted, but it continued to be incidental, at best, until the development of the modern science of political economy. Montesquieu devoted two books to commerce but saw nothing in the city as such to require his attention, nothing remotely comparable to the third book of Adam Smith's *Wealth of Nations* a generation later, with its well-known opening:

The great commerce of every civilised society is that carried on between the inhabitants of the town and those of the country . . . We must not . . . imagine that the gain of the town is the loss of the country. The gains of both are mutual and reciprocal, and the division of labour is in this, as in all other cases, advantageous to all the different persons employed in the various occupations into which it is subdivided.

That last point was soon challenged, for example by Marx and Engels in *The German Ideology*: 'The division of labour inside a nation leads at first to the separation of industrial and commercial from agricultural labour, and hence to the separation of town and country and *a clash of interests between them*' (my italics).[7] Such a disagreement is, in itself, evidence of the arrival of the town as a subject of investigation.

My subject, however, is not the pre-industrial city in general but the ancient city. I ask you to bear with me while I assume that the ancient city is a distinct and distinguishable category.[8] What criteria have historians or sociologists established with which to differentiate the ancient city from cities in other eras and other societies, and then to differentiate among the various kinds of ancient city? In purely quantitative terms, the sad answer is: very little worthy of serious consideration. Most historians of antiquity appear never to have asked themselves that question; a few, in a famous polemic that began late in the last century and continued into the first decades of our own, *argued* that the differences between the ancient and the modern city were merely quantitative: small population, less commerce, less manufacture. The *auctoritas* of Eduard Meyer, Julius Beloch and, more recently, Michael Rostovtzeff stilled opposition and even discussion, at least among ancient historians.[9]

Whereas ever since Gordon Childe discovered the 'urban revolution' there has been a growing and increasingly sophisticated literature about the beginnings of urbanism in Mesoamerica, Mesopotamia and ancient China,[10] and whereas the unceasing literature from the early nineteenth century has reached an unmanageable quantity about the 'rise of towns' (a curiously preemptive label for the rise of the medieval city), the intervening thousand years appear as a vacuum, or perhaps I should say a prohibited space. There is a considerable publication about what is sometimes grandiloquently called 'ancient town-planning', and no one will dispute that this is part of urban history, as are demography, drains and sanitation.[11] But a town is more than the mere arithmetical total of layout and drains and inhabitants, and it is remarkable that the ancient city *qua* city has aroused so little interest. Had it not 'disappeared' at the end of antiquity, it would not have had to 'rise' again: that simple logic alone should have forced attention on it.

There have been exceptions, of course, and perhaps even more *apparent* exceptions. Momigliano has recently written, 'When one talks of the ancient city (*città*) as a society within which institutions operate and ideas circulate, the first modern historian whose name comes to mind is Fustel de Coulanges.'[12] Fustel's *La Cité antique* was published in 1864 and had a tremendous impact in certain circles. Writing in 1891, W. J. Ashley pointed out that 'especially in England . . . it fell in with all that current of thought which was then beginning to turn into the direction of social evolution, comparative politics, and the like. For a year or so, the final piece of advice which schoolmasters gave to men who were going up for scholarships at the Universities was to read the *Cité antique*.'[13] Willard Small's translation was published in the United States in 1873, and the copy in my possession, dated 1894, is called the eighth edition. In the academic world, on the other hand, interest was largely restricted to France among historians and apparently to Roman lawyers in Italy.[14]

Now the first, and for our purposes most important, thing to be said of *La Cité antique* is that its subject is the city-state, not the town. The French and Italians have not adopted the 'city-state' convention, so that *cité* (or *città*), like *polis*, can mean *ville*, an urban centre, or, in the words of the dictionary of the Académie, 'la Constitution de l'Etat'. Fustel clearly did not mean, or concern himself with, *ville*. His subject was the origin of private property, the origin of the state, and the 'revolutions' within the ancient state, and his book has a thesis, drummed in repeatedly. I quote one typical passage:

There are three things which, from the most ancient times, we find founded and solidly established in these Greek and Italian societies: the domestic religion; the family; and the right of property – three things which had in the beginning a manifest relation, and which appear to have been inseparable. The idea of private property existed in the religion itself. Every family had its hearth and its ancestors. These gods could be adored only by the family, and protected it alone. They were its property.[15]

The inextricable family-religion-property link then moved into the larger kinship unit, the *gens*, and ultimately into the earliest state. Clearly the succession, family-*gens*-state, was for Fustel an historical one, not merely a conceptual one; to that extent he was following Aristotle, who, however, never imagined ancestor worship and the cult of the fire (the hearth) to be the fountainhead of private property. Nor did, nor could, any ancient author have shared Fustel's addiction to the newfangled Aryan doctrine: he included the Indians of the *Rigveda* and (because of a then common error) the Etruscans along with the Greeks and the Italians in his scheme of evolution. That was the extent and the limit in this book of Fustel's famed pioneering role as a comparativist.

For a historian, like myself, who greatly admires Fustel's subsequent work, such as his fundamental study of the late Roman colonate or his work on medieval France and Germany, *La Cité antique* is not easy to come to terms with. Its deployment of massive knowledge of the Greek and Latin sources goes hand in hand with a lack of source criticism that is almost incredible. Despite the deliberate refusal to mention a single modern author, the book is polemically ideological in a subtle and complex way; so was its reception, as Ashley perceived; so, too, as Ashley explained sadly, was the cool reception of Fustel's later, medieval works. In the latter his wide reading emerged on every page, his way with the sources was impeccable, the centrally creative force of religion was allowed to drop from sight, but the insistence that as far back as we can trace civilised societies there was private property, not communal ownership, remained a central theme.

Yet *La Cité antique* was by no means without notable academic impact in certain directions. In the first place, the book became decisive in the development of Durkheim's school.[16] Second, Fustel, along with Maine and Morgan, all three working independently in the halcyon days of social evolutionism, gave kinship the central role it holds to this day in social anthropology. And third, through Paul Guiraud and even more Gustave Glotz, the book has left its stamp on French ancient historians. In Glotz's classic *La Cité grecque*, published in 1928, which is also a work on the city-state, not the town, the opening pages are devoted to Fustel. 'The grandiose construction of Fustel de Coulanges,' he said 'impels admiration. . . . Nevertheless today it is impossible to accept all his conclusions' (a verdict echoed by Henri Berr in the introduction). And what were Glotz's reserves? 'History does not allow a rectilinear road': in addition to the family and the city, we must consider the individual.

'In the era when the *Cité antique* was published,' Glotz also wrote, 'no one since the time of Montesquieu had employed [the comparative method] with such mastery.' I am unable to explain so uninformed a judgment by a major historian; not even Glotz's overt refusal to employ the comparative method himself is a sufficient explanation. The 'comparative method' of La Cité antique is largely an illusion, since Fustel claimed to be revealing a *single*, Aryan pattern of evolution – a typical statement is, 'The religion of the dead appears to be the oldest that has existed among his race of men'[17] – and, anyway, in the century after Montesquieu the volume of genuine comparative studies had grown to immense proportions. Yet, as Durkheim pointed out, by ignoring the available ethnographic evidence, Fustel came to a false conception of the Roman *gens*.[18] We may nevertheless concede to Evans-Pritchard that *La Cité antique* marked 'the dividing-point between the speculative and dogmatic treatises of such writers as Turgot, Condorcet, Saint-Simon and Comte on the one side' and the 'detailed analyses' and 'scholarly treatment' that characterise the work of Durkheim, Hubert and Mauss.[19] We may also agree that Fustel made a considerable contribution in the recall from near-oblivion of the persistence of kinship institutions within the ancient city-state. However, the history of the city (whether town or city-state), ancient or medieval or modern, cannot be sufficiently analysed in terms of the cult of ancestors, worship of fire and the conflict within the developed state between the kinship group and the individual.

The most notable of the theories of social evolution to have emerged, on the basis of comparative studies, in the century between Montesquieu and Marx was the theory of the four stages, hunting, pastoral, agricultural and commercial, through which early man evolved. Its main proponents were in Scotland and France, and with John Millar we have what Meek has now called 'in effect' 'a materialist conception of history'. In the introduction to his *Observations concerning the Distinction of Ranks in Society*, first published in 1771, Millar listed among 'the causes of those peculiar systems of law and government which have appeared in the world' the following: 'the fertility or barrenness of the soil, the nature of its (a country's) productions, the species of labour requisite for procuring subsistence, the number of individuals collected together in one community, their proficiency in arts, the advantages which they enjoy for entering into mutual transactions and for maintaining an intimate correspondence.'[20]

There is no trace of the four-stages theory in *La Cité antique*. Yet not only was Fustel cognisant of the theory, at least in its French forms, but he himself accepted it up to a point. In the opening paragraph of his *The Origin of Property in Land* (first published in 1872), he wrote in reply to critics: 'it is obvious that when men were still in the hunting or pastoral

stage, and had not yet arrived at the idea of agriculture, it did not occur to
them to take each for himself a share of the land. The theory of which I
speak applies to settled and agricultural societies.'[21] But then he departed
radically, as he departed from Aristotle, replacing the mode of subsistence by religion as the focus of attention and the key to the formation
and change of institutions. Ashley correctly observed that even in his
work on the colonate Fustel failed to take proper account of 'the economic as well as the constitutional or legal'.[22]

So far as I know, the first man to insist on, and to formulate, an
'economic theory of town formation (*Städtebildung*)', of 'the necessary
relationship between the phenomenon of the town and the prevailing
economic system', was Werner Sombart in *Der moderne Kapitalismus*,
originally published in Leipzig in 1902.[23] In that work he presented a
series of models, starting with the obvious working definition, 'A town is
a settlement of men who rely for their maintenance on the products of
foreign (or alien) agricultural labour.'[24] In the second edition, fourteen
years later, he introduced a slight modification by adding the admittedly
vague word 'larger' – 'a larger settlement'.[25] This definition, he explained, was designed to exclude the *Landstädte* of the Middle Ages, in
which the majority of the inhabitants exploited the land themselves, as
well as the 'giant cities' of the ancient Near East, of ancient India or of the
type represented by Teheran today. That he did not specify the cities of
Graeco-Roman antiquity, or at least some of them, can be explained by
his concentration on his subject, the rise of modern capitalism and
therefore the rise of the city in the Middle Ages. And the key idea in his
definition of a town goes back to Adam Smith – Sombart placed at the
head of this section the same passage from Book III of the *Wealth of
Nations* that I quoted earlier, and he said explicitly that his models were
'"variations on a theme," a theme formulated in Adam Smith's words'.[26]

In the long and historiographically fecund period between Smith and
Sombart there had of course been massive research into, and publication
about, towns. But the interest, in so far as it was more than mere local
history in the antiquarian sense, had always been in the evolution from
feudalism to capitalism, in the rise of the medieval city, in the Renaissance city, and in the subsequent modern developments. Occasional
remarks about the ancient city can be found, some of them penetrating,
from Adam Smith on (and David Hume, too, one should always remember), but they were by the way, incidental to the subject at hand and
never elaborated. It would repay the effort to collect and examine these
remarks, but I can stop briefly only for one man, Karl Bücher.

In 1893 Bücher, who had already produced a remarkable 'social-statistical' study of the city of Frankfurt in the fourteenth and fifteenth centuries, published his *Die Entstehung der Volkwirtschaft* (*The Rise of the National Economy*), in which, building on an idea of Rodbertus's, he extended the old four-stage evolutionary theory by suggesting three further stages in the history of the last, the commercial one, which he called closed household-economy, city-economy and national economy.[27] This was the book that sparked off the dispute with the ancient historians, now commonly referred to as the Bücher-Meyer controversy, which was 'won' by the latter, to their own satisfaction, as I have already indicated.[28]

The year of Bücher's *Entstehung*, 1893, was also the year of the first of Henri Pirenne's three famous articles in the *Revue historique* on 'The Origin of the Urban Constitutions of the Middle Ages', in which he formulated the leading ideas that were to preoccupy him for so much of his life.[29] The rise of the medieval city, he insisted time and again, was in the first instance 'the product of certain economic and social causes'.[30] These 'economic and social causes', alas, turn out to be nothing more than a mysterious 'natural' process set in train by merchants, and Pirenne quickly slid back to the very stress on jurisdiction and constitutional history he had so powerfully condemned in others. Apart from banalities about the 'sterility' of the town, there is nothing that rises above the purely descriptive level, intelligent, learned and invaluable as he certainly was on that level. He admired Bücher's book on Frankfurt, but in the latter's theoretical work, Pirenne warned his students in lectures, he 'was too much the economist and not enough the historian, . . . his theories on economic development, however stimulating, were not related to historical evidence'.[31] Only once, to my knowledge, did Pirenne deign to discuss and dispute Bücher and Sombart, in a paper which I can best summarise as a medievalist's echo of the arguments of the 'modernising' ancient historians, concluding, with the latter, that the difference between modern capitalism and the 'capitalism' that began in the twelfth century was 'only a difference of quantity, not a difference of quality, a simple difference of intensity not a difference of nature'.[32] Pirenne later heard, we are told, that Weber, not surprisingly (if true), 'caustically referred to him as that Belgian medievalist who knew no medieval economic and social history'.[33]

Weber elsewhere protested that the historians had misunderstood Bücher's avowedly 'ideal type' approach,[34] but historians, whether of antiquity or of any other era, are customarily either allergic or totally deaf to ideal types. Thus, the distinguished medievalist Georg von Below, more sympathetic than most to Bücher's contribution, nevertheless concluded that the enterprise was doomed from the start because of the concern for 'norms': 'It is precisely the deviations which are interesting, or at least no less important than the rule.'[35] Eduard Meyer was less comprehending, and Bücher had refused an invitation from the editor of the *Jahrbücher für Nationalökonomik und Statistik* to reply to Meyer on the ground, in his own words, that Meyer revealed 'so little understanding of the economically essential'.[36] A few years later he could not resist, and in a long essay, full of erudition and wit, he examined in detail the Athenian evidence adduced by Meyer and Beloch, and he left their conclusions in tatters.[37]

Bücher, in short, knew perfectly well that the closed household was not the sole or universal economic formation in Graeco-Roman antiquity. That he did not discuss Graeco-Roman towns at any length is another matter – his chapters on *Stadtwirtschaft* deal with the Middle Ages – but he incorporated the ancient city into his evolutionary schema by stressing the shift in town-country relations: 'The Greek and Roman town-dweller was a possessor and exploiter of the land, even if he allowed the labour to be performed by slaves or tenants. . . . *That* the inhabitants of our medieval towns were not. . . . Town and country had separated in economic function.' The medieval town 'was not a mere centre of consumption, as were the towns of the Greeks and Romans'.[38] Sombart then elaborated and refined the notion: 'By a consumption city I mean one which pays for its maintenance (*Lebensunterhalt*) . . . not with its own products, because it does not need to. It derives its maintenance rather on the basis of a legal claim (*Rechtstitel*), such as taxes or rents, without having to deliver return values.' He then added a qualification: 'The original, primary city creators were consumers, the derived secondary (tertiary, etc.) creators were producers', and the latter were a dependent element, 'whose existence was determined by the share of the consumption fund allowed to them by the consumption class.'[39]

And that brings us at last to Max Weber. The intellectual relationship between Weber and Sombart was a very close one: they were joint co-editors of the revitalised *Archiv für Sozialwissenshaft und Sozialpolitik* for one thing.[40] Bücher was not a member of the Weber circle, but Weber's *Agrarverhältnisse* opens with a powerful defence, though not an unqualified acceptance, of Bücher's *Entstehung der Volkswirtschaft*.[41] My concern with showing that Weber's infinitely better known work on the city had important forerunners and, in a sense, co-workers has more than

antiquarian interest for my subject. We need Sombart and Bücher to help
us fill out the picture, for Weber's one sustained analysis of the city is a
posthumous, unannotated, book-length essay, subsequently included
within a context that is often overlooked in his *Wirtschaft und Gesellschaft*.
The latter is itself not only a posthumous work on which he had been
working for more than a decade (and therefore with changing styles and
aims) but one left by Weber in such a state that not even the sequence of
the sections was indicated.[42] And, it should be added, Weber's style in
his latter works, like his thought-processes, was extraordinarily dense
and complex; in the two works that concern me, so much so that the
available English translations are unreliable at best, and at worst
blundering.

Weber was of course the most profoundly historical of sociologists. He
began his career as a legal historian, interested particularly in two large
subjects, the history of the organisation of land-exploitation (with its
political and social implications or consequences) and the development
of commercial practices and institutions. In that first period he wrote his
Römische Agrargeschichte (1891), a brilliant piece of historical research still
within the recognisable framework of an established academic discipline. Thereafter his only substantial work on antiquity was a *tour de
force*, a full-length book written in four months in 1908 and published the
following year in the encyclopaedia which commissioned it and which is
responsible for the misleading title, *Die Agrarverhältnisse des Altertums*
(even worse in the English title, chosen for the translation that has
recently appeared: *The Agrarian Sociology of Ancient Civilizations*). His
widow characterised it, not inaccurately, as 'a sort of sociology of antiquity' prefaced by 'an economic theory of the world of ancient states',[43]
among which he included not only the Greek and the Roman but also the
Near Eastern (Egypt, Mesopotamia and Judaea). For all Weber's concern
with the dynamics of social institutions and social-cultural interrelations,
the *Agrarverhältnisse* is not a history, whether of ancient agriculture or of
ancient society. Weber had abandoned the writing of history. Still less
historiographical is the somewhat later 'book' on the city, though the
data about antiquity are largely taken over from the *Agrarverhältnisse*. It is
not insignificant that each section of the later study begins with either
general concepts or medieval material before the ancient world is introduced for purposes of clarification or contrast.

In sum, Weber never published a study of the ancient city, and his
views on the subject, as on other aspects of the ancient world, must be
elicited, with effort (including what amounts to decoding), from his

whole *oeuvre*, not merely from the writings overtly dealing with antiquity, with constant alertness to changed nuances in his thinking.[44] Some of the pivotal concepts have an obviously close kinship with those of Bücher and Sombart. He, too, began with an economic definition, which turns out to be a refined and elaborated statement of Sombart's: a town is a place in which 'the resident population satisfy an economically essential portion of their daily needs in the local market, and that in an essential part by means of products which the residents and the inhabitants of the immediate vicinity have produced or otherwise acquired for sale in the market.' When the large consumers derive their income in one form or another as rentiers, the city is a consumer-city, as in antiquity. For, 'if today we rightly conceive of the typical townsman as one who does not secure his sustenance from his own land, originally the opposite was true of the mass of the typical cities (*poleis*) of antiquity'.[45]

Two words in that last quotation require the closest attention: 'originally' and 'typical'. *Originally* the ancient city arose around the town-dwelling large landowners, but as it grew, more and more of its inhabitants were neither large nor small landowners. Yet it remained a consumer-city: even in its late, 'democratic' phase the social conflicts within the ancient city were sparked by the demands of 'essentially debtor interests. Therefore consumer interests,' unlike the 'manufacturing' interests underlying the parallel conflicts in the medieval city.

In order to explain that fundamental difference in development, an independent variable has to be introduced into the analysis, namely, slavery.[46] The widespread use of slaves in agriculture and manufacture severely restricted the scope for free labour and blocked expansion of the market, especially of the market for mass-consumed manufactures. It also hindered, and effectively prevented, increasing rationalisation of production: given the uncertainty of the market and the fluctuating costs of slaves (for both procurement and maintenance), the slaveowner had to be free to dispose of a portion of his slave force at a moment's notice, or to exploit them in ways other than direct employment in production. Extensive division of labour and other forms of rationalization would have destroyed the owner's flexibility. In sum the slaveowner of antiquity, like the landowner and the 'money-owner', was a rentier, not an entrepreneur.[47] The contrast with the development of manufacture in the Middle Ages is self-evident.

From these distinctions there flowed equally sharp differences in policy, and now a new variable must be introduced. In the opening section of the later work, Weber began with the 'economic' definition of the city, as I have mentioned, but he quickly went on to indicate that it was not a complete definition. 'The mere fact of a residential agglomeration of traders and manufacturing interests and the regular satisfaction of daily needs in the market do not *of themselves* exhaust the concept "city".' It is also 'an economy-regulating association' encompassing 'characteristic objects of economic-policy regulation on behalf of the association and a matrix of characteristic measures'.[48] The focus had shifted from that of the *Agraverhältnisse*, though much of the later work can be discerned in the earlier one.

Bluntly and therefore over-sharply stated, policy and political authority moved to the centre. When 'The City' reappears in *Wirtschaft und Gesellschaft*, it has a longer title, 'Non-legitimate Domination (Typology of Cities),' and it is but one section of a much larger one, on *Herrschaft* (Domination), which includes, among others, bureaucracy and charisma.[49] As early as 1895, in his Freiburg Inaugural Lecture, he had argued that the preservation and growth of the nation-state overrode all other considerations and interests.[50] Although this strong nationalist stance and its concomitant political stress were less visible in the historical writings of the succeeding years, they were never absent (as we shall see shortly). They reemerged in full force in the final decade of his life, both in his political activity and in his theoretical work.[51] In *Wirtschaft und Gesellschaft*, with its two fundamental themes, rationality and domination, he sealed the 'fateful connection between industrialisation, capitalism and self-preservation'.[52]

And at last we turn to the second of the two words I said we must attend to with care, 'typical'. Of course Weber knew that cities survived for centuries under the Roman Empire, though they had lost all capacity for 'economic-policy regulation'; that cities in fact proliferated in that era and sprang up in new territories, under direct stimulus and sometimes compulsion from the central authority. But his 'typology of cities' – the subtitle of the later work – was intended, and can only be understood, as a typology of 'ideal-type cities'. As he himself wrote, 'In the reality the types were everywhere fluid among themselves. That, however, is true for all sociological phenomena and should not prevent the establishment of the predominantly typical.'[53] Hence his frequent employment of inverted commas, especially in the *Agrarverhältnisse*, for such terms as 'feudal' and 'capitalistic' (usually as adjectives rather than as nouns in these critical instances), a formal sign of what he, with equal frequency, calls *Ansätze* (preliminaries) as an indication of fluidity, of the genesis within one type of elements characteristic of another type. Rarely, if ever, does he dodge the obligation to explain the failure (when that was the case) of *Ansätze* to mature and eventually to dominate.

Thus the final section of the *Agrarverhältnisse* attempts to explain why the Roman Empire and the *pax Romana* destroyed, rather than nourished, the *Ansätze* of capitalism he had detected in the ancient town. The argument is dense, but it may reasonably be summarised in this way. The *pax Romana* put an end to extensive territorial expansion and to the accumulation of booty, including vast quantities of human booty, both essential processes for the growth of wealth in the Graeco-Roman economy. Previous expansion had brought into the empire for the first time large tracts of inland territory, away from the sea and therefore with inadequate access to routes of trade and communication. The consequent tendency on inland estates was for rural settlement around a villa where the basic requirements of mass consumption were produced, thereby 'disarming' the town by reducing its opportunities for gainful activity. The decisive blow fell in the political sphere: the absolute monarchy replaced city administration by the 'dynastic professional army and bureaucracy', ending in a 'liturgy-state' (a state relying on compulsory services). 'Since the capitalism of antiquity was politically anchored and depended on private exploitation of political relations of domination in an expanding city-state, it came to a standstill with the disappearance of this source of capital-formation . . . The bureaucratic system killed the political initiative of its subjects as well as the economic initiative, for which the appropriate opportunities were lacking.' And then the despairing coda: 'Every bureaucracy has the tendency to accomplish the same effect by self-expansion (*Umsichgreifen*). Ours too.'[54]

For historians who are allergic to ideal types, there is nothing here to discuss; there are no propositions deserving examination and testing. One can find sufficient comfort and refuge in the 'discovery' that Weber's knowledge of the Greek world was very much less extensive and accurate than of the Roman;[55] in the demonstration that Weber can now be shown to be wrong when he called the Roman *equites* 'a pure national capitalist class'.[56] One can (legitimately) challenge Weber's conception of the feudal and capitalist elements in antiquity, or his political definition of the city. But when the demolition has been completed, the phenomena have not stolen away silently. It still remains true, and needing an explanation, that the peasant was an integral element in the ancient city, but not in the medieval; that the guild was an integral element in the medieval city, but not in the ancient. Perhaps I may be allowed to repeat what I wrote recently on the second point: 'it seems commonly overlooked that the excavators of Tarsus have found no Cloth Hall, that all ancient cities lacked the Guildhalls and Bourses which, next to the cathedrals, are to this day the architectural glories of the great medieval cities of Italy, France, Flanders, the Hansa towns, or England. Contrast the Athenian Agora with the Grande Place in Brussels.'[57] Furthermore, it still remains true, and needs an explanation, that ancient urbanism decayed so badly as to require a second 'rise of towns' in the Middle Ages. If Weber does not offer satisfactory explanations, even partial ones, where do we turn?

To Karl Marx perhaps? Marx was the spectre haunting Weber (and of course Sombart) throughout his life, much more so than might be inferred from the rare and even crude comments on Marx and Marxism to be found in Weber's writings.[58] I have no intention of entering into the subject, except to note that it is more complex than some current, oversimplified and dogmatic accounts suggest. Merely to dismiss Weber as an 'idealist', whose emphasis on 'spirit' and trade led him to see 'capitalism' where it never existed, is a caricature, an idle playing about with words. In his 1857 notebooks, Marx wrote about 'the *civilising influence* of external trade', though at first only a *'passive* trade',[59] in a passage that cannot but remind us sharply of Weber's thesis that the archaic shift from passive to active trade was the first step leading to the gulf between the western and the eastern city. For Marx (and Engels), there was never any doubt that 'commercial capital', 'commercial cities' and even 'commercial people' (Phoenicians and Carthaginians) were widespread ancient phenomena, and that in some instances, ancient Corinth for example, trade led to a highly developed manufacture.[60]

Weber, like Marx, had at the centre of his interests the phenomenon of capitalism.[61] That the two analyses ultimately diverged sharply, to a point of conflict, is undeniable (quite apart from the violent disagreement over political action and future goals). Marx's theories were 'absolutely unpalatable' to Weber 'as ontological propositions'. On the other hand, he saw 'Marx's interpretation of history, in terms of the various forms of production, as a most useful hypothesis which might help to gain important insights into the development of modern industrial society.'[62] In consequence, for the pre-industrial ages, and for the ancient city in particular, there was a large area of overlap and agreement between them.

Marx, of course, never made a systematic inquiry into the ancient world in general, or the ancient city in particular. On the latter, his few scattered remarks all stem from the proposition I quoted earlier from *The German Ideology*, repeated in the first volume of *Capital*:

The foundation of every division of labour which has attained a certain degree of development and has been brought about by the exchange of commodities, is the separation of town from country. One might well say that the whole economic history of society is summed up in the movement of this antithesis. However, for the moment we shall not go into this.[63]

Not only 'for the moment', I may add: in the whole Marxian corpus no more is to be found about the ancient town than an occasional statement, propositions about ideal types which are often more or less Weberian in substance.[64] Thus, we read in the *Grundrisse*: 'In the world of antiquity, the city with its territory is the economic totality. . . . Urban citizenship resolves itself economically into the simple form that the agriculturist is a resident of the city.'[65]

This is not the place for an extended analysis of the parallels (or the divergences), but two further examples may be useful. 'The modern proletariat, as a class, was absent. For ancient culture either rested on slavery at its centre of gravity (as in late Republican Rome), or, where "free" labour in a private-law sense predominated (in the Hellenistic world and in the Roman Empire), it was still permeated by slavery to a degree that never existed in medieval Europe.' That is Weber,[66] but few Marxist historians could reasonably disagree, except perhaps to transfer the first two centuries of the Roman Empire in the west to the first of the alternatives. 'Military power was more closely locked to economic growth than in perhaps any other mode of production, before or since, because the main single origin of slave-labour was normally captured prisoners of war, while the raising of free urban troops for war depended on the maintenance of production at home by slaves.' That is Perry Anderson, in a recent, subtle Marxist account,[67] and the Weberian parallel is evident from the summary I have already given of Weber's view on the impact of the *pax Romana*.

Suppose one accepts that these propositions, and others I have drawn from my survey of the history of theories of the ancient town, are, at the least, interesting enough to be pursued by a detailed examination of the available data, literary, epigraphical, archaeological. What are the implications for further historical inquiry? Not even the most sociologically minded historian is willing to stop with the formulation of ideal types. The variations within each type, the changes and developments, the implications over the whole range of human thinking and acting require detailed, concrete exposition – an exposition which would at the same time be a test of the ideal type.[68]. Such an account does not yet exist of the ancient town. There are, to be sure, a growing number of 'histories' of individual towns, Greek and Roman, from the archaic age to the end of antiquity. With scarcely an exception, however, they lack a conceptual focus or scheme: everything known about the place under examination appears to have equal claim – architecture, religion and philosophy, trade and coinage, administration and 'international relations'. The city *qua* city is flooded out. The approach is usually descriptive and positivistic, 'collecting evidence and interrogating it with an open mind':[69] the unexpressed assumptions about the economy are usually 'modernising'. I do not underestimate the contribution to knowledge that has been made by these studies, nor the difficulties inherent in the attempt, nor such conceptual advances as there have been in the past decade or two.[70] However, it is the case that the considerations I have raised, the issues presented by Marx, Bücher, Sombart and Weber, are peripheral, at best, in current study of the ancient town.[71]

In the end, I believe that the history of *individual* ancient towns is a *cul-de-sac*, given the limits of the available (and potential) documentation, the unalterable condition of the study of ancient history. It is not wholly perverse to see an advantage in the weakness. There is mounting criticism of contemporary urban history for allowing the deluge of data to obscure the questions being asked and their purpose,[72] a danger the ancient urban historian is happily safe from. But what questions do we wish to ask about the ancient city, whether they can be answered satisfactorily or not? That is the first thing to be clear about, before the evidence is collected, let alone interrogated. If my evaluation of the current situation is a bleak one, that is not because I dislike the questions that are being asked but because I usually fail to discover any questions at all, other than antiquarian ones – how big? how many? what monuments? how much trade? which products?

To *understand* the place of the town as a pivotal institution in the Graeco-Roman world and its development, the starting-point must surely be two facts. First, the Graeco-Roman world was more urbanised than any other society before the modern era. Second, the city-state, the closely interlocked town-country unit, remained the basic module even after the state component in city-state had lost its strict original meaning. Did it also remain a 'consumer-city'?

That there were such consumer-cities throughout antiquity is indisputable. In 385 B C Sparta defeated Mantinea in Arcadia and laid down as a peace condition that the town be razed and the people returned to the four villages in which they had once lived. 'At first they were discontented', comments Xenophon (*Hellenica* 5.2.7), 'because they had to demolish their existing houses and build new ones. But when the property owners were living near the estates they possessed around the villages, and they had an aristocracy and were rid of the burdensome demagogues, they were pleased with the state of affairs.' Xenophon's political comments are irrelevant for my purposes; the viability of the Spartan demands is what matters. And when the town of Mantinea was eventually restored, it continued for centuries as a centre for landowning residents, as it had been when the Spartans destroyed it.[73]

How typical was Mantinea? Capua, Cicero tells us (*On the Agrarian Law*, 2.88), was preserved by the victorious Romans in the interest of the Campanian farmers, among other things so that, 'wearied by the cultivation of the lands, they would have the use of the homes in the town'. The steady urban growth in central and northern Italy during the late Republic produced towns of the same kind.[74] So did the 'Romanisation' of the Danubian region incorporated into the province of Pannonia under the Empire.[75] Rome itself was of course the prototype of a consumer-city, as it has been throughout its history. Antioch, too, the fourth city of the empire: for the fourth century the urban population has been estimated at between 150,000 and 300,000; its extensive territory was at least 300 times as great as the area within the town walls, and the foundation of its wealth was in the land and in its leading place within the imperial administrative system.[76] The extra-urban districts were thick with villages, each with its own local production and distribution through rural fairs. In consequence, Libanius explains (*Orations*, 11.230), the villagers 'have little need for the town, thanks to the exchange among themselves'.

Present-day overtones of the word 'consumer' should not be allowed to intrude and mislead. No one is suggesting that the urban lower classes were a host of beggars and pensioners, though it has become a favourite scholarly pastime to 'disprove' that contention for the city of Rome; though, too, the extent of beggary, unemployment and famine is not to be underestimated. The issue implicit in the notion of the consumer-city is whether and how far the economy and the power relations within the town rested on wealth generated by rents and taxes flowing to, and circulating among, town-dwellers.[77] Even the quintessential consumer-city, Rome, required innumerable craftsmen and shopkeepers for intra-urban production and circulation. In so far as they were engaged in

'petty commodity production', the production by independent craftsmen of goods retailed for local consumption, they do not invalidate the
notion of a consumer-city.

It is also not suggested that the examples I have given – a handful from
many available instances – were all identical towns. If it is the case that
they were all in some respects consumer-cities, the next step in the
inquiry is to examine the variations of (or from) the ideal type, to
establish a typology of ancient towns. Consider Cyzicus on the Sea of
Marmara, a harbour-town identified by historians as 'a great clearing-
house for the trade of the Euxine (Black Sea)',[78] famous for its widely
circulated 'white gold' (electrum) coins. In 319 BC, in the course of the
wars among Alexander's successors, it was attacked by the satrap of
Hellespontine Phrygia in a surprise move that found the town unpre-
pared, with only a few people within the walls while the majority were
out in the fields. There is no ground for disbelieving the historian
Diodorus (18.51.1–2) on this score. Where, then, do we locate Cyzicus in
a typology? Unless we are content with the familiar and meaningless
serial formulation – 'the economic life' of Noricum 'depended on agricultural production, pastoralism, mining, industry – above all iron-
smelting and metal-working – and trade'[79] – proper factor analysis is
essential. The factors may not often coincide with the modern ones and
the opportunities for genuinely quantitative and dynamic analysis are
few and frustrating; the procedure is nevertheless unavoidable.

It is not my intention in this essay to enumerate the variables or to
formulate a typology. Much of what I should include is anyway implicit
(and sometimes explicit) in what I have already said – the extent (and in
rare cases, the absence) of agricultural territory appertaining to the town;
the size of the town and of its population; access to waterways; the extent
and 'location' of the slave-labour force; self-sufficiency on the large
estates; peace or war; the changing role of the state with the development of the large territorial empires. This is not an exhaustive list, but it
will suffice for present purposes. It points back to the questions which
distinguish theory from antiquarianism.

I have come to the end, still referring to *the* ancient city. Is it a
defensible category? Mere chronology is no argument in its favour, nor is
the undeniable variety among ancient towns an argument in its disfavour. My defence is a simple one. The city does not exist in isolation: it
is an integral part of a larger social structure, in the Graeco-Roman world
a pivotal institution. Unless and until the kind of concrete investigation I
have suggested demonstrates that, allowing for exceptions, Graeco-

Roman towns did not all have common factors of sufficient weight to warrant both their inclusion in a single category and their differentiation from both the oriental and the medieval town, I hold it to be methodologically correct to retain the ancient city as a type. And so 'type' has crept back, as my final word.

- 2 -

SPARTA AND SPARTAN SOCIETY

I

The Sparta I shall consider falls within a rather restricted period, from about the middle of the sixth century to the battle of Leuctra in 371 BC. I exclude the earlier history, apart from a few certain events and general trends, because I believe that our information is almost wholly fictitious (especially anything referring to Lycurgus); that all attempts to reconstruct that early history in detail, with names and exact dates, rest on totally unsound methodological principles; and that the excessive concentration on assumed distant origins in a legendary migration period is equally unsound in method.[1] I stop at Leuctra because I accept the virtually unanimous Greek tradition of qualitative change fairly early in the fourth century. Thereafter, despite certain continuities, Sparta was being transformed into a different kind of society again.

What this means is that I accept that the decisive turning-point in Spartan history came in or about the reign of Leon and Agasicles (Herodotus 1.65–66), soon after 600 BC, as the culmination of internal troubles going back perhaps a century, a period in which the so-called Second Messenian War was the main catalytic occurrence, and which produced persistently revolutionary potentialities and threats. Much about that war is obscure, not to say legendary, but the poetry of Tyrtaeus is contemporary and illuminating. It demonstrates that the Spartan army was in a disorder and turmoil unlike anything known from the later, classical period, the community in a state of civil disturbance (stasis); and that the Lycurgus legend was not yet current. Once the war was finally won, a number of profound changes were introduced: political, economic and ideological. I do not know how rapidly they were brought about (a question to which I shall return), or by whom, but in the end we have the Sparta which was a unique structure in the Greek world, which

Originally published in *Problèmes de la guerre en Grèce ancienne*, ed. J.-P. Vernant (Paris and The Hague, 1968), and reprinted with the permission of the publishers, Mouton & Co, and the Ecole Pratique des Hautes Etudes.

the Sparta of the poet Alcman was not. I stress the word *structure* in order to divert attention from the customary over-concentration on certain elements in the system, and on what regularly goes with them in the modern literature, namely, a mystique about Dorians and Dorianism in general and a few largely irrelevant Cretan parallels in particular, the latter, in my judgment, essentially misleading constructs of fourth-century theories or propaganda (in which Carthage also figured, at least for Aristotle, let it be noted).

If the excavations of the shrine of Artemis Orthia were as revealing of the transformation in Sparta as it is sometimes said, we could date the break rather near the year 600 (or several decades later in Boardman's chronology).[2] However, apart from the rather problematical dis-appearance of ivory from the deposits, I do not see that Artemis Orthia provides evidence from which to prove anything. The 'evidence', which it had been rather more fashionable to stress ten or twenty years ago than it is now, turns out to consist of little more than highly subjective judgments about the quality of Laconian pottery in various periods, on which the experts do not agree. Besides, we do not know whether the Spartans ever made this pottery themselves or whether much (or even all) of it was already in the hands of the *perioikoi* (citizens of neighbouring communities who, though free men probably enjoying local self-government, were subject to Sparta in military and foreign affairs) well before 600, in which case the decline is irrelevant anyway, even if it really could be placed in the middle of the sixth century. On the other hand, if those who believe the ephor Chilon to have been the great reforming 'lawgiver' could be shown to be right, then we should have a firm date about 550, although I cannot imagine how we should fill out the very long interval between the end of the Second Messenian War and 550. Since all this is largely irrelevant to my subject, I propose to by-pass the chronological puzzles and speak, as a kind of shorthand, of the 'sixth-century revolution'.[3]

Let me elaborate a bit on this 'revolution'. Schematically (and rather inexactly) one may divide the classical Spartan structure into three broad strands: (1) the infrastructure of land allotments, helots and *perioikoi*, with everything that includes with respect to labour, production and circulation; (2) the governmental system (including the military); (3) the ritual system: *rites de passage*, the *agoge*, the age-classes, *syssitia*, etc. (*Agoge* is a conventional label for the system by which all Spartan boys were brought up by the state. There is good Greek authority for the term; 'education' in the normal modern sense is too narrow a translation.

Syssitia were the dining-groups or mess-companies to which every Spartan male belonged as a necessary condition of full citizenship.)

These strands had different origins and a different history; they did not develop and shift *en bloc*; and they did not have the same unchanged functions at all times. The 'sixth-century revolution' was therefore a complex process of some innovation and much modification and re-institutionalisation of the elements which appear to have survived 'unchanged'. I use the word 'revolution' even more loosely than is perhaps customary, but I do not use it capriciously. It is loose because I do not for a moment suggest, or believe, that the classical Spartan system was created at one stroke, or even in one reign. After all, the introduction of the hoplite army was one of its necessary conditions, and that must go back early in the seventh century, at least before the Second Messenian War. Helotage in some form was even older. And we must not rule out the possibility that other elements were effectively introduced, or raised to new prominence, as late as the fifth century (as we know certain changes in the army organisation to have been). On the other hand, it was not a system that somehow just evolved. Some innovations and modifications had to be introduced at a single stroke (whether one at a time or in combination). The Great Rhetra, for example, reflects something very fundamental of this kind.[4] In a negative way, the prohibition of the use of silver coinage by Spartiates was another obviously sharp decision made by somebody at some moment (and one, incidentally, which more than most can be almost exactly dated to the time of Leon and Agasicles).

By speaking of the 'sixth-century revolution', in sum, I am trying to underscore the necessity for looking at the structure, not at isolated elements and their antiquity or persistence. I include the whole of the ritual system in this argument, particularly in what I have called rather awkwardly 're-institutionalisation', because even if it were the case that the ritual externals were all very old and unaltered (a most unlikely possibility), their function within the new structure was necessarily a new one in significant respects, in effect if not always by deliberate intent. No one will pretend that the whipping ceremony at Artemis Orthia in Roman times, when a great theatre was built for the convenience of the spectators, bore any meaningful connection with the superficially similar rite of Xenophon's day.[5] A *priori* we must assume the same discontinuity in function between the fifth century and, say, the eighth, and sometimes we have evidence to confirm the assumption, for example, in the case of the *krypteia*, as we shall see shortly.

Classical Sparta may have had an archaic and even a pre-archaic look about it, but the function of the 'survivals' is what chiefly matters, not the mere fact of survival. Before the reign of Leon and Agasicles, writes Herodotus, the Spartans were the worse governed (*kakonomotatoi*) of all the Greeks; they then switched to good order (*eunomia*). Translation destroys the full sense of the judgment: both *eunomia* and *kakonomos* characterise a whole way of life, not only (or perhaps not at all) a form of constitution.[6] That transformation was the 'sixth-century revolution'.

II

At this stage I want to consider the structure as an ideal type. In what follows, furthermore, I am not much concerned with the accuracy of any individual text. Unless one believes that the picture the Greeks have left us is altogether a fiction, few of the details are of themselves crucial for an apprehension of the ideal type.

I go immediately to the adult male citizens, the *homoioi* as they were frequently called, who are our subject. We must, at the start, take the word in its full connotation – Equals.[7] At birth, if they were permitted to remain alive, all Spartan males were strictly 'equal' with two exceptions: (1) two of them were potential heirs to the kingship; (2) some were richer than others – the rich men (*anthropoi olbioi*) of Herodotus (6.61; 7.134); the wealthy (*plousioi*) of Xenophon (5.3),* who provided wheaten bread for the *syssitia*; or the winners of Olympic chariot-races, of whom there are eleven within my time-limits in Moretti's catalogue, one a king and another the daughter of a king.[8] Being equal meant sharing a common, well defined life-cycle, including: (1) a common, formalised, compulsory upbringing designed to inculcate obedience, valour, discipline and professional military skill; (2) a single vocation or profession, that of a hoplite soldier or officer; (3) economic security and complete freedom from economic concerns, all productive and ancillary services being provided by two distinct categories of dependents, helots and *perioikoi*; (4) a public (rather than private) life in an all-male community, with maximum conformity and anti-individualism.

Structurally, however, the system then generated two further, unavoidable, closely interrelated inequalities apart from those inherent in each child at birth. One was the inequality, not very tangible but none the less real, that followed from inequality of performance, whether in

* All references in this chapter to Xenophon, unless otherwise indicated, are to his pamphlet which goes under the inaccurate title, *Constitution of the Lacedaemonians*.

the *agoge* or in games and hunting or in war. The other arose from the need for leadership and élites, not only at the top (kings, ephors and council of elders), but also in the smaller military units, and, because of the Spartan *agoge*, in the age-classes beginning at a remarkably early age. Xenophon's 'love of victory' (*philonikia*) produced losers as well as winners (4.4), a self-evident fact which is often overlooked by modern scholars, who then write as if everyone passed through every stage a prizewinner.

All this was massively buttressed, psychologically and institutionally. Living in public for so much of their lives, the Spartans were more strongly susceptible than most people to the pressures of public opinion and of the network of rewards and punishments, with its great stress in childhood on corporal punishment, and in adulthood on a rich and imaginative variety of expressions of social disfavour or even ostracism. Everything was harnessed into service, including piety and *rites de passage*. Perhaps the most dramatic example is the transformation of the *krypteia*. This ancient rite of initiation at the age of eighteen became rationalised, that is, re-institutionalised, by being tied to a new police function assigned to an élite youth corps. Significantly, policing the helots was one of their duties.[9]

An important part of the buttressing was negative, so to speak, the reduction to the barest minimum of the disruptive, centrifugal effects of property and the family. We may permit ourselves to be more 'sociological' and less moralistic than Xenophon, for example, in analysing the functions of the Spartan regime of property and family.

Property – extensive comment is unnecessary at this point, though I shall have to return in the next section to the inequality in wealth. The total withdrawal from economic (and not merely banausic) activity, the austerity, the sharing were meant to be cohesive factors, and they were.

Family – a mere enumeration of certain rites and institutions is sufficient to reveal the scale of the effort to transfer allegiance away from the family or kinship group to various male groups: the steps taken to insure procreation, with which Xenophon opens his booklet; the right of any father or indeed of any adult Spartiate to exercise authority over any child; the singularly joyless marriage ceremony with its rare transvestite ritual; the barrack life. The family, in sum, was minimised as a unit of either affection or authority, and replaced by overlapping male groupings – the age-classes, the homosexual pairings between younger and older men (whether 'Platonic' or not), the élite corps, the *syssitia*. Two details are perhaps worth mentioning here, though I shall have to return to them at the end:

1. The age-class system was unusually ramified. I have no precise idea of what its effects were, but at least the complexity greatly increased the occasions for ritual reinforcement.

2. On entry into adulthood, the Spartiate was at least partly divorced from his age-class by the practice of individual cooptation into a *syssition*. Any device which cuts across a 'natural' grouping, whether family or age-class, can be seen as one more way of strengthening the structure as a whole against its individual parts.

So much buttressing was necessary, in part at least, because the Equals turned out, in the end, to be meshed in a complex of inequalities. There were leaders, élites, at all levels, and the primary principles of selection were appointment and cooptation – never, it should be stressed, selection by lot, the standard Greek device for imposing equality. All *homoioi* were eligible in principle, and that fact differentiated the Spartan army from those, like the Prussian, which had an officer corps drawn solely from a pre-existing and exclusive élite. The end-result, however, was the same in one respect: there was a chain of command in which the authority-obedience syndrome moved in one direction only, from the top down. To be sure, there were two exceptions in the method of selection: the council of elders and the ephors were elected in open competition. It is a pity that we know virtually nothing about this procedure or about the men elected. Were they usually the same men who had already come out on top through cooptation? That is what I should expect in this society, and I shall come back to the question shortly.

In so far as the success of the system is to be measured by its military successes, the verdict must, of course, be favourable. The Spartan army was better than any other, with more stamina and greater manoeuvrability, thanks to superior physical condition, better training and discipline, more obedience. Thought seems to have been given to military organisation; at least the not infrequent changes in organisation suggest that. On the other hand, there is no evidence of interest in tactics or weaponry beyond the maintenance of both at the best traditional level.

The production and distribution of weapons remain something of a puzzle. I think we can take it that the procurement of metals and the manufacture of arms were the responsibility (and also the privilege) of the *perioikoi*. But how did the individual Spartiate obtain his arms and armour? The traditional Greek conception of the hoplite as by definition the citizen (or metic) rich enough to equip himself, does not apply. All

Spartiates were 'rich' enough, but none had the proper market mechanism. The choice lies between (a) individual procurement from *perioikoi* by
payment in kind (or, conceivably, iron spits), and (b) procurement and
distribution by the state. I know of no ancient text which gives the
answer. Nor does archaeology help in the absence of systematic excava-
tion of any perioecic community. One can argue either way from the
shields, all of which were required to have a Lambda inscribed on them,
but many (if not all) of which also had a personal blazon. My own
preference is for the public supply system, because the other seems
insufficiently reliable and because we do have textual evidence that once
the army had marched off, the state took responsibility for repair and
replacement (as it must have done for the initial procurement even at
home when helots were enrolled as hoplites).[10]

III

So much for the ideal type. In actual practice the system was filled with
tensions and anomie.

  1. To begin with, the Spartan army was not always big enough for its
needs – needs which were more cause of the system than consequence.
Perioikoi were an equal part of the hoplite army, and, at least on major
occasions such as the Peloponnesian War, substantial numbers of helots
and ex-helots (*neodamodeis*) were also enlisted. I have no answer to the
very important question of how helots were selected and trained for
hoplite fighting (or to any possible connection with the mysterious
mothakes). Spartans were regularly accompanied by helot orderlies or
batmen and there is no particular problem in using such people as
light-armed auxiliaries. Hoplite training, however, could not be
achieved casually; the essence was movement in formation, and it was
for their unique skills at this in particular that the Spartans were commended by ancient writers. That helot and ex-helot hoplites were a
serious flaw in the system is self-evident, psychologically as well as in its
overt functioning.

  2. For Aristotle the greatest vice was financial corruption. Perhaps he
was thinking primarily of the changed Sparta of the later fourth century,
but bribery is already a major theme in Herodotus.[11] The infrastructure
was flawed. The regime of property and inheritance, like the political
system, was a compromise. Heavy as the pressures of austerity and
withdrawal from all economic activity may have been, they were insufficient to overcome completely the counter-pressures of inequalities in

wealth, or the fears of impoverishment whether through large families
or otherwise. The prohibition of business activity (*chrematismos* is
Xenophon's carefully chosen word) does not eliminate a desire for – and
an ability to employ – wealth, not even if the prohibition can be perfectly
enforced. Xenophon's statement (7.6) that the possession of gold and
silver was prohibited must be understood, in my opinion, to refer only to
coin, as his context implies. But gold and silver have other functions,
revealed by Herodotus, perhaps unconsciously, when he employs the
good old Homeric *keimelion* (treasure) in his story (6.62) of how King
Ariston acquired his third wife, the mother of Damaratus. Coined
money is not essential for exchange, and there were exchanges in Sparta.
Even if one were for some reason unwilling to accept the accuracy of
Thucydides' inclusion of buying and selling among the activities forbid-
den to a Spartiate when he suffered loss of civil rights (5.34.2), there is no
getting away from the sportsmen Darmonon and his son Enymacritidas,
who made a dedication to Athena Chalkioikos, probably in the middle of
the fifth century B C, recording twenty or more victories.[12] The text
stresses that they won with their own horses and their own chariots, and
the latter had to be acquired by the exchange of wealth in some form.
Presumably a sufficient equilibrium could be maintained despite the
pressures so long as the Spartans remained safely cocooned within their
own world. But not when they were drawn abroad.

3. There was structural tension within and about the leadership. I am
not concerned with disagreements over policy which are inevitable
whenever there is shared leadership – examples are abundant, as with
respect to the situation in Athens after the overthrow of the Pisistratids,
or whether to go to war with Athens in 431 – but with the tensions
inherent in the positions themselves, in the efforts to attain and then to
maintain and enhance positions of leadership. We must not allow
ourselves to be bemused by the Greek obsession with the 'lawgiver': the
sixth-century revolution had to strike some sort of balance among the
social elements that were then in existence, and this balance meant
failure to institute a unified leadership principle. Hence there were
hereditary kings, elected elders and ephors, and appointed leaders at
other levels. Again we must not be bemused by a Greek obsession, this
time with the 'mixed constitution'. Instead of an equilibrium there was
permanent conflict, which could not be cushioned by the self-confidence
and stability which are generated, for example, by an exclusive leadership caste. Even the kings, in Aristotle's words, were compelled to court
(*demagogein*) the ephors (*Politics* 1270b14).

The leitmotif, I think, was not so much a conflict between kings and ephors, as such, as between men of energy and ambition – the men imbued with excessive 'love of victory', a Lysander as well as a Cleomenes, actual and potential – and the rest. One source of *stasis*, Aristotle noted (*Politics* 1306b31–33), was the dishonourable treatment of men of virtue by others whose virtue was no greater but who had more honour, and the specific example he gave was the treatment of Lysander by the kings. That the kings were a persistently disruptive force of a special kind and magnitude in classical Spartan history needs no demonstration. What deserves notice, however, is that they were potentially disruptive by definition, so to speak, that their very existence was a contradiction of the ideal type of Spartan equality. Cleomenes I, wrote Herodotus (5.39), reigned not because of his own manliness but by heredity. That sums it up. Given the psychological underpinning of being born to high office and the various charismatic practices and institutions attached to Spartan kingship – Herodotus knew what he was saying when he called the royal funeral rites 'barbarian' – it depended solely on the personality of the individual king whether he was a force for civic peace or for strife, or no force at all.

The hereditary principle also injected the family into the picture, again in violation of the Spartan ideal. The various recorded manoeuvres on behalf of younger sons and other kin of kings, including the classic employment of allegations of illegitimacy, belong to the courts of tyrants and barbarian monarchs, not to a Greek *polis*. It then becomes necessary to consider whether kinship did not also play some part in the leadership struggles outside the kingship. I have already said that it is my guess that the men chosen for the council of elders, the ephorate and the magistracies were those who had earlier come out on top through the appointment procedures. All *homoioi* were, in a formal sense, equally eligible. But were they in practice? Who, then, were the men whom Herodotus called 'among the first by birth' (7.134); and what did Aristotle mean when he said that election to the council was 'oligarchical' (*dynasteutikos*, which implies manipulation as well), whereas everyone was eligible for the ephorate (*Politics* 1306a18, 1294b29–31)? It is true that such texts are very rare: the more common reference is to individuals being or wishing to be 'first' or 'among the most powerful', which need mean nothing more than to achieve leadership by their own efforts. But the few texts remain, and they say what we should have guessed without them, namely, that there were families who were able to influence the appointment procedures in favour of their own members, beginning at the first opportunity, among the children. That means, in effect, that there developed an element of hereditary aristocracy within the system, far from closed, but not without considerable influence nevertheless. And I have no doubt that wealth played its part here (as Herodotus 7.134 implies). There were others, in sum, besides Cleomenes who achieved positions, lower or higher in the ranking, by birth rather than by manliness.

Inevitably when there is struggle for leadership, disagreements over policy reflect calculations of personal advantage in the struggle alongside, and confused with, calculations about the desirability of a proposed policy as such. Sometimes these differences were brought before the people in assembly, and that raises one further question respecting equals and unequals. The time has long passed when any serious historian or political scientist thinks in nineteenth-century liberal terms about voting behaviour, with its image of the 'reasonable man' weighing the issues 'rationally' and free from all prejudices, pressures and emotions. It is nevertheless legitimate to ask whether there was something in the Spartan structure which makes the 'reasonable man' approach even less applicable, even more of a caricature, than, say, for the Athenian assembly. I will put the question very bluntly. Can we imagine that the obedient, disciplined Spartan soldier dropped his normal habits on those occasions when he was assembled not as a soldier but as a citizen, while he listened to debates among those from whom he otherwise was taught to take orders without questioning or hesitation?[13] I do not think we have any evidence from which to answer concretely, but my guess is that the Spartan assembly was much closer to the Homeric than to the Athenian in function and psychology. Archidamus and Stenelaidas harangued each other before the assembled people as Agamemnon and Achilles did. That is not open discussion. But neither is it mere puppetry: when the leadership divided over policy, someone had to make the decision, and that was the people in assembly.[14]

4. There was too much social mobility in both directions, too much, that is, for a society which in principle was completely closed and rigid and which therefore lacked the mechanism (and the psychology) necessary to adjust the mobile elements properly in their new statuses:

(a) There were Spartiates who lost status, yet somehow remained within the community in a curiously inferior position (as distinct from exiles). These were not always economic failures (men who could not maintain their *syssition* quotas); a depreciation in status could also follow from failure at some stage in the *agoge*, failure in battle, loss of civic rights, or the like. (b) There were helots who rose in status, many even achieving membership in the *damos*, the citizenry (for that is what *neodamodeis* has to mean, whatever inferior shading it may imply). I am frankly unable to visualise these people, how they lived or even, in many cases, where they lived. The helots who fought under Brasidas, says Thucydides (5.34.1), were first given permission to reside where they wished, but then they were settled with the *neodamodeis* at Lepreon on the Elean border to help serve as buffers against the hostile Eleans. Neither Thucydides nor anyone else explains what it meant in practice to be 'settled' or to reside where they wished, or where and how the degraded Spartiates lived. That all these groups were an undigested lump within the system is self-evident; the Spartan prisoners who had surrendered to the Athenians at Sphacteria were on their release treated as such by the regime, too, simply because they could anticipate loss of civic rights. Interestingly enough, this particular group came from the first families.[15]

Yet it must be recorded that neither separately nor together were the misplaced elements able to destroy the system directly. We are told of only one actual attempt, and that a failure, the abortive revolt led by Cinadon in 397 BC. Several aspects of that revolt are neatly symbolic. Cinadon himself had been employed by the ephors on secret missions. Aristotle (*Politics* 1306b34) described him as 'manly' (*androdes*), and it would be nice to know whether Aristotle had any more information than we have on which to base that perhaps surprising adjective. When asked why he had conspired, Cinadon's reply was, 'in order to be inferior to no one in Sparta' (Xenophon, *Hellenica* 3.3.11). Appropriately, the chief agents in suppressing the revolt before it started were drawn from the élite youth corps.

5. For the sake of completeness, I record without discussion two further sources of tension: (a) the women, if Plato and Aristotle are to be believed; and (b) experience abroad.

IV

I have said very little so far about war or warriors. The paradox is that militarism in Sparta was in low key. Among the more than 100,000 lead figurines found in the ruins of Artemis Orthia, neither soldiers nor arms are particularly prominent (though they exist). There were no war games, no warrior-graves. The latter disappeared abruptly throughout the Greek world, save for strikingly few exceptions on the fringes, more or less at the same time as the appearance of the hoplite, that is, with the

extension of the military role from the 'heroic' aristocrat to a broader
sector of the population. Sparta was no exception. Sparta seems not even
to have included removal from the army among the punishments for
military disgrace. At least that is the implication in Herodotus' story
(7.229–31 + 9.71) about Aristodamos, the survivor of Thermopylae who
was permitted to die a glorious death (though officially not recognised as
such) at Plataea. And the men who surrendered at Sphacteria, tempor-
arily deprived of civic rights though they were, soon found their rights
restored. There is also no trace of the 'war habit' characteristic, for
example, of the Assyrians, the tendency to go out and fight simply
because that is what warriors are for. After the Second Messenian War
and the sixth-century revolution, Sparta was, if anything, less quick to
join battle than many other Greek states. The Corinthians were not
wrong when, in Thucydides' account in his first book, they made a
special point of that.[16]

   If we look on the whole of Laconia and Messenia as a unit, then of
course we see a pyramidal social structure with the Spartiates as a
military élite at the top. However, it was not a military élite in the sense of
the Prussian Junkers or even of the Theban Sacred Band. Instead we
must think of a (conceptually) closed system as a whole, which had a
military function but not a wholly militaristic stamp. I am using these
words as they are distinguished by Alfred Vagts: 'The military way is
marked by a primary concentration of men and materials on winning
specific objectives of power with the utmost efficiency. . . . Militarism,
on the other hand, presents a vast array of customs, interests, prestige,
actions and thought associated with armies and wars and yet transcend-
ing true military purposes.' In a sense both are of course visible in Sparta,
but a further quotation from Vagts's book will show why I said 'not a
wholly militaristic stamp'. Vagts continues: 'An army so built that it
serves military men, not war, is militaristic; so is everything in any army
which is not preparation for fighting, but merely exists for diversion or to
satisfy peace-time whims like the long anachronistic cavalry today . . .
enterprises for sheer glory or the reputation of leaders, which reduce the
fighting strength of armies and wreck them from within, come under
that head.'[17]

   That may conceivably describe a Cleomones I, for example, but he was
rejected. It is not until the fourth century B C that the refrain becomes
insistent in Greek writers that the Spartan state was like an army camp;[18]
that was the sole aim of the lawgiver was war; that in consequence
Spartans were too underdeveloped in all other human aspects (or,

36   THE ANCIENT CITY

contrariwise, that they were praised for precisely those narrow qualities which Plato and Aristotle condemned); that, in sum, they were not only efficiently military but also excessively militaristic. All this is well known and requires no elaboration. But it is not unnecessary or out of place to say that this was not the whole picture even in fourth-century writers. Why did Plato, who criticised Sparta so brutally in the eighth book of the *Republic* (547D–549A), not simply dismiss her? Why did he instead select a Spartan to be one of the trio who were to set up the new state of the *Laws*?

The answer, of course, is that for Plato Sparta had much to offer despite her one-sidedness, not in her laws or institutions narrowly conceived (which are hardly reflected in Plato's book) but in her fundamental conception of a total community, in her *eunomia* as a way of life, one which he wished to strip of its militaristic side (but not of its military function). Sparta had long been a bulwark against tyranny, after all, both at home and abroad; that may not be very true, especially not about Sparta's activities abroad, but it was firmly believed to be true by many Greeks, and it was repeated *ad nauseam*. Pindar believed it. There are not many references to Sparta in Pindar's surviving poems, but they are more significant than their rarity might imply precisely because they are all gratuitous. Pindar wrote no odes for Spartan victors and he did not have to drag Sparta in at all. In the *First Pythian*, celebrating a victory by Hiero I of Syracuse, the poet comments in these words on Hiero's new foundation at Etna (lines 61–70):

> that city in liberty built
> of gods, and ordinances of Hyllos' rule, and the
>   descendants of Pamphylos,
> those, too, of Heracles' seed,
> who dwell beside Taygetos' slopes, are minded to abide
>   for ever in the decrees of Aigimios,
>
> Dorians . . .
> By your (Zeus's) aid, this leader of men,
> enjoining it upon his son also, might glorify his people
>   and turn them to peace and harmony.[19]

Some quite remarkable nonsense has been, and is still being, written about those lines. The absurd suggestion is offered that Hiero, following a brutal expulsion of population of the type so familiar in Sicilian history, actually planned to introduce the Spartan constitution and *agoge* at Etna under the kingship of his son Deinomenes.[20] If it is not obvious that all Pindar had in mind was a traditional royal and aristocratic set-up, in

which the people would find its freedom in discipline, piety and hon-
ourable rule by their betters, then Edouard Will has settled the point by
drawing attention to the remarkably parallel lines in a fragment about
Aegina.[21] If there was anything political, in the narrow sense, in Pindar's
mind, then it was to whisper a reminder of Sparta's anti-tyrant tradition.
There is never anything more in Pindar, never a suggestion that Sparta
was somehow peculiar or unique; in particular, not that Sparta was
militaristic in a way that set it apart from the states and the aristocracies
of the old school in which the values he accepted were to be found.

> There they surpass in counsels of elders,
> And in the spears of young men,
> And in choirs, and the Muse, and Glory.[22]

That was sung about Sparta in another fragment; it could as well have
been used for Thebes, Thessaly, Aegina or Cyrene, or even for the kind
of Athens that Miltiades and Cimon stood for in his eyes.

Nor is the picture in Herodotus very different on the essential question. Given his subject-matter, Herodotus was bound to stress the military skill of the Spartans and their unfailing obedience to the rule never
to retreat in battle. Being Herodotus, he was also bound to dwell on
certain oddities, such as the honours and rituals surrounding the kings
or the penalties meted out to cowards. Herodotus was alert to, and often
very subtle about, nuances differentiating Greek states from one
another. But that was still some way from the altogether odd Sparta of
the fourth-century mirage. For him the Greek world was divided into
two kinds of communities, those ruled by tyrants, which were a bad
thing, and those ruled by themselves. The latter in turn were either fully
democratic or they were not, and Sparta was the most important, the
most powerful and the most interesting of those which were not.

I have gone on at some length about the way in which Sparta was
classed with a whole category of Greek *poleis* because it is essential to be
clear on what was really different and unique about Sparta. At the
beginning I made the point that we must not think of the various strands
in the Spartan structure as monolithic in their history and movement. If
we look at these elements again, this time from the point of view of their
uniqueness of familiarity, we find the following (details apart):

1. Helotage was not altogether rare; it was found in Thessaly, in Crete,
in Sicily, and probably throughout the Danubian and Black Sea areas of
Greek settlement. (I do not ignore the probability that the proportion,
and therefore the potential menance, of helots to citizens was greater
than elsewhere, as will be evident shortly.)

2. The Spartan governmental machinery had its peculiarities, to be sure, but not a single feature of significance other than the kings that can be legitimately be called unique among the Greeks.

3. Every Greek community had its *rites de passage* – at birth, on entering adulthood, at marriage, at death. The variations were endless, and, looked at in isolation, the only things that stand out about the Spartan rites were their perhaps greater frequency and their apparently greater stress on physical punishment and brutality.

4. There is absolutely nothing to my knowledge in Spartan cults or cult practices deserving of notice in our context.

5. Not even the *syssitia* or the age-classes were of themselves unique.

This last point requires elaboration. Some form of table fellowship can be found in all human societies. The association of *syssitia* with age-classes is specifically attested in several Greek communities, and there is every reason to suspect that our information is fragmentary and incomplete. Age-classes, in turn, are common under a great diversity of circumstances. Armies regularly employ them whenever there is conscription, both for the initial training and for call-up when their services are required. On the other hand, there was a proliferation of societies of the youths in Hellenistic and Roman times, precisely the period when they had lost all military function and turned instead to the gymnasium and the palaestra.[23] Love of victory could take a sporting form just as well as a military – as Pindar bears witness.

What was unique about Sparta was the way all these elements were combined into a coherent structure, and the pivotal organising mechanism, the *agoge*. I must insist that there is nothing inherent in age-classes which has to end in the Spartan *agoge*, or even in its ethos of obedience and self-effacement before the interests of the state. There is no self-evident reason why an organisational division into young and old should evolve into the complexity of the Spartan age-class system. It is the complexity and the function that are unique in Sparta, not the division into confraternities of the old and the young. Nor is there any inherent reason why helotage should have led precisely to the Spartan system; and so on through each of the elements. But when the system finally emerged, each element was re-institutionalised in a process that never quite came to an end. And the *agoge* was invented. That last is a pure speculation, of course, but of all the elements in Sparta the *agoge* is the one of which it is most impossible to find traces in our earliest Greek record or traditions, the one which alone 'makes' the Spartan system, so to speak. Therefore I am driven to the inference that, as a pattern of life for the young and as an attempt to fix the individual Spartan's behaviour and ideology for a lifetime, the *agoge* was a late invention, however old some of the initiation rites and other external aspects of it may have been. It was the *agoge*, finally, and the *eunomia* it was held responsible for, which in the end caught the Greek fancy and lay at the heart of the Spartan mirage. 'One of the finest of your laws', said Plato's Athenian (*Laws* 634D), 'is the one absolutely prohibiting any of the young men from inquiring whether any of the laws is good or not.'

The one phenomenon which remains a complete puzzle is the survival of kingship, worse still, of a dual kingship. I have no explanation to put forward, but I will suggest that 'survival' may not be the precisely correct word. What do we know about Spartan kings or kingship between the legendary Menelaus and Leon (or Cleomenes I for that matter)? Genealogies and stories told by Plutarch add up to very little history. Prerogatives in sacrifice and the like were commonplace in Greece whenever anyone exercised the priestly function, whatever his title; guards of honour are so obvious that they can, and have been, thought up time and again in history; double rations in the *syssitia* are really not the same as the Homeric perogatives, no matter how often they are said to be; and above all, the funeral rites – which Herodotus found to be the most striking thing of all about the Spartan kings – cannot be survivals in any sense, since we know of no precedent in the Greek tradition, nor did Herodotus, who called them 'barbarian'. It is at least a defensible hypothesis that the Spartan kingship in the institutional form that we know was as much, or more, a product of the sixth-century revolution, stimulated by the failures of the Second Messenian War, as of inertia, which, in the absence of an explanation, we have the habit of calling 'survival'.

There remains, finally, to look at one other unusual feature of Sparta. No other Greek state was a territorial state like her, in which *polis* and territory were not synonymous, so to speak (as they were between Athens and Attica); in which the *polis*, at least ideally, consisted of a single class of Equals ruling over a relatively vast subject population. The Second Messenian War was decisive in this respect, too. Thereafter the military function became primarily a police function, aimed against an enemy within rather than at enemies real or potential without. To preserve the difficult position of a ruling class in those special circumstances, the whole society was structured to fulfil the police function. Even the efforts expended to found and maintain the Peloponnesian League, though they required repeated warfare, may be accurately described as part of the police function. Sparta's tragedy thereafter stemmed from a familiar cause: she did not live in a vacuum. The Persian invasions foreshadowed what was to come in the Peloponnesian War. Against her will almost, Sparta was drawn into extensive military activity, genuinely military. That entailed severe pressure on manpower and a dangerously extensive incorporation of non-equals into the army if not into the ruling class, unprecedented opportunities for ambitious individuals, extensive travel abroad and a breach in the traditional xenophobia, the impossibility of holding the line against the seductions of wealth. The system could not and did not long survive. And so the final paradox is that her greatest military success destroyed the model military state.

- 3 -

THE ATHENIAN EMPIRE:
A BALANCE SHEET

I

'Every doctrine of imperialism devised by men is a consequence of their second thoughts. But empires are not built by men troubled by second thoughts.'[1]

I start with that aphoristic formulation, the truth of which has been demonstrated in the study of modern imperialisms, as an antidote to the familiar practice of *beginning* a discussion of the Athenian empire with aims and motives and quickly sliding over to attitudes and even theory, thereby implying that the men who created and extended the empire also began with a defined imperialist programme and theories of imperialism. An outstanding current example of the procedure I have in mind is the attempt to date a number of Athenian laws and decrees (or to support a proposed date) by what may be called their imperialist tone. If they are 'harsh', it is argued, they smack of Cleon and should be dated in the 420s BC, and not in the time of the more 'moderate' Periclean leadership, the 440s or 430s.[2] In so far as the argument is not circular, it implies the existence of an identifiable programme of imperialism, or rather of both successive and conflicting programmes, and that requires demonstration, not assumption.

A second source of confusion is the unavoidable ambiguity of the word 'empire'. Stemming from the Latin *imperium*, 'empire' becomes entangled with the word 'emperor', and much of the extensive discussion throughout the Middle Ages and on into modern times ends in a tautological cul-de-sac: an empire is the territory ruled by an emperor.[3] Everyone knows that there are, and have been in the past, important empires not ruled by an emperor, and I see no purpose in playing word-games in order to get round that harmless linguistic anomaly. To suggest, for example, that we should abandon 'empire' as a category in Greek history and speak only of 'hegemony' does not seem to me helpful

Originally published in *Imperialism in the Ancient World*, ed. P. D. A. Garnsey & C. R. Whittaker (1978), and reprinted by permission of the Cambridge University Press.

or useful.[4] It would have been small consolation to the Melians, as the Athenian soldiers and sailors fell upon them, to be informed that they were about to become the victims of a hegemonial, not an imperial, measure.

This is not to question the legitimacy of efforts to differentiate among empires. All broad classificatory terms – 'state' is the obvious analogy – embrace a wide spectrum of individual instances. The Persian, Athenian and Roman empires differed among themselves in important ways, as do modern empires. It then becomes necessary, as with all classifications, to establish the canons for inclusion or exclusion. Those who play with 'hegemony' seem to me to give excessive weight to purely formal considerations, which, if adopted rigorously, would fragment the category 'empire' so much as to render it empty and useless. Common sense is right in this instance: there have been throughout history structures that belong within a single class on substantive grounds, namely, the exercise of authority (or power or control) by one state over one or more other states (or communities or peoples) for an extended period of time. That is admittedly imprecise, but large-scale human institutions can never be classified by other than imprecise canons: again I cite 'state' as an analogy.

A notable example of the formalistic approach is the concern of some historians to define and date the point at which a voluntary association of states was converted into an Athenian empire. The year 454 is a favourite date, because, it is generally believed, the 'league treasury' was then transferred from Delos to Athens.[5] At most, such an action was a symbol, a brutal statement of the reality, but not the reality itself. The word 'voluntary' is not even a good symbol, leading historians into remarkable verbal contortions. 'It seems possible to go farther and to state that though coercion of members apparently was regarded as legitimate – and probably even compulsion against states that did not wish to join – the reduction even of revolting members to the status of subjects was contrary to the constitution'.[6] Matters are not improved by a sprinkling of 'Weberian' terminology: 'indirect domination consists in the fact that it builds on, or attempts to evoke, an interest of the ruled in the process of being ruled.'[7]

Thucydides, with his incomparable eye for reality, did not confuse it with the symbols and the slogans. 'First', he writes in opening his narrative of the half-century between the Persian and Peloponnesian wars (1.98.1), 'they (the Athenians) besieged Eion on the Strymon River', still in Persian hands, and then the island of Skyros in the north

Aegean. Their populations were enslaved and *their territories were colonised by Athenian settlers*. Next Athens compelled Carystus on Euboea to join the league; clearly the 'voluntary' principle had had a very short run. Soon Naxos tried to withdraw from the league (the precise date is uncertain), only to be besieged and crushed by Athens. Naxos 'was the first allied city to be enslaved against established usage', comments Thucydides (1.98.4), employing his favourite metaphor for Athenian interference with the autonomy of the subject-cities in the empire.

Of course the Athenian empire underwent significant changes in the more than half a century of its existence. So has every other empire of similar (or longer) duration in history. To establish and explain the changes is a valid historical concern, but I find it a misconceived enterprise to seek one point along a continuous line which permits us to say that there was no empire before and that there was an empire thereafter. Carystus refused to join the alliance and was forced in; Naxos sought to leave and was forcibly prevented. And they were only the first of many city-states in that position, subject to the authority of another state which acted to advance its own interests, political and material.

I do not dispute that the 'Delian league' (a modern name for which there is no ancient authority) was welcome when it was created in 478 BC, both because of the popularity of the vengeance appeal and, fundamentally, because of the need to clear the Aegean Sea of Persian naval forces. The Persians had twice invaded Greece unsuccessfully, and no one in 478 could have had the slightest confidence that the Great King would accept the defeats passively and would not return in a third attempt. Control of the Aegean was the most obvious protective measure, and Athens successfully won the leadership of such an undertaking. An Athenian, Aristides, was given the task of fixing the amount of money or the number of ships equipped and manned which each member-state would provide for the combined league fleet. The Athenians suppled the league treasurers (*Hellenotamiai*) and the military-naval command. Within a dozen years (the exact number depends on the date of the battle of Eurymedon, which no scholar dates later than 466 BC), the league's formal objective was achieved. The Persian fleet of 200 triremes, most of them Phoenician, was captured and destroyed in a great land-and-sea battle at the mouth of the Eurymedon River in southern Asia Minor. Yet the 'league' remained in existence without a moment's faltering and its membership grew, willingly or by compulsion as the case may have been in each instance, exactly as before Eurymedon.

The chief executant of Athenian policy in those years and the commander-in-chief at Eurymedon was Cimon. He had been personally in charge at Eion, and again in 465 BC, shortly after Eurymedon, when Thasos, the largest and wealthiest island in the north Aegean, tried to withdraw from the alliance. After a siege lasting more than two years, Thasos capitulated and was condemned to surrender her fleet (henceforth paying tribute in money), to dismantle her walls, to pay Athens a large indemnity, and to surrender the ports and the mines she possessed on the mainland. And Cimon, of course, far from being a 'radical democrat' or 'demagogue' like Pericles, let alone Cleon, represented the traditional, oligarchically inclined, landowning aristocracy of Athens. Had he lived longer, he no doubt would have opposed many of the policies adopted by both Pericles and Cleon with respect to the empire. However, his oppostion would not have been on moral grounds. There is no difference in 'harshness' between the treatment of the people of Eion and Skyros in Cimon's day and Cleon's proposal nearly half a century later to massacre the people of Mytilene. Our sources, in fact, do not reveal a single Athenian who opposed the empire as such, not even Thucydides son of Melesias or his kinsman and namesake, the historian.[8]

Certainly neither Athens nor her allies anticipated all the consequences of the first step of association in 478, in particular what would happen if a member-state chose to 'secede'. Nor can anyone today know what decision-making individuals in Athens hoped or desired. What, for instance, were the long-range aspirations of Themistocles and Aristides for Athens and Athenian power? The Delian league was the first of a number of major instances in classical Greek history of the deployment of Panhellenism, with or without the name, 'to justify the hegemony and mastery of one *polis* over the other states by proposing a common aim, war against the barbarians'.[9] Hope and aspirations do not imply a defined programme, but their presence in Athens in 478 is demonstrated by the rapidity with which Athens not only acquired the decision-making power for the league but also was prepared, in manpower, ships and psychology, to exert force in the strictest sense, to impose her decisions and to punish recalcitrants.

This is not to underestimate the Panhellenic appeal, any more than the real fear of further Persian invasions. The pull of ideology is never to be underestimated, nor is it easy to untangle ideology and reality. In a conflict, how does one measure the respective importance of the two elements in determining the decision of a weaker state? A prudent state could 'voluntarily' save itself from the frightful consequences of resistance and 'involuntary' subjection, but some did not. An early British juridical distinction between ceded and and conquered territories was soon abandoned precisely because the two overlapped much of the time.[10] Lacking, as we do, the data from the Athenian empire with which to attempt such refined distinctions, we may still examine that empire operationally, that is, analyse as best we can, and as concretely, the observed behaviour patterns, and assess the gains and the losses of both the imperial state and the subject states.[11]

For that purpose, a crude typology of the various ways in which one state may exercise its power over others for its own benefit will suffice: (1) restriction on freedom of action in inter-state relations; (2) political, administrative and/or judicial interference in internal affairs; (3) compulsory military and/or naval service; (4) the payment of 'tribute' in some form, whether in the narrow sense of a regular lump sum or as a land tax or in some other way; (5) confiscation of land, with or without subsequent emigration of settlers from the imperial state; (6) other forms of economic subordination or exploitation, ranging from control of the seas and Navigation Acts to compulsory delivery of goods at prices below the prevailing market price and the like.

The present essay will focus on the economics of imperial power. I do not imply by that concentration that the politics of the Athenian empire do not merit analysis or that economics and politics were separable, autonomous aspects of the story. However, I have nothing new to contribute on the foreign-policy aspect, except perhaps to ask: Why was Athens concerned to convert other Greek *poleis* into dependent agents in inter-state relations, and, in particular, what material benefits did Athens obtain (whether deliberately envisaged or not) from her success in the endeavour? Interference in internal affairs is less well understood, largely because of the inadequacy of the evidence, and again I shall restrict myself to those which either had or may possibly have had an immediate economic impact.

Because of the paucity and one-sidedness of the sources, no narrative is possible, and that means no adequate consideration of development and change. If what follows therefore has a static appearance, that is not because I hold the improbable view that the relations between Athens and her subjects were fundamentally unchanged from 478 to 404 but because I know of no way to document significant change, and no other way to avoid falling into the harshness-of-Cleon trap I have already discussed. We have the impression, for example, that over the years Athens interfered with increasing frequency and toughness in the internal affairs of some or all of the subjects: certain criminal cases had to be tried in Athens before Athenian juries, the right to coin money was taken away for a period, and there were other measures. What little we know about these actions rests almost entirely on epigraphical finds, and although it is usually possible to offer a plausible reason for the introduction of a particular measure at the time of a particular inscription, there has been too much unhappy experience with the crumbling of such logic upon the discovery of a new inscription. Besides, the dates of some of the most critical measures, such as the coinage decree, remain the subject of open controversy.

We know, too, that the Athenians developed a considerable administrative machinery for the empire, 700 officials, says Aristotle (*Constitution of Athens* 24.3), about as many as the number for internal affairs. Apart from suspicion about the duplication of the figure 700, there is no valid reason to question his accuracy. 'We do not know enough to say that 700 is an impossible figure'[12] is needlessly sceptical. And again the sources let us down: the evidence for the administration is almost entirely epigraphical; it does not take us back earlier than the Erythrae decree (*IG* 1² 10), probably of the mid-450s; it allows barely a glimpse into the division of functions.[13] Nothing can be deduced from silence here: there are virtually no Athenian inscriptions (other than dedications) before the mid-fifth century, and even the tribute drops from site between the original assessment by Aristides and 454. We may safely assume, I believe, that administrative officials (both military and civilian, in so far as that distinction has any meaning in this context) other than the *Hellenotamiai* began to appear at least as soon as there was resistance to membership, that their numbers increased and so did their duties and powers as the years went on. No long-range or systematic Athenian planning is implied in that assumption. What is indisputable is the existence and scale of this administration in the end, not only very large by Greek standards but also, as has apparently not been noticed, relatively larger than the formal administation in the provinces of the Roman empire.

II

In any study of the Athenian empire, two of the categories in my typology – military-naval service and tribute – must be considered together, because they were manipulated together by Athens for most of the history of the empire. When the league was founded, the member-states were divided into those which contributed cash and those which contributed ships together with their crews. As time went on, the latter group was whittled down until only two members remained, Chios and Lesbos, although others are recorded as having contributed a few ships to a campaign on a few later occasions, as did Corcyra, an ally outside the league. We have no list of the original muster of ship-contributing states nor any statement of the principles on which the states were assigned to one category or the other.[14] In a general way it is obvious that ships would have been required of the larger maritime states with proper harbour facilities, not of inland states or of very small ones. Honour would have also played its part. In 478, at any rate, Chios or Lesbos would not lightly have surrendered their warships and everything that their possession implied; a few decades later, they pathetically clung to their continued ship-contribution as a symbol of 'autonomy' in contrast to the tribute-paying mass of subject states.[15]

However, if the surviving ancient texts fail us on the situation at the foundation of the league, Thucydides is explicit enough about the reason for the change in the pattern: 'reluctance to go on campaign led most of them, in order to avoid serving abroad, to have assessments made in money corresponding to the expense of producing ships' (1.99.3). 'To avoid serving abroad' cannot be taken at face value; these states had not in the past built, equipped and manned warships merely in order to repel attackers, and there are enough instances of their willingness to 'serve abroad'. Now, however, they were serving an alien, imperial state on its terms and at its command. Hence the reluctance, which first showed itself in a refusal to meet the required contributions (Thucydides 1.99.1), and after the high price of refusal had several times been revealed, turned into the most abject surrender, the conversion of the 'league' fleet into an Athenian fleet in the narrowest sense, part of it consisting of ships confiscated from the subjects (Thucydides 1.19) and another part paid for out of their annual tribute. Thucydides openly condemns the subjects for thus reducing themselves to impotence. But I suggest that the difference in naval power between 478 and, say, 440 was basically only a quantitative one. Athenian control of the combined fleet was near enough complete at the beginning to justify H. D. Meyer's judgment that the league was 'from the moment of its creation an Athenian instrument of compulsion (*Zwangsinstrument*)'[16]

Some of the purposes for which the instrument was employed will be considered later. Here I want to examine the financial implications, without resorting to the arithmetical guessing-games that litter the scholarly literature. The few figures in the surviving sources are too skimpy, too unreliable, and often too contradictory to underpin the mathematics, and the epigraphical data add to the confusion rather than help to clear it. I shall therefore restrict myself to a few considerations by way of example, none of which is undermined by a large margin of error.

First, however, it is necessary to get rid of two fetishes. One is a single numeral: 'The original tribute assessment totalled 460 talents' (Thucydides 1.96.2). It requires a powerful will-to-believe to accept that figure as credible, and a mystical faith to bring contributions in ships within the total.[17] The expenditure of ingenuity in the attempt to reconcile 460 with other amounts scattered among the sources could be indulged as a harmless pastime were it not that they divert attention from the realities of the situation. The objective was a fleet, not coin, yet scholars debate whether Aristides began his survey with a target of 460 talents or merely ended his work with a bit of meaningless addition, producing the meaningless total of 460. Can it be seriously suggested that in the early fifth century BC anyone would have begun the difficult task of assembling a coalition fleet by setting a target in cash, not in ships? And what is the point to a tribute total without a ship total, of which there is not a trace in the sources?

A major difficulty in the attempts at reconciliation is created by the totals of payments, normally under 400 talents, that appear (or are conjectured) on the 'Athenian tribute lists', a group of inscriptions which collectively are my second fetish.[18] Their discovery and study have of course been the greatest modern boon to our knowledge of the Athenian empire, but it has become necessary to insist that the 'tribute lists' are not a synonym for the empire, and that they do not represent the whole of the monetary inflow into Athens from the empire. I believe that the only figure of money income from the empire which can be defended, both substantively and contextually, is the one Thucydides (2.13.3) attributes to Pericles at the beginning of the Peloponnesian War – 600 talents. The tribute was the largest component, but from the viewpoint of Athens it was fiscally irrelevant whether the cash arrived as tribute, as indemnities or as income from confiscated mines.[19] But even if my faith in 600 talents should prove to be ill-founded, my analysis of the financial implications of the empire would not suffer in the least.

The figure of 600 talents certainly did not include the 'cash value' of ship-contributions, by then restricted to Lesbos and Chios. For the earlier period of the empire, however, it is essential to obtain some notion of the relative burden of the two types of contribution.[20] Unfortunately, the cost of building and equipping a warship is unknown; the widely quoted figure of between one and two talents in the mid-fifth century is a guess, but it will serve our purposes. The normal life of a trireme was twenty-plus years, against which must be offset damage or loss in storms, shipwreck and battles, all varying greatly from year to year and incalculable. Then there was much the largest cost item, the pay for the crews, 200 in round numbers on each trireme, 170 of them rowers. That ranged from one third or one half a drachma early in the fifth century to one drachma a day at the beginning of the Peloponnesian War, or one talent per ship per month at the higher rate. Again there are too many uncontrollable variables – the number of ships on regular patrol duty, on guard duty or on tribute-collecting assignment, the number and duration of campaigns year by year and the number of participating warships, the numbers of days devoted annually to training, essential for the rowers in triremes,[21] the share of 'allied' ships in the total activity of the league in all these respects.

We must therefore attempt a comparative assessment without precise figures, and one fairly late instance will serve as a point of departure. In the spring of 428 BC ten triremes from the Lesbian *polis* of Mytilene arrived in the Piraeus 'according to the alliance' (Thucydides 3.3.4.). The ten triremes, Blackman writes, were 'a small squadron for routine service; more could of course be called for if necessary for a particular campaign'.[22] Yet this small squadron cost Mytilene five talents a month in pay, at the half-drachma rate, in addition to the costs of construction, maintenance, repair and equipment. The fragmentary 'tribute lists' for the years 431–428 show such annual tribute payments, in round numbers, as 10–15 talents from Abdera, 10 from Lampsacus, 15 or 16 from Byzantium, 9 from Cyzicus – all in the higher range of recorded contributions, not exceeded by more than half a dozen or so states. The comparison with the cost of ships' crews therefore suggests that, once the Persian fleet was shattered at Eurymedon, the move by the subject-states to shift from ships to tribute was motivated not only by patriotism and love of freedom but also by public finance. For the maritime states, tribute often meant a reduced financial burden, in some years a substantial reduction. One comparative figure may help assess the burden: the average annual outlay on the Parthenon, a very expensive temple, was 30–2 talents,[23] equal to the highest recorded tribute, a sum which the crews of twelve triremes would have earned in pay (at the lower rate) in one five-month sailing season (and there were times when warships remained at sea outside the 'normal' season).

Two offsetting considerations are commonly introduced into the calculation, as in the following statement by Blackman: '. . . but the pay
was mainly if not entirely going to their own citizens. A long season
probably meant active campaigning rather than routine patrols, and this
gave greater hope of booty to offset expenditure'. They 'may well have
expected to cover their costs as a result; this was probably the case in the
early years, at least until after Eurymedon and perhaps until the early
450s.'[24] The 'social welfare' consideration may be dismissed out of hand:
it is not a fifth-century conception, especially not among the oligarchies
which still controlled some of the larger maritime states: besides, many
of 'their own citizens' quickly found employment as rowers in the
Athenian navy. As for booty, which everyone no doubt hoped for, so
long as they had to campaign and fight, there is little evidence in the
ancient sources about any campaign during the relevant period except
for Eurymedon. The silence of the sources is not a compelling argument
on one side, but it seems to me impermissible on the other side to fill out
that silence with 'may well have expected to cover their costs'. As for
Eurymedon, it is a flight of the wildest imagination to think that the
Delian league gambled its combined fleet, with their men, and the
independence of Greece on a major naval battle chiefly, or even significantly, for the booty they would collect if they won.[25]

Large-scale naval (and military) engagements were both expensive
and unpredictable, to the participants if not to later historians, even
those with heavy advantages on one side. It required something like a
full year, from about April 440 to about April 439, for Athens to subdue
Samos.[26] The island was then still a ship-contributor and was able to
muster 70 warships, 50 of them in fighting condition, and posed the
further threat, real or imaginary, of support from a 'Persian' fleet.
Athens sent several large flotillas, perhaps totalling more than 150 (a
portion of which was diverted against the 'Persian' threat), and a military
force with siege equipment; she also summoned Chios and Lesbos to
make their contributions, 25 triremes together in the first year, 30 in the
second. There were victories on both sides, and then an eight-month
siege forced Samos to surrender. There was considerable loss of life and
material (including triremes). The financial cost to Athens may have
been 1,200 talents (though that figure is reached by too many textual
emendations for comfort). The victor's terms included a heavy indemnity, paid to Athens, and the surrender of the Samian fleet, marking her
permanent disappearance from the roster of ship-contributors. We have
no details of the Lesbian-Chian involvement, but each month would

have cost them 12–15 talents in pay alone, and they received not a penny for their pains, either in indemnity or in booty.

Triremes were purpose-built warships fit for no other use. There was no interchangeability with merchant ships or fishing vessels, nor was there any other professional employment for tens of thousands of rowers.[27] Hence, as states lost genuine freedom to make war, there was little point, and great expense, in constructing, maintaining and manning a squadron. So they sought relief by inviting Athens to transfer them to the tribute-paying category, a request that could not have been imposed on an unwilling Athens. That Athens did agree indicates that she could afford the fiscal loss as the price for a fully Athenian navy, with all that it meant in power and self-satisfaction. She could afford it because the state's finances were in a healthy condition, thanks to the imperial revenues, direct and indirect. We are unable to do the sums, just as we cannot properly calculate how Athens managed to put aside so much of her public revenues as a reserve fund, reaching 9,700 talents at one moment (Thucydides 2.13.3). That is a pity, but it does not alter the reality.

III

Tribute, in its narrow sense, is of course only one way that an imperial state drains funds from subject states for its treasury. It is probably neither the most common nor the most important, as compared, in particular, with a tithe or a monetary tax on the land of the subjects. Of the latter there is no trace in the Athenian empire, and indeed there is only one recorded instance of state exploitation of confiscated property, that of the gold and silver mines on the mainland taken from Thasos after her unsuccessful revolt.[28] These mines continued to be worked by individuals, as they had been before – most famously by Thucydides (4.105.1), presumably as an inheritance from his Thracian ancestors – but the Athenian state took its share of the profits, as from the mines of Laurium at home.

It was in the area of private enrichment, not public, that land played a major role in the Athenian empire. The number of Athenian citizens, usually from the poorer strata, who were given either allotments of confiscated land or, at least in Lesbos after the unsuccessful revolt there in 428, a substantial, uniform (and therefore arbitrary) 'rent', roughly equivalent to a hoplite's pay for a full year, on holdings retained and worked by the islanders, may have totalled 10,000 in the course of the imperial period.[29] The most naked kind of imperial exploitation therefore directly benefited perhaps 8–10 per cent of the Athenian citizen body.[30] Some confiscations were in places from which the defeated population had been totally expelled, but many were in areas in which the local people remained as a recognised community, and there the settler pattern that has dominated so much of the history of later imperialism was evident,[31] though rather in embryo because the settlements were short-lived.

Colonies and cleruchies are not the whole story, though most accounts of the empire rest with them, 'too preoccupied in studying the misdeeds of Athenian imperialism through official institutions and collective decisions' to give due weight to 'the action of individuals who played their part in the general concert'.[32] Individual Athenians, most of them from the upper end of the social and economic spectrum, acquired landed property in subject territories where there were neither colonies nor cleruchies. The evidence is scarce, but one piece is remarkable enough for a closer look. In the surviving fragments of the very detailed record, inscribed on stone, of the sale by public auction of the property confiscated from men convicted of participation in the double sacrilege of 415 BC, the profanation of the mysteries and the mutilation of the herms, there are included a few landed estates outside Attica, in Oropus on the Boeotian border, on Euboea and Thasos, and at Abydos on the Helles-pont and Ophryneion in the Troad.[33] One group of holdings, dispersed in at least three regions of Euboea, belonged to one man, Oionias. It went for 81 ⅓ talents,[34] a sum to be compared with the largest (composite) landed holding recorded for Attica itself, that of the banker Pasion at his death in 370/69 BC, which, we are told, was worth twenty talents (Ps.-Demosthenes 46.13).[35]

It must be emphasised that men like Oinias were not from the classes who were assigned land in the colonies and cleruchies, and that the properties sold up following their conviction (or flight) were not within 'cleruchic' blocks.[36] They had acquired their holdings by 'private enterprise', though we have no idea how that was achieved. Throughout the Greek world in this period, land ownership was restricted to citizens, unless a *polis* by a sovereign act granted special permission to a non-citizen, which it appears to have done rarely and then only for notable services to the state. It is wildly improbable that Alcibiades and his friends had each individually been granted this privilege by Oropus, Euboea, Thasos, Abydos and Ophryneion in gratitude for their benefactions. It is equally improbable that only men caught up in the escapades of 415 were in this privileged group. Were it not for the chance find of a batch of fragmentary inscriptions, we should have known nothing about the whole operation beyond four or five off-hand general remarks in the literary sources, yet Oionias, otherwise unknown, turns out to be one of the richest Athenians of any period in its history. Nor, finally, have we any idea of the number of properties abroad held by the men sold up: only some twenty of the known fifty victims have been identified in the surviving epigraphical fragments, and by no means all of their possessions are listed in the texts we have.

As I have already said, we do not know how these acquisitions were brought about. Were they obtained 'legally' or 'illegally'? Only the Athenian answer is clear: the Athenian state accepted the legitimacy of the title and sold the estates as the property of the condemned men. That the Athenian empire was the operative element seems certain to me: I need not again note the ambiguity of the concept of 'voluntary action'; we are here concerned with men who had influence and power inside Athens, men to be courted by subjects. It is even more certain that there was a great resentment in the empire over this breach of the principle of citizen monopoly of the land, hence the Athenian concession in the decree founding the so-called second Athenian league in 378/7 BC, that neither the Athenian state nor any of its citizens will be permitted 'to acquire either a house or land in the territories of the allies, whether by purchase or by foreclosure or by any other means whatsoever' (IG II² 43.35–41). No one would have requested and been granted the inclusion of such a blunt prohibition unless there were strong feelings on the subject, which are reflected in the excessive formulation and which can have resulted only from the bitter experience of the 'first Athenian league'.[37]

IV

The moment we turn to the sixth category of my typology, 'other forms of economic exploitation or subordination', we are immediately plunged into the contentious field of Greek 'trade and politics'. On that I have stated and argued my views at length elsewhere.[38] My chief concern at present is with the consequences of Athenian imperial power in assisting individual Athenians to derive direct economic advantage other than through employment in the navy and related industries or through the acquisition of land in subject territories. Indirect gains were inevitable: power always attracts profits, as in the much vaunted plenitude and

variety of commodities available in Athens, from which shippers, artisans and peddlers made gains. Many of the latter were not Athenians,
however, and Hellenistic Rhodians were in the same advantageous
position without the same political power behind them. Nevertheless,
that such gains were a by-product of the Athenian empire is indisputable, though the magnitude of the gain cannot be measured and its
place, if any, in Athenian policy cannot be deduced simply from its
existence. *Handelspolitik* (commercial politics) is not a synonym for
Machtpolitik (power politics), no matter how often historians make the
slide.

The problem can be stated in this way. Control of the Aegean was for
Athens an instrument of power. How was that instrument employed to
achieve ends beyond collection of tribute, land settlement, interference
in internal political arrangements, suppression of petty wars and the
more or less complete elimination of piracy? More precisely, was it in fact
employed for any ends other than those I have just listed, and, in
particular, for commercial ends?

Given the nature of the ancient economy, two of the most important
and profitable forms of modern colonial exploitation were ruled out,
namely, cheap labour and cheap raw materials; in more technical
language, the employment, by compulsion if necessary, of colonial
labour at wages well below the market wage at home, and the acquisition, again by compulsion if necessary, of basic raw materials at prices
substantially below the market prices at home. A third form of exploitation, which was available and which loomed so large in republican
Rome, seems to have been absent in the Athenian empire. I refer to the
lending of money to subject cities and states at high rates of interest,
usually in order to provide the latter with the cash required by them for
their tax (or tribute) payments to the imperial state. The possibilities of
Handelspolitik are therefore narrowed to competitive commercial advantages sought by non-economic means, that is to say, by the exercise of
power without manipulating prices and wages.

The evidence is notoriously slight, almost to the point of non-
existence. In the second chapter of his *Constitution of the Athenians*,
Pseudo-Xenophon hammers the point, repeated in blunt words in the
next century by Isocrates (8.36), that imperial Athens 'did not permit
others to sail the sea unless they were willing to pay the tribute'. These
two writers are so notoriously tendentious that any of their generalisations is suspect, but not *ipso facto* false. Not so easily dismissed is the
provision in the Athenian decree of 426 BC allowing Methone on the

Thermaic Gulf to import a fixed amount (lost) of grain annually from Byzantium, upon registering with Athenian officials there called *Hellespontophylakes* (Hellespont Commissioners). Similar permission was given in the same period to Aphytis (near Potidaea). Only two texts, but they go some way towards documenting Pseudo-Xenophon and Isocrates. The inscriptions do not say that Methone and Aphytis could not sail the sea without paying tribute; they say both less and more; both cities were guaranteed the right to 'sail freely' but neither could purchase Black Sea grain without Athenian permission.[39]

The presence of the *Hellespontophylakes* implies that all other cities were, or could be, similarly controlled. Whether or not the *Hellespontophylakes* represented 'a system of strict organisation'[40] cannot be determined but they deserve more attention than they customarily receive. Potentially, with the backing of the Athenian navy, they could deny any and every Greek city access to the Black Sea, and therefore access to the main seaborne route not only for grain, but also for slaves, hides and other important products. When were they installed? The temptation to label them a 'wartime measure' must be resisted. Not only does it introduce the argument from silence, about which I have already said enough, but it ignores the fact that very few years since 478 were not 'wartime years'.[41]

I do not suggest that the *Hellespontophylakes* were introduced early in the history of the empire. They were, after all, only the capstone of the structure, an organisation designed to bring about a closed sea. What I do suggest is that such an aim was the automatic consequence of naval power, within the Greek *polis* system, and that steps in that direction would have been taken by the Athenians when and as they were able, and found it advantageous, to do so.[42] Short of going to war, there was no more useful instrument for punishing enemies, rewarding friends, and persuading 'neutrals' to become 'friends'.[43] And if employment of the instrument meant going to war, *tant pis*. The revolt of Thasos, Thucydides writes (1.100.2), arose from a quarrel 'about the *emporia* on the Thracian coast and about the mines the Thasians exploited'. That was as early as 465 BC, and, though we do not know the issue dividing Athens and Thasos over the *emporia*, it can scarcely be unrelated to the 'closed sea' ambitions of the imperial state, which then simply took over the *emporia* after Thasos was defeated. Of course Athens did not yet have the ability to close the sea which she was to have later, but it is surely wrong to say that the aim itself was *unthinkable* in the 60s and 50s.[44] That is to commit the hegemony-into-empire error once again.

The question, in sum, is not when or whether the 'closed sea' was thinkable but when and how Athens was able to close the sea to suit herself. And why. As we shall see in a moment, Athenian purposes did not require total control, even if that were within their reach. The Corinthian warning, in 432, that inland states would soon learn what maritime states already knew, that Athens was able to prevent them from bringing their produce to the sea and from buying what they required in turn (Thucydides 1.120.2), is meaningful but must be understood correctly in practical terms. So is the 'Megarian decree'. Not even the most monumental special pleading has succeeded in diluting the plain words, repeated three times by Thucydides (1.67., 1.139, 1.144.2), that a decree, moved by Pericles in 432, among other provisions excluded the Megarians 'from the harbours of the Athenian empire'. All the elaborate arguments about the impossibility of blockade by triremes and about the ease of 'sanction-busting', founded in fact though they are, are irrelevant.[45] The Athenians claimed the right to exclude the Megarians from all harbours, and they could have enforced that claim *had they wished*. The long story that began with Eion and Skyros was known to every state which had a harbour, and there were Athenian officials (as well as *proxenoi* and other Athenian friends) in every important harbour-town.

That Athens did not wish to *destroy* Megara is patent, and significant. What she wished, and accomplished, was to hurt Megara and at the same time to declare openly and forcefully that she was prepared to employ the 'closed sea' ruthlessly as an instrument of power. The coinage decree, whenever one dates it, was precisely the same kind of declaration.[46] Both were expressions of *Machtpolitik* – but not, in the normal sense of that term, of *Handelspolitik*. At this point, we must introduce into the discussion the distinction first formulated clearly in the field of Greek history by Hasebroek, the distinction between 'commercial interests' and 'import interests' (specifically food, shipbuilding materials, metals).[47] Athens could not survive as a great power, or indeed as any kind of large autonomous *polis*, without a regular import on a considerable scale of grain, metals and shipbuilding materials, and she could now guarantee that through her control of the sea. In not a single action, however, did Athens show the slightest concern for private Athenian profits in this field: there were no Navigation Acts, no preferential treatment for Athenian shippers, importers or manufacturers, no efforts to reduce the large, perhaps preponderant, share of the trade in the hands of non-Athenians.[48] Without such moves, there can be no *Handelspolitik*, no 'monopolisation of trade and traffic'.[49] And on this score there was no difference between the landowner Cimon and the tanner Cleon.

Many Greek *poleis*, and especially most larger and ambitious ones, had a comparable need to import. Athens could now block them, partially if not completely, and that was the other use of the 'closed sea' instrument. When the Athenians sent a fleet in 427 BC to support Leontini against Syracuse, their real aim, explains Thucydides (3.86.4), 'was to prevent corn from being exported from there to the Peloponnese'. How often and under what circumstances Athens used her fleet this way in the course of the half-century after 478 cannot be determined from the pitiful evidence. The very existence of her navy normally made an open display of force unnecessary, and there is no reason to think that Athens block-aded other states merely for practice or sadistic amusement. In the absence of genuinely commercial and competitive motives, interference in the sailing and trading activities of other states was restricted to specific situations, as they arose *ad hoc* in the growth of the empire. Only during the Peloponnesian War (or so it seems), which radically altered the scale of operations and the stakes, did it become necessary to make massive use of the 'closed sea' instrument. And even then the volume of traffic in the Aegean was considerable enough for the Athenians in 413 BC to abandon the tribute for a five per cent harbour tax (Thucydides 7.28.4) *in an attempt to increase their revenue*.[50]

Obviously a steady flow of food and other materials was a benefit to many Athenians individually. But to include such a gain under the rubric, 'other forms of economic subordination or exploitation', would strain the sense unduly.

V

'Athens' is of course an abstraction. Concretely, who in Athens ben-efited (or suffered) from the empire, how and to what extent? In what follows, I shall remain within my narrow framework, restricting 'benefits', 'profits', to their material sense, excluding the 'benefits' (not unimportant) arising from glory, prestige, the sheer pleasure of power. I shall also ignore such side-benefits as the tourist attraction of every great imperial city.

The traditional Greek view is well known, as it was 'quantified' by Aristotle (*Constitution of Athens* 24.3): the common people of Athens, the poorer classes, were both the driving force behind, and the beneficiaries

of, the empire. Their benefits are easily enumerated. At the head of the
list is the extensive land confiscated from subjects and distributed in
some fashion among Athenians. Perhaps as important is the navy:
Athens maintained a standing fleet of 100 triremes, with another 200 in
drydock for emergencies. Even 100 required 20,000 men, and, though
we do not know how many ships were kept at sea regularly on patrol
duty and for practice,[51] or how many ships campaigned for how long
through all the fighting of the periods 478–431 and 431–404, there seems
little doubt that thousands of Athenians earned their pay for rowing in
the fleet through the sailing-season annually, and that tens of thousands
(including many non-Athenians) were engaged for longer or shorter
periods on campaigns in many years. Add the work in the dockyards
alone and the total cash benefit to poor Athenians was substantial
though not measurable; to a large percentage of all the poor, furthermore.

To be sure, Athens maintained a navy before she had an empire, and
continued to do so after the loss of the empire, but the later experience
demonstrates that, without the imperial income, it was impossible to pay
so large a body of crewman regularly. Similarly with corn supply: Athens
succeeded in maintaining imports in the fourth century, too, but in the
fifth century everyone knew how imperial power guaranteed those
imports (as it supported the navy), even if not everyone knew the text of
the Methone decree or had heard of the *Hellespontophylakes*. And it is
always the poor who are most threatened by shortages and famines.

Finally, there was pay for office, on which Aristotle laid his greatest
stress in his attempt at quantification. No other Greek state, so far as we
know, made it a regular practice to pay for holding public office or
distributed the offices so widely.[52] That was a radical innovation in
political life, the capstone of 'Periclean' democracy, for which there was
no precedent anywhere. Fundamental radical measures require powerful stimuli and unprecedented necessary conditions. I believe that the
empire provided both the necessary cash and the political motivation.[53]
'Those who drive the ships are those who possess the power in the state',
wrote Pseudo-Xenophon (1.2), and I have already indicated that this
unpleasant writer did not always miss the mark with his gnomic propaganda statements.

What, then, of the more prosperous Athenians in the upper classes,
the *kaloi kagathoi*? The paradox, in modern eyes, is that they both paid the
bulk of the domestic taxes and constituted the armed forces. Yet, as we
have already seen, they also supported the imperial advance of Athens,

surely not out of idealistic or political interest in the benefits to the lower classes. How did they benefit? Did they? There is total silence in the literary sources of this question, save for a remarkable passage in Thucydides (8.48.5–6). During the manoeuvres leading to the oligarchic coup of 411, Phrynichus spoke against the proposal to recall Alcibiades and replace the democracy. It is false, he said (in Thucydides' summary), to think that the subjects of Athens would welcome an oligarchy, for 'they saw no reason to suppose that they would be any better off under the *kaloi kagathoi*, considering that when the democracy had perpetrated evils it had been under the instigation and guidance of the *kaloi kagathoi*, who were the chief beneficiaries'.

Phrynichus was a slippery character and we are not obliged to believe everything (or anything) he said in a policy debate. However, Thucydides went out of his way, to an unusual degree, to stress the acuity and correctness of Phrynichus' judgments,[54] and that puts a different light on his assertion about upper-class benefits from the empire. It at least suggests something more than glory and power-as-such as the aims of the long line of *kaloi kagathoi* beginning with Cimon who built, defended and fought for the empire. The puzzle is that we are unable to specify how the upper classes could have been the chief beneficiaries. Apart from the acquisition of property in subject territories, I can think of nothing other than negative benefits. That is to say, the imperial income enabled the Athenians to construct splendid public buildings and to float the largest navy of the day without adding to the taxpayers' financial burdens. How much of a burden the navy could impose became clear in the fourth century. That is something, but it is hardly enough to resolve the puzzle Phrynichus has left us with.

Be that as it may, the conclusion seems to me compelling that the empire directly profited the poorer half of the Athenian population to an extent unknown in the Roman empire, or in modern empires. There was a price, of course, the costs of constant warfare. Men were lost in naval engagements and sometimes in land battles, most shatteringly in the Sicilian disaster. Athenian farmers suffered from periodic Spartan raids in the first stage of the Peloponnesian War, and even more from the permanent Spartan garrison at Decelea in the final decade of the war. The connection between those evils and the empire was obvious, but what conclusions were drawn? War was endemic: everyone accepted that as fact, and therefore no one seriously argued, or believed, that surrender of the empire would relieve Athens of the miseries of war. It would merely relieve them of certain particular wars, and the loss of empire and its benefits did not seem worth that dubious gain. Athenian morale remained buoyant to the bitter end, reflecting their calculus of the profits and the losses.

VI

No doubt the subject states would have preferred freedom from Athens to subjection, other things being equal. But the desire for freedom is often a weak weapon, and other things are rarely equal in real life. I am referring not merely to the staggering difficulties of staging a successful revolt – Naxos tried and was crushed, Thasos tried and was crushed, later Mytilene tried and was crushed – but to the more complex relationships inherent in all situations of subjection and domination. 'The allies (or subjects)' are as much an abstraction as 'Athens'. Athens had friends in every subject city.[55] In 413, before the final battle at Syracuse, when the position of the Athenian army had become hopeless, the Syracusans offered the allied contingents their freedom and a safe-conduct if they deserted. They refused and accepted the Athenian fate. Two years later, the people of Samos reaffirmed their loyalty to Athens and remained faithful to the bitter end.

We do not know why the Samians reacted in this way in 411, the Mytileneans in the opposite direction in 428. We lack the necessary information. The history of empire reveals a similarly divergent pattern everywhere: the view from the imperial state is more or less unitary, whereas the view from the receiving end varies from community to community, and within each community from group to group. Among some of Athens' subjects, the common people preferred democracy backed by Athenian power to oligarchy in an autonomous state. That would be one explanation of a particular reaction (though Athens did not always oppose oligarchies). In this connection, it is worth remembering that we are never told how the tribute was collected *within the tributary state*. If the normal Greek system of taxation prevailed – and there is no reason to believe that it did not – then the tribute for Athens was paid by the rich, not by the common people. That burden would therefore not have caused the latter any concern. In sum, the material costs borne by the subjects were uneven, and by and large their weight and impact elude us.

In Thucydides' account of the debates at Sparta that ended with a declaration of war against Athens, the historian attributes the following words to an Athenian spokesman (1.76.2):

We have done nothing extraordinary, nothing contrary to human practice, in accepting an empire when it was offered to us and then in
refusing to give it up. Three very powerful motives prevent us from
doing so – honour, fear and self-interest. And we were not the first to act
in this way. It has always been a rule that the weak should be subject to
the strong; besides we consider that we are worthy of our power.

There is no programme of imperialism there, no theory, merely a
reassertion of the universal ancient belief in the naturalness of domination. Looking back, the historian is free to make his own moral
judgments; he is not free to confuse them with practical judgments. Too
much of the modern literature is concerned, even obsessed, with trying
to determine whether Athens 'exploited her allies in any extensive way'
or 'how much exploitation and oppression took place'. Such questions
are unanswerable, when they are not meaningless. Athenian imperialism employed all the forms of material exploitation that were available
and possible in that society. The choices and the limits were determined
by experience and by practical judgments, sometimes by miscalcu-
lations.

- 4 -

LAND, DEBT
AND THE MAN OF PROPERTY
IN CLASSICAL ATHENS

When Alexander the Great's father, Philip II of Macedon, organised the Greek cities into a League of the Hellenes, one important task of the new body was the suppression of sedition in the Greek world. The catalogue of seditious acts included the redistribution of land and cancellation of debts (Ps. Demosthenes 17.15). For Plato these measures betokened the tyrant and the demagogue.[1] All the citizens of Itanos in Crete swore, 'I will not bring about a redistribution of lands or houses or building lots, nor a cancellation of debts', in an oath preserved on a marble pillar of the early third century before Christ.[2] Earlier, a law of Delphi made it a crime under pain of malediction merely to propose either step in the assembly.[3]

The common theme is no mere rhetorical stereotype but the reflection of a deep concern solidly grounded in the character of the Greek economy and the history of Greek political struggles. Beginning no later than the eighth century BC and continuing uninterruptedly for more than five hundred years until the Roman conquest, Greeks were constantly on the move, either as migrants (singly or in groups) or as exiled revolutionists. The Athenian military-agricultural colonies (cleruchies) of the fifth century BC, totalling 10,000 men or more at the peak;[4] the huge number of fourth-century Greek mercenaries, of whom Xenophon's Ten Thousand are but the most famous example; the civil war in third-century Sparta under Agis, Cleomenes and Nabis – these are instances that can be repeated at almost any moment in Hellenic history, if not always with the same dramatic impact. And it was land hunger that was the driving force. Land hunger, in turn, stemmed frequently from private expropriation, with debt the effective instrument.

The debt-ridden farmer may be a universal figure in one sense, but he is at the same time a personification of economic factors that change; and as they change, he, too, takes on an altered appearance, sometimes

Reprinted with permission from the *Political Science Quarterly* 68 (1953), 249–68.

radically so. Natural conditions apart, significant variables would include the market, the size and type of the holding, the land-tenure
régimes, the division of labour between town and country, the quality
and extent of credit facilities and operations, the economic position of the
moneylender, and the degree and kind of intervention by the state. To
say flatly, with a leading economic historian, that 'like the consumption
loan . . . the agricultural loan becomes a basis for extortion and
oppression,'[5] is to formulate a generalisation which, though undoubtedly valid, also conceals a trap for those who ignore the variables. The
elimination of such a trap at a focal point in Greek history is one aim of
this paper.

I

Solon is the Greek name that comes first to mind when land and debt are
mentioned together. Shortly after 600 B C he was designated 'lawgiver' in
Athens, with unprecedented constitutional powers, because the demand for redistribution of land and cancellation of debts could no longer
be blocked off by the landholding oligarchy through force or minor
concessions. In one of his poems, Solon spoke of the 'dark earth, whose
horoi affixed in so many places I once removed; once she was a slave, now
free'.[6] Just what measures Solon had in mind when he wrote these two
lines is widely disputed today, as are most aspects of his economic
reform programme. It is certain, however, that in some fashion he lifted
the encumbrances that were squeezing the small Attic farmers off their
land.[7] *Horoi* were slabs of stone used to mark boundaries between
adjoining holdings. At some point, the Athenians found another, quite
distinct, use for the *horoi*, and it was this second type that Solon removed, markers placed on farms in order to make public the fact that
those particular holdings were legally encumbered. In a sense, the
Athenians had hit upon a very crude way of achieving some of the
purposes of the modern register of titles and deeds. Removal of the
stones symbolised release from the encumbrance.[8]

   Whatever Solon may have accomplished for the farmers of his day, he
neither intended nor effected a prohibition for all time of land-secured
loans. Farmers continued to fall into debt, and now that they were no
longer permitted to offer their persons or their families as security – a
permanent reform of Solon's – only their land gave them borrowing
capacity. The use of *horoi* for public notice continued, too, not merely for
agricultural property but eventually also for houses in the city when they

were put up as security. Archaeologists have discovered more than two hundred of these stones in Attica and in four Aegean islands under Athenian influence. The time period for these finds is roughly 400–250 BC. The texts of 222 had been published by 1951, 182 of them in a sufficiently complete state to be analysed.[9]

A typical *horos*, translated very literally, reads as follows:

[In the archonship] of Praxibulos [i.e. 315–314 BC]. *Horos* of the land and house put up as security to Nicogenes of [the deme] Aixone, 420 [drachmas], according to the agreement deposited with Chairedemos of [the deme] Rhamnus.[10]

Few of the stones have longer texts; most are shorter, for a date is given in only 27 or 28, a written agreement is mentioned in but fifteen, even the name of the creditor and the amount of the debt are sometimes omitted. Thus, one marble block (*IG* II², 2760) found in the city of Athens proper says merely: '*Horos* of a workshop [*ergasterion*] put up as security, 750 [drachmas]' – three words and a numeral in the Greek.

Such a concentrated, homogeneous body of texts from a single community is a rarity in Greek source materials. The time is significant, too, for the fourth century BC, in which the majority of the *horoi* can be placed, is the century of the 'breakdown' of the Greek city-state, however historians may understand and interpret that phenomenon. And there lies the trap. The considerable number of fourth-century *horoi* is regularly adduced to prove that, during that critical century, 'the small farmers ran more and more into debt, and were frequently forced to give up their farms'.[11] The memory of Solon and the picture of the mortgaged homestead farm of today are easily discernible. In fact, the *horoi* tell us nothing whatsoever about the small farmer and his debts: they stood on the property of the wealthier landowners.

But, first, what was a large holding in ancient Athens? The persistent failure of the sources to give figures is a notable instance of the non-quantitative approach that characterises Greek writing whenever it touches upon economic matters. I know of precisely five land figures in the whole of Athenian literature and not one usable figure in the Athenian inscriptions. In a forensic speech written somewhat later than 330 BC, the estate of a man named Phainippos is given in linear measure; the acreage was somewhere between 700 and 1,000, depending on the contour of the land.[12] Then there is Alcibiades' patrimonial estate of some 70 acres, matched by the holding of a certain Aristophanes, not the playwright, confiscated by the state in 390 BC.[13] In these three instances,

the rule is broken and the dimensions given because the speakers
wished to emphasise that they were large holdings. The fourth figure is
45 acres, the land in Euboea given by the Athenian state to Aristides'
impoverished son Lysimachus in the latter part of the fifth century BC.[14]
Finally, there is a 14-acre figure in an oration dated about 389 BC (Isaeus
5.22). This last figure was given to underscore the small size of the
farm.

There is good reason to believe that 45- and 70-acre holdings, though
not unusual, were above average. Phainippos' farm was certainly in the
very highest bracket, shared by few Athenians. According to Dionysius
of Halicarnassus, a proposal was made and rejected in 403 BC to restrict
political rights in Athens to landholders, which, if carried, would have
disfranchised 5,000 citizens.[15] The figure is difficult to control, for Dionysius lived 400 years later, but if it has any basis in fact it means that only
20 or 25 per cent of the Athenian citizens owned no land of any kind at
the end of the fifth century BC. Some support comes from the estimate
that nearly two thirds of the citizen population lived in the rural districts
in 430 BC, slightly more than half one century later; and many of the
city-dwellers were themselves farm owners.[16]

Since no *horos* indicates the dimensions of the holding which it
marked, the determination of the stratum of landowners involved must
be somewhat circuitous. Thirty-two of the stones are linked with dowries. In Athenian law the dowry did not become the outright property of
the husband. Under certain conditions, the death of a childless wife for
example, the marriage portion had to be returned to her father or
guardian. To guarantee the dowry's return in such cases, the dowry-
giver often demanded adequate security, usually in the form of real
property. The property remained the husband's but, should he become
obligated to surrender the dowry and fail to do so, then he would lose the
security exactly as if he had offered that piece of property to guarantee a
loan. Of the thirty-two *horoi* that indicate this type of legal situation,
seventeen give the amount of the dowry. The range is from 300 to 8,000
drachmas, with the median 1,900 and the average 2,650.[17]

These figures are easily evaluated. There was no law requiring a man
to dower his daughter. Economic and social pressures, however, not
only made dowries more or less mandatory, they also tended to fix the
amount appropriate for a given social status. Roughly, 3–6,000 drachmas
seems to have been the accepted standard for the wealthiest Athenians,
Authenticated dowries exceeding 6,000 drachmas are so rare that we
may set that figure as the normal maximum. The *horoi* linked with

dowries therefore take us into the world of the wealthier, indeed of the wealthiest, Athenian citizens. There are only three sums under 1,000 drachmas – one of 300 and two of 500 – and even they are dowries far beyond the reach of the poorer section of the population.

Sums inscribed on the other *horoi* represent debts of various kinds, rarely specified. They range from a low of 90 drachmas to a high of 7,000, with a median of 1,000. For proper application in the present context, these figures require a substantial upward adjustment. In the first place, the property involved need not have been the whole of the individual debtor's holding. In the second place, some of the smaller debts were secured by houses alone. The farm-secured debts, in other words, would show a median substantially greater than 1,000 drachmas. Even 1,000-drachma debts, like 1,000-drachma dowries, were not possible for the small farmers. In 322 B C the Macedonian general Antipater, wishing to establish an oligarchy in Athens, imposed a 2,000-drachma property qualification on the right to vote and hold office, thereby disfranchising a majority of the citizen body.[18] If we assume that the property marked by a *horos* was as a rule worth at least twice the amount of the indebtedness – an assumption for which there is some supporting evidence – then considerably more than half of these landed estates fell within the aristocratic range as defined by Antipater.

The astonishing point is that, once the *horoi* have been eliminated as evidence of the decline of the small farmer and of the growing concentration of agricultural properties in fourth-century Athens, no evidence at all remains. An examination of the modern authorities cited early in this discussion reveals that their picture of a shift from small to large holdings, mediated through land credits, is drawn from a combination of two arguments: a misreading of the significance of the *horoi* coupled with an analysis of the economics of agriculture (capital needs, markets, and the like) that pertains to modern farming, not to the ancient Greek, and that rests on no discoverable basis in Athenian sources. Ultimately we seem to be reduced to the conviction that the small farmer 'must have' been squeezed off the land in the fourth century as he had been in the seventh. But why? According to the best estimates of population, the citizen body increased steadily in the fourth century (at least until 322 B C), following the sharp drop during the Peloponnesian War; the rate of urbanization seems to have been no greater than the growth rate; nor is there any evidence of increasing size of families. More important, there is no trace in Athens of a genuine demand for, or even fear of, redistribution of land and cancellation of debts at any time during the century.[19] In this respect, Athens was not typical of the Greek world, as the programme of the League of the Hellenes demonstrates.

That the fourth century saw the finale of the classical Greek *polis* is indisputable. That the democratic *polis* had lost some of its vitality, even where it maintained a formal existence, is clear. That in Athens the rich were living more comfortably, the poor more miserably, is possible. But that all this had anything to do with a shift in the property régime on the land seems quite certainly wrong.

II

'Where a loan is involved,' wrote the Peripatetic author of a book of *Problems* attributed to Aristotle, 'there is no friend, for if a man is a friend he does not lend but gives.'[20] This ethical judgment, like Plato's recommendation (*Laws*, 742C) that interest-bearing loans be prohibited altogether, no longer coincided fully and literally with prevailing Athenian norms, but it still reflected a substratum of aristocratic solidarity which remained operative in the fifth, fourth and third centuries BC. For that we have indisputable testimony, for example in the case of Apollodorus.

After the death of his father, Pasion, the most successful and most famous of all Athenian bankers, Apollodorus involved himself in a series of legal manoeuvres, probably in the years 368–365 BC, against a certain Nicostratus and the latter's brother. Nicostratus had been captured in a battle and then ransomed. He had succeeded in repaying 1,000 drachmas of the ransom money but he could not raise the balance and was threatened with enslavement, in accordance with Athenian law on the subject. In this emergency, he appealed for help to his boyhood friend Apollodorus. What happened is told to the court by Apollodorus in the following way:

'Nicostratus,' I said, . . . 'since at the present time you cannot find the entire sum of money, nor have I any cash any more than yourself, I will lend you as much of my property as you wish and you shall hypothecate it for as much money as is lacking; you may have the use of the money for one year without interest and pay off the strangers. When you have collected the *eranos*-loan, as you yourself say, release my property.' Hearing this, he thanked me and urged me to act as quickly as possible . . . I therefore hypothecated my multiple-dwelling to Arceasas of [the deme] Pambotadai, whom this man himself recommended to me, for 1,600 drachmas at interest of 8 obols per mina per month [i.e. 16 per cent per annum].[21]

The *eranos*-loan which Nicostratus was to arrange in order to repay Apollodorus was a familiar and very common device all over the Greek world. It was a friendly loan tendered by an *ad hoc* group (more properly, a plurality) of individuals; it was characterised not only by the fact of group participation but also by the absence of interest and by a provision for repayment over a period of years in regular instalments. *Eranoi* were resorted to by everyone, from slaves who raised money in this fashion to purchase their freedom (more often than not it was the master who assembled the loan) to the wealthy landowners and social leaders of the community. Willingness to lend ranked high among the civic and social virtues;[22] it was perfectly consonant with the Peripatetic's 'if a man is a friend, he does not lend but gives'. Aristotle's pupil and successor, Theophrastus, reflected the same notion when he depicted a braggart as one who ran up on his abacus the fantastic sum of ten talents (60,000 drachmas) in paid-out *eranoi* (*Characters*, 23.6).

Nicostratus needed financial assistance to extricate himself from his ransomers. In probably the best known of all Athenian instances of personal indebtedness, the fictional case of Strepsiades in Aristophanes' *Clouds*, the rich, elderly, old-fashioned farmer went to Socrates to learn how to cheat two creditors from whom he had borrowed 1,500 drachmas for the purchase of horses – not farm animals, the playwright underscores, but show horses for the conspicuous consumption of Strepsiades' socially ambitious wife and son.

A third example of motive in borrowing is given us in another of Apollodorus' lawsuits, a successful action against the leading Athenian general Timotheus to recover a total of nearly 4,500 drachmas that Pasion had lent the latter on several occasions in 373–372 B C. According to the plaintiff, Timotheus was in a hopeless financial position when Pasion out of friendship lent him various sums with which to meet obligations incurred in the course of his military and political activities on behalf of the state. The loans were made without witnesses or documents, they were unsecured, and they bore no interest. After Pasion's death the general denied the existence of the obligations, hence the suit by Apollodorus as his father's heir.[23]

Eranoi, ransom, conspicuous consumption, the personal financial troubles of generals in the turbulent fourth century – the pattern that emerges is one of borrowing for non-productive purposes. The distinction between personal, consumption loans and business, productive loans is not always easy to draw. 'From a historical point of view,' Sieveking points out, 'the differentiation . . . became possible only when the merchant began to maintain special accounts for the management of his business undertakings and when the firm became clearly distinguished from the private household.'[24] Apollodorus was entitled to sue Timotheus because Pasion's 'firm' and private household were one and the same; there was no distinction, in fact or in law, between bank property and the banker's personal wealth. Apollodorus' claim against the general rested on his position as son and heir, not on the continuity of the bank, with which he never had any connection. Nevertheless, the difference between personal loans and business loans does emerge with considerable clarity, especially when the transactions under consideration are counterposed to maritime loans, which were indubitably business operations on both sides.

It seems to have been almost a fixed rule of Athenian commercial practice, attributable to the great risks of sea traffic and the inadequate accumulation of liquid capital, that merchants used borrowed funds, in whole or in part, for their maritime ventures. In the fourth century BC, from which our information about bottomry comes, a set pattern can be seen. The loans rarely, if ever, exceeded 2,000 drachmas; they were made for the duration of the voyage (weeks or months, no more); the articles of agreement were detailed and always in writing; interest rates were high, even an annual figure of 100 per cent was not unheard of; all the risks of the voyage, though not of economic failure, were borne by the lender, who held the ship or cargo or both as security for prompt repayment once the vessel was safely back in the harbour of Athens. Land-secured loans, in contrast, *average* only a little less in amount than the maximum for bottomry and frequently ran to far larger sums. They were often arranged verbally and without interest. When interest was charged, the rate was roughly 10 to 18 per cent. One year seems to have been a common term, perhaps the customary one. And of course the kind of risk element inherent in bottomry transactions was lacking.

The available information is altogether too meagre for any sort of statistical presentation. But it is significant, even decisive, that in the instances known to us from our best source, the Athenian orators, whenever a substantial sum was borrowed on real security, the borrower's purpose was not a productive one. Occasionally landed Athenians no doubt did borrow on their holdings for productive reasons, but the pattern was unmistakably in the opposite direction, 'to cover the conventional needs of a social class accustomed to elaborate expenditures'.[25]

Paramount among the conventional needs, in Athens as in all earlier socio-economic systems, were the financial requirements of marriage, in particular a large dowry. Fully one third of the *horoi* are explicitly linked with family matters; how many of the others may also have been is not determinable from the texts and their elliptical language. Thirty-two *horoi* indicated dowry security, as we have already seen. Twenty-one others were connected with an institution known officially as 'leasing of the family estate' (*misthosis oikou*). If a guardian designated by will was unwilling or unable to administer the child's property, he could arrange to have the estate leased by auction, under governmental supervision, for the duration of the child's minority. The successful bidder was required by law to offer adequate real security guaranteeing payment of the annual rent and the return of the estate when the orphan attained his majority. The twenty-one *horoi* stood on properties so encumbered. The lessors of course acted from motives of gain, not charity. However, these texts contribute nothing to the discussion of the motive for indebtedness on the part of men of property who *borrowed* on their holdings. Leases are not under consideration, and the *misthosis oikou* was nothing but a lease under peculiar circumstances.

Apart from dowry and *misthosis oikou*, the *horoi* maintain almost complete silence about the reasons for the indebtedness they publicised. But the orators and other literary sources leave little doubt that in most instances the underlying obligation was like those described by Apollodorus. Particular stress must be given the point that, whereas the modern mortgage loan serves primarily to finance either the purchase or the improvement of real property, these two reasons for borrowing were virtually unknown in Athens.

Among the Greeks, sales were cash sales in fact as well as in law. The Greek city-states never recognised a promise to buy and sell to be a legally binding contract, not even when accompanied by transfer of possession and partial payment. In this respect the law merely kept step with actual practice. Some credit sales were made, to be sure, but they constituted the exception and they could be given legal force only through a fiction, usually in the form of a loan agreement. I know exactly two unequivocal references in the Athenian sources to a piece of real property being put up as security to cover its purchase price. One is a *horos*, found in a rural district and dated in either 340–339 or 313–312 BC. It marked a plot of land that was encumbered for 2,000 drachmas owing on the price.[26] The other is in a speech (no. 37) by Demosthenes, probably dated 346–345 BC, written for a lawsuit in a very complicated case involving an ore-crushing mill in the silver-mining district of Attica, purchased together with some slaves with the help of a loan of 10,500 drachmas, by far the largest private credit transaction in extant Athenian records.

The fact is that there was no real-estate market, properly speaking, in Athens at all, that land was not a commodity in any significant sense. The Greek language had no word for 'real property'. Nor was there a word for 'seller of real estate' or 'broker'; 'grain-seller', yes, 'perfume-seller', 'bread-seller', even comic inventions like Aristophanes' 'decree-seller', but no 'land-seller' or 'house-seller'. Not one Athenian is known to us who earned his livelihood by dealing in real estate. The city itself kept no formal record of property holdings and no record of any kind of transactions on property. That explains why a creditor posted a *horos* in order to protect himself against possible legal complications, should the owner be tempted to borrow further on his already encumbered land or to alienate it. A would-be buyer or lender could not turn to registers of deed or title, but he could see the telltale stone markers.

Not a single Athenian text is available to exemplify the modern practice of mortgaging property in order to raise funds for purposes of building and improvement. All in all, there are not a dozen references in any context in Greek literature to increasing the value of a farm or of urban realty. And the few to be found scattered in the sources attribute the results to zeal, hard work, temperance, or some other moral quality, rather than to an outlay of funds or skilful managerial manipulation bringing about a change in the economic quality and potentiality of the property.

One group of documents is particularly instructive in this respect. It was a standard practice for Athenian cult associations, public, quasi-public, and private, to rent their land to individual farmers on long-term leases (ten to forty years). Some twenty individual and model agreements have been preserved on stone. They are rather detailed: among the provisions to be found in one or another are clauses requiring the tenant to restore the property at the end of the rental period with the same number of trees and vines he had received, to keep the buildings in repair, to cut the olive trees in a designated way, to employ the fallow system, and the like. Only once is there mention of improvements in the proper sense of the term, and that a singularly unimpressive one. The fourth-century B C lease of a garden owned by worshippers of the Hero Physician gave the tenant, who took a thirty-year lease, the right to make any construction he wished, at his own expense, in a designated section of the property. At the end of the term, he was to remove the roof, doors and window frames, unless a prior agreement was made to the contrary.[27]

That farmland was maintained for years and years on a fixed level of operations is revealed most clearly by the inventories of the temple of Apollo on Delos.[28] Whatever it was that prevented the Delian temple from developing its landed holdings, it was not lack of cash, for the temple possessed large sums, some of which it hoarded while the remainder was placed on loan, always at 10 per cent. The Athenian man of property may not have had the cash. If he did not, neither did he borrow on his property for economic expansion. His mentality was non-productive. Freedom from the burden of earning one's living was what distinguished the *plousios* from the *penes*; this standard Greek antinomy has a shade of meaning that differs significantly from our 'rich' and 'poor'. For the latter word-pair there is no precise rendition in Greek, except through a circumlocution. Wealth was good and desirable, in fact necessary for the life of the good citizen. But its function was to liberate its owner from economic activity and concern, not to provide him with a base for continued effort toward more and more acquisition.[29]

Institutionally, a major inhibition to the building of a bridge between property and money was the citizens' monopoly of land ownership. All Greek cities limited the right to own land to their citizens; non-citizens could acquire the right only by special enactment and there is ample evidence that such privileges were not easily cḻ 'ained except in times of gravest crisis. The Athenians in particular jealously guarded their prerogative. Obviously, a man who could not own land would not accept land as security for a debt; such security would be worthless to anyone who could not seize the property in case of default.[30] Non-citizens played a leading rôle in the economic life of Athens, particularly in financial dealings. As non-citizens, however, their financial activities were necessarily cut off from the economic base of the society, its landed property. They could lease farms, houses and mines, but they could not purchase them or lend on them.

However one may explain the unbroken insistence upon the citizens' monopoly of real property, the fact remains that in large measure land and money remained two separate spheres; for a large section of the financial community, entirely so. There were twenty or thirty thousand metics (resident aliens) and an incalculable number of transients in Athens. Their contribution to the city's economic life was welcomed, even sought after. In the fourth century BC, important changes in legal procedure were introduced to facilitate and expedite the settlement of disputes in which they were involved and to make their commercial and financial dealings simpler and therefore more attractive. But their exclusion from the land remained untouched; as far as we know, no one ever proposed a change in that law. It follows that there were not productive drives sufficient in strength to overcome the political-psychological resistance of the traditional land-citizenship tie. And neither a genuine market in land, a significant concentration of holdings, nor a continually intensified exploitation of the land was possible divorced from fluid wealth.

III

Moneylending was fundamentally non-institutional and discontinuous. Neither the firm nor true partnership made an appearance; agency was known in a rudimentary way, but it was very much the exception. In the overwhelming mass of land-secured debts, individual X was directly and personally indebted to individual Y, no more.[31] Though there is little information about the Ys, that few of them were vocationally lenders of money seems certain. Not thirty Athenians are known from the whole of the fourth century who are specifically identified as bankers, a reflection of the rarity of the occupation, not of a defect in the available sources. Most often the loans came either from merchants and *rentiers* who seized a particular opportunity to make a profit or from men of wealth willing to assist a friend without monetary return. Occasionally two or more men made a loan jointly. Their relationship, too, like that between creditor and debtor, was accidental and disjunctive. Thus, the two men who made the 10,500-drachma loan on the ore-crushing mill and slaves, already cited, were neither business associates nor even friends; and this is the largest transaction of its kind on record.

From the whole pattern it necessarily follows that no continuity or rationality of financial connection was established; that 'credit rating' was a matter of gossip and repute, not of economic analysis; and that no machinery existed for building up large cash funds in private hands, not to mention credit balances, which would transcend the relatively small sums any given individual was able and prepared to venture in any single, isolated loan transaction. When the loan was sufficiently large and when the creditor was a citizen (or one of the rare non-citizens who had received from the state the privilege of owning realty), he often requested land or a house as security, at times even for an interest-free, friendly loan. This practice is not to be confused with investment in mortgages.

In the first place, short-term lending was the rule. For the lender this meant a brief outlay of cash for a high return, not a long-range placement of capital. For the borrower it meant generally the satisfaction of a social-personal need, not the expansion of his economic potential. If the mere number of *horoi* now available proves anything, it is the wide prevalence of indebtedness among the propertied Athenians in the fourth and third centuries before Christ.

In the second place, book clearance and negotiable paper were foreign to the Athenian economy. The banker was little more than a money-changer and pawnbroker; his system of deposits and payments did not rise even to the giro level. Much of the available coin never found its way into the banks, but remained in homes and buried hoards. The state, too, handled its money in a rudimentary, strongbox method, doling out coins as needed to the appropriate officials.[32] Oral transactions were common. The receipt was unknown: proof of payment was secured by the presence of witnesses. 'Some of you', Demosthenes (27.58) says to a jury, '. . . saw [Theogenes] count out this money [a 3,000-drachma payment] in the Agora.' If a written agreement were in existence, it was destroyed and that was the end of the affair. A clearance procedure and, to a lesser extent, negotiable paper are essential for payment in credit, in turn a necessary technical condition if the economy is to grow beyond the narrow limits imposed by the necessity of holding and transporting large quantities of coin or bullion. And there is a simple, logical connection between non-negotiability and a legal system that clings to the strict principles of cash sales.

In the third place, security was substitutive, not collateral. In its early form, security is always substitution, a forfeit. X owes Y something, an object, money, a performance, which he does not render, and Y accepts a substitute – land for money – in full satisfaction of X's obligation to him. Athenian security practice remained on that level right down to the Roman conquest, and perhaps for centuries thereafter. Occasional exceptions were made when the two parties had special reasons for introducing them, but the original conception continued unbroken. Collateral security involves economic thinking of quite another order. The security now becomes a guarantee of payment, not a substitute; default entails not simple forfeit but compulsory sale and a division of the proceeds according to the respective monetary values of the debt and the property. Between substitution and collateral there lies a profound economic transformation. 'We are not to seek in the law of pledge itself for the reasons of the change. The change came about as soon as the community recognised credit widely and developed varieties of obligation and forms of action for them.'[33] Conversely, failure to make the change suggests failure of the community to recognise (that is, need) credit widely.

It scarcely requires demonstration that an investor must have collateral security as much as negotiability. The average, casual, non-professional Athenian lender of two or three or even ten thousand drachmas was seeking either the emoluments of friendship or ten or twelve per cent together with the return of the principal at the end of perhaps a year. He would have preferred not to take the security as a substitute, not merely because of the nuisance involved in foreclosure but because he might very well be burdened for a considerable period with a farm or house for which he had no use or desire. If he did take the security, under the law it could be only as a substitute, in full and final satisfaction of the debt.

It is commonly said today that land was a 'preferred investment' in ancient Greece because it was less risky than any other form of 'investment'. How strange, then, that the numerous cult bodies, whose psychology was certainly not that of the speculator, did not put their money into land but always put it to work in small loans, when they did not simply hoard it. Only one instance is known of the purchase of property by such a group, and that one in the first century after Christ.[34] The great majority owned some realty, no matter how small a plot, *which they invariably acquired by gift*. But they did not 'invest' their funds in land when they sought a regular, secure cash income with which to meet the expenses of their religious activity.

In so far as land was in fact preferred to other forms of wealth, the choice was a psychological, social and political one: land was the proper wealth for a self-respecting gentleman and citizen. No economic judgment about investments was implied, merely a generally non-productive mentality. But when a man made a loan at interest, he was seeking profit, not social standing, and he wanted his own money back and more, not a substitute in reality.

When Lord Nottingham in the seventeenth century ruled that 'The principal right of the mortgagee is to the money, and his right to the land is only as security for the money', the collateral idea was finally triumphant in England.[35] Implicit in that transformation was a conception of property wherby everything is readily translated into money. The post-Nottingham English creditor who accepted a landed estate as collateral security thought of it not so much as land but as so many pounds sterling concealed in the form of land, valuable to him only because in that form his money could not easily escape him. With pardonable exaggeration we may say that his Athenian counterpart saw nothing but the land.

Hazeltine has interpreted the shift from substitution and forfeit to collateral and the right of redemption as, in part at least, a victory of the debtor class in England.[36] It is doubtful that this line of reasoning offers a useful analogy for classical Athens. Under Solon there was a debtor class and it did score some sort of victory. But the relatively heavy, land-based indebtedness of the fourth and third centuries BC was largely an intra-class phenomenon. There was no struggle then between small farmer and usurer or between landowner and merchant capitalist. The usurer was not missing from the picture, to be sure, but we find him – and the complaints against him – circulating among the petty shopkeepers and craftsmen in the market-place and the harbour, not in the countryside. Interest rates were untouched by legislation. Plato proposed the aboli-tion of interest in his *Laws*. This he did as a philosopher with a fully systematized ethical theory, not as the spokesman of a debtor class. There is no trace in classical Athens of any popular agitation against usury, just as there is no serious evidence of a demand for cancellation of debts – and for the same reasons.

THE FREEDOM OF THE CITIZEN
IN THE GREEK WORLD

Men have for centuries exercised their minds in vain to find a workable definition of 'freedom'. I do not propose to add yet another attempt to the mountain of failures, for I do not believe the term to be definable in any normal sense of the word 'definition', and that for two related reasons. The first is that 'the concept of "freedom" can properly be formulated (only) as the antithesis of "unfreedom"'.[1] The statement, 'X has a right', has no content until it is accompanied by 'Y has a correlative duty'. My second reason is that the gamut of claims, privileges, powers and immunities, and of their correlative duties, 'unprivileges', liabilities and disabilities, is too vast over the whole range of human activity, and too varied not only from society to society but also among the members within any known society. The rights recognised in a given society constitute a bundle of claims, privileges, powers and immunities, un-evenly distributed among the individual members, even among those who are called 'free', so that a definition of freedom encompassing them would be either a tautology or a misrepresentation of the reality.[2] A man who possessed claims, privileges and powers in all matters against the whole world would be a god, not a man, to paraphrase Aristotle.

In lieu of a definition, I shall begin by pointing up some of the analytical difficulties inherent in any account of the subject and the instability over time of essential conceptions. I start with a quotation from the classic statement of what we may call the 'libertarian position', by John Stuart Mill. 'The object of this essay', he wrote in the introduction to his *On Liberty*,

is to assert one very simple principle, as entitled to govern absolutely the dealings of society with the individual in the way of compulsion and control, whether the means used be physical force in the form of legal penalties, or the moral coercion of public opinion. The principle is, that the sole end for which mankind are warranted, individually or collectively,

Originally published in *Talanta* 7 (1976) 1–23, and reprinted by permission of the editors and publisher.

in interfering with the liberty of action of any of their number, is self-protection. That the only purpose for which power can be rightfully exercised over any member of a civilised community, against his will, is to prevent harm to others. . . . The only part of the conduct of any one, for which he is amenable to society, is that which concerns others. In the part which merely concerns himself, his independence is, of right, absolute. Over himself, over his own body and mind, the individual is sovereign.

Mill's 'one very simple principle' may be easily asserted, it is less easily elaborated: if nothing else, 'self-protection', 'harm to others', turn out to be almost as slippery as 'liberty' itself. Mill had to acknowledge that later in the same essay: 'there are many acts which, being directly injurious only to the agents themselves, ought not to be legally interdicted, but which, if done publicly, are a violation of good manners, and coming thus within the category of public offences, may rightfully be prohibited.'[3]

That qualification of course opens the door to the conflict over the relationship between law and morals which has lost little of its sharpness even in our more permissive societies today. Mill managed to keep it within the tight frame of 'harm to others'. Even when he extended the notion of 'public offences' slightly, he went no further than 'good manners'. Contrast to this doggedly negative approach the following selections from the Universal Declaration of Human Rights proclaimed by the General Assembly of the United Nations in 1948: 'Everyone, without any discrimination, has the right to equal pay for equal work' (Article 23, sect. 2); 'Everyone has the right to form and to join trade unions for the protection of his interests' (Article 23, sect. 4); 'Elementary education shall be compulsory' (from Article 26, sect. 1).[4]

These clauses exemplify a positive approach, that is to say, they establish claims for individuals (for 'everyone' in fact) which, by their very nature, reduce the claims of others – in my first two quotations the claims of employers of labour to liberty of action. Hence enforcement of these rights would cause them 'harm'.

John Stuart Mill came at the end of one period of sharp political conflict and he codified in an extreme form some principles of the victors. The central issue in the conflict (though not for Mill) may be reduced for our purposes to the freedom of the citizen from the arbitrary authority of a monarch or a foreign power; a freedom, it is important to remember, in which taxation and the autonomy of private economic activity were major components. When the English crown was offered to William and Mary in 1689, the accompanying Declaration of Rights not only dealt with elections, trial by jury, the standing army and the right to bear arms, but also declared expressly that 'levying of money without consent of Parliament is illegal'. The provisions were all concrete, not abstract statements of freedom or of rights, and they reflected the struggle with the Crown which had been brought to a successful conclusion.

Both the American and the French revolutions, a century or so later, also had their proximate causes in a conflict over taxes and various economic restrictions. The outcome transcended these limited concerns – transcended, but did not eliminate. The most famous rhetoric emerged from the American Revolution, in the second paragraph of the Declaration of Independence: 'We hold these truths to be self-evident, that all men are created equal, that they are endowed by their Creator with certain inalienable Rights, that among these are Life, Liberty and the pursuit of Happiness.' The rhetoric was not meant to be taken literally: not 'all men' since the numerous slaves were excluded; 'inalienable' only with important exceptions, for the right to liberty did not prohibit imprisonment, nor did the right to life prohibit capital punishment or conscription into the armed forces. The rhetoric was translated into practical propositions in the Constitution, where we find freedom of speech and religion and so on, in the first ten amendments collectively known as the Bill of Rights, but, no less important, we read in the fifth amendment that no person shall 'be deprived of life, liberty, or property, without due process of law; nor shall private property be taken for public use, without just compensation'. There is no reference to a right of property in the Declaration of Independence, but clearly 'the pursuit of Happiness' implied both its existence and its protection.

The road from the conception of rights in the American Constitution to the very different conception in the Declaration of the United Nations was a long and difficult one, strewn not only with debate but also with overt conflict. In the United States, to give but one example, it required an amendment to the Constitution, the sixteenth (not formally adopted until 1913), to permit Congress to levy an income tax, the courts having previously ruled such a tax unconstitutional. I do not propose to pursue that history. I have called attention to certain contemporary aspects of the problem of rights and freedom solely in order to lay the foundation for several conceptual and methodological points that I believe one needs to formulate expressly in an account of the ancient Greek situation (the classical *polis*, more narrowly, in which citizenship was acquired by birth in all but exceptional cases; I shall not be concerned with the Greek cities in the Hellenistic monarchies or in the Roman empire). They are commonplace points. My justification for taking time to state and document three of them is that recent extensive reading of the learned literature has brought home to me how common is the tendency to overlook, ignore and even flout the obvious.

1. My first point is that rights are not fixed entities but historically conditioned variables; that so-called universal or inalienable or natural rights are merely those which a given society, or a given sector of a society, or even a particular individual favours. The dialectic is that specific 'natural rights' arise as a positive demand against authority, only to be transformed into an argument against further changes in the social and political arrangements. Freedom was once used as an argument against the income tax; it is now deployed as an argument against the right to equal pay for equal work. The latter is not traditional, it is argued, it embodies no *universal* moral right (it cannot apply to those who do not work for pay), it is not enforceable. The poverty of such arguments requires little demonstration.[5] Freedom of speech was not always traditional either, it too cannot apply to various categories of people, it is not always enforceable.

2. Changes in the matrix of rights that prevail in any society normally begin in a struggle over specific issues, not over abstract concepts or slogans. The rhetoric and the abstractions come later, and then are reified. Consider *stasis*, civil strife, in the Greek world. Although the dominant line of Greek writers, from Thucydides to Aristotle, called it the greatest of evils, they had little impact on the Greek people, who went on with their *staseis* unrelentingly. Why? Because, Aristotle concluded in our textbook on Greek *stasis*, the fifth book of his *Politics*, one sector of the community sought more *kerdos*, profit, gain, material advantage, and more *time*, honour (1302a32): two concrete, definable objectives. The methods employed ranged from normal political means to open civil war; the intellectual argument, when there was one, centred round the concept of equality, the only abstraction which Aristotle introduced into his analysis.

3. Any attempt to gain more rights and privileges for one man or one class or one sector of the population necessarily involves a corresponding reduction of the rights and privileges of others. In all hitherto existing societies, ever since the expulsion from the Garden of Eden, rights have clashed. At least in those spheres of human behaviour that involve goods or power or honour, one man's claims and privileges are another man's duties and disabilities. That is not one jot less true if we resort to Greek and say *agōn*, as anyone knows who has read his Pindar with an

eye to the values expressed. A gain on either side automatically entailed a corresponding loss on the other side, and naturally led to resistance from that side. That is what underlay *stasis* in the Greek city-states, and *stasis* was by definition restricted to the citizen-body, to the free men, to those who already had rights which they wished either to increase or to protect.

One reason for their ability to indulge in so much fratricidal activity was the presence of others who possessed no rights. On this subject the Greek view was virtually unanimous: there was no contradiction, in their minds, between freedom for some and (partial or total) unfreedom for others, no notion that all men are created free, let alone equal. 'It was no easy matter', wrote Thucydides (8.68.4) of the oligarchic coup of 411 BC, 'some hundred years after the expulsion of the tyrants to deprive the Athenian people of their freedom, a people not only unused to subjection but for more than half this period accustomed to rule over others.'[6]

Thucydides was thinking not of slaves at this point, but of the citizens of the other communities within the Athenian empire. When he used the verb 'to enslave' repeatedly as a metaphor for Athenian treatment of subject-states, he was dividing the spectrum of rights very near one end: 'freedom' became 'unfreedom', 'enslavement', the moment the autonomy of the community in foreign and military affairs was lost. Normally, a Greek divided the line very much nearer the other end, the complete loss of what we call personal freedom.[7] He would not have considered the *perioikoi* of Laconia unfree, though they, like the Athenian subjects, had no autonomy in military or foreign affairs. Nor, turning to the domestic field, would he have called the numerous metics in Athens unfree despite their serious disabilities, such as their debarment from political life, their incapacity to own landed property, their exclusion from state grain requisitions and other public perquisites, their liability to be taken before a magistrate by force when served with a summons in a private lawsuit.

In sum, the citizens possessed a larger share of the bundle of claims, privileges, powers, and immunities than anyone else, though not all citizens had equal shares. The freedom of the Greek citizen cannot be examined solely as an antithesis to unfreedom, to slavery: one must acknowledge the range among the free. In particular, it must be recognised that what we commonly call privileges or immunities are not something apart from rights but a proper class within the genus 'rights', and therefore a component of freedom. A public distribution of grain, the gift of an African prince to Athens in 445 BC, led to a purge of the citizen roster because some non-citizens, falsely inscribed as citizens, were claiming a privilege to which they were not entitled.[8] At first sight that might appear a minor instance, almost a caricature of the subject of rights and freedom, but behind it there looms a major consideration, namely, the positive right of the citizen to assistance with respect to food supply. Hence two items were regularly on the agenda of the first assembly meeting in each prytany, defence of the city and the corn supply (Aristotle, *Constitution of Athens* 43.4). No doubt few Athenian citizens actively wished the metics to starve, but only the citizen had the right to demand that the state help prevent such an eventuality.

One of the most important privileges of the Greek citizen was the freedom to engage in *stasis*. I am being neither frivolous nor perverse. A quarter of a century ago Loenon made the acute, and still generally neglected, observation that 'illegality is simply not the *constant* hallmark of *stasis*. The label *stasis* was always also applied to completely legal groups, existing or arising, between whom there were permanent oppositions and tensions which did not burst into spectacular forms.'[9] Freedom that does not include the freedom to advocate change is empty. So is the freedom of advocacy that does not include the freedom to combine with others. And change, as I have already said, entails the loss of some rights by some members of the community. They resist, hence *stasis*.

Now, it is inherent in a political society – and the Greek *polis* was a quintessentially political society – that conflict over important matters of substance, in every sphere of life, is sooner or later translated into a political conflict. Our ancient authorities therefore deal with *stasis* solely on that level, as conflict between oligarchy and democracy, as conflict within the oligarchic minority, as conflict between democratic factions. But, then as now, politics was a way of life for very few members of the community. Even when we make allowance for the satisfaction that comes from the right to vote in the assembly or to sit on juries, the fact remains that for most people political rights are purely instrumental: they are means for achieving non-political ends. So are the now traditional, negative rights, such as freedom of speech, freedom of the press, freedom of assembly. These are understandably the rights most dear to intellectuals, to professors, playwrights and publicists. They could also become important to ordinary men in autocracies: the troubles of the good soldier Schweik began when he said in his local café that the flies had left their trademark on the emperor, referring to the portrait hanging over the bar. We are not in the present context concerned with such systems. When Aristotle (*Constitution of Athens* 16.8) reported that Pisistratus, once accused of murder, was so eager to maintain the rule of law that he appeared in person before the Areopagus to defend himself, but that the frightened accuser failed to appear, the philosopher permitted himself the only joke known to me in the entire corpus of his surviving works. Freedom under a tyranny is not a fruitful subject for discussion. In Sparta, I believe, a citizen could safely have said that the flies have left their trademark on King Archidamus, or on Lysander. But could he have advocated a radical change in the *agoge*, abolition of the *syssitia* or the introduction of silver coinage? That is a meaningful question, and, though advocacy would have been a political act, the objectives I have mentioned would not have been.

Modern discussions of the subject of Greek freedom are too narrowly, too obsessively, concerned with political rights and with the negative freedoms. They are also, I believe, too narrowly concentrated on abstract rights, with insufficient attention to their enforceability in practice. If Aristotle's joke about Pisistratus and the rule of law does not strike one as a cogent example, I offer *isegoria*, the right of every citizen to speak and make proposals in the Assembly, a topic which has recently produced a spate of scholarly articles.[10] That was a right which Spartans lacked, but what happened in practice in the Athenian Assembly? A fifth-century Athenian Thersites could not have been beaten by a nobleman for his presumption; he would usually have been shouted down by his equals.[11]

Why? Because even the Athenian *demos*, for all its drive towards the right of every individual to full participation in the activity of government, accepted certain limits on the exercise of its political rights. The Athenians extended the use of the lot widely, for example, and they insured rotation of office by the one-year rule, but they exempted the *strategia* from both. The people claimed *isegoria* but left its exercise to a few. Again we must ask, Why?, and one part of the answer is that the *demos* recognised the instrumental role of political rights and were more concerned in the end with the substantive decisions, were content with their power to direct those decisions through their power to select, dismiss and punish their political leaders.[12] On this score they were favoured by an important and genuine equality – equality of the vote. Wherever there was a popular assembly in Greece, the principle of 'one man, one vote' prevailed. There was no weighted group voting, as in the Roman centuriate assembly, for example, or in the French Estates General.

In employing such phrases as 'the *demos* accepted', 'the *demos* recognised',

I am of course not suggesting that these were deliberate choices made after due examination and weighing of the issues and the possibilities in the rather abstract, conceptual terms I used. The history of struggles for political rights has never been like that. There were a number of critical moments in the prehistory and history of Athenian democracy – the crisis which produced the reforms of Solon, the seizure of power by Pisistratus, the struggle leading to the reforms of Cleisthenes, the internal problems created by the two Persian invasions, the *stasis* of the late 460s which saw the assassination of Ephialtes and which brought Athens to the brink of civil war. Each of these moments was one of struggle, of overt conflict; each centred round specific concrete issues, not round abstract theories about rights or freedom.

The antagonists produced their rhetoric, of course, and I do not underestimate political rhetoric, an expression of basic ideology. If any one term is to be singled out as the 'banner' of the ultimately victorious democracy, it is the word *isonomia*, which has two distinct connotations.[13] The dominant one is 'equality through the law', virtually a synonym for 'democracy',[14] and therefore regularly employed in the context of political rights. But the other sense, 'equality before the law', takes us into a different sphere of behaviour. 'With written laws,' says Theseus in the *Suppliant Women* (lines 433–7) of Euripides,

> People of few resources and the rich
> Both have the same recourse to justice. Now
> A man of means, if badly spoken of,
> Will have no better standing than the weak;
> And if the lesser is in the right, he wins
> Against the great.[15]

The boldness and rarity of such a notion cannot be overstressed. The Romans of the Republic never attained it and never seriously desired to, the Roman emperors openly rejected it.[16] There is no reason in principle why an oligarchy should not accept equality before the law in private relations and there is evidence to suggest that some Greek oligarchies in fact did.[17] Then, with the demise of the independent Greek *polis*, the western world had to wait until recent times before the doctrine was reasserted and reintroduced. And modern experience, including our own, has shown that there is no principle more difficult to translate fully into practice than that of equality before the law. What was the ancient Greek reality?

To begin with, there was a grave technical weakness: there was insufficient governmental machinery for the purpose. To a considerable extent in the case of public offences, and almost wholly in the case of private legal disputes (including many accusations of what we call 'crimes', murder for one), legal redress depended on self-help, from the initial summons to the final execution of a judgment. At the beginning of his year in office the Athenian archon proclaimed by herald that everyone shall possess and control to the end of the year whatever property he held at the beginning (Aristotle, *Constitution of Athens* 56.2), but the archon was largely powerless to fulfil that intention against an obstinate and sufficiently powerful miscreant. Self-help is a workable procedure between equals: it weighs the scales heavily in the case of unequals.[18]

Consider the behaviour of the wealthy Midias, son of Cephisodorus. In 349 BC, Demosthenes undertook the liturgy of preparing a male chorus for the Greater Dionysia of the following year. His old enemy Midias then embarked on a career of disruption, including nocturnal entry into a goldsmith's shop in order to destroy the garments and golden crowns that were being prepared for the chorus, bribery of the chorus-master to prevent proper rehearsals, and a number of hooligan actions at the festival itself. Demosthenes' chorus failed to win first prize and the orator took Midias to court. In the course of his long address to the jury he said the following (21.20): Some of Midias' previous victims 'remained silent because they were cowed by him and his insolence, his henchmen, his wealth and all his other resources; others chose to go to court and failed; still others came to terms with him'. Demosthenes won his case – and promptly came to terms with Midias, for 3,000 drachmas (Aeschines 3.52).

Demosthenes' oration against Midias has been an embarrassment to modern scholars. It has been ignored, rejected, dismissed as an unfinished draft of an undelivered speech in a case that never came to trial – not on the evidence of the oration itself, but, one must assume, on a reluctance to believe that such things could go on in classical Athens and the wealthy rascal remain unpunished, and on an equal reluctance to believe that the great Demosthenes would have so demeaned himself as to allow himself to be bought off cheaply by Midias.[19] Similar disbelief is less in evidence with respect to the opposite view, repeatedly stated by Greek pamphleteers, theorists and comic poets, that the Athenian juries took every opportunity to plunder the rich. 'Court verdicts', we read, 'amounted to pure arbitrariness, which could not be overcome because of the primitive procedure and the pettifogging of the advocates.'[20] The words are those of a professor of Hamburg, not of the anonymous oligarchic author of the late fifth-century work known as the *Constitution*

of Athens, but a close study of the surviving forensic speeches has shown
that the conclusion is based on political preconceptions akin to those of
Pseudo-Xenophon, and on the professional preconceptions of a modern
continental jurist.[21] Midias had no fear of being plundered, and rightly
so: the family fortune remained sufficiently intact to permit his sons to
perform expensive liturgies half a century after the affair with
Demosthenes.[22]

Athens was no Utopia. Injustices were committed there, both by
individuals and by official bodies. *Isonomia* in practice cannot be assessed
by the evocation of individual instances, or by literal acceptance of the
rhetoric on either side. I am doubtful that a proper assessment, with all
the necessary nuances, is possible today, given the available evidence.
But there is one sphere in which we can be confident that the rule was
inequality, not equality, before the law. I refer to the law of debt, which
lay heavily and onesidedly on the defaulting debtor. His property was
subject to forceable seizure by self-help, though after due process, and in
many Greek states also his person.[23] Solon put an end to personal
bondage in Athens, and the magic of Solon's name induces forgetfulness
of the fact that he was an Athenian, not a Greek, lawgiver. Solon greatly
influenced political theory and political ideals; he made less impact on
the law outside his native city. Cancellation of debts and redistribution of
land together were the perennial 'revolutionary' demands in the Greek
cities. Debtors are 'very dangerous' when a city is under siege, wrote the
fourth-century BC mercenary captain Aeneas (14.1).

The incompatibility of freedom and demands for equality is a familiar
dogma throughout the history of political theory. There were many
Greeks, however, who believed that the fundamental incompatibility
was between freedom and inequality, though they are not easily to be
found among those who wrote books. In the political field, narrowly
understood, steps were taken to create an artificial equality, carried
furthest in Athens: they included the widespread use of selection by lot,
pay for office, annual rotation of office, ostracism. But there were limits:
it is hard to imagine how the education and leisure necessary for political
leadership could have been equally distributed, and no one tried. It is
equally hard to imagine devices aimed at an artificial equality in the
juristic sphere, in private relations between individuals, short of either
the abolition or the equalisation of wealth. And no one tried in practice,
though a rare Utopian writer, notably Phaleas of Chalcedon, showed a
realisation of this central issue.[24]

Nevertheless, it is an absurdity to dismiss Athenian, or any other

Greek, judicial procedure as 'pure arbitrariness', to relegate *isonomia* to the realm of empty rhetoric. Classical Greek communities would have torn themselves apart long before Philip and Alexander brought the curtain down on the city-state. They were not Utopian communities, neither were they the victims of pure arbitrariness, caprice and anarchy. Under the best conditions, they practised the principles of the rule of law and equality before the law as well as could be expected, though always setting the citizen above all other men in both respects. In matters of property and contract they allowed wide, though of course not absolute, freedom to the individual,[25] and sought to protect that freedom against fraud and duress. Restrictions on the individual's freedom in this broad sphere were as likely to arise from social pressures as from the law, for example in the preference for certain forms of income-producing wealth against others.

To catalogue and examine the rights and disabilities through the whole gamut of property relations would require another essay. I shall restrict myself to one example because of two important implications, and that is the virtually unlimited freedom of a slaveowner to manumit his slaves. In Rome, when a citizen slaveowner did that the freedmen automatically became Roman citizens (with exceptions that are irrelevant in the present context). But never in Greece, so far as I know. More broadly a Greek had his freedom severely restricted by law in any activity that entailed the introduction of new members into the closed circle of the citizen-body.[26] That meant, in particular, tight restriction in the field of marriage and family law. The state determined the legitimacy of a marriage, not only by laying down the required formalities but also by specifying the categories of men and women who could, or could not, marry each other, and in so doing they went well beyond the incest taboos. Pericles' law of 451 or 450 BC, prohibiting marriage between a citizen and a non-citizen, is only the most famous instance.[27] Violators may not have been punished personally, but their children paid the heavy penalty of being declared bastards, *nothoi*, and therefore being excluded from the citizenship roster as well as having their inheritance rights reduced.

Such disabilities, such limitations on the freedom of the citizen, were accepted without a murmur. A Diogenes did not accept them, of course, but Diogenes renders all discussion impossible. Furthermore, family law cut across political rights and political systems, and that is the second implication arising from my initial example of manumission. In this field of behaviour, and it is not the only one, democracy did not necessarily entail an extension of rights, greater freedom, beyond those existing in oligarchies. On the contrary, Pericles' law of 451/0, for example, was more restricting than any other we know, in any Greek community of that period. Similarly, Athenian women had fewer claims to an inheritance than the women of Sparta or Crete; conversely, Athenian male citizens had less freedom to dispose of their property with respect to their wives, daughters and female relations.

In short, when we turn, as I now do, to the freedom of the Greek citizen in his relations with the state, as distinct from his relations with other individuals, we must try to rid our minds of the false unitary notion that all rights, political and non-political, moved in tandem. I must stress this particularly because I shall be concentrating on classical Athens, the only *polis* other than the very atypical Sparta that is accessible to systematic analysis, and Athens was an exceptional *polis* because of the quality of its democracy and also because of its fifth-century empire.

I begin with the state and the individual in the military sphere. It has been calculated that, during the century and a half from the end of the Persian wars in 479 B C to the defeat by Philip of Macedon in 338, Athens was engaged in war on an average of two out of every three years, and never enjoyed a period of peace for as long as ten consecutive years. No wonder that defence of the city was on the agenda of the Athenian assembly ten times a year at a minimum. Who performed the necessary military service and under what conditions? If we put aside such marginal groups as archers and slingers, normally mercenaries, the Greek ideal can be formulated in two parts: (1) the propertied sector of the population, both citizens and non-citizens, were obligated to serve as hoplites, paying for their equipment themselves, with the wealthiest performing the even more expensive duties of cavalrymen; (2) the poorer sector of the citizen-body were eligible, but normally not compelled, to serve as rowers in the fleet, supplemented by foreigners and even slaves. That the ideal could not be maintained in grave emergencies or in such a protracted conflict as the Peloponnesian War is obvious and easily documented. Sparta, for example, then had eventually to enrol helots as hoplites, Athens to use slaves as rowers (though she normally was more able than other states to resist this practice).[28] And in the fourth century B C the professional general and the mercenary soldier became increasingly important.

Had we the information, therefore, a full account of military and naval service in classical Greece would reveal endless variations, according to place, time and circumstance. Nevertheless, the reality approximated the ideal sufficiently, for much of the classical period, to permit us in the present context to assume the existence of the ideal.[29] And the fundamental distinction between the richer and the poorer must be carried one step further than I have so far taken it. While on active service, soldiers and rowers were paid a *per diem* sum, the same for both whenever possible except that the hoplite was expected to have a batman, and indeed needed one because of his armour, and he was given a second, identical allowance for his servant. In fifth-century Athens the amount varied from a half-drachma to a drachma a day, according to the state of the treasury and the size of the demand.[30] The sources call the *per diem* 'pay' and 'rations' indiscriminately, a usage which has the implication of a trifling sum, and which may accordingly mislead. Hoplites were usually on active duty for periods of only days or weeks and rarely in full force, and, it is worth repeating, they were not compensated for the considerable cost of their equipment. Their pay was therefore in fact a trifle. A substantial number of triremes, on the other hand, were on duty in fifth-century Athens for seven or eight months of the year, quite apart from the ships called out in an emergency. For those poorer citizens who rowed regularly, their pay thus ranged from perhaps 100 drachmas a year in times of peace to over 200 in the Peloponnesian War – no longer a trifle.[31]

If we now combine the pay situation with the distinction between compulsory military service and voluntary naval service, we are drawn to say that contribution to the defence of the city was a duty of the richer citizens and a privilege of the poorer. That may not be the whole truth: the Greek *polis* was not the only society in history in which army service was transformed from a duty to a privilege, a right, through powerful ideological pressures. But the paradox is valid nonetheless. I shall restate it brutally: the poorer Athenian citizen had the freedom to choose between serving and not serving and to be maintained by the state if he chose to serve, whereas the wealthier Athenian citizen had no freedom in this sphere. I have carefully said 'Athenian', not 'Greek', because Athenian exceptionalism is very marked here. The obligation of hoplite service was more or less universal, irrespective of the political regime, but the naval side of the paradox existed only in the maritime states, and we may doubt that others were able to pay on the Athenian scale with any regularity.

In so far as non-citizens were drawn into the same structure of military and naval service, political rights were reduced, in this sphere, to a minor, almost irrelevant, factor. However, that is not the important approach. The decision to deploy the army and navy was a sovereign one. In democracies the power lay with the assembly. Since Greek democracies were direct, not representative, many of the men who, on the day, voted for war with Sparta or for the Sicilian expedition, were voting to take themselves off on campaign, with the distinction between hoplite service and naval service I have drawn certainly in their minds. Only in an imaginary world of disembodied spirits could they have been unaware of the personal implications, or unaffected by them.

A similar distinction was to be found in the fiscal sphere. The classical Greeks looked upon direct taxes as tyrannical and avoided them whenever possible.[32] The two exceptions in Athens, the only city about which we know enough in these matters, are most revealing. One was the *metoikion*, a flat-rate head-tax paid by every non-Athenian residing in the city for even short periods, a 'tyrannical' kind of tax which by its mere existence marked the free non-citizen off from the citizen.[33] The other was the *eisphora*, a capital levy imposed from time to time to meet special military costs, from which the poor, roughly everyone below the hoplite status, were exempt. The rich therefore paid for the wars as well as fighting in them (unless they could pass the costs to subject-states). Otherwise normal governmental income was derived from state property, court fees and fines, and such indirect taxes as sales taxes and harbour dues. Again with one exception: the 'liturgies', the device by which the state got certain things done, not by paying for them by the treasury but by assigning to richer individuals direct responsibility both for the costs and for the actual performance, such as the training of a festival chorus or the command and maintenance of a trireme. The honorific element in liturgies was a strong one, but so was the financial burden.

I called attention at the beginning of this paper to the well-known importance of taxation in the modern struggles for citizens' rights. In Greece, by contrast, taxation was no issue at all in the analogous struggles (except, I believe, against tyranny once again),[34] and the explanation lies ready to hand. Whatever the grievances and the demands of citizens with restricted rights, they did not refer to a tax burden. In all the vast catalogue of complaints which Aristophanes was able to compile, much helped by his fertile imagination, not once does a peasant or townsman grumble about his taxes. But we do find in Aristophanes, notably in the *Wasps*, the soak-the-rich charge I mentioned earlier. And it is a fact that only in *staseis* designed to overthrow democracy, not in those aimed to introduce or advance it, did fiscal burdens feature prominently, those borne by the rich. Thucydides says so explicitly (8.48, 63.4) about the oligarchic coup of 411 BC. In the fifth book of the *Politics* (1304b20–05a7) Aristotle gives five instances in which oligarchic revolts were provoked by the 'wantonness' of the 'demagogues', in Cos, Rhodes, Heraclea, Megara and Cyme. Characteristically there are no dates and little concrete information, but it is certain from his concluding sentences that financial charges, particularly liturgies, were an essential element in the conflicts.

For Athens there is the oft-quoted remark of Pseudo-Xenophon (*Constitution of Athens* 1.13): the *demos* 'demand payment for singing, running, dancing and sailing on ships in order that they may get the money and the rich become poorer'. That comes from a skilfully contrived political pamphlet, with an unconcealed oligarchic bias. The expressed motive, that the rich should become poorer, need not detain us: the egalitarianism runs counter to all the contemporary evidence, such as the openness with which wealthy Athenians, from Alcibiades to the minor figures in the forensic orations, paraded their wealth in the assembly and the courts as points in their favour because they employed that wealth in the public interest.[35] The uses of wealth, not its possession, were the crux of the matter. However, it does not follow that the remainder of the quotation is as easily dismissible. Pay for a wide range of public activity had become the order of the day in Athens, varying from the *per diem* of the jurors to the naval payments which sometimes amounted to annual salaries, on to the monetary rewards for Games victors and the pensions of war-orphans. Non-citizens were sometimes admitted, when there was no alternative, but the fundamental divide is symbolised by a decree of 402 BC, which voted maintenance for the orphans of men killed in the fighting that overthrew the Thirty Tyrants, and explicitly restricted the benefit to the legitimate sons of citizens.[36] The number of boys involved, and therefore the sums of money, were tiny; that is precisely why the decree is so revealing.

I am not for a moment suggesting that a notable proportion of the citizen-body were idlers living at public expense. Most Athenians, like most Greeks, had a low standard of living and worked for it, none harder than the rowers in the fleet, the largest body of men receiving pay from the state. My point is, rather, one which is implicit in the formal language of government – 'the Athenians', not 'Athens', passed laws, levied taxes, declared war and so on – that in practice the Greek concept of rights was closer in spirit to the one revealed by the United Nations Declaration than to the libertarian position of John Stuart Mill. A citizen had positive claims on the state, not merely the right not to be interfered with in the private sphere. Such claims, if pressed, quickly produced financial crises: I need not review the history of fourth-century Athens on this score, with its chronic difficulties in financing the navy or with the characteristic difficulties of Demosthenes in getting public monies transferred to the war fund from the theoric fund, which provided free admissions to the theatre. Elsewhere *stasis* was endemic, but not in Athens, though no city carried the claims of its citizens to public pay and assistance so far. The key to this Athenian exceptionalism, I have already suggested, will be found in the empire, discussed in another chapter.

Except in moments of desperation when they called for the cancellation of debts and redistribution of the land, Greek citizens failed to press their claims as far as one might imagine they could and would. Despite Pseudo-Xenophon and his co-believers, not even the Athenian *demos* ever mounted an assault on the fortunes or the honours of the Athenian wealthy. Nor, to look at the matter from another angle, did the Greek state exercise its powers in many spheres of behaviour. It did not restrict interest rates, as the Romans did, or (save for Sparta) introduce compulsory education. Neither did it build highways: that is to say, the limits of observable governmental intervention in the realm of rights and duties were set by the structure and value-system of the society, not by transcendental doctrines, just as in the normally neutral realm of technological activities. There were no inalienable rights guaranteed by a higher authority. There were no natural rights. The secular discussion of *physis* and *nomos*, nature and convention, initiated by the Sophists and continued by philosophers of different schools, ultimately found its way into political rhetoric (among the Romans rather than among the Greeks), but it is difficult to discover any significant impact on the practical behaviour of citizens and governments.

That is not to say that the Greeks were determined immoralists. In matters of the family and sexual relations, most notably, there was a common belief that some practices and relations were somehow natural and universal (at least among civilised people), others unnatural, though even here there was a wide latitude for legislation and change. What was wholly lacking was a conception of precisely those inalienable rights which have been the foundation of the modern libertarian doctrine: freedom of speech, of religion and so on. In the family field, the Athenian state could narrow the range of legitimate marriage; it would have found it impossible to abolish the incest taboos. But it could make inroads into freedom of speech and thought, and did so when it chose.

The operative phrase is 'when it chose'. Provided the procedures adopted were themselves lawful, there were no limits to the powers of the *polis*, other than self-imposed (and therefore changeable) limits, outside the sphere in which deep-rooted and ancient taboos remained powerful. In 411 BC, after all, the Athenian assembly voted to abolish democracy.

What, then, were the sources of rights and duties, of freedom, and what were the sanctions? Where, particularly, were the gods in this whole story? The pervasiveness of rituals, of sacrifices, oaths and oracles is too familiar to require retelling. So is the strength of the public outcry against a blasphemous outrage, or the ubiquity of the curse, public and private. However, it is also true that Greek law had undergone a process of thorough de-sacralisation by the classical period.[37] Although the religious externals were scrupulously retained, there is silence about divine command, divine favour or divine sanction in the substantive provisions. Athena received gifts and her share of the tribute, she was even given confiscated counterfeit coins carrying her portrait (as was Poseidon in Corinth),[38] but she was not invoked in the massive legislative reform of the end of the fifth century. Zeus Xenios protected strangers; he was never invoked to increase the rights of metics: even the pious Xenophon restricted himself to purely utilitarian arguments in the *Poroi* when he called for various benefits, within narrow limits, designed to attract more metics to Athens. In other historical periods, religion has sometimes been a positive ideology on behalf of rights and freedom, in the peasant revolts at the end of the Middle Ages, for example, or in the Calvinist support against autocracy in the sixteenth and seventeenth centuries. Not in Greece, however.

I have oversimplified, of course, under the compulsion of brevity, and I have concentrated almost entirely on the state and its governmental machinery, leaving aside the important role of informal social pressures, all the stronger because the Greek *poleis* were small, face-to-face communities, in which men lived out their lives in public, so to speak. Granted the need for qualification that a more extended and nuanced treatment would require, the conclusion seems to me to be warranted, nevertheless, that the classical Greek *polis* had evolved an institutional system which, of itself, was capable of formulating, sanctioning, and when necessary changing the intricate network of rights and duties that are subsumed under the label 'freedom'. The weaknesses which the ancient theorists pursued relentlessly were the strengths of the system seen from within. The greatest flaw, from our standpoint, the underpinning of the *polis* by a majority with restricted rights or with no rights at all, was not one of the weaknesses condemned by the theorists. On the contrary, they held the democratic *polis* to be insufficiently hierarchical, the extension of *isonomia* (in both its senses) to peasants, shopkeepers and craftsmen to be its greatest fault.

Historians have an understandable affinity with their own predecessors, the intellectuals of antiquity, and tend to see ancient realities through their eyes, which means as refracted through their values. There is another way of looking at the Greek realities. It was no one less a man than Pseudo-Xenophon who concluded (3.1): 'As for the Athenian system of government, I do not like it. However, since they decided to become a democracy, it seems to me that they are preserving the democracy well.'

PART TWO

SERVITUDE, SLAVERY AND THE ECONOMY

괴5괴5괴5

- 6 -

WAS GREEK CIVILISATION
BASED ON SLAVE LABOUR?

I

Two generalisations may be made at the outset. First: at all times and in all places the Greek world relied on some form (or forms) of dependent labour to meet its needs, both public and private. By this I mean that dependent labour was essential, in a significant measure, if the requirements of agriculture, trade, manufacture, public works, and war production were to be fulfilled. And by dependent labour I mean work performed under compulsions other than those of kinship or communal obligations.[1] Second: with the rarest of exceptions, there were always substantial numbers of free men engaged in productive labour. By this I mean primarily not free hired labour but free men working on their own (or leased) land or in their shops or homes as craftsmen and shopkeepers. It is within the framework created by these two generalisations that the questions must be asked which seek to locate slavery in the society. And by slavery, finally, I mean the status in which a man is, in the eyes of the law and of public opinion and with respect to all parties, a possession, a chattel, of another man.[2]

How completely the Greeks always took slavery for granted as one of the facts of human existence is abundantly evident to anyone who has read their literature. In the Homeric poems it is assumed (correctly) that captive women will be taken home as slaves, and that occasional male slaves – the victims of Phoenician merchant-pirates – will also be on hand. In the early seventh century BC, when Hesiod, the Boeotian 'peasant' poet, gets down to practical advice in his *Works and Days*, he tells his brother how to use slaves properly; that they will be available is simply assumed. The same is true of Xenophon's manual for the gentleman farmer, the *Oeconomicus*, written about 375 BC. A few years earlier, an Athenian cripple who was appealing a decision dropping him from the dole, said to the Council: 'I have a trade which brings me in a little,

Originally published in *Historia* 8 (1959) 145–64. I have reduced the annotation considerably to eliminate now outdated debates.

but I can hardly work at it myself and I cannot afford to buy someone to replace myself in it' (Lysias 24.6). In the first book of the Pseudo-Aristotelian *Oeconomica*, a Peripatetic work probably of the late fourth or early third century BC, we find the following proposition about the organisation of the household, stated as baldly and flatly as it could possibly be done: 'Of property, the first and most necessary kind, the best and most manageable, is man. Therefore the first step is to procure good slaves. Of slaves there are two kinds, the overseer and the worker (1344a22). Polybius, discussing the strategic situation of Byzantium (4.38.4), speaks quite casually of 'the necessities of life – cattle and slaves' which come from the Black Sea region. And so on.

The Greek language had an astonishing range of vocabulary for slaves, unparalleled in my knowledge.[3] In the earliest texts, Homer and Hesiod, there were two basic words for slave, *dmos* and *doulos*, used without any discoverable distinction between them, and both with uncertain ety-mologies. *Dmos* died out quickly, surviving only in poetry, whereas *doulos* remained the basic word, so to speak, all through Greek history, and the root on which there were built such words as *douleia*, 'slavery'. But Homer already has, in one possibly interpolated passage (*Iliad* 7.475), the word (in the plural form) *andrapoda* ('man-footed' = human being) which became very common, having been constructed on the model of *tetrapoda* ('four-footed' = animal). These words were strictly servile, except in such metaphors as 'the Athenians enslaved the allies'. But there was still another group which could be used for both slaves and free men, depending on the context. Three of them are built on the household root, *oikos* – *oikeus*, *oiketes*, and *oikiatas* – and the pattern of usage is variegated and complicated. For example, these *oikos*-words sometimes meant merely 'servant' or 'slave' generally, and sometimes, though less often, they indicated narrower distinctions, such as house-born slave (as against purchased) or privately owned (as against royal in the Hellenistic context).[4]

If we think of ancient society as made up of a spectrum of statuses, with the free citizen at one end and the slave at the other, and with a considerable number of shades of dependence in between, we shall quickly discover different 'lines' on the spectrum: the Spartan helot (with such parallels as the *penestes* of Thessaly); the debt-bondsman, who was not a slave although under some conditions he could eventually be sold into slavery abroad; the conditionally manumitted slave; and, finally, the freedman. These categories rarely, if ever, appeared concurrently within the same community, nor were they equal in importance or equally significant in all periods of Greek history. By and large, the slave proper was the decisive figure (to the virtual exclusion of the others) in the economically and politically advanced communities; whereas helotage and debt-bondage were to be found in the more archaic communities, whether in Crete or Sparta or Thessaly at an even late date, or in Athens in its pre-Solonian period. There is also some correlation, though by no means a perfect one, between the various categories of dependent labour and their function. Slavery was the most flexible of the forms, adaptable to all kinds and levels of activity, whereas helotage and the rest were best suited to agriculture, pasturage, and household service, much less so to manufacture and trade.

II

With little exception, there was no activity, productive or unproductive, public or private, pleasant or unpleasant, which was not performed by slaves at some times and in some places in the Greek world. The major exception was, of course, political: no slave held public office or sat on the deliberative and judicial bodies (though slaves were commonly employed in the 'civil service', as secretaries and clerks, and as police-men and prison attendants). Slaves did not fight as a rule, either, unless freed (although helots apparently did), and they were very rare in the liberal professions, including medicine. On the other side, there was no activity which was not performed by free men at some times and in some places. That is sometimes denied, but the denial rests on a gross error, namely, the failure to differentiate between a free man working for himself and one working for another, for hire. In the Greek scale of values, the crucial test was not so much the nature of the work (within limits, of course) as the condition or status under which it was carried on.[5] 'The condition of the free man', said Aristotle (*Rhetoric* 1367a32) 'is that he does not live under the constraint of another.' On this point, Aristotle was expressing a nearly universal Greek notion. Although we find free Greeks doing every kind of work, the free wage-earner, the free man who regularly works for another and therefore 'lives under the constraint of another' is a rare figure in the sources, and he surely was a minor factor in the picture.[6]

The basic economic activity was, of course, agriculture. Throughout Greek history, the overwhelming majority of the population had its main wealth in the land. And the majority were smallholders, depending on their own labour, the labour of other members of the family, and the occasional assistance (as in time of harvest) of neighbours and casual hired hands. Some proportion of these smallholders owned a slave, or even two, but we cannot possibly determine what the proportion was, and in this sector the whole issue is clearly not of the greatest importance. But the large landholders, a minority though they were, constituted the political (and often the intellectual) elite of the Greek world; our evidence reveals remarkably few names of any consequence whose economic base was outside the land. This landholding elite tended to become more and more of an absentee group in the course of Greek history; but early or late, whether they sat on their estates or in the cities, dependent labour worked their land as a basic rule (even when allowance is made for tenancy). In some areas it took the form of helotage, and in the archaic period, of debt-bondage, but generally the form was outright slavery.

I am aware, of course, that this view of slavery in Greek agriculture is contested. Nevertheless, I accept the evidence of the line of authors whom I have already cited, from Hesiod to the pseudo-Aristotelian *Oeconomica*. These are all matter-of-fact writings, not utopias or speculative statements of what ought to be. If slavery was not the customary labour form on the larger holdings, then I cannot imagine what Hesiod or Xenophon or the Peripatetic were doing, or why any Greek bothered to read their works.[7] One similar piece of evidence is worth adding. There was a Greek harvest festival called the Kronia, which was celebrated in Athens and other places (especially among the Ionians). One feature, says the Athenian chronicler Philochorus, was that 'the heads of families ate the crops and fruits at the same table with their slaves, with whom they had shared the labours of cultivation. For the god is pleased with this honour from the slaves in contemplation of their labours.'[8] Neither the practice nor Philochorus' explanation of it makes any sense whatever if slavery was as unimportant in agriculture as some modern writers pretend.

I had better be perfectly clear here: I am not saying that slaves outnumbered free men in agriculture, or that the bulk of farming was done by slaves, but that slavery dominated agriculture in so far as it was on a scale that transcended the labour of the householder and his sons. Nor am I suggesting that there was no hired free labour; rather that there was little of any significance. Among the slaves, furthermore, were the overseers, invariably so if the property was large enough or if the owner was an absentee. 'Of slaves,' said the author of the *Oeconomica*, 'there are two kinds, the overseer and the worker.'

In mining and quarrying the situation was decisively one-sided. There were free men, in Athens for example, who leased such small mining concessions that they were able to work them alone. The moment, however, additional labour was introduced (and that was by far the more common case), it seems always to have been slave. The largest individual holdings of slaves in Athens were workers in the mines, topped by the one thousand reported to have been leased out for this purpose by the fifth-century general Nicias.[9] It has been suggested, indeed, that at one point there may have been as many as thirty thousand slaves at work in the Athenian silver mines and processing mills.[10]

Manufacture was like agriculture in that the choice was (even more exclusively) between the independent craftsman working alone or with members of his family and the owner of slaves. The link with slavery was so close (and the absence of free hired labour so complete), that Demosthenes, for example, could say 'they caused the *ergasterion* (work-shop) to disappear' and then he could follow, as an exact synonym and with no possible misunderstanding, by saying that 'they caused the slaves to disappear'.[11] On the other hand, the proportion of operations employing slaves, as against the independent self-employed craftsmen, was probably greater than in agriculture, and in this respect more like mining. In commerce and banking, subordinates were invariably slaves, even in such posts as 'bank manager'. However the numbers were small.

In the domestic field, finally, we can take it as a rule that any free man who possibly could afford one, owned a slave attendant who accompanied him when he walked abroad in the town or when he travelled (including his military service), and also a slave woman for the household chores. There is no conceivable way of estimating how many such free men there were, or how many owned numbers of domestics, but the fact is taken for granted so completely and so often in the literature that I strongly believe that many owned slaves even when they could not afford them. (Modern parallels will come to mind readily.) I stress this for two reasons. First, the need for domestic slaves, often an unproductive element, should serve as a cautionary sign when one examines such questions as efficiency and cost of slave labour. Secondly, domestic slavery was by no means entirely unproductive. In the country-side in particular, but also in the towns, two important industries would often be in their hands in the larger households, on a straight production for household consumption basis. I refer to baking and textile making, and every medievalist, at least, will at once grasp the significance of the withdrawal of the latter from market production, even if the withdrawal was far from complete.

It would be very helpful if we had some idea how many slaves there were in any given Greek community to carry on all this work, and how they were divided among the branches of the economy. Unfortunately we have no reliable figures, and none at all for most of the *poleis*. What I consider to be the best computations for Athens suggest that the total of slaves reached 60–80,000 in peak periods in the fifth and fourth centuries BC.[12] Athens had the largest population in the classical Greek world and the largest number of slaves. Thucydides (8.40.2) said that there were more slaves in his day on the island of Chios than in any other Greek community except Sparta, but I suggest that he was thinking of the density of the slave population measured against the free, not of absolute totals (and in Sparta he meant the helots, not chattel slaves). Other places, such as Aegina or Corinth, may at one time or another also have had a higher ratio of slaves than Athens. And there were surely communities in which the slaves were less dense.

More than that we can scarcely say about the numbers, but I think that is really enough. There is too much tendentious discussion of numbers in the literature already, as if a mere count of heads is the answer to all the complicated questions which flow from the existence of slavery. The Athenian figures I mentioned amount to an average of no less than three or four slaves to each free household (including all free men in the calculation, whether citizen or not). But even the smallest figure anyone has suggested, 20,000 slaves in Demosthenes' time[13] – altogether too low in my opinion – would be roughly equivalent to one slave for each adult citizen, no negligible ratio. Within very broad limits, the numbers are irrelevant to the question of significance. When Starr, for example, objects to 'exaggerated guesses' and replies that 'the most careful estimates . . . reduce the proportion of slaves to far less than half the population, probably one third or one quarter at most',[14] he is proving far less than he thinks. No one seriously believes that slaves did all the work in Athens (or anywhere else in Greece except for Sparta with its helots), and one merely confuses the issues when one pretends that somehow a reduction of the estimates to only a third or a quarter of the population is crucial. In 1860, according to official census figures, slightly less than one-third of the total population of the American slave states were slaves. Furthermore, 'nearly three-fourths of all free Southerners had no connection with slavery through either family ties or direct ownership. The "typical" Southerner was not only a small farmer but also a nonslaveholder.'[15] Yet no one would think of denying that slavery was a decisive element in southern society. The analogy seems obvious for ancient Greece, where, it can be shown, ownership of slaves was even more widely spread among the free men and the use of slaves much more diversified, and where the estimates do not give a ratio significantly below the American one. Simply stated, there can be no denial that there were enough slaves about for them to be, of necessity, an integral factor in the society.

There were two main sources of supply. One was captives, the victims of war and sometimes piracy. One of the few generalisations about the ancient world to which there is no exception is this, that the victorious power had absolute right over the persons and the property of the vanquished.[16] This right was not exercised to its full extent every time, but it was exercised often enough, and on a large enough scale, to throw a continuous and numerous supply of men, women, and children on to the slave market. Alongside the captives we must place the so-called barbarians who came into the Greek world in a steady stream – Thracians, Scythians, Cappadocians, etc. – through the activity of full-time traders, much like the process by which African slaves reached the new world in more modern times. Many were victims of wars among the barbarians themselves. Others came peacefully, so to speak: Herodotus (5.6) says that the Thracians sold their children for export. The first steps all took place outside the Greek orbit, and our sources tell us virtually nothing about them, but there can be no doubt that large numbers and a steady supply were involved, for there is no other way to explain such facts as the high proportion of Paphlagonians and Thracians among the slaves in the Attic silver mines, many of them specialists, or the corps of Scythian archers (slaves owned by the state) who constituted the Athenian police force.

Merely to complete the picture, we must list penal servitude and the exposure of unwanted children. Beyond mere mention, however, they can be ignored because they were negligible in their importance. There then remains one more source, breeding, and that is a puzzle. One reads in the modern literature that there was very little breeding of slaves (as distinct from helots and the like) among the Greeks because, under their conditions, it was cheaper to buy slaves than to raise them. I am not altogether satisfied with the evidence for this view, and I am altogether dissatisfied with the economics which is supposed to justify it. There were conditions under which breeding was certainly rare, but for reasons which have nothing to do with economics. In the mines, for example, nearly all the slaves were men, and that is the explanation, simply enough. But what about domestics, among whom the proportion of women was surely high? I must leave the question unanswered, except to remove one fallacy. It is sometimes said that there is a demographic law that no slave population ever reproduces itself, that they must always be replenished from outside. Such a law is a myth: that can be said categorically on the evidence of the southern states, evidence which is statistical and reliable.

III

The impression one gets is clearly that the majority of the slaves were foreigners. That is to say, it was the rule (apart from debt-bondage) that Athenians were never kept as slaves in Athens, or Corinthians in Corinth. However, I am referring to the more basic sense, that the majority were not Greeks at all, but men and women from the races living outside the Greek world. It is idle to speculate about the proportions here, but there cannot be any reasonable doubt about the majority. In some places, such as the Laurium silver mines in Attica, this meant relatively large concentrations in a small area. The number of Thracian slaves in Laurium in Xenophon's time, for example, was greater than the total population of some of the smaller Greek city-states.

No wonder some Greeks came to identify slaves and barbarians (a synonym for all non-Greeks). The most serious effort, so far as we know, to justify this view as part of the natural arrangement of things, will be found in the first book of Aristotle's *Politics*. It was not a successful effort for several reasons, of which the most obvious is the fact, as Aristotle himself conceded, that too many were slaves 'by accident', by the chance of warfare or shipwreck or kidnapping. In the end, natural slavery was abandoned as a formal concept, defeated by the pragmatic view that slavery was a fact of life, a conventional institution universally practised. As the Roman jurist Florentinus phrased it, 'Slavery is an institution of the *ius gentium* (law of all nations) whereby someone is subject to the *dominium* of another, contrary to nature.'[17] That view (and even sharper formulations) can be traced back to the sophistic literature of the fifth century BC, and, in a less formal way, to Greek tragedy. I chose Florentinus to quote instead because his definition appears in the *Digest*, in which slavery is so prominent that the Roman law of slavery has been called 'the most characteristic part of the most characteristic intellectual product of Rome'.[18] Nothing illustrates more perfectly the inability of the ancient world to imagine that there could be a civilised society without slaves.

The Greek world was one of endless debate and challenge. Among the intellectuals, no belief or idea was self-evident: every conception and every institution sooner or later came under attack – religious beliefs, ethical values, political systems, aspects of the economy, even such bedrock institutions as the family and private property. Slavery, too, up to a point, but that point was invariably a good distance short of abolitionist proposals. Plato, who criticised society more radically than any other thinker, did not concern himself much with the question in the *Republic*, but even there he assumed the continuance of slavery. And in the *Laws*, 'the number of passages . . . that deal with slavery is surprisingly large' and the tenor of the legislation is generally more severe than the actual law of Athens at that time. 'Their effect, on the one hand, is to give greater authority to masters in the exercise of rule over slaves, and on the other hand to accentuate the distinction between slave and free man.' Paradoxically, neither were the believers in the brotherhood of man (whether Cynic, Stoic, or early Christian) opponents of slavery. In their eyes, all material concerns, including status, were a matter of essential indifference. Diogenes, it is said, was once seized by pirates and taken to Crete to be sold. At the auction, he pointed to a certain Corinthian among the buyers and said: 'Sell me to him; he needs a master.'[20]

The question must then be faced, how much relevance has all this for the majority of Greeks, for those who were neither philosophers nor wealthy men of leisure? What did the little man think about slavery? It is no answer to argue that we must not take 'the political theorists of the philosophical schools too seriously as having established "the main line of Greek thought concerning slavery" '.[21] No one pretends that Plato and Aristotle speak for all Greeks. But, equally, no one should pretend that lower-class Greeks necessarily rejected everything which we read in Greek literature and philosophy, simply because, with virtually no exceptions, the poets and philosophers were men of the leisure class. The history of ideology and belief is not so simple. It is a commonplace that the little man shares the ideals and aspirations of his betters – in his dreams if not in the hard reality of his daily life. By and large, the vast majority in all periods of history have always taken the basic institutions of society for granted. Men do not, as a rule, ask themselves whether monogamous marriage or a police force or machine production is necessary to their way of life. They accept them as facts, as self-evident. Only when there is a challenge from one source or another – from outside or from catastrophic famine or plague – do such facts become questions.

A large section of the Greek population was always on the edge of marginal subsistence. They worked hard for their livelihood and could not look forward to economic advancement as a reward for their labours; on the contrary, if they moved at all, it was likely to be downward. Famines, plagues, wars, political struggles, all were a threat, and social crisis was a common enough phenomenon in Greek history. Yet through the centuries no ideology of labour appeared, nothing that can in any sense be counterpoised to the negative judgments with which the writings of the leisure class are filled. There was neither a word in the Greek language with which to express the general notion of labour, nor the concept of labour 'as a general social function'.[22] There was plenty of grumbling, of course, and there was pride of craftsmanship. Men could not survive psychologically without them. But neither developed into a belief: grumbling was not turned into a punishment for sin – 'In the sweat of thy face shalt thou eat bread' – nor pride of craftsmanship into the virtue of labour, into the doctrine of the calling or anything comparable. The nearest to either will be found in Hesiod's *Works and Days*, and in this context the decisive fact about Hesiod is his unquestioning assumption that the farmer will have proper slave labour.

That was all there was to the poor man's counter-ideology: we live in the iron age when 'men never rest from toil and sorrow by day, and from perishing by night'; therefore it is better to toil than to idle and perish – but if we can we too will turn to the labour of slaves. Hesiod may not have been able, even in his imagination, to think beyond slavery as *supplementary* to his own labour, but that was the seventh century, still the early days of slavery. About 400 BC, however, Lysias' crippled client could make the serious argument (24.6) in the Athenian Council that he required a dole because he could not afford a slave as a *replacement*. And half a century later Xenophon put forth a scheme whereby every citizen could be maintained by the state, chiefly from revenues to be derived from publicly owned slaves working in the mines.[23]

When talk turned to action, even when crisis turned into civil war and revolution, slavery remained unchallenged. With absolute regularity, all through Greek history, the demand was 'Cancel debts and redistribute the land.' Never, to my knowledge, do we hear a protest from the free poor, not even in the deepest crises, against slave competition. There are no complaints – as there might well have been – that slaves deprive free man of a livelihood, or compel free men to work for lower wages and

longer hours.[24] There is nothing remotely resembling a workers' programme, no wage demands, no talk of working conditions or government employment measures or the like. In a city like Athens there was
ample opportunity. The *demos* had power, enough of them were poor,
and they had leaders. But economic assistance took the form of pay for
public office and for rowing in the fleet, free admission to the theatre (the
so-called theoric fund), and various minor doles; while economic legislation was restricted to imports and exports, weights and measures,
price controls. Not even the wildest of the accusations against the demagogues – and they were wholly unrestrained as every reader of Aristophanes or Plato knows – ever suggested anything which would hint at
a working-class interest, or an anti-slavery bias.

    Nor did the free poor take the other possible tack of joining with the
slaves in a common struggle on a principled basis. The Solonic revolution in Athens at the beginning of the sixth century B C, for example,
brought an end to debt-bondage and the return of Athenians who had
been sold into slavery abroad, but not the emancipation of others,
non-Athenians, who were in slavery in Athens. Centuries later, when
the great wave of slave revolts came after 140 B C, starting in the Roman
west and spreading to the Greek east, the free poor on the whole simply
stood apart. It was no issue of theirs, they seem to have thought;
correctly so, for the outcome of the revolts promised them nothing one
way or the other. Numbers of free men may have taken advantage of the
chaos to enrich themselves personally, by looting or otherwise. Essentially that is what they did, when the opportunity arose, in a military
campaign, nothing more. The slaves were, in a basic sense, irrelevant to
their behaviour at that moment.[25]

    In 464 B C a great helot revolt broke out, and in 462 Athens dispatched a
hoplite force under Cimon to help the Spartans suppress it. When the
revolt ended, after nearly five years, a group of the rebels were permitted
to escape, and it was Athens which provided them refuge, settling them
in Naupactus. A comparable shift took place in the first phase of the
Peloponnesian War. In 425 the Athenians seized Pylos, a harbour on the
west coast of the Peloponnese. The garrison was a small one and Pylos
was by no means an important port. Nevertheless, Sparta was so frightened that she soon sued for peace, because the Athenian foothold was a
dangerous centre of infection, inviting desertion and eventual revolt
among the Messenian helots. Athens finally agreed to peace in 421, and
immediately afterwards concluded an alliance with Sparta, one of the
terms of which was: 'Should the slave-class rise in rebellion, the

Athenians will assist the Spartans with all their might, according to their power.'[26]

Obviously the attitude of one city to the slaves of another lies largely outside our problem. Athens agreed to help suppress helots when she and Sparta were allies; she encouraged helot revolts when they were at war. That reflects elementary tactics, not a judgment about slavery. Much the same kind of distinction must be made in the instances, recurring in Spartan history, when helots were freed as pawns in an internal power struggle. So, too, of the instances which were apparently not uncommon in fourth-century Greece, but about which nothing concrete is known other than the clause in the agreement between Alexander and the Hellenic League, binding the members to guarantee that 'there shall be no killing or banishment contrary to the laws of each city, no confiscation of property, no redistribution of land, no cancellation of debts, no freeing of slaves for purposes of revolution'.[27] These were mere tactics again. Slaves were resources, and they could be useful in a particular situation. But only a number of specific slaves, those who were available at the precise moment; not slaves in general, or all slaves, and surely not slaves in the future. Some slaves were freed, but slavery remained untouched. Exactly the same behaviour can be found in the reverse case, when a state (or ruling class) called upon its slaves to help protect it. Often enough in a military crisis, slaves were freed, conscripted into the army or navy, and called upon to fight.[28] And again the result was that some slaves were freed while the institution continued exactly as before.

In sum under certain conditions of crisis and tension the society (or a sector of it) was faced with a conflict within its system of values and beliefs. It was sometimes necessary, in the interest of national safety or of a political programme, to surrender the normal use of, and approach to, slaves. When this happened, the institution itself survived without any noticeable weakening. The fact that it happened is not without significance; it suggests that among the Greeks, even in Sparta, there was not that deep-rooted and often neurotic horror of the slaves known in other societies, which would have made the freeing and arming of slaves *en masse*, for whatever purpose, a virtual impossibility. It suggests, further, something about the slaves themselves. Some did fight for their masters, and that is not unimportant.

Nothing is more elusive than the psychology of the slave. Even when, as in the American South, there seems to be a lot of material – autobiographies of ex-slaves, impressions of travellers from non-slaveholding societies, and the like – no unambiguous picture emerges. For antiquity there is scarcely any evidence at all, and the bits are indirect and tangential, and far from easy to interpret. Thus, a favourite apology is to invoke the fact that, apart from very special instances as in Sparta, the record shows neither revolts of slaves nor a fear of uprisings. Even if the facts are granted, the rosy conclusion does not follow. Slaves have scarcely ever revolted, even in the southern states.[29] A large-scale rebellion is impossible to organise and carry through except under very unusual circumstances. The right combination appeared but once in ancient history, during two generations of the late Roman Republic, when there were great concentrations of slaves in Italy and Sicily, many of them almost completely unattended and unguarded, many others professional fighters (gladiators), and when the whole society was in turmoil, with a very marked breakdown of social and moral values.[30]

At this point it is necessary to recall that helots differed in certain key respects from chattel slaves. First, they had the necessary ties of solidarity that come from kinship and nationhood, intensified by the fact, not to be underestimated, that they were not foreigners but a subject people working their own lands in a state of servitude. This complex was lacking among the slaves of the Greek world. The Peripatetic author of the *Oeconomica* made the sensible recommendation that neither an individual nor a city should have many slaves of the same nationality.[31] Secondly, the helots had property rights of a kind: the law, at least, permitted them to retain everything they produced beyond the fixed deliveries to their masters. Third, they outnumbered the free population on a scale without parallel in other Greek communities. These are the peculiar factors, in my opinion, which explain the revolts of the helots and the persistent Spartan concern with the question, more than Spartan cruelty.[32] It is a fallacy to think that the threat of rebellion increases automatically with an increase in misery and oppression. Hunger and torture destroy the spirit; at most they stimulate efforts at flight or other forms of purely individual behaviour (including betrayal of fellow-victims), whereas revolt requires organisation and courage and persistence. Frederick Douglass, who in 1855 wrote the most penetrating analysis to come from an ex-slave, summed up the psychology in these words: 'Beat and cuff your slave, keep him hungry and spiritless, and he will follow the chain of his master like a dog; but feed and clothe him with physical comfort, – and dreams of freedom intrude. Give him a *bad* master, and he aspires to a *good* master; give him a good master, and he wishes to become his *own* master.'[33]

There are many ways, other than revolt, in which slaves can protest.[34] In particular they can flee, and though we have no figures whatsoever, it seems safe to say that the fugitive slave was a chronic and sufficiently numerous phenomenon in the Greek cities. Thucydides estimated that more than 20,000 Athenian slaves fled in the final decade of the Peloponnesian War. In this they were openly encouraged by the Spartan garrison established in Decelea, and Thucydides makes quite a point of the operation. Obviously he thought the harm to Athens was serious, intensified by the fact that many were skilled workers.[35] My immediate concern is with the slaves themselves, not with Athens, and I should stress very heavily that so many skilled slaves (who must be presumed to have been, on the average, among the best treated) took the risk and tried to flee. The risk was no light one, at least for the barbarians among them: no Thracian or Carian wandering about the Greek countryside without credentials could be sure of what lay ahead in Boeotia or Thessaly. Indeed, there is a hint that these particular 20,000 and more may have been very badly treated after escaping under Spartan promise. A reliable fourth-century B C historian attributed the great Theban prosperity at the end of the fifth century to their having purchased very cheaply the slaves and other booty seized from the Athenians during the Spartan occupation of Decelea.[36] Although there is no way to determine whether this is a reference to the 20,000, the suspicion is obvious. Ethics aside, there was no power, within or without the law, which could have prevented the re-enslavement of fugitive slaves even if they had been promised their freedom.

The *Oeconomica* (1344a35) sums up the life of the slave as consisting of three elements: work, punishment, and food. And there are more than enough floggings, and even tortures, in Greek literature, from one end to the other. Apart from psychological quirks (sadism and the like), flogging means simply that the slave, as slave, must be goaded into performing the function assigned to him. So, too, do the various incentive plans which were frequently adopted. The efficient, skilled, reliable slave could look forward to managerial status. In the cities, in particular, he could often achieve a curious sort of quasi-independence, living and working on his own, paying a kind of rental to his owner, and accumulating earnings with which, ultimately, to purchase his freedom. Manumission was, of course, the greatest incentive of all. Again we are baffled by the absence of numbers, but it is undisputed that manumission was a common phenomenon in most of the Greek world. This is an important difference between the Greek slave on the one hand, and the helot or

American slave on the other. It is also important evidence about the degree of the slave's alleged 'acceptance' of his status.[37]

IV

It is now time to try to add all this up and form some judgment about the institution. This would be difficult enough to do under ordinary circumstances; it has become almost impossible because of two extraneous factors imposed by modern society. The first is the confusion of the historical study with moral judgments about slavery. We condemn slavery, and we are embarrassed for the Greeks, whom we admire so much; therefore we tend either to underestimate its role in their life, or we ignore it altogether, hoping that somehow it will quietly go away. The second factor is more political, and it goes back at least to 1848, when the *Communist Manifesto* declared that 'The history of all hitherto existing society is the history of class struggles. Free man and slave, patrician and plebeian, lord and serf, guild-master and journeyman, in a word, oppressor and oppressed, stood in constant opposition to one another. . . .' Ever since, ancient slavery has been a battleground between Marxists and non-Marxists, a political issue rather than a historical phenomenon.

Now we observe that a sizable fraction of the population of the Greek world consisted of slaves, or other kinds of dependent labour, many of them barbarians; that by and large the elite in each city-state were men of leisure, completely free from any preoccupation with economic matters, thanks to a labour force which they bought and sold, over whom they had extensive property rights, and, equally important, what we may call physical rights; that the condition of servitude was one which no man, woman, or child, regardless of status or wealth, could be sure to escape in case of war or some other unpredictable and uncontrollable emergency. It seems to me that, seeing all this, if we could emancipate ourselves from the despotism of extraneous moral, intellectual, and political pressures, we would conclude, without hesitation, that slavery was a basic element in Greek civilisation.

Such a conclusion, however, should be the starting point of analysis, not the end of an argument, as it is so often at present. Perhaps it would be best to avoid the word 'basic' altogether, because it has been preempted as a technical term by the Marxist theory of history. Anyone else who used it in such a question as the one which is the title of this chapter, is compelled, by the intellectual (and political) situation in which we work, to qualify the term at once, to distinguish between *a* basic institution and *the* basic institution. In effect what has happened is that, in the guise of a discussion of ancient slavery, there has been a desultory discussion of Marxist theory, none of it, on either side, particularly illuminating about either Marxism or slavery.[38] Neither our understanding of the historical process nor our knowledge of ancient society is significantly advanced by these repeated statements and counter-statements, affirmations and denials of the proposition, 'Ancient society was based on slave labour.' Nor have we gained much from the persistent debate about causes. Was slavery the cause of the decline of Greek science? or of loose sexual morality? or of the widespread contempt for gainful employment? These are essentially false questions, imposed by a naive kind of pseudo-scientific thinking.

The most fruitful approach, I suggest, is to think in terms of purpose, in Immanuel Kant's sense, or of function, as the social anthropologists use that concept. The question which is most promising for systematic investigation is not whether slavery was the basic element, or whether it caused this or that, but how it functioned. This eliminates the sterile attempts to decide which was historically prior, slavery or something else; it avoids imposing moral judgments on, and prior to, the historical analysis; and it should avoid the trap which I shall call the free-will error. There is a maxim of Emile Durkheim's that 'The voluntary character of a practice or an institution should never be assumed beforehand.'[39] Given the existence of slavery – and it is given, for our sources do not permit us to go back to a stage in Greek history when it did not exist – the choice facing individual Greeks was socially and psychologically imposed. In the *Memorabilia* Xenophon says that 'those who can do so buy slaves so that they may have fellow workers'. That sentence is often quoted to prove that some Greeks owned no slaves, which needs no proof. It is much better cited to prove that *those who can*, buy slaves – Xenophon clearly places this whole phenomenon squarely in the realm of necessity.

The question of function permits no single answer. There are as many answers as there are contexts: function in relation to what? And when? And where? Buckland begins his work on the Roman law of slavery by noting that there 'is scarcely a problem which can present itself, in any branch of law, the solution of which may not be affected by the fact that one of the parties to the transaction is a slave'.[40] That sums up the situation in its simplest, most naked form, and it is as correct a statement for Greek law as for Roman. Beyond that, I would argue, there is no problem or practice in any branch of Greek life which was not affected, in some fashion, by the fact that many people in that society, even if not in the specific situation under consideration, were (or had been or might be) slaves. The connection was not always simple or direct, nor was the impact necessarily 'bad' (or 'good'). The historian's problem is precisely to uncover what the connections were, in all their concreteness and complexity, their goodness or badness or moral neutrality.

I think we will find that, more often than not, the institution of slavery turned out to be ambiguous in its function. Certainly the Greek attitudes to it were shot through with ambiguity, and not rarely with tension. To the Greeks, Nietzsche said, both labour and slavery were 'a necessary disgrace, of which one feels *ashamed*, as a disgrace and as a necessity at the same time'.[41] There was a lot of discussion: that is clear from the literature which has survived, and it was neither easy nor unequivocally one-sided, even though it did not end in abolitionism. In Roman law 'slavery is the only case in which, in the extant sources . . . , a conflict is declared to exist between the *Ius Gentium* and the *Ius Naturale*'.[42] In a sense, that was an academic conflict, since slavery went right on; but no society can carry such a conflict within it, around so important a set of beliefs and institutions, without the stresses erupting in some fashion no matter how remote and extended the lines and connections may be from the original stimulus. Perhaps the most interesting sign among the Greeks can be found in the proposals, and to an extent the practice in the fourth century B C, to give up the enslavement of Greeks.[43] They all came to nought in the Hellenistic world, and I suggest that this one fact reveals much about Greek civilisation after Alexander.[44].

It is worth calling attention to two examples pregnant with ambiguity, neither of which has received the attention it deserves. The first comes from Locris, the Greek colony in southern Italy, where descent was said to be matrilineal, an anomaly which Aristotle explained historically. The reason, he said, was that the colony was originally founded by slaves and their children by free women. Timaeus wrote a violent protest against this insulting account, and Polybius, in turn, defended Aristotle in a long digression (12.6a), of which unfortunately only fragments survive. One of his remarks is particularly worth quoting: 'To suppose, with Timaeus, that it was unlikely that men, who had been the slaves of the allies of the Spartans, would continue the kindly feelings and adopt the friendships of their late masters is foolish. For when they have had the good fortune to recover their freedom, and a certain time has elapsed, men, who had been slaves, not only endeavour to adopt the friendships of their late masters, but also their ties of hospitality and blood; in fact, their aim is to keep them up even more than the ties of nature, for the express purpose of thereby wiping out the remembrance of their former degradation and humble position, because they wish to pose as the descendants of their masters rather than as their freedmen.'

In the course of his polemic Timaeus had said that 'it was not customary for the Greeks of early times to be served by bought slaves'.[45] This distinction, between slaves who were bought and slaves who were captured (or bred from captives), had severe moral overtones. Inevitably, as was their habit, the Greeks found a historical origin for the practice of buying slaves – in the island of Chios. The historian Theopompus, a native of the island, phrased it this way: 'The Chians were the first of the Greeks, after the Thessalians and Lacedaemonians, who used slaves. But they did not acquire them in the same manner as the latter; for the Lacedaemonians and Thessalians will be found to have derived their slaves from the Greeks who formerly inhabited the territory which they now possess, . . . calling them helots and *penestae*, respectively. But the Chians possessed barbarian slaves, for whom they paid a price.'[46] This quotation is preserved by Athenaeus, who was writing about 200 A D and who went on to comment that the Chians ultimately received divine punishment for their innovation. The stories he then tells, as evidence, are curious and interesting, but I cannot take time for them.

This is not very good history, but that does not make it any less important. By a remarkable coincidence Chios provides us with the earliest contemporary evidence of democratic institutions in the Greek world. In a Chian inscription dated, most probably, to the years 575–550 B C, there is unmistakable reference to a popular council and to the 'laws (or ordinances) of the *demos*'.[47] I do not wish to assign any significance other than symbolic to this coincidence, but it is a symbol with enormous implications. I have already made the point that, the more advanced the Greek city-state, the more it will be found to have had true slavery rather than the 'hybrid' types like helotage. More bluntly put, the cities in which individual freedom reached its highest expression – most obviously Athens – were cities in which chattel slavery flourished. The Greeks, it is well known, discovered both the idea of individual freedom and the institutional framework in which it could be realised.[48] The pre-Greek world – the world of the Sumerians, Babylonians, Egyptians, and Assyrians; and I cannot refrain from adding the Mycenaeans – was, in a very profound sense, a world without free men, in the sense in which the west has come to understand that concept. It was equally a world in which chattel slavery played no role of any consequence. That, too, was a Greek discovery. One aspect of Greek history, in short, is the advance, hand in hand, of freedom *and* slavery.

BETWEEN SLAVERY
AND FREEDOM

I

I have taken my title from the *Onomastikon*, or *Word-Book*, of an Alexandrian Greek of the second century of our era named Julius Pollux. At the end of a longish section (3.78–83) listing, and sometimes exemplifying, the Greek words which meant 'slave' or 'enslave', in certain contexts at least, Pollux noted that there were also men like the helots in Sparta or the *penestae* in Thessaly who stood 'between the free men and the slaves'. It is of no use pretending that this work is very penetrating or systematic, at least in the abridged form in which it has come down to us, but the foundation was laid in a much earlier work by a very learned scholar, Aristophanes of Byzantium, who flourished in the first half of the third century BC. The interest in the brief passage I have cited is that it suggests in so pointed a way that social status could be viewed as a continuum or spectrum; that there were statuses which could only be defined, even if very crudely, as 'between slavery and freedom'. Customarily Greek and Roman writers were not concerned with such nuances. To be sure, the Romans had a special word for a freedman, *libertus*, as distinguished from *liber*, a free man. When it came to political status, furthermore, distinctions of all kinds were made, necessarily so. But for social status (which I trust I may be permitted, at this stage, to distinguish from political status), and often for purposes of private law, they were satisfied with the simply antinomy, slave or free, even though they could hardly have been unaware of certain gradations.

There is a Greek myth which neatly exemplifies the lexical point, a myth certainly much older than its first surviving literary reference in the *Agamemnon* of Aeschylus produced at Athens in 458 BC. Heracles was afflicted with a disease which persisted until he went to Delphi to consult Apollo about it. There the oracle informed him that his ailment was a punishment for his having killed Iphitus by treachery, and that he could

Originally published in *Comparative Studies in Society and History* 6 (1964) 233–49, and reprinted by permission of the journal.

be cured only by having himself sold into slavery for a limited number of years and handing over the purchase price to his victim's kinsmen. Accordingly he was sold to Omphale, queen of the Lydians (but originally a purely Greek figure), and he worked off his guilt in her service. The texts – which are fairly numerous and scattered over a period of many centuries – disagree on several points: for example, whether Heracles was sold to Omphale by the god Hermes or by friends who accompanied him to Asia for the purpose; whether his term of servitude was one year or three, and so on.[1]

One has no right to expect neatness in a myth, of course, or, for that matter, in the legal institutions of the archaic society in which this particular myth arose. The ancient texts all speak of Heracles being 'sold', and to describe his status while in Omphale's service they employ either *doulos*, the most common Greek word for 'chattel slave', or *latris*, a curious word that meant 'hired man' and 'servant' as well as 'slave'. The word *latris* upsets modern lexicographers and legal historians, but the historical situation behind the lexical 'confusion' is surely that in earlier Greece, as in other societies, 'service' and 'servitude' did in fact merge into each other. The Biblical code was explicit (*Deuteronomy* 15.12–17): 'If thy brother . . . be sold unto thee and serve thee six years; then in the seventh year thou shalt let him go free from thee . . . And it shall be, if he say unto thee, I will not go out from thee; because he loveth thee and thy house, because he is well with thee; then thou shalt take an awl, and thrust it into his ear unto the door, and he shall be thy servant for ever.'

Cynical remarks are tempting. Quite apart from the very real possibility that the six-year limitation was, as one distinguished authority has phrased it, 'a social programme rather than actually functioning law',[2] there is an odd ring about 'if he say unto thee, I will not go out from thee; because he loveth thee and thy house'. One suspects that the transition from a more limited bondage to outright slavery was neither so gentle nor so voluntary; that, unlike Heracles, the victims in real life, once caught up in bondage, had little hope of release; that, as in peonage, their masters could find devices enough by which to hold them in perpetuity. The sixth-century Athenian statesman Solon, referring to debt-bondsmen, used these words: 'I set free those here (in Athens) who were in unworthy enslavement, trembling at the whim of their masters.'[3] And the Greek words he employed were precisely those which became the classical terminology of chattel slavery: *douleia* – slavery; *despotes* – master; *eleutheros* – a free man. Modern scholars, too, regularly speak of enslavement for debt. Why not? Why play with words? Why draw elaborate, abstract distinctions?

The men Solon liberated belonged to a restricted though numerous class: they were Athenians who had fallen into bondage to other Athenians in Athens. His programme did not extend to non-Athenians, outsiders, who were slaves in Athens, just as the Biblical six-year limitation was restricted to 'thy brother', a fellow-Hebrew, and did not extend to the Gentile. Nor was this merely a sentimental distinction, empty rhetoric holding up vain hopes to the in-group, pretending that they were different from the outsiders when in fact they shared the latter's fate. The whole story of Solon (like the closely analogous struggles in early Roman history) proves that the distinction was meaningful, though it may have been in abeyance in any individual case or in any given span of time. For Solon was able to abolish debt-bondage – indeed, he had been brought to power for that express purpose – following a political struggle that bordered on civil war. Athenian bondsmen had remained Athenians; now they re-asserted their rights as Athenians, and they forced an end to the institution – servitude for debt – which had deprived them *de facto* of all or most of these rights. They were not opposed to slavery as such, only to the subjection of Athenians by other Athenians. Hence, whatever the superficial similarity, this was not a slave revolt; nor did ancient commentators ever make such a connection, despite their resort to slave terminology.

I am not concerned with the history of debt-bondage and its abolition (on which see Chapter 9) or of clientage in Athens or Rome, nor for the moment with giving precise content to the notion of 'rights'. I am merely trying, as a preliminary, to establish the need to distinguish among kinds of servitude, even though contemporaries were themselves not concerned to do so, at least not in their vocabulary. The matter of revolts is worth pursuing a little further in this connection. The debt-revolt syndrome was one of the most significant factors in the early history of both Greece and Rome, and it even survived into classical history. Helot revolts were equally important and very persistent in the history of Sparta. Chattel slaves, on the other hand, showed no tendency at any time in Greek history and only for a brief period, between 135 and 70 BC, were there massive slave revolts in Roman history.[4] Towards the end of antiquity, finally, there was more or less continual revolt in Gaul and Spain by depressed and semi-servile peasants and slaves acting in concert.[5]

To explain the differences in the revolt pattern and particularly in the propensity to revolt, by the differences in treatment, by the relative harshness or mildness of the masters, will not do. The one distinction which stands out most clearly is this, that the chattels, who were both the most rightless of all the servile types and the most complete outsiders in every sense, were precisely those who showed the weakest tendency to cohesive action, the weakest drive to secure freedom. Under certain conditions individual slaves were permitted considerable latitude and eventual emancipation was often held out as an incentive to them. That is another matter, however. Slaves as slaves showed no interest in slavery as an institution. Even when they did revolt, their objective was either to return to their native lands or to reverse the situation where they were, to become masters themselves and to reduce to slavery their previous masters or anyone else who came to hand. In so far as they thought about freedom, in other words, they accepted the prevailing notion completely: freedom for them, as individuals, included the right to possess other individuals as slaves. Debt-bondsmen and helots, in contrast, fought – when they fought – not only to transfer themselves, as individuals, from one status to the other, but to abolish that particular type of servitude altogether (though not, significantly, to abolish all forms, and particularly not chattel slavery).

II

To a Greek in the age of Pericles or a Roman in Cicero's day, 'freedom' had become a definable concept, and the antinomy, slave–free, a sharp, meaningful distinction. We are their heirs, and also their victims. Sometimes the results are amusing, as in the first efforts in the Far East in the nineteenth century to cope with the word 'freedom' for which they had no synonym and which till then was 'scarcely possible' in, say, Chinese.[6] And sometimes the results are very unfunny, as when western colonial administrators and well-meaning international organisations decree the immediate abolition of such practices as the payment of bride-wealth or the 'adoption' of debtors on the ground that they are devices for enslavement.[7] My subject, however, is not current social or political policy but history; the simple slave–free antinomy, I propose to argue, has been equally harmful as a tool of analysis when applied to some of the most interesting and seminal periods of our history. 'Freedom' is no less complex a concept than 'servitude' or 'bondage'; it is a concept which had no meaning and no existence for most of human history; it had to be invented finally, and that invention was possible only under very special conditions. Even after it had been invented, furthermore, there remained large numbers of men who could not be socially located as either slave or free, who were 'between slavery and freedom', in the loose language of Aristophanes of Byzantium and Julius Pollux.

Let us look at one particular case which came before the royal court of Babylonia in the middle of the sixth century BC, in the so-called neo-Babylonian or Chaldaean period.[8] A man borrowed a sum of money from a woman who was head of a religious order, and gave her his son as a debt-bondsman. After four years the woman died and both the debt and the debt-bondsman were transferred to her successor. The debtor also died and his son, now his heir, found himself in the position of being simultaneously the debtor and the debt-bondsman (an oddity in the ancient Near East, I may add parenthetically, where the transfer of wives and children for debt was common, but the transfer of the debtor himself was rare, unlike the Graeco-Roman practice). After ten years the bondsman paid over a quantity of barley from his own resources and went to court. The judges made a calculation, according to the conventional ratios, translating each day's service into barley and then translating the barley (both the real barley and the fictitious barley) into money; this arithmetic produced a sum which was equal to the original loan plus twenty per cent interest per annum for ten years; the court ruled, accordingly, that the debt was now paid up and the bondsman was liberated.

During his ten years of service was the bondsman who was working off his father's debt (which became his debt) a free man or a slave? Were the Israelites in Egypt slaves because they were called upon, as were most native Egyptians, to perform compulsory labour for the Pharaoh? The answer seems clearly to be, 'Neither', or better still, 'Yes and no'. In analogous situations the Greeks and Romans defined such service obligations as 'slave-like', and that catches the correct nuance. There were in Babylonia and Egypt chattel slaves in the strict property sense, whose services were not calculated at so much barley or so much anything per day, who could not inherit, own property or take a matter to court. But there was no word in the languages of these regions to encompass all the others, those who were not chattel slaves. To call them all 'free' makes no sense because it wipes out the significant variations in status, including the presence of elements of unfreedom, among the bulk of the population.

If one examines the various law codes of the ancient Near East, stretching back into the third millennium BC, whether Babylonian or

Assyrian or Hittite, the central fact is the existence of a hierarchy of statuses from the king at the top to the chattel slaves at the bottom, with rules – in the penal law, for example – differentiated among them. Translators often enough employ the term 'a free man', but I believe this to be invariably a mistranslation in the strict sense, the imposition of an anachronistic concept on texts in which that concept is not present. It is enough to read the commentaries appended to the translations to appreciate the error: each such rendition required the most complex contortions in the commentry if the various clauses of the codes are not to founder in crass inner contradictions once 'free man' has been inserted. What the codes actually employ are technical status-terms, which we are unable to render precisely because in our tradition the hierarchy and differentiation of statuses has been different. Hence, for example, careful Hittitologists resort to such conventional renditions as 'man of the tool', which may not be very lucid but has the great advantage of not being downright misleading. The English word 'slave' is a reasonable translation of one such status-term, but it is then necessary to emphasise the fact that slaves were never very significant and never indispensable in the ancient Near East, unlike Greece or Rome.

The neo-Babylonian case I have discussed took place sixty or seventy years before the Persian Wars, by which time the Greek city-state had achieved its classical form, in Asia Minor and the Aegean islands as well as on the mainland of Greece, in southern Italy and Sicily. Proper analysis of classical Greece would require far more space than I have at my disposal, for the society was not nearly so homogenous throughout the many scattered and independent Greek communiities as we often pretend. I shall confine myself to two cities, Athens and Sparta, in the fifth and fourth centuries B C, the two cities which the Greeks themselves considered the best exemplars of two sharply contrasting social systems and ideologies.

Athens is, of course, the Greek city that comes first to mind in association with the word 'freedom'. And Athens was the Greek city which possessed the largest number of chattel slaves. The actual number is a matter of dispute – as are nearly all ancient statistics or, better, statistical guesses – but much of the debate is largely irrelevant since no one can seriously deny that they constituted a critical sector of the labour force (in a way which slaves never did in the ancient Near East). My own guess is of the order of 60–80,000, which could give a ratio to the free population about the same as in the southern states of the United States in the first half of the nineteenth century, but with a different distribution pattern.

Proportionally more Athenians than Southerners owned slaves, but there were few if any great concentrations in single hands because there were no plantations, no Roman *latifundia*.

For our present concern there are a number of points to be made about slavery in Athens, which I shall run through briefly.

1. There were no activities in which slaves were not engaged other than political and military, and even those two categories must be understood very narrowly, for slaves predominated in the police and in what we should call the lower civil service. Contrariwise, there were no activities in which free men were not engaged, which slaves monopolised: they came nearest to achieving that in mining and domestic service. In other words, it was not the nature of the work which distinguished the slave from the free man but the status of the man performing the work.

2. Slaves were outsiders in a double sense. After Solon's abolition of debt bondage, no Athenian could be a slave in Athens. Hence all slaves to be found there had either been imported from outside the state or had been born within to a slave mother. 'Outside the state' could mean a neighbouring Greek as well as Syria or southern Russia – the law never forbade Greeks to enslave other Greeks, as distinct from Athenians and Athenians – but the evidence seems to show that the great majority were in fact non-Greeks, 'barbarians' as they called them, and that is why I say 'outsiders in a double sense'.

3. Slaveowners had the right, essentially without restriction, to free their slaves, a right which seems to have been exercised with some frequency, especially among domestic servants and skilled craftsmen, though, as usual, we are unable to express the pattern numerically.

4. The contemporary attitude was summed up by Aristotle when he wrote (*Rhetoric* 1367a32): 'The condition of the free man is that he does not live under the constraint of another.' In that sense, manumitted slaves were free men, if we ignore, as we legitimately may in this outline analysis, conditional manumissions and minor obligations towards the ex-master. But in another sense 'free man' is an excessively loose category. The distinction between citizens and free non-citizens was not merely political – the right to vote or hold office – but went much deeper: a non-citizen could not own real property, for example, except by special grant of that privilege by the popular assembly, a grant which was rarely made. Nor, for much of the period under consideration, could a non-citizen marry a citizen; their children were by definition bastards, subject to various legal disabilities and excluded from the citizen-body. Manumitted slaves were not citizens, though free in the loose sense, and hence

they suffered all the limitations on freedom I have just mentioned. In addition, it should be noted that in so far as slaves were often freed relatively late in life, and in so far as any children born to them were not freed along with them – practices which existed though we do not know in what proportion of the cases – to that extent freed women were effectively denied the right to procreate free children.

Now let us look at Sparta in the same period, the fifth and fourth centuries BC, and in the same schematic way.

1. The Spartiates proper were a relatively small group, perhaps never more than 10,000 adult males and declining from that figure more or less steadily during our period.

2. Such chattel slaves as existed were wholly insignificant. In their place there existed a relatively numerous servile population known as helots (a word with a disputed etymology) who were scattered over extensive territories in the southern and western Peloponnese, in the districts of Laconia and Messenia. Again we lack figures, but it is certain that the helots outnumbered the Spartiates, perhaps several times over (in contrast to Athens, where the proportion of slaves to free was probably of the order of 1:4, of slaves to citizens less than 1:1).

3. Who the helots were in origin is disputed. They may even have been Greeks to begin with, but whether so or not, they were the people of Laconia and Messenia, respectively, whom the Spartans subjugated and then kept in subjection in their own home territories. That immediately distinguished them – and distinguished them sharply – from the chattel slave 'outsiders', not only genetically but also in later history, for they were bound together by something far more than just the weak negative factor of sharing a common fate, by ties of kinship, nationhood (if I may use the term) and tradition, all perpetually reinforced through their survival on their native soil.

4. In so far as it makes any sense to use the terminology of property, the helots belonged to the state and not to the individual Spartiates to whom they were assigned. (Parenthetically I should say that the word 'belonged', which explains the willingness of the Greeks to call the helots 'slaves', is justified by the existence of a further Peloponnesian population who were politically subject to Sparta but were at the same time free and citizens of their own communities, the *perioikoi*, whom I am ignoring in this discussion.)

5. It follows from the previous point that only the state could manumit helots. They did so only in one type of situation: when military service by helots was unavoidable, those selected were freed, either beforehand or

as a subsequent reward. Once freed they did not become Spartiates but acquired a curious and distinct status, as did Spartiates who lost their standing for one reason or another, so that, as in Athens, the category of 'free men' was a conglomeration, not a homogeneous single group.

These points do not exhaust the picture, nor do they by any means exhaust the range of differences between Athens and Sparta, but I trust I have said enough to make it clear not only that the differences were very sharp but also that the number of status possibilities was very considerable. It remains to add that whereas for our subject Athens was typical of the more highly urbanised Greek communities on the mainland of Greece and in the Aegean islands, Sparta was, taken whole, unique. However, if we narrow our focus solely to the helots, then parallels were far from uncommon, less so in Greece proper than in the areas of Greek dispersion east and west, such as Sicily or the regions bordering on the Black Sea, where native populations were reduced to a status sufficiently like that of the helots to warrant their being bracketed with them, as Pollux did, under the rubric 'between the free men and the slaves'.[9]

Now, merely to illustrate the variety which actually existed, I want to look briefly at the institution we know from the so-called law code of Gortyn in Crete.[10] The text we have was inscribed on stone in the fifth century BC but the provisions may be much older. The code is far from complete, and there are some devilishly difficult problems in interpretation. It is clear, however, that there was a servile population which in some sense 'belonged' to individual Gortynians who could buy and sell them (apparently with restrictions hinted at, but not clarified, in the code), unlike the situation in Sparta with which too easy comparisons are often made. Yet this same servile population had rights which slaves in Athens lacked. For example, the rules regarding adultery and divorce and the provisions regulating relations between bondsmen and free women leave no doubt that it is proper to speak of marriage, of a relationship which was more than the Roman *contubernium* between slaves, because it created enforceable rights, but which was at the same time far less than a marriage between free persons. For one thing, an unfree husband was not his wife's tutor; that role was fulfilled by her master. For another, such a marriage did not lead to the creation of a kinship group, although it created the elementary family for certain purposes. Hence a composition payment for adultery could be arranged with the kinsmen of a free woman, but only with the master of a servile woman. (I should also note that debt-bondsmen are clearly differenti-ated in the code from the bondsmen I have been discussing.)

After the conquests of Alexander the Great, finally, when Greeks and Macedonians became the ruling class in Egypt, Syria and other lands of the ancient Near East, they found no difficulty in adapting themselves to the social structure which had been in existence there for millennia, modifying the top of the pyramid more than the bottom. A city in the Greek style like Alexandria had its chattel slaves just as in Athens; in the Egyptian countryside, however, the peasantry remained in its trad-itional status, neither free nor unfree. Royal grants of land to favourite ministers included whole villages along with their inhabitants. Compul-sory labour services of various kinds were imposed on them, precisely as on the Israelites a thousand years earlier. Our greatest historian of this era, Rostovtzeff, has written of this peasantry that 'They possessed a good deal of social and economic freedom in general and of freedom of movement in particular, . . . And yet they were not entirely free. They were bound to the government and could not escape from this bondage, because on it depended their means of subsistence. This bondage was real, not nominal.'[11] Which both makes my point and illustrates, in the vagueness and inadequacy of its formulations, how far we still are from a proper analysis of the social pattern.

The Romans, who eventually replaced the Greeks as rulers of this whole area, had a history of servitude more like that of Athens than of Sparta or the Near East, but with features of their own worth our notice. They, too had an internal crisis in the archaic period brought about by massive debt-bondage. They, too, then turned to chattel slaves on a large scale, the form of dependent labour which was characteristic of Rome in what I shall arbitrarily define as its classical period, roughly speaking, the three centuries between 150 BC and AD 150. 'Rome' is here am-biguous: we normally use it to refer both to the city on the Tiber and to the whole of the Roman empire, which by the end of the classical age extended from the Euphrates to the Atlantic. I want to focus on neither, however, but on Italy, the Latin heartland of the empire, which had become sufficiently uniform socially and culturally to warrant our treat-ing it as a unit. And I want to single out a few characteristics of slavery in Italy which contribute new dimensions to the picture I have drawn so far.

1. The great landed estates of Italy, the *latifundia*, which specialised in ranching, olive and wine production, remained, at least until the Amer-ican South replaced them, the western model of slave agriculture *par*

excellence. Slave numbers there, and in the rich urban households, reached proportions far exceeding anything in Greece. In the final struggle between Pompey and Caesar, for example, Pompey's son enlisted 800 slaves from his shepherds and personal attendants to add his father's army (Caesar, *Civil Wars*, 3.4.4). In a law of 2 BC Augustus restricted to 100 the number of slaves a man could manumit in his will, and only an owner of 500 or more was permitted to free that many (Gaius, *Institutes*, 1.43). A certain Pedanius Secundus, who was prefect of the city in AD 61, maintained 400 slaves (Tacitus, *Annals*, 14.43.4). These are examples at the upper end of the scale, to be sure, but they help fix the whole level.

2. Upon manumission a freedman acquired the status of his ex-master, so that the freed slave of a Roman citizen became a citizen himself, distinguished by certain minor disabilities (chiefly with respect to his former master) but none the less a citizen with the right to vote and to marry in the citizen class. This last had interesting and amusing implications. Within the Roman imperial territory there was a complicated variety of free statuses in the sense that there were numerous non-Romans, free men and citizens of their communities, who lacked both the political rights of Roman citizenship and the *ius conubii*, the right to contract a legitimate marriage with a Roman citizen. But an ex-slave, by the mere private act of manumission, which required no approval from the government, automatically jumped the queue, in law at any rate, provided that his master was a Roman citizen.

3. A significant proportion of the industrial and business activity in Rome and other cities was carried on by slaves acting independently, controlling and managing property known as a *peculium*. This was a legal device invented in the first instance to permit adults to function independently while still technically in *patria potestas*, the tenacity of which in Rome is one of the most remarkable features of the social history of that civilisation. The extension of *peculium* to slaves created legal problems of great complexity – in the event of a lawsuit, to give the most obvious example – but they do not concern me now, apart from one notable anomaly. It was possible, and by no means rare, that a *peculium* included one or more slaves, leaving the slave in charge of the *peculium* in the position of owning other slaves *de facto*, though not *de jure*. The reasons I have singled out *peculium* can perhaps best be clarified by some rhetorical questions. In what sense were a slave loaded with chains in one of the notorious agricultural *ergastula* and a slave managing a sizable tannery which was his *peculium* both members of the same class we (and the

Romans) call 'slaves'? Who was more free, or more unfree, a slave with a *peculium* or a 'free' debt-bondsman? Can the concept of freedom be usefully employed at all in such comparisons?

4. In order to insure their administrative control, the early emperors, beginning with Augustus and reaching a crescendo under Claudius and Nero, made extensive use of their own *familiae* in running the empire. The *servi* and *liberti Caesaris*, the emperor's own slaves and freedmen, took charge of the bureaus and even headed them for a time. Careful investigation has shown that even among these imperial slaves their children were not as a rule freed along with them if they were also slaves – there are complications here, arising from the status of the mothers, which I need not go into – but stayed on as *servi Caesaris*, advancing in the service if they were capable and earning their own freedom in time. Hence the interesting situation was created in which important civil servants not only came out of the slave class but left their children behind in that class. And more interesting still, the generalisation may be made that in Rome of the first century of our era, much the greatest opportunity for social mobility lay among the imperial slaves. No one among the free poor could have risen to a status like that of head of the bureau of accounts, or, for that matter, to anything like the many lower posts in the administration. I doubt if I need make further comment.

III

All the societies I have been discussing, from those of the Near East in the third millennium BC to the end of the Roman Empire, shared, without exception and throughout their history, a need for dependent, involuntary labour. Structurally and ideologically, dependent labour was integral, indispensable. In the first book of the Pseudo-Aristotelian *Oeconomica* we read: 'Of property, the first and most necessary kind, the best and most manageable, is man. Therefore the first step is to procure good slaves. Of slaves there are two kinds, the overseer and the worker.' Just like that, without justification or embellishment. There is no need to pile on the quotations; it is simpler to note that not even the ancient believers in the brotherhood of man were opponents of slavery: the best that Seneca the Stoic and St Paul the Christian could offer was some variation on the theme, 'status doesn't matter'. Diogenes the Cynic, it is said, was once seized by pirates and taken to Corinth to be sold. Standing on the auction block he pointed to a certain Corinthian among the buyers and said: 'Sell me to him; he needs a master' (Diogenes Laertius, 6.74).

Most revealing of all is the firm implication in many ancient texts, and often the explicit statement, that one element of freedom was the freedom to enslave others. Aristotle wrote the following in the *Politics* (1333b38ff., translated by Barker): 'Training for war should not be pursued with a view to enslaving men who do not deserve such a fate. Its object should be these – first, to prevent men from ever becoming enslaved themselves; secondly, to put men in a position to exercise leadership . . .; and thirdly, to enable men to make themselves masters of those who naturally deserve to be slaves.' It may be objected that I am unfair to select a text from Aristotle, the most forthright exponent of the doctrine of natural slavery, a doctrine which was combatted in his own day and generally rejected by philosophers in later generations. Let us then try another text (Lysias, 24.6). About the year 400 B C an Athenian cripple who had been taken off the dole on the ground that the amount of property he owned made him ineligible, appealed formally to the Council for reconsideration of his case. One of his arguments was that he could not yet afford to buy a slave who would support him, though he hoped eventually to do so. Here was no theorist but a humble Athenian addressing a body of his fellow-citizens in the hope of gaining a pittance from them. The implications – and the whole psychology – could scarcely be brought out more sharply.

I do not propose to revive the old question of the origin of the inequality of classes, to ask why dependent labour was indispensable. My starting-point is the fact that everywhere in the civilisations under consideration, as far back as our documentation goes (including the new documentation provided by the Linear B tablets), there was well established reliance on dependent labour. All these societies, as far back as we can trace them, were already complex, articulated, hierarchical, with considerable differentiation of functions and division of labour, with extensive foreign trade and with well-defined political and religious institutions.

It is rather what happened thereafter which interests me now: the essentially different development as between the Near East and the Graeco-Roman world, and, in the latter, the sharp differences in different periods as well as the unevenness of development in different sectors. I have already indicated the most fundamental difference, namely, the shift among Greeks and Romans from reliance on the half-free within to reliance on chattel slaves from outside, and as a corollary, the emergence of the idea of freedom. A wholly new social situation emerged, in which not only some of the components were different from anything known before but also the relationships and spread among them, and the thinking. We may not be able to trace the process but we can mark its first literary statement beyond any doubt, in the long poem, the *Works and Days*, in which Hesiod, an independent Boeotian landowner of the seventh century B C, presumed freely to criticise his betters, the 'gift-devouring princes' with their 'crooked judgments'.

In another poem, the *Theogony*, also attributed to Hesiod – and it does not matter whether the attribution is right or not, for the *Theogony* and the *Works and Days* were approximately contemporary, which is enough for this discussion – the same new social situation found expression in another area of human behaviour, in man's relations with his gods. As Henri Frankfort phrased it, the author of the *Theogony* 'is without oriental precedent in one respect: the gods and the universe were described by him as a matter of private interest. Such freedom was unheard of in the Near East . . .'[12] It was a firm doctrine in the ancient Near East that man was created for the sole and specific purpose of serving the gods: that was the obvious extension by one further step of the hierarchical structure of society. Neither Greek nor Roman religion shared that idea. Man was created by the gods, of course, and he was expected to serve them in a number of ways, as well as to fear them, but his purpose, his function, was not that, and surely not that alone. Institutionally the distinction may be expressed this way: whereas in the Near East government and politics were a function of the religious organisation, Greek and Roman religion was a function of the political organisation.

Hesiod is often called a peasant-poet, which is inexact, for Hesiod not only was himself an owner of slaves but assumes slavery as an essential condition of life for his class. From the first, therefore, the slave-outsider was as necessary a condition of freedom as the emancipation of clients and debt-bondsmen within. The methods by which outsiders were introduced into the society need not concern us. But it is worth a moment to consider one aspect of the outsider situation, the 'racial' one, which is being much discussed today, both by historians and sociologists, chiefly with reference to the American South. It is important to fix in mind that 'outsiders' were often neighbours of similar stock and culture; that though the Greeks tried to denigrate the majority of their slaves with the 'barbarian' label and though Roman writers (and their modern followers) are full of contemptuous references to 'Orientals' among their slaves and freedmen, the weaknesses of this simple classification and its implications were apparent enough even to them. The decisive fact is that widespread manumission and the absence of strict endogamy together destroy all grounds for useful comparison with the American South on this score. When the Roman lawyers agreed on the formulation, 'Slavery is an institution of the *ius gentium* (the law of all nations) whereby someone is subject to the *dominium* of another, contrary to nature' (*Digest*, 1.5.4.1), they were saying in effect that slavery was indispensable, that it was defensible only on that ground, and that one was liable to be enslaved just because one was an outsider. An outsider, in short, was an outsider. That tautological definition is the best we can offer. Hence the expansion of the Roman empire, for example, automatically converted blocks of outsiders to free insiders.

Why, we must then ask, was the historical trend in some Greek communities, such as Athens, and in Rome towards the polarity of the free insider and the slave outsider, while elsewhere no comparable development occurred (or where incipient signs appeared, they soon proved abortive)? Max Weber suggested that the answer lay in the loosening of the royal grip on trade and the consequent emergence of a free trading class who acted as social catalysts.[13] I have no great confidence in this hypothesis, which can neither be verified nor falsified from Greek or Roman evidence. The decisive changes occurred precisely in the centuries for which we lack documentation, and for which there is no realistic prospect of new documentation being discovered. I must confess immediately that I have no alternative explanation to offer. Reexamination of the body of Greek and Roman myth may help, but the hope lies, in my opinion, in the very extensive documentation of the ancient Near East.

I say 'hope', and no more, because it is no use pretending that study of Near Eastern servitude has taken us very far. One reason is the primitive classification into slave and free which has been my theme, and I now want to return to this and suggest an approach. Merely to say, as I have thus far, that there were statuses between slavery and freedom is obviously not enough. How does one proceed to formulate the differences between a Biblical bondsman who hoped for release and the man who chose to remain a slave in perpetuity and had his ear bored to mark his new status? Or between a helot in Sparta and a chattel in Athens?

The Sicilian Greek historian Diodorus, writing as a contemporary of Julius Caesar, gives us the following variation on the Heracles-Omphale myth. Heracles, he says, produced two children during the period of his stay with the Lydian queen, the first by a slave-woman while he was in servitude, the second by Omphale herself after he had been restored to freedom. Unwittingly Diodorus has pointed the way. All men, unless they are Robinson Crusoes, are bundles of claims, privileges, immunities, liabilities and obligations with respect to others. A man's status is defined by the total of these elements which he possesses or which he has (or has not) the potential of acquiring. Actual and potential must both be considered: the potential of the *servi Caesaris*, for example, was always a factor in the psychology of status in the early Roman Empire, and sometimes it became an actuality, when one of them climbed high enough on the civil ladder and was freed. Obviously none of this can be expressed in numerical, quantitative terms: it is not a matter of one man having one more privilege or one more liability than another. Rather it is a matter of location on a spectrum or continuum of status; the *servi Caesaris* as a class, in this language, stood nearer the freedom end than did the slaves of any private owner in Rome.

It is possible, furthermore, to work out a typology of rights and duties. By way of illustration, I suggest the following rough scheme:[14]

1. Claims to property, or power over things – a category which is itself complex and requires further analysis: for example, the difference between the power of a slave over his *peculium* and the power of an owner in the strict sense; or differences according to the different categories of things, land, cattle, money, personal possessions, and so forth.

2. Power over human labour and movement, whether one's own or another's – including, of course, the privilege of enslaving others.

3. Power to punish, and, conversely, immunity from punishment.

4. Privileges and liabilities in judicial proceedings, such as immunity from arbitrary seizure or the capacity to sue and be sued.

5. Privileges in the area of the family: marriage, succession and so on – involving not only property rights and rights of *conubium*, but, at one step removed, the possibility of protection or redemption in case of debt, ransom or blood–feud.

6. Privileges of social mobility, such as manumission or enfranchisement, and their converse: immunity from, or liability to, bondage, penal servitude and the like.

7. Privileges and duties in the sacral, political and military spheres.

I have said enough, I trust, to forestall any suggestion that I am proposing a mechanical procedure. In Athens chattel slaves and wealthy free non-citizens (Aristotle, for example) were equally barred from marriage with a citizen; in terms of my typology, they both lacked the privilege of *conubium*. It would be absurd, however, to equate them in a serious sense just on that score. Or to take a more meaningful instance of quite another kind: Athenian slaves and Spartan helots both belonged to someone, but the fact that the someone was a private individual in the one case, the Spartan state in another, introduced a very important distinction. These various combinations must be weighed and judged in terms of the whole structure of the individual society under examination.

If I am then asked, What has become of the traditional property definition of a slave? Where on your continuum do you draw the line between free and slave, free and unfree? – my answer has to be rather complicated. To begin with, the idea of a continuum or spectrum is metaphorical: it is too smooth. Nevertheless, it is not a bad metaphor when applied to the ancient Near East or to the earliest periods of Greek and Roman history. There one status did shade into another. There, although some men were the property of others and though the gap between the slave and the king was as great as social distance can be, neither the property-definition nor any other single test is really meaningful. There, in short, freedom is not a useful category and therefore it is pointless to ask where one draws the line between the free and the unfree.

In classical Athens and Rome, on the other hand, the traditional dividing line, the traditional distinction according to whether a man is or is not the property of another, remains a convenient rule of thumb for most purposes. For them the metaphor of a continuum breaks down. But the problem has not been to understand those two, relatively atypical, societies, but the others, societies which we have not understood very well just because, in my view, we have not emancipated ourselves from the slave-free antinomy. And if my approach proves useful, I suggest it will lead to a better understanding of Athens and Rome, too, where the category of 'free man' needs precise subdivision.

I might close with a highly schematic model of the history of ancient society. It moved from a society in which status ran along a continuum towards one in which statuses were bunched at the two ends, the slave and the free – a movement which was most nearly completed in the societies which most attract our attention for obvious reasons. And then, under the Roman Empire, the movement was reversed; ancient society gradually returned to a continuum of statuses and was transformed into what we call the medieval world.

- 8 -

THE SERVILE STATUSES
OF ANCIENT GREECE

I

As I mentioned at the beginning of Chapter 7, the third book of the *Onomastikon* of Julius Pollux, a writer of the second century A D from Alexandria, contains a block of eleven chapters devoted to the language of servitude. Pollux rarely defines his words, in any proper sense, nor does he often illustrate their use. Nevertheless, it is clear that the numerous words in chapters 73–83 can all, without exception, be rendered 'slave', 'slavery' in many contexts. The section concludes, in chapter 83, with a few terms like 'helot' and *penestes*, men who, says Pollux, stand 'between the free men and the slaves', followed by a short bit on freedmen.

Incomplete as it is, the list of slave-words includes a dozen distinct roots: a variety and profusion of servile terminology which one would find difficult, if not impossible, to parallel in other societies. The distinctions vary in kind: for example, purchased or house-born slave (*argyronetos-oikogenes*), branded slave (*stigmatias*), or regional peculiarities, as when Pollux says that the Athenians call their slaves *paides* (children) even when they are older. These are self-evident distinctions. Others are more subtle and elusive: in the fourth century B C, for example, there was a demonstrable tendency (not noted by Pollux) to say *doulos* when the stress was on the personal element, but *andrapoda* when the property aspect was to brought to the fore.[1]

Some of these distinctions are sociologically interesting and revealing, but they do not of themselves indicate anything deeper. Others imply something more basic: the slave and the helot were two different categories in a sense in which the house-born slave and the purchased slave normally were not. The question I wish to pursue goes still further: apart from helot and *penestes* and the like, is there a range of statuses concealed

Originally published in *Revue internationale des droits de l'antiquité*, 3 ser., 7 (1960) 165–89, and reprinted by permission of the editors. I have reduced the more scholarly annotation somewhat.

in the group we tend to bring together under the single rubric 'slave'? *A priori* I should assume that there must be, that what we call slavery was an institution which varied considerably and significantly in different parts of the Greek world. By 600 B C – to take a rough starting point, for I propose to by-pass the very difficult question of the servile population in the worlds of Homer and Hesiod – the Greeks had a long and complicated history behind them, filled with conquests, migrations (both inner and external), social changes, revolutions, technological advances, and all kinds of contact with other societies. This history was by no means the same everywhere in Greece, nor was the history in the centuries which followed the year 600. The economy, the government, laws regarding land and inheritance and trade all differed, to a greater or lesser degree, from century to century and from area to area. Slavery, or the labour regime more generally, was not something autonomous, and therefore it is only by an artificial insistence on some mystical kind of Greek unity that historians of antiquity start, as they customarily do, with the assumption that the word *doulos* indicates exactly the same category of persons wherever it appears. That may or may not be the case in any given instance, but this is a matter for demonstration, not prior assumption.

There is a fetishism about words which must be overcome. The Greeks had altogether too many slave words (quite apart from the helotage words); even after we exclude 'branded slave' and similar terms, there remain too many. As Collinet showed in an analogous situation, regarding the Roman colonate, such a profusion of terminology is likely to mirror historical reality.[2] In principle, there are a number of possibilities. There may have been an original diversity in the institutions, paralleling the diversity in the terminology; and these differences may have continued, or they may have been gradually eliminated by a process of convergence while the multiple terminology remained. Or different words may have been coined, at the start, to describe essentially the same status or institution in different localities. Here again both divergence and convergence in the subsequent development are equally possible. Finally, there is always the possibility of a word remaining unchanged while the institution diverges in one region or another. I do not believe that there are any rules in this matter; examples are available of each of these possibilities in the area of technical social terminology. We must start with the individual words – the labels – but we must immediately transcend them.

In this chapter I shall chiefly be concerned with one type of distinction, namely, the more or less formal differences of a juristic nature. In so restricting myself, I do not suggest that this is the most important aspect of status, or that it is an autonomous aspect. Complete analysis would require consideration of the economic roles of the unfree and of the psychology of status (as revealed, for example, in the hierarchy of employments). It would also require consideration of the political history of the different Greek communities, of early conquests, for example, or of the impact of tyranny or democracy on the evolution of the social structure. I do suggest, however, that a proper juristic analysis will provide an essential tool for the larger study, and that is the limited end to which this chapter is directed.

II

One important servile word (built on the household root) which is overlooked in Pollux is the familiar *oikeus* of the Gortyn code (he also fails to include the Gortynian word for master, *pastas*). The situation with respect to the servile population of Crete is notoriously confused, thanks to the fact that the language of the code is different from the language of the other Cretan inscriptions, and to the fact that the literary evidence, in Aristotle and fragments of Hellenistic writings, is incomplete, inconsistent, and in large part unintelligible. However, the code when taken alone provides coherent information, sufficient for my purposes, and I shall therefore restrict the discussion of Crete to that one source.[3] Such a limitation would be illegitimate, of course, if I were attempting a complete analysis of Cretan servitude, which I am not. Then I should have to deal with a number of words like *aphamiotai*, *klarotai* and *mnoia*, with which the literary sources are chiefly concerned. None of these words appears in the code, which is satisfied with two servile terms, *oikeus*, and *doulos*. Most modern scholars take these two words to represent two different statuses, usually rendered 'serf' and 'slave', respectively.[4] Fifty years ago Lipsius argued that this is a wrong interpretation, that the two words are synonymous in the code, and that only one unfree status category appears there.[5] His arguments have never been effectively countered, to my knowledge: they have merely been ignored, and an examination of the text shows that he was right.

To begin with, there are passages in the code in which *oikeus* and *doulos* are synonymous and interchangeable: everyone is agreed on this. If, then, the two words mean the same thing in one provision and different things in another provision of the same code, the product is confusion,

and nothing else, as is abundantly evident in modern exegeses. Vagueness of this order in legal matters is perfectly possible in poetry and even
in historical writing, but not in a law code. Second, there is not a single
provision in the code in which there is one rule stated for an *oikeus* and
another for a *doulos*.[6] Third, there are rules about *douloi* followed by
silence regarding *oikees*, and there are rules about *oikees*, followed by
silence regarding *douloi*. For example, in column II there is a penalty fixed
in the case that a *doulos* rapes a free woman, but not if an *oikeus* does it,
and there are penalties if a free man or a male *oikeus* rapes a female *oikeus*,
but not if a *doulos* does it; there are penalties fixed for adultery between a
doulos and either a free woman or a *doule* but not a word about adultery
involving an *oikeus*, male or female, until some lines later, when rules of
evidence are laid down, and suddenly the word for the unfree adulterer
is no longer *doulos* but *oikeus*. All this is perfectly intelligible on the view
that *oikeus* equals *doulos*; it becomes nonsense on the other view.

I am not suggesting that everything about the *douloi* of Gortyn is
perfectly clear. The code is much too incomplete for that, and there are
more insoluble difficulties than certainties in the situation, but they
remain difficulties on either hypothesis. Nor am I suggesting that there
was no distinction in origin between an *oikeus* and a *doulos*. But my
concern is solely with the situation in the code, not with what it may have
been at some earlier date. Furthermore, it is likely that, in ordinary
speech, there was a tendency to say *doulos* for some categories of the
unfree, domestics for example, and *oikeus* for other categories, just as
fourth-century Athenian orators tended to draw a subtle line between
douloi and *andrapoda*. No doubt there were practical distinctions too,
between a recently purchased slave restricted to household chores, let us
say, and a servile family on the land for several generations. But such
distinctions exist wherever slavery exists in a complex society, without
touching the essence of the institution. With regard to rights, privileges
and duties, I do not find in the Gortyn code, as we have it, anything that
requires a distinction for purposes of the present analysis.

For both terms the word for 'master' is *pastas*, which has in it a
property-tone that is sharper, or at least more obvious, than in the far
more common Greek *despotes*. And to a considerable extent the *doulos–
oikeus* did 'belong' to his master: the latter could sell him and buy others
(apparently with restrictions, hinted at but not clarified sufficiently in the
code); his children belonged to the master, a child born to a divorced or
unmarried servile woman belonged to her ex-husband's master, or to
her own father's master, or to some other *pastas*, according to fixed rules;

the master had legal responsibility for delicts of his *doulos* and, in my opinion, received the fines incurred by others for delicts against his *doulos* (not, as some believe, that the fines were paid to the servile victim for him or her to keep).[7]

On the other hand, when a Gortynian said *doulos* or *oikeus* he clearly had something in mind which differed, in some essentials, from what a fifth-century Athenian meant by *doulos*. The unfree of Gortyn had at least two privileges which the code protected in its regulations on succession, namely, the right of domicile and the right to cattle (if they possessed any).[8] Whether these can in any proper sense be called proprietary rights is not a crucial question here. They also seem to have had the right to possess their own clothing and household goods (for that is how I interpret the clause that if two *oikees* are separated by death or divorce, the woman 'may take what is hers').[9] Some scholars believe they also possessed money, but there is no evidence, and surely they did not possess the quantities required to meet the statutory fines (reaching 200 staters for a *doulos* who rapes a free man or woman). Nor do I share the interpretation of the law of succession which allows an *oikeus* to take his deceased master's estate in the absence of near kin.[10]

Even on my narrow interpretation of the privileges, however, the unfree had certain proprietary or quasi-proprietary rights unknown in Athens and many other classical cities. With these (and perhaps even more important) went certain personal rights, above all, the right of marriage. The rules regarding adultery, divorce and relations between *douloi* and free women leave no doubt that it is proper to speak of marriage here, of a relationship which was more than a *contubernium*, because it created certain enforceable rights, but which was at the same time far less than a marriage between free persons. For one thing, the unfree husband was not his wife's *kyrios* (tutor): that role was fulfilled by his or her master, as the case may be. For another, such a marriage did not lead to the creation of a kinship group, although it created the elementary family for certain purposes. The simplest proof is in the provision regarding composition in cases of adultery: agreement is to be made with the kin of a free woman, but with the master of a *doule*.[11]

Still another distinction emerges from the opening section of the code, which deals with procedure in legal disputes over a man's status (whether he is free or unfree) or over the ownership of a slave. In such cases, says the law, the person in dispute may not be carried off prior to the court judgment. However, it continues, a *nenikamenos* or *katakeimenos* may be carried off. This remark is not amplified, but the contrast must mean that both – the man who lost a court action and failed to pay up (a *nenikamenos*), and the man who entered bondage by direct agreement (a *katakeimenos*) – are somehow neither free nor slave. What that means with respect to the *katakeimenos* is explained, in part, in the so-called second code. If a *katakeimenos* commits an offence, he shall pay the penalty; but if he lacks the wherewithal to pay, then the aggrieved party and the master (called *katathemenos* and not *pastas*, significantly enough) shall consult and do something (unknown because the stone unfortunately breaks at that point). If, on the other hand, a *katakeimenos* is aggrieved, his master shall sue for him 'as for a free man' and the two shall divide the award equally. If the master fails to take action, the *katakeimenos* may do so himself, provided he first pays off his debt (and therefore, presumably, releases himself from bondage).[12]

At all points in this one field, clearly, the *katakeimenos* was neither free nor unfree, but shared some of the privileges and limitations of both conditions. How much further this halfway status prevailed is another question. There is no mention of the *katakeimenos* in the sections on rape, adultery, and divorce, and no informative discussion in the section on succession. Nor do we know anything at all about the *nenikamenos* other than the fact that he could be 'carried off'. The Greek verb (*agein*) can imply either taken for service at home or sold abroad, a distinction of great importance since in the latter case the result is outright enslavement, in the fullest sense of the word. The others, those kept in servitude at home, had a superior status, at least in principle. It was always possible, either in law or by private agreement, that the period of servitude was fixed and would come to an end. Furthermore, these men retained their place within the kinship structure of society, and the possibility remained that their kinsmen might pay the debt and release them. Finally, they were still in some sense members of the political community (assuming that they held membership before they fell under obligation). Their political rights were no doubt in abeyance, but the Solonic crisis in Athens shows that they were not altogether meaningless under certain conditions.

In the absence of specific provisions in the code, three possibilities must be reckoned with for the *nenikamenos*. Either he must be sold abroad, or the successful party has the choice of keeping him or selling him, or he becomes a bondsman in Gortyn precisely like the *katakeimenos*. I do not see how, in the present state of our knowledge, it is possible to choose among these possibilities. Failure of the code to deal with the *nenikamenos* in the section on delicts seems to suggest that he is to be distinguished from the *katakeimenos*. On the other hand, it is a fact that the two are bracketed as being *agogimos* (subject to being carried off) and that nothing is said which would indicate that their fates differed. I take it that the *katakeimenos* could not be sold abroad, and such a possibility is not indicated explicitly for the *nenikamenos*. Elsewhere, in a decree of fifth-century Halicarnassus or in the so-called *dikaiomata* of Alexandria, for example, the law expressly required sale abroad, precisely as in the ancient Roman *trans Tiberim* provision.[13] But I do not believe we have enough examples to warrant the view, commonly held, that this was a universal Greek rule of law. In one analogous situation, the Gortyn code points in the opposite direction. He who has been ransomed from abroad, it says, shall belong to the ransomer until he has repaid the amount. The final clause of this provision would have been meaningless if the man ransomed from abroad were again sold abroad.[14] Of course, it does not necessarily follow that the *nenikamenos* was in the same position, but this is at least a Gortynian parallel, and I suggest that it more compelling than the Halicarnassian decree or the Alexandrian *dikaiomata*.

III

Nothing can be argued about the Gortyn code *e silentio*. After all, it is not a code in the strict sense, like the *Code Napoléon* or the *bürgerliches Gesetzbuch*: whole areas of behaviour are completely neglected, areas which beyond doubt were covered by law despite their absence in the code.[15] We may be certain that the status of the *nenikamenos* was similarly covered, and therefore perfectly clear in Gortyn, if not to us. The same is true of the provision which says that if a son stands surety in his father's lifetime, the son is responsible with his person and with such property as he has acquired. Clauses with similar wording are known from as widely scattered places as Boeotia, Heraclea in South Italy, and Delos, and in each instance the text we have provides no detail about execution on the person.[16] We must conclude that we cannot be certain of the exact consequences in any of these instances, nor can we be certain that they were the same in each community and each century.

It is precisely this obvious point, that each of our texts works with a clear local reference, which cannot be ignored when we try to establish a *Greek* pattern. The lexicographer's approach is dangerous. If one looks up any 'technical' social term in Liddell and Scott, one finds a few meanings or shades of meaning with hardly any indication (and sometimes none at all) that the variations around an essential core-idea may signify local institutional distinctions of considerable magnitude. It would be impossible, I have suggested, for the Gortyn code to use the word *doulos*, without qualification, for a variety of statuses. But it is perfectly proper for this code, or any other legal document, to use the word in a sense different in some respects from its use in other Greek communities (exactly like month names, coin denominations, or units of weight). Because of the way in which the Greek world was split into small units and because the history of these various units was not all of one piece, their social and legal institutions varied in the course of time. Often, however, the individual words were the same in widely scattered regions. That creates grave difficulties for us, but not for the people who used them.

Thus far, without trying to be either systematic or complete, I have suggested some half a dozen more or less different unfree statuses (or situations of servitude), found in one or another Greek community. How are we to establish a classification which will have meaning, if the terminology is an insufficient and often misleading clue? We cannot get much help from Greek writers. Legal documents, whether laws, decrees, agreements, or letters, deal with specific cases or rules, not with jurisprudential analysis. There were no jurists, or at least no juristic writing has survived. Philosophers, orators and historians were satisfied with the simplest possible antinomy: free man and slave, *eleutheros* and *doulos*. For their purposes they were not interested in a sociology or jurisprudence of servitude, and they could call helots *douloi* in most contexts, for example, even though they knew perfectly well that helots and Athenian *douloi* were by no means the same. Even so crude a text as the few lines in Pollux enumerating some local words for a status between slavery and freedom is a rare exception in the available literature.

Aristotle's *Politics* by itself offers sufficient illustration of both the actual lexical situation and the fundamental indifference of ancient authors to the ramifications of servitude. In discussing states which have been held up as models or approaches to the ideal, Aristotle complains (1269a34 ff.) that no one has solved the admittedly difficult problem of establishing a workable system of helotage. It may be significant that he uses *heiloteia* and *penesteia* here, not *douleia*, when he is talking about Sparta, Thessaly and Crete. The Cretans, he admits, have not had to face revolts of their *perioikoi*, and a few pages later he fixes a direct correspondence between this word in its Cretan use and the Spartan helot.[17] Elsewhere in the book he writes (1264a21) that the Cretan *douloi* have all the privileges of free men save access to the gymnasium and the right to possess arms, and in still other passages (though not in an explicitly Spartan or Cretan context), he seems to distinguish *douloi* from *perioikoi*.[18] I do not believe that it is possible to sort out the confusions (and probably, the contradictions) in these passages. That is one important point. A second is that, although Aristotle believed that the word *perioikos* was used for two quite different statuses in Sparta and Crete, he did not find this fact so anomalous or disquieting as to demand special comment.

Obviously Aristotle felt that the status situation among the unfree was complicated and often opaque. A thinking Greek could hardly have been totally unaware of the complexities, yet the texts reveal a persistent lack of interest in pursuing the subject, often with (to us) comic consequences in the terminology. There is a long fragment of Menander's *The Hero*, for example, involving a brother and sister who are in debt-bondage. In a conversation between two slaves in the household, one asks the other about the girl. 'Is she a slave?' The second replies, 'Yes – partly – in a way',[19] and then goes on to tell how she came to be in debt-bondage. This is comedy, to be sure, and this particular story raises very difficult historical and legal questions. But they need not delay us. Lysias, Isocrates and Diodorus all testify to the existence of servitude for debt in classical and post-classical times.[20] They were not writing comedy. Nor was the philosopher Theophrastus when he wrote in his will: 'Of the slaves I manumit Molon and Timon and Parmenion, who are already free.'[21] Nor was the lexicographer Harpocration, when he said in his definition of the legal proceeding known as *dike apostasiou*: 'And those who are condemned necessarily become slaves, but those who win, already being free men, become so completely.' I could continue to pile up other instances, but nothing would be gained thereby. The evidence is unmistakable that in all sorts of terminology the Greeks recognised the existence of half-way statuses, but neither sought nor made a systematic analysis. When a distinction was needed, they were satisfied to make (or report) local rules about procedure, property, marriage, or whatever else was required for a specific status-category, as we saw in some detail in Gortyn.

In truth, Menander's vague phrase, 'Yes – partly – in a way', is as far as we have advanced ourselves. And it was an important step to have got that far. Half a century ago, Arangio-Ruiz found it necessary to begin the first chapter of his book, 'Persons and Family in the Law of the Papyri', with these remarks:

The Romanist who asks of the papyri what regime the Graeco-Egyptian world adopted with respect to the problems of personality, inevitably starts from the (Roman jurist) Gaius, to seek the principles pertaining to the *status libertatis*, the *status civitatis*, the *status familiae*. But the first contact with the new juristic environment is enough to persuade him that such an investigation will be in vain. For all that there were in Egypt, too, free men and slaves, participants and non-participants in the various national communities, *patres* and *filiifamiliae*, there were lacking the rigid boundary-lines which only a people with a true juristic vocation is able to draw.

A year later, in 1931, Koschaker in his classic study of the institution we have labelled *paramone* spoke even more sharply against the Romanist preconceptions which still dominated – and therefore vitiated – the study of Greek and Graeco-Egyptian statuses.[22] A person in *paramone*, he argued, was half-slave, half-free.

Today, the juristic literature on the subject is fairly clear that Arangio-Ruiz and Koschaker were right, at least with respect to the papyri. Philologists and historians have tended to try another tack, when dealing with Greece proper, one which seems to me to be altogether unhelpful and misleading. They often turn not to Rome for their concepts but to the medieval world, and bring serfs and serfdom into the Greek picture. Serfs appear everywhere: in Aristotle's account of the Solonic crisis, in Crete, in Sparta, to name the most obvious and most common examples. The trouble with this is, first, that serfdom is itself a term which tends to cover a very considerable range of statuses;[23] secondly, that there are too many differences between the Spartan helot, let us say, and the serf of feudal society; thirdly, that it is wrong to blanket every unfree person who is not an outright chattel under a single term like 'serf'; and fourthly, that serfdom (no matter how loosely defined) cannot be extended to include either the debt-bondsman or the person in *paramone*, two categories which, we are now learning, were very widespread in the Greek-speaking world for many centuries. We are in thrall to a very primitive sociology which assumes that there are only three kinds of labour-status: the free, contractual wage-earner, the serf, and the slave. Everyone must somehow be fitted into one of these categories. A striking example occurs in the Far East, where missionaries, colonial administrators, and scholars alike pinned the slave label on a fantastic variety of statuses in China, Burma and Indonesia, with unfortunate consequences both to learning and administration. Modern anthropology has successfully re-examined that field and demonstrated that human status possibilities are far from exhausted by the triple classification which we

have inherited from Rome and medieval Europe.[24] Ancient Greece, it
seems clear to me, is exactly comparable in this respect, and we must
take seriously, and literally, the idea of a broad status-spectrum. When
Pollux, and Aristophanes of Byzantium before him, wrote 'between
slavery and freedom', they meant *between* slavery and freedom.

Merely to say that someone is half-slave, or half-free, important step as
that may be, is hardly sufficient, or even very meaningful. To define this
mid-position, Koschaker turned to property, and suggested that *paramone* constituted a case of *geteiltes Eigentum* (divided property rights). He
developed this idea by bringing together a number of apparently different practices and institutions. One is 'antichretic' debt-bondage, in
which the debtor gives personal service in place of interest. No certain
instance is known from Greece proper, and Koschaker's analysis started
from a Greek parchment dated A D 121 found on the site of Dura-Europus
on the Euphrates River. The document is a loan agreement which provides that, instead of interest, 'Barlaas (the borrower), staying
(*paramenon*) with Phraates (the lender) until the time of repayment, will
perform for him slave-like services (*doulike chreia*), doing everything
which is ordered him, and absenting himself neither day nor night
without the permission of Phraates'. Further, if Barlaas does not repay
the loan when it falls due, he 'will remain with Phraates, performing the
same services according to the above provisions until the repayment of
the money'.[25] This is a late text from a peripheral area, to be sure, but if
something like it was inherent in the Attic situation at the time of Solon
(and in the position of the *katakeimenos* in Gortyn), as Koschaker
suggested with much plausibility, then this would have been the oldest
form of *paramone*. The second and best attested form is *paramone* in
connection with manumission, whereby a slave is freed but is to 'remain'
in service (expressed in language very much like that of the Dura parchment). For this form we have documentation from the fourth century B C
on, in an extensive area of the Greek world. The third is the so-called
'service contract' of the papyri.

A few of the *paramone* documents actually specify the element of
servitude by saying, in one phrase or another, that the work performed
shall be 'that of a slave', 'slave-like', or that the person shall serve 'as a
slave'. What distinguishes service as a free man from service as a slave is
the fact that the latter is total and that malfeasance is directly punishable
without recourse to formal procedure. 'He will do whatever he is told' is
the operative formula. *Paramone*, as Koschaker said, 'does not lie simply
in the sphere of obligations but creates . . . a power relationship'.[26] Nor is

this merely a question of fine juristic distinction. From a very early stage in their history, the Greeks thought of personal and domestic service as 'slave-like' by its nature. That is why free Greeks simply cannot be found as servants, and that in turn is why words like *oiketes* and *therapon*, which in the strictest sense mean no more than 'servant', were regularly employed to mean 'slave' without creating confusion or a feeling of ill-usage.

In a sense, it is correct to say that the Greeks came to sum up this particular situation in the simple verb *paramenein* (remain with). Not all the various institutional forms of *paramone* were equally old. I do not believe we have enough information with which to make a decision about priorities, but the wide spread of this language in a split-up world without systematic juristic analysis or writing is very striking. And it is very tempting for us to conceptualise the language into a single uniform institution. 'May we', Koschaker asked, 'carry over to *paramone* for debt the juristic concept of divided property rights discovered in the manu-mission *paramone*?' His answer was an unconditional yes, supported, he thought, by 'the kinship, if not the juristic identity, of both institutions, having the same name, the same juristic terminology, and a far-reaching agreement in their content'.[27] However, this undeniable agreement is an abstraction, and only an abstraction. On the one hand, a man who has been a slave is freed, but his freedom is partly withdrawn in the same action in which it is given to him: for a period, sometimes definite and sometimes indefinite, he remains bound to total service 'like a slave', like the slave he has been all along. On the other hand, a free man 'freely' surrenders a portion of his freedom in return for maintenance or a loan or perhaps even a wage. One moves on the road from slavery to freedom, the other in the reverse direction, and they meet. That meeting-point, that half-state, is *paramone* – so runs the Koschaker doctrine. But is it so complete an identity? What, for example, if the free man had financial or military obligations to the state, which the manumitted slave in *paramone* would in principle not have? What was the status of their children and who determined it? What were their respective positions in disputes at law with third parties? Where did they stand with regard to the owner-ship of property and to rights of succession and testament? Above all, what were the penalties for failure to perform the required services? The manumitted slave in *paramone* would then return to slavery: the manu-mission, say some of the texts very explicitly, becomes null and void. But surely it was not so simple in the case of the debt-bondsman.

I have already indicated by the example of Gortyn that we cannot yet answer these questions with any clarity or precision, at least not for Greece proper. Perhaps our evidence will never permit us to do so. I suggest, however, that the answer is likely to be, first, that there were significant differences in some of these matters between the manumitted slave in *paramone* and the free man who had entered that state; secondly, that the rules and principles were not uniform regardless of time or place, that, in other words, they sometimes varied with the different social and political structures which made up the Greek world through most of its history. I am not thinking of minor variations in detail, of which there are not a few examples in the available manumission documents, such as the duration of the *paramone* or the precise maintenance requirements or the provisions regarding children. What I have in mind is more basic, something which affects the nature of the institution itself, the precise definition of the particular status or statuses. I suggest, in other words, that bringing these various situations together under the single rubric, *paramone*, is an excessive abstraction. Granted the important common element, there remain differences, rooted in the fact that *paramone* was reached from totally different starting-points. These differences should not be wiped out as the Koschaker position in effect does. I suggest, further, that ownership is too narrow a yardstick. 'Divided property rights' is a useful concept up to a point, but there are aspects of the question of half-statuses which, it seems to me, cannot be understood in that way except by straining the notion too hard.

More recently Westermann has tried another approach, which emphasises personal rights, so to speak, rather than property. He starts from the fact that there is a regular formula in the Delphic manumissions (with parallels from other communities). The manumitted slave, the texts say in one variation or another, 'shall be free, shall not be subject to seizure, may do as he pleases, and may go where he pleases.' This formula, which Westermann believes 'to have been devised at Delphi by the local priests of Apollo', he then treats as a more or less formal and complete 'Greek' definition of freedom. 'To the Delphic priests, therefore,' he writes, 'individual liberty consisted of the possession of four freedoms – status, personal inviolability, freedom of economic activity, right of unrestricted movement.'[28]

The weaknesses of this analysis are grave. In the first place, there are not four elements but only three at best. The first, which Westermann calls 'status', is pure tautology. The texts say that the manumitted slave shall be free, and freedom is obviously not one element of freedom. Nor are 'do what you please' and 'go where you please' two distinct categories of action. It is only by interpretation that the former can be rendered 'freedom of economic activity', and such freedom cannot exist without freedom of movement. In the second place, the very same documents promptly remove both these freedoms in the case of *paramone*, leaving Westermann in the curious position of arguing that the manumitted slave in *paramone* is at least half-free despite his lack of the two most essential elements of freedom. In the third place, freedom of movement, on which Westermann places greatest stress, turns out to be remarkably shaky as a test of free status. In Gortyn, for example, freedmen lacked it: they were restricted to a place (or district) called Latosion.[29] Or, to take a quite different example, consider the Spartan élite, the *homoioi*, who, in a very real sense, lacked freedom of movement almost completely.

IV

After all, the composers of these Delphic documents, as Koschaker correctly noted, were not professional jurists, 'their formulas were often inaccurate and contradictory, and they . . . muddled disparate formal elements together'.[30] I am far from convinced, on the evidence, that it was the priests of Apollo who worked out the categories, as Westermann asserts, and I feel confident that whoever did, had no notion that they were 'defining' the status of a free man in any fundamental sense. These inscriptions had one purpose, and one only, to give public notice of a formal act which changed the status of an individual (or individuals). It was not their function, or aim, to offer a juristic treatise on freedom. Therefore they gave such information as custom dictated to be necessary, and then they stopped. Because manumission was often incomplete, qualified either by suspensive conditions or by *paramone*, and because the manumittor had wide latitude in a number of details regarding children, future succession, repayment of an *eranos* loan and the like, what was necessary included those things which he, the manumittor, might or might not grant. Hence the repeated reference to doing as one pleased and going where one pleased, whenever that was the case. But there were other elements of freedom which it was not in the power of the manumittor to determine, which were matters of the law of the *polis*, and they obviously did not appear in the inscriptions. If, for example, the law in the central Greek states restricted land ownership to citizens, as it very probably did, it would not be for the manumittor either to grant or to refuse to grant this privilege to his ex-slave, or to make any reference to the subject. Nor could he say anything meaningful in the areas of legal

capacity, taxation, military obligations, and cult (apart from requirements regarding his own burial and the upkeep of his tomb).

It may be objected that I am now confusing political and social categories with proper juristic ones. To that I would reply that such 'confusion' is inherent in Greek thinking and in Greek institutions. To separate
them might be more elegant, more Roman, but it would no longer be
Greek. When Diodorus, for example, tried to explain the rationale of the
law of the Egyptian pharaoh Bocchoris prohibiting loans on the security
of the person, he wrote as follows (1.79.3): 'The bodies of citizens should
belong to the state, to the end that the state might avail itself of the
services which its citizens owed it, in times of both war and peace. For it
would be absurd, he felt, that a soldier, at the moment perhaps when he
was setting forth to fight for his fatherland, should be carried off by his
creditor on account of a loan, and that the greed of private individuals
should in this way endanger the safety of all.' The historicity of Diodorus' account of the legislation of Bocchoris is beside the point: there
can scarcely be any dispute that here he was expressing the classic Greek
conception of the individual's relation to the *polis*. The *polis* was above all
else a community, and a community was imperfect if some of its members could thus be withdrawn from service in the common interest, from
complete membership in other words. Hence Aristotle (*Constitution of
Athens* 9.1) quite rightly included Solon's prohibition of loans on the
person among the greatest and most 'demotic' of all his measures.

No definition of freedom would be complete, within such a
framework, if it overlooked the community aspect. Ideally, one end of
the spectrum of statuses would be the pure chattel, the slave who was
only a thing. Such a status probably never existed, but it was certainly
approached quite closely at times in Greek history. But what is the other
end, the opposite of the chattel? Logically one might say the status of
absolute freedom from restraint, the anarchist's ideal. Apart from the
fact that such a status, too, never existed (which is not a serious objection
conceptually), this is false logic, that is to say, it is false to the realities of
Greek life and Greek thinking. The opposite of the chattel was the full
citizen, the man who was capable of performing all the roles, both the
privileges and the obligations, of citizenship. Not only was the metic
lower down on the spectrum, but also the citizen whose position was
restricted for one reason or another, whether by property qualifications
in an oligarchic *polis*, for example, or by loss of civil rights in so democratic a community as Athens. Obviously the sharpest line was somewhere in the middle of the spectrum. The metic was a free man in

comparison with the slave or helot or bondsman in *paramone*. In establishing that line, however, one must always bear in mind social and political categories (historical categories in other words) as well as narrowly legal categories.

How these various categories interacted may be illustrated in two ways, both of which demonstrate that in certain respects men who, on a narrow view, were apparently on the free side of the line, turn out, on further examination, to have held insecure tenure there. If we view status as implying potentialities as well as a present condition, then one element of freedom is the possibility or impossibility of its loss.[31] In classical Athens, a citizen could not be enslaved, by public or private action, except in that peculiar survival, the law regarding ransom. A non-citizen, however, was subject to penal slavery for certain offences, and there was further differentiation in this respect among them, as between freedmen and metics (free men coming from abroad).[32] My other instance is in the area of the extension of status to descendants. It is impossible to state the rules in this area without distinguishing city from city, and within the individual cities, era from era. It is enough to cite the Gortyn code on the one hand, and on the other the Athenian law of 451/50 establishing full bilaterality as a requirement for legitimacy. A man's freedom to marry, culminating in the Greek view in freedom to choose a mother of legitimate children – and legitimacy was, above all, a community-political concept – can therefore not be defined except by combining what we should call private-law with political notions. And, as we saw earlier, there were ranges of possibilities in this respect as well.

In sum, my argument is that status in ancient Greece can be analysed effectively only by borrowing an approach which has been developed in contemporary jurisprudence particularly in the analysis of property. This involves first breaking up the traditional notion of rights into a number of concepts, including claims, privileges, immunities, powers, and their opposites (duties and so on).[33] Second it involves envisaging status (or freedom) as a bundle of privileges, powers, and so on, and therefore the definition of any particular status, or of any individual's status, in terms of the possession and location of the individual's elements of the bundle. This cannot be done in terms of possession alone, for clearly certain privileges – such as the right of marriage – may be totally absent, that is, the unfree person may not have them, but neither does anyone else have them with respect to him. Nor can the analysis be made only in terms of the unfree person and his master. The Spartan state, for example, had certain powers over the helot which the helot's master did not possess.[34]

Here I can do no more than repeat the necessary categories of analysis: (1) claims to property, or power over things – a complex of elements requiring further differentiation both in its range (from *peculium* to full ownership) and in its application to different categories of things (e.g. cattle or land or agricultural produce or money); (2) power over a man's labour and movements; (3) power to punish; (4) privileges and liabilities in legal action, such as immunity from arbitrary seizure or the capacity to sue and be sued; (5) privileges in the area of the family: marriage, succession, and so on; (6) privileges of social mobility, such as manumission or enfranchisement (and their inverse); and (7) privileges and duties in the sacral, political, and military spheres.[35]

Such a method of analysis, I suggest, will enable us to clarify the Greek status pattern, with its half-statuses and mixed statuses, and to introduce a precision into the picture which is lacking so far. It provides a technique for defining *paramone*, for example, or for differentiating the Cretan system from the Spartan. More important perhaps, it will help us see the historical development and tendencies of Greek social structures and social concepts in proper relationship to the history of the *polis* as a political structure. It is a fact, I believe, that social and political progress in the Greek *poleis* was accompanied by the triumph of chattel slavery over other statuses of dependent labour. But it is also a fact that much of the Greek world did not take this step (or did not take it fully), and that the Hellenistic age was filled with debt-bondage and kindred practices – in the eastern regions more than on the Greek mainland and in the west.[36] These are more than formal distinctions: they are substantive clues to the social and political system as a whole, to its institutions and values. The latter include legal institutions, and in this field, surely, vague generalisations about a common Greek law (and Greek juristic thinking) must founder on the indisputable evidence for the existence of profound qualitative differences in both time and place.

9

DEBT-BONDAGE AND
THE PROBLEM OF SLAVERY

I

We may begin with the details of the mythical story concerning the Greek hero Heracles, to which I alluded at the beginning of Chapter 7. At Delphi the god told Heracles that the disease with which he was afflicted was a punishment for the treacherous murder of Iphitus, and that he could be cured only by having himself sold into slavery for a limited number of years and handing over the purchase price to his victim's kinsmen. Accordingly he was sold to Omphale, queen of the Lydians, and he worked off his guilt in her service. The texts disagree on several points: whether he was sold by Hermes or by friends who accompanied him to Asia for the purpose, whether his period of servitude was one year or three, and so on.

The details themselves do not matter. One must not press a myth too hard, or the language in which it is repeated by writers as far apart in spirit and time as Sophocles and Diodorus. Nevertheless, several points emerge which are not without interest. The first is lexical. Sophocles calls Heracles a *latris* of Omphale's (*Trachiniae* 70, equated by the scholiast with *doulos*)[1] and he twice uses a verb meaning 'to sell' in this connection (lines 250,252).[2] Apollodorus (2.6.2–3) employs *latreuo* and *douleuo* interchangeably in his account, Diodorus (4.31.5–8) only *doulos* and its derivatives. The word *latris* has been a lexicographer's nightmare from Hellenistic times to the chaotic entry in Liddell and Scott, for it means 'hired man', 'servant' and 'slave', a confusion which is intolerable not only to lexicographers but also to many legal historians accustomed to developed rules of law and to technical terms appropriate to them.[3] But in the 'pre-law' stage (and often enough after 'pre-law' has given way to 'law'[4]) 'service' and 'servitude' did in fact merge into each other. That is when debt-bondage had its origins, in Greece as in Rome, and it is noteworthy that the Greek language, so far as we know, had no specific

Originally published in French in *Revue historique de droit français et étranger*, 4 ser., 43 (1965) 159–84, and reprinted (for the first time in English), with some revisions, by permission of the editors.

word in general use meaning 'debt-bondsman' (hence Dionysius of Halicarnassus could not translate the Latin *nexum* and *nexus* into Greek except by circumlocution).

I have chosen the Heracles story to introduce my analysis despite the fact that it speaks of 'sale' into bondage rather than of debt-bondage proper and that it has complications (such as sale abroad) which would, if pursued, take us too far afield.[5] As we shall see, 'sale' into bondage and debt-bondage cannot be distinguished very sharply. In ordinary speech even today the words 'debt' and 'obligation' are vague and broad at the same time: they take in not only obligations in their strict legal sense, debts arising from loans and commercial transactions or obligations arising from a tort or delict, but also 'moral' obligations which are not enforceable in a court of law. In the discussion of the critical period with which we shall be chiefly concerned a more exact discrimination is unnecessary, and often misleading. All 'debts' were equally enforceable or unenforceable, as the case may be, without a meaningful difference between 'legal' and 'moral' obligations. Men lived in a network of obligations. Some arose from status alone, within a kinship group or *familia* or community: the obligation to provide bride-wealth, for example, or to support parents or patrons. Others arose from hostile acts, as in blood-guilt; still others arose from friendly acts, a gift or other service.

No doubt there were distinctions in the weight of these different kinds of debt, but it is anachronistic to dismiss certain common expressions of the idea as metaphorical or to insist on some form of prior, bilateral agreement. There were no disinterested actions in primitive and archaic societies: one cast one's bread upon the waters in the firm and legitimate expectation of a return.[6] The line which divided a gift from a loan was perhaps not invisible, but it was thin and fragile, as is readily apparent from the semantic cluster surrounding the Latin *mutuum* and its cognates. *Si datum quod reddatur, mutuum* ('if something is given which is to be returned, it is called *mutuum*'), writes Varro (*On the Latin Language*, 5.179), and he goes on to quote the old Sicilian Greek dialect form *moitos* from the fifth-century writer Sophron, a word which Hesychius equates with Greek *charis*. 'We set up a shrine of the Charites (Graces) in a public place', Aristotle explains (*Ethics* 5.5.7), 'that there may be a requital; for this is a characteristic of grace, since it is proper not only to make a return to one who has shown grace but another time to take the initiative in an act of grace oneself.' And Hesiod, as one might expect, ties the whole complex together in all its harsh practicality (*Works and Days*

349–55): 'Take fair measure, or better, if you can; so that if you are in need afterwards, you may find him sure. . . . Give to one who gives, but do not give to one who does not give. A man gives to the free-handed, but no one gives to the close-fisted.'

On the other hand, loans slide away from gifts and into theft. Why, asks Plutarch in his *Greek Questions* (*Moralia* 303 B), was it the custom in Knossos for borrowers to snatch the money? he replies with another question: 'Was it so that, if they default, they could be charged with violence and punished all the more?' This is a curious text, unique, so far as I know, among Greek and Roman writers. But a fifth-century B C law of Thasos provides that the action against anyone who buys grapes on the vine before the month of Plyntherion shall be 'as for violence'.[7] Although the original editor comments that this was only 'a simple procedural reference without any implication of kinship between the offences,'[8] it is a suggestive inference, nonetheless, and not an inevitable, or self-evident one.[9] The crucial point with regard to debt, at least, is that in early law it is regularly assimilated to delict and thence to crime. As Ihering wrote nearly a century ago, personal execution in the XII Tables was 'an act of the civil law . . . and achieved the most extreme misalliance between debt and punishment . . .; *by law* the debtor paid with the ruin of his entire existence for his inability to pay up.' Greek law, he noted in a postscript, never eliminated the 'penal element in private law and civil procedure' and he adduced a parallel which is unusually apt for our purposes (though he did not cite the Plutarch passage and he could not have known the Thasian text), namely, provisions in the old Norwegian laws which explicitly assimilated civil-law obligations to robbery (*rán*).[10] I shall restrict myself to one example. If a man refused to pay his share of the bishop's fee for conducting divine services and if he continued in his refusal even after formal notice, 'he shall be summoned before the *thing* on the charge of robbery'.[11]

The extreme harshness of the laws of debt is a well-known and ubiquitous fact of early and archaic societies (and often much later, too, as the debtor-prisons testify), in particular when debtor and creditor came from different social classes. It was a cruel joke to legislate, as they did in Gortyn, that if a debt-bondsman (*katakeimenos*) suffered an actionable injury and his master failed to sue on his behalf, he could do so himself provided he first paid off his debt.[12] The whole of the Roman system of *legis actiones* was another cruel joke, in particular *sacramentum* and *manus iniectio*, to those 'who lacked the backing of a mighty house'.[13] Twist and squirm as one will, the words *partis secanto* (he shall be cut into portions) cannot be expunged from the Twelve Tables, nor their ugly sound, accepted as such by all later Roman writers.[14]

II

The obsession with debt one perceives in primitive and archaic societies must therefore be differentiated according to the threat implied. Save in exceptional cases, it was only between classes, between rich and poor, to put it in loose and simple terms, that debt led to bondage in practice. By 'bondage' or 'servitude' I mean any relationship of personal dependence, other than familial or economic (as in the modern wage-labour situation), whether chattel slavery or helotage or the statuses which can be described, in the phrase of the ancient lexicographer Pollux (3.83), as being 'between the free men and the slaves'. A very broad general word is required, no less all-embracing than the word 'debt': power over a person took various specific forms, as did the obligations which were so often the occasion for its coming into play.

It is easy enough to understand how the poor fell into debt, but the other side of the operation was perhaps more complicated than we usually allow. Why should a rich man lend – for we must come to loans in the end – except to another rich man? The conventional answer is that he seeks profit through the interest he charges (at excessive rates, of course). At best, however, that is a partial answer, for the earlier stages, indeed, largely a false answer. A very short digression about the fairly abundant Near Eastern documents, dealing with both 'sales' and 'loans', may help to explain why. For example, nine tablets from a small family archive found at Nippur in 1950–51 reveal how, during a siege of the city in the seventh century B C, young children (all but one of them girls) were sold for token sums, and two of the texts employ a very impressive formula: 'Take my small child . . . and keep her alive . . . that I may eat.'[15] There are other cuneiform texts in which no money is paid over at all;[16] still others in which the transaction takes the form of a loan, the child (or an adult) being handed over to the 'creditor' either as security or in lieu of interest or both.[17] In Nuzi agreements of the latter type, either no time limit is fixed or there is a long term, up to fifty years in some cases. As Mendelsohn says, we must assume that few such pawns were ever redeemed, since the labour service was 'the most essential feature of the transaction and not the loan itself'.[18]

When a Nuzi text provides that for three talents of copper a man gives over his son, a weaver, for fifty years; that if the 'debtor' breaks the agreement, he shall return the copper, receive back his son and supply another weaver – it is perfectly obvious that the loan was purely fictitious and that labour service was the sole objective, the money being in effect payment in advance for the fifty years.[19] More than a millennium and a half later, a very well-known Greek parchment from Dura-Europos, dated A D 121, reveals how the same effect could be achieved in a more complicated and more sophisticated way.[20] In lieu of interest on a 'loan' of 400 drachmas, the debtor agreed, in the typical language of the Greek *paramone*, to remain with the 'creditor' performing slave-like services and to repay the money after one year. There follows a renewal clause which, as Welles says, seems 'designed to prevent the borrower from repaying the loan', thereby perpetuating the 'slave-like' relationship, and I do not believe there can be any doubt that this was understood and intended by both parties from the outset.[21] Scholars commenting on the covenant have debated the question of 'nationality' excessively.[22] The social situation which lay at the base of the transaction was Parthian, but the formulas in the document and the legal institutions were familiar enough in the Hellenistic Greek world. The important point, at least for our purposes, is the survival in this mixed frontier civilisation in the second century of our era of an age-old principle common to both Graeco-Roman and Near Eastern societies in their early stages, and to many other civilisations as well. In the words of a distinguished authority on southeast Asia, 'The concept of labour as a saleable commodity, apart from the person of the seller, is relatively recent in the history of civilisation.'[23]

This is not to suggest either that all loans were fictitious and that all agreements in this form were purely service-arrangements, or that labour power was *never* disposed of apart from the person, even in quite early situations. The family whose archive included the Nippur 'siege documents' were neither slave-dealers as such nor an industrial establishment hungry for labour power. The evidence, though incomplete, suggests that they had an entrepreneurial approach which led them to a variety of activities, like Balunamhu of Larsa a thousand years earlier, in the generation preceding Hammurabi. He, like his father before him, was a very wealthy landed magnate who also hired out ships, lent money at interest and sometimes without interest, took both slaves and free persons as pawns and then hired them out to others.[24] To such a man it presumably made little difference whether he profited by having his loan repaid with interest or by using, in whatever way, a pledge, a person or a thing (usually land). And the law, because it gave him this double chance, shielded him from risk and almost guaranteed him absolutely against it.

The range of possibilities is nicely exemplified in a group of neo-Assyrian documents from the latter half of the second millennium.[25] The loans there recorded are in money or corn or both, for varying terms, and sometimes with the proviso that interest shall accrue if the loan is not repaid on time. The security takes the form of land, houses, slaves, wives, sons and daughters. The motive, either of the lender or the creditor, is of course not stated, and that is just what we should like to know. When we read in no. 60, referring to a loan of corn for eleven months, that land and houses are pledged as security, and that 'if he (the creditor) does not obtain satisfaction from these fields and houses, he shall obtain it from his (the debtor's) sons and daughters', the objective of the creditor seems clear enough. In no. 56, however, the provision is this: 'As a pawn the wife of the debtor shall live in the house of the creditor. On the day he (the debtor) pays the corn, the money and the interest on them, he shall redeem his wife.' Can we be certain in this case that the creditor had made a loan rather than a service agreement, that, in other words, he really wished repayment rather than, as in the Dura parchment and some of the Nuzi agreements, that he preferred (or at least was equally willing) to retain the lady's services and not to have his 'loan' repaid? Commentators automatically tend to the first alternative, but I suggest that, though it may be the more probable, it is decidedly not the only possible one.

It is just this kind of one-sided assumption, I also suggest, which has prevented a correct appreciation of the notorious debt-bondage cruces in the early history of Greece and Rome. We are too quick with talk of default and personal execution, a possibility, of course, but not the only possibility. 'Debt' may also have been arranged in order to *create* a state of bondage, just as, between equals, its purpose may have been to maintain bonds of solidarity or to provide a kind of insurance against a future need (as the Hesiod passage I have already quoted indicates very explicitly). Indeed, I will go further and say that labour power and solidarity were historically prior to profit in the form of interest. In early Greece and Rome, how did the rich and well-born, the holders of the large estates, obtain and increase their labour force? Both hired labour and chattel slaves are known from our earliest sources, the Homeric poems and the Twelve Tables, but it is clear that they were not the answer. Labour was essentially dependent labour – clients, helots, *pelatai* or whatever else they were called – and debt-bondsmen. That is to say, as between the social orders, debt was a deliberate device on the part of the creditor to obtain more dependent labour rather than a device for enrichment through interest.[26]

III

It was labour in the form of personal servitude which lay at the heart of the Solonic crisis in Athens, the only such situation in archaic Greece about which we are sufficiently informed to attempt a more systematic analysis. 'The poor together with their children and their wives were enslaved to the rich' – that is how, Aristotle opens his account (*Constitution of Athens*, 2.2). We need not take 'enslaved' (*edouleuon*) literally, for Greek writers regularly used *doulos* and *douleuo* for any form of subjection, whether strictly that of a chattel slave or not. But that Aristotle understood Solonic Athens to be one in which a large section of the Athenian population were somehow unfree is beyond question (and I stress 'Athenian', since foreign chattel slaves are in no way part of the story). So did all other later writers, Greek or Roman.

Aristotle and later writers were also unanimous in their preoccupation with debt as the key issue, and they have been followed so enthusiastically by modern writers that certain complexities and shadings have escaped notice. To begin with, it seems not to have been noticed that no ancient writer unequivocally equates the *hektemoroi* ('sixth-parters'), who are also involved in Aristotle's account of Solon, with debt-bondsmen.[27] For Aristotle *hektemoros* was synonymous with *pelates*, and in the scholia and lexica, as in Plutarch, *thes* is introduced as a third synonym. The precise sense of *pelates* is by no means clear today, but so far as I know it was never applied in antiquity to a debt-bondsman. Dionysius of Halicarnassus (2.9.2) used it to translate the Latin *cliens* (as did other writers), but never in the context of *nexum*, for which, as I have already observed, he had no single Greek word. *Hektemoroi* therefore constituted a distinct status whose roots are lost in the Dark Age of Greek history, men who worked land on terms of a fixed rent of one sixth of the crop, presumably not free to leave it, but not caught up in what we normally refer to when we speak of a debtor-creditor relationship.[28] They were not the stratum from which the debt-bondsmen emerged as a rule, and as a class they may therefore be excluded from our discussion.[29]

We cannot exclude them yet, however, until they are allowed to reveal one very important further distinction. If the *hektemoroi* failed to pay their one-sixth, Aristotle says, they and their children were *agogimoi*, and, he continues, 'all loans were on the person until Solon'. The word *agogimoi* has a cluster of meanings, but here it can be pinpointed to 'carried off for sale abroad'. The crucial question is whether *agogimoi* refers only to defaulting *hektemoroi* or to the debtors as well. One must judge as well as one can from Aristotle's wording, with the further assistance of the long quotation from Solon in which the lawgiver enumerates the actions he took:

1. By removing the *horoi* I freed the land which had been enslaved;
2. I brought back from abroad three categories of Athenians: (a) those who had been sold legally, (b) those who had been sold unlawfully, and (c) those who had fled;
3. I set free those who were in shameful bondage at home.

That there is a measure of unclarity in both Solon's poem and Aristotle's terse summary can scarcely be denied. Yet it seems to me that a straight, unforced reading produces some clear features. Solon's 'lifting of the burden' from the Athenian poor consisted of three distinct steps: (1) he abolished the status of *hektemoros*; (2) he brought back, in so far as he could, Athenians who had been sold abroad under the law, the *agogimoi*, among whom were defaulting *hektemoroi*;[30] (3) he cancelled existing debts and prohibited debts on the person in the future, thereby both freeing the debt-bondsmen of his day and abolishing the category from Athens henceforth.

Three questions then remain. Were there also defaulting debtors among the *agogimoi*? Were those 'enslaved' at home debtors who had defaulted or were they in bondage as an immediate consequence of going into debt? Was there a choice of possibilities in the treatment of defaulting debtors, and, if so, how and by whom was the choice exercised? I hope I have demonstrated in the early part of this paper that it is not self-evident, as modern accounts take it, that all the troubles arose from failure to meet debt payments. The comparative evidence suggests, on the contrary, that we must allow for the alternative I have put in my questions, an alternative in which default plays no significant part. But the Greek evidence will take us no further.[31] We must turn to Rome for help.

The parallel between the Solonic crisis and the *nexum*-struggle could not possibly have escaped the notice of the learned men in antiquity. Indeed, Dionysius of Halicarnassus (5.65.1) even has Marcus Valerius cite Solon as a precedent in a great debate with Appius Claudius in 494 B C, which tells us a good deal about Dionysius as a historian if nothing of any value about the history itself. But Cicero in the *Republic* (2.34.59) and elsewhere is no more precise or helpful. The plain fact is that by the late Republic *nexum* was so long dead and the kind of relationship it represented so incomprehensible, that the Romans themselves knew no more than that such an institution has once existed, that it meant debt-bondage, and that it had been abolished in the fourth century. The jurists and the antiquarians had the XII Tables, of course – that is what kept the memory of *nexum* alive. The annalists and historians then told their dramatic tales, but no one can seriously argue today that their stories rest on any deep insight into the nature of the institution, or even of the underlying social situation.

On one point, however, the stories are unanimous. The victims could be abused in every way, fettered, overworked, beaten, assaulted sexually, starved, but never were they threatened with death or with sale abroad, the latter being the consequences of the formal judicial procedure following default on a payment or other obligations, known as *manus iniectio*, explicitly spelled out in the XII Tables. *Nexum* and *manus iniectio*, in short, were two distinct institutions,[32] the former creating, in Solon's words, those who were in bondage at home, trembling before their masters, the latter sending Romans across the Tiber into slavery abroad. The Athenian-Roman parallel seems to me to be compelling, the explanation for the distinction in both cases, though hypothetical, ready to hand. Given the harshness of the law of debt, those driven into debt – and I must stress again that for the present I am speaking only of debts between the classes – protected themselves from the ultimate sanctions by debt-bondage. They had no other protection, no other choice.[33]

Thus far I believe we are on safe ground. But we are driven to very difficult speculation the moment we try to visualise the actual situation in any detail. Imbert has argued that we must strip away from *nexum* not only the false link with *manus iniectio* but also the obsession with default. The very act of establishing the *nexum*-bond, in his view, at once placed the debtor in the full power of his creditor, *in fidem*.[34] I think he is right; the comparative material I have already produced does not prove him right, but it at least establishes the possibility. It is no objection to point out that the Roman sources reveal the original power-sense of *fides* unconsciously, so to speak, while on the conscious level they refer only to defaulting debtors. In Livy's world, as in Plutarch's, debt was frightening because of usury or because one could not repay when it fell due. Hence when they thought about *nexum* or Solon at all, they naturally assumed that bondage followed default. Their assumption proves nothing. Nor were they moved to think about the further steps. What

happened to the debt-bondsman in the end? Livy is concerned solely
with maltreatment; Dionysius mentions work for the creditor; neither
seems to have asked himself if the status went on to death, unless
Dionysius' 'they used them like bought slaves' (5.53.2) is to be taken as a
deliberate answer, which I doubt.

Only a learned antiquarian like Varro gives the impression of some
thinking. 'A free man who gives his labour in servitude for money which
he owes, until he has worked off (*dum solveret*) the debt, is called a
nexus.'[35] For Varro the idea behind *nexum* was therefore that a man who
could not meet his obligation by payment could compensate by work
(slave-like, exactly as in the Greek texts from archaic times to the Dura
parchment). Unfortunately there is one possible ambiguity in the text.
How shall we understand *dum solveret*? Does it mean 'until he pays up' as
it is regularly translated (and which was the standard meaning in the first
century B C), in which case we are back with our cruel jokes again? Or
does it mean 'until he has paid through his work' (as I have translated),
which would be a logical consequence of 'gives his labour for money
which he owes'? Varro, with his antiquarian interest, may have had the
distinction in his mind, but again, even if we knew, it would tell us about
Varro, not about *nexum*. One should not overestimate Varro. He ends
the sentence I quoted with these words: *ut ob aere obaeratus* ('as a debtor
bound by debts'), a typical bit of misleading etymological display. Elsewhere in the *De re rustica* (1.17.2), he says that among the types of
non-slave agricultural labour are those 'whom we called *obaerati* (or
obaerarii) and who still exist in large numbers in Asia, Egypt and Illyria.'
Which goes to prove how dangerous a little learning is, for Varro, having
discovered that some form of dependent labour was common in the
Hellenistic east and among northern barbarians, jumped to the false
conclusion that they were *all* debt-bondsmen in the ancient Roman
style.[36] On this point we have controls; on *nexum* we have none, but it is
reasonable not to assume more knowledge on Varro's part for one than
for the other.

The injection of *obaerati* points up the inability of Varro and his contemporaries to imagine a debt in any terms other than monetary. Some
scholars have been quick to seize on what looks like an anachronism.
Nexum, they note, is a considerably earlier institution than coinage (and
numismatists agree that Athens did not begin to coin until after Solon).
There is a confusion here, however: money need not be coin, and in
Mesopotamia money was used in sales and loans millennia before
anyone ever thought of coinage. In a largely non-monetary agrarian

economy it is not money the peasant or landless labourer needs when in distress so much as food, seed-corn or beasts of burden, and, despite the absence of evidence, I believe we must assume that loans often took that form, in archaic Greece and Rome, just as they did in Mesopotamia (for which we have ample documentation). Later Roman practice, with its insistence that all judgments must be expressed in monetary terms, is not relevant to the earlier period.

If that is correct, however, it creates a new difficulty for the view of *nexum* I am putting forward. Is it conceivable that a peasant who borrowed seed-corn could enter a state of bondage immediately? How then could he possibly grow his corn, reap his crop and repay his debt? Is it not more reasonable to accept the sequence, related by Livy in most pathetic terms (2.23.5–6): first, loss of land and crops, and only then, when nothing was left to seize, loss of liberty?

I do not underestimate the difficulties, and yet I have no hesitation in rejecting the 'more reasonable' view. To begin with, there is the elementary point that real security is a late development in Rome; that originally the creditor's claim to the debtor's property was a consequence of his claim to the debtor's person.[37] Then there is the comparative evidence that real and personal security need not be alternatives but may be employed jointly. That was the case in some of the Middle Assyrian documents I have already cited (e.g. nos. 39 and 55). The Dura parchment gave the ultimate right of execution, in a case in which the bondage was certainly immediate, on both the person and the possessions.[38] Finally, and most important of all perhaps, are considerations of the social situation as a whole. We must, I think, accept the unanimous opinion of the sources, vague and inaccurate through they are in most respects, that in both Athens and Rome the debt-bondage crisis involved a substantial section of the citizenry. Aristotle's 'the poor were enslaved to the rich' may be exaggerated, but neither Solon's reforms nor the complex history of the patrician-plebeian struggle in Rome makes any sense at all unless the generalisation is near enough true. Are we to believe that they were a great crowd of landless families? Doing what? And who was lending money or seed-corn or anything else to such people, without the faintest hope that they could repay?

Frankly I am quite unable to imagine such a state of affairs, and yet that is the only possible implication of the traditional view. The chief fallacy, I suggest, lies in a misconception of the nature of the bondage. We have allowed ourselves to be completely misled by Livy with his debtors languishing in private patrician prisons. That might do for the brief waiting-period before sale abroad in *manus iniectio*; it is nonsense otherwise.[39] Nor is the model of the chattel slave on the *latifundia* binding. Labour was what was wanted from the bondsmen (and also enhancement of the status of the 'creditors'), and it is not ruled out that many provided the labour, and its products, from holdings of their own. This is necessarily speculative, of course, and to discover the permissible channels of speculation we must turn to other societies because there is no Graeco-Roman documentation whatsoever.

In one neo-Babylonian instance, for example, a court ruled that a money debt was paid off, after ten years, with accruing interest, through a combination of personal service in bondage and a lump payment of corn, the latter presumably coming from an estate the debt-bondsman had inherited from his father (along with the debt, which he also inherited).[40] This was no vague judgment, furthermore, but a precise calculation made by the court on the basis of 20 per cent interest (so that the debt was trebled in ten years) and a conventional ratio between months of service and *gur* of corn. An altogether different example comes from the present world, among the Apa Tanis, who live in a secluded valley in the eastern Himalayas, untouched by European adminstrative intervention when they were first studied in 1944 and 1945. There a debt-bondsman can work off a debt either by direct service for the creditor or by work for others or both. If the debt remains uncleared for a length of time, 'his position turns gradually into that of a slave'. As such, he might be attached to the household and be property-less, or he might be 'separated', allotted land to cultivate and the right to acquire property.[41]

If Apa Tanis and neo-Babylonians could find such solutions to the problem, or if Heracles could work off his debt in a fixed term, that still does not tell us what the Athenians or the Romans did. But it tells us, in my opinion, that we must think of a flexible procedure. The only fixed point is that there was a sharp class division, in which all the power, including the right to protect one's interests, was on one side. A debtor had little chance. In fact, he had little chance before he even became a debtor, because he was poor and essentially defenceless, against bad harvests and famine, against war and its depredations, against the one-sidedness of the law. When his luck was bad his only defence was to put himself *in fidem*, in the power of the powerful. In practice that could – and I suspect did – mean a range of possibilities, including actual loans and fictitious loans (as in Nuzi), immediate servitude or delayed servitude, permanent or temporary bondage. The one thing it excluded was the full force of the law of debt as expressed in *manus iniectio*. It was to protect themselves from stravation and death, in sum, that the poor accepted debt-bondage.[42]

IV

The element of social conflict hovers about the history of debt-bondage everywhere in the ancient world. There are distinctions, however, both in the institution and in its later history, which reflect differences among the social systems in which debt-bondage flourished. One must be careful here, given the varied nature and the limits of the sources. For archaic Greece and Rome we have no private documents and only the most fragmentary contemporary references, but considerable annalistic and historical tradition. For the ancient Near East we have masses of private documents and a fair scattering of provisions in 'law codes' – the two being remarkably difficult to reconcile – but no historical accounts. Ancient Israel stands apart, with its codes but no documents, and with the addition of fleeting, yet not insignificant, records of protest. Hellenistic Egypt is in a direct line of descent from the Near Eastern pattern. And none of these societies, finally, has left us any systematic juristic analysis.

Despite these differences in the character of the sources, I believe we may draw one very sharp distinction: in Greece and Rome the debtor-class rebelled, whereas in the Near East they did not. Stated differently, reform, amelioration, abolition came in Greece and Rome as a direct consequence of struggle from below, at times reaching genuinely revolutionary proportions; elsewhere the initiative came from above, from the rulers, in response to grumbling and dissatisfaction, no doubt, but on the whole with little effect, and none at long range on the social system itself.[43]

Debt-bondage is not an institution which simply withers away without any reason.[44] Nor can it be abolished by simple fiat unless sufficient force is present to back up the decrees and workable alternatives exist for both classes – a substitute labour force for the creditor class and guarantees for the emancipated (and potential) debtors.[45] There is more than a suspicion that in the ancient Near East the famous ameliorative laws and moratoria were rarely enforced, at least not for any length of time. There is no support in the private documents, for example, for par. 117 of Hammurabi's code setting a three-year limit to the servitude for debt of a man's wife or children.[46] Four reigns later, King Ammizaduga declared a moratorium soon after ascending the throne: a common act of clemency by a new king, proving precisely that such ameliorative acts and provisions were essentially without practical meaning.[47] And there is no ground other than sentiment for believing that the seventh-year release of the Biblical codes was anything but 'a social programme rather than actually functioning law'.[48] There is no documentary evidence one way or the other, but the persistent refrain, especially among the prophets, seems a pretty clear pointer, as does Nehemiah's reduction of interest rates in response to the plea, 'we bring into bondage our sons and our daughters'.[49]

With Nehemiah we are in the second half of the fifth century BC. Among the Israelites the problem was apparently still acute, and the lawgiver's response was only a mild palliative. Thereafter, it seems probable, despite the paucity and difficulty of the evidence, that the situation continued more or less unchanged for about three centuries, until the conquests and expansion of the Hasmonean period made available, for the first time, a large enough supply of foreign chattels. But Jewish history in this and the succeeding period provides no model because of the unique problems imposed upon the institutions of bondage, of whatever kind, by religious considerations, which were further exacerbated by the revolts of AD 66–70 and 132–35, the consequent dispersal of vast numbers of Jews and the loss of a central political and ecclesiastical authority. In the Talmudic period, indeed, there seems to have been a revival under the Sassanids of enslavement of Jews by Jews, in which debt and poverty again played a significant role.[50]

For the two centuries before Nehemiah's time there is a rich body of neo-Babylonian material. In his study of these documents, Petschow concludes that, by contrast with some earlier periods in Babylonian and Assyrian history, the number of examples of the handing over of children in bondage is markedly smaller and there is only one known instance of self-enslavement.[51] Petschow notes, however, that we completely lack documents about execution, whether real or personal; and that the unique judicial text I have already discussed[52] reveals that the principle of 'self-mortgage' must have existed, since by law a son (or daughter) remained in bondage even after his father's death and his succession to the inheritance. Although there may have been a decline, therefore, the practice went on, not only until Alexander conquered Babylonia, but to the end of antiquity, through much of the area east of the Aegean Sea (and it was not unknown to the west). That is the implication of, for instance, Dio Chysostom's remark (15.23) that 'myriads' of free men 'sell themselves and so become slaves by contract'; or of the repeated prohibitions by later Roman emperors preserved in the law codes of Theodosius and Justinian.[53]

The failure of late Roman emperors to stamp out 'voluntary enslavement' of children and adults is merely the last act of a very long story that goes back before the second millennium B C. Why should these royal enactments have been so persistently unenforceable? Not all the emperors – Babylonian, Ptolemaic, Roman – were powerless. Far from it. Nor were they trying to foster freedom, in any sense of that word which an Athenian or a Roman of the Republic would have recognised. Near Eastern society was always a stratified one, in which large sections of the population were never wholly free (quite apart from the chattel slaves). Just what that meant is not easily defined or even apprehended today. As Rostovtzeff wrote of the peasantry of Ptolemaic Egypt: 'they possessed a good deal of social and economic freedom in general and of freedom of movement in particular . . . And yet they were not entirely free. They were bound to the government and could not escape from this bondage, because on it depended their means of subsistence. This bondage was real, not nominal'.[54] The operative phrase is 'bound to the government', for, as he went on to suggest with much plausibility (although in careless language), the Ptolemaic resistance to chattel slavery in general and to enslavement of 'free' peasants in particular, both in Egypt and, when they controlled it, in Syria, is best explained on the grounds that the spread of the latter practice 'would deprive him, the king, of valuable free labour, especially that of the *laoi* in agriculture and industry'.[55]

It is along such lines, I suggest, that one can understand why Near Eastern rulers so often tried to ameliorate and sometimes even to suppress one type of bondage alone. In a world in which there were degrees of unfreedom, rather than of freedom, there could be clashes of interest in which one type of bondage interfered with another. In particular, if the royal interest clashed with others, royal edicts on debt and bondage were unlikely to be enforceable for very long.[56] The same late Roman emperors who seem to have had not very much success with their orders that free-born may not 'be in servitude to creditors' (a practice which spread into the Balkans, North Africa, and even Italy itself eventually), were wholly successful in fostering a new kind of bondage, the later 'colonate' (a form of tied peasantry).[57] Their motive for the latter was openly fiscal; the language they used is wonderfully reminiscent of the phrasing repeatedly noted in this chapter with regard to debt-bondage –

e.g. 'compelled by a servile penalty to perform the duties appropriate to them as free men', or 'though they may appear to be free-born they are to be considered as slaves of the land'[58] and, significantly, this time imperial interests coincided with the interests of the large landowners seeking an immobile labour force.

Now, what can 'be in servitude to creditors' have meant in actual practice at the end of the third century of our era, or 'those who ignorant of the law receive your sons or free men for the money which you owe to them'?[59] I do not think we know, nor do I think there was a single answer. But the trend, I am prepared to argue, was towards wiping out the distinction between the debt-bondsman and the slave. It was always possible for the debtor to slide into slavery *de facto* and sometimes *de iure* as well, as in the Biblical provisions of Exodus 21.2–6 and Deuteronomy 15.16–17. Now, however, in the last centuries of antiquity, it may be significant that the texts refer most often to sale (as Dio Chrysostom had already done), and particularly to sale of children. Once they were thrown onto the slave market and transported by slave-dealers, theoretical rights of redemption, if any, became utterly meaningless. And so did imperial prohibitions of the practice. Traditional debt-bondage had finally lost much of its point now that the poorer classes as a whole were being levelled down to a more uniform status of bondage, with the colonate as the key institution. But there were still enough individuals glad to make a quick profit and there were enough hungry men for them to take advantage of. Therefore pawning and sale of free individuals still went on, but now as increasingly marginal phenomena, especially the former, where once they had been an integral part of the labour situation.

Broadly speaking the trend throughout the late Empire was towards uniformity in this respect. If the old classical core, Greece and Italy, still looked somewhat different, that was because there the history of debt-bondage had been utterly different centuries earlier. To begin with, the institution had been more complete and drastic. Unless the sources have misled us completely, in Greece and Rome there came a time when, as the ancient writers themselves phrased it, one whole class was 'enslaved' to another. In the Near East, debt-bondage, for all its importance, never reached such proportions and often it seems to have been narrowed down to the employment of dependent members of the family as pawns, while the *pater* himself remained free from bondage.

Then came the break in Greece and Rome, and it too was complete and drastic. That break did not just happen, nor was it merely the result of a long accumulation of misery and grumbling – it never is. Something new had entered the situation in seventh-century Attica and fifth-century Rome. To attempt to define the changes would be out of place here, for that would require a basic re-examination of the social history of early (post-Mycenaean) Greece and Rome. The effect, in any event, was that debt-bondage was abolished *tout court*, by political action, and its return was prevented by the growing political power of the emancipated class as they became part of a self-governing community, in which they could use their position for both political and economic ends. (It does not matter for this discussion whether the community which emerged in classical times was democratic or oligarchic.) The possessing classes, in their turn, solved their continuing need for a labour force by the employment on an increasingly large scale of chattel slaves, drawn from outside. In the Near East there was no such political development, no general emancipation of the various categories of dependent 'insiders', and therefore little development of chattel slavery as an essential institution.

10

THE SLAVE TRADE IN ANTIQUITY:
THE BLACK SEA AND DANUBIAN
REGIONS

I

The silence of both Greek and Latin sources about the slave trade – at any time or any place – is well known. Usually it was broken only when some special circumstance attracted a writer. Thus among the innumerable references to war captives, the method of disposal and dispersal is customarily ignored. We may assume that Thucydides' exceptional narrative (6.62; 7.13) of how the Athenian expedition under Nicias seized the Sicilian town of Hyccara, removed the entire population and sailed them to Catania, there to sell them for 120 talents, was motivated by the political and military implications of the incident, not by any particular interest in the procedure as such. Similarly, Herodotus' detailed story about the slave-dealer Panionion of Chios and the appropriate punishment he finally suffered, was stimulated by the fact that Panionion specialised in eunuchs (he had young free-born boys castrated and then sold them).[1] Eunuchs aroused a moral indignation among Greek writers which ordinary slavery did not.

The Danubian and Black Sea regions follow the normal pattern in this respect. With the possible exception of one dubious passage in Demosthenes' speech against Phormio (34.10), I have been unable to find any reference to the procurement of slaves from these areas either in the relevant orations of Demosthenes and Isocrates, or in the surviving geographical and ethnographic writings other than Strabo, or in the Borysthenic discourse of Dio Chrysostom, or in Ovid's Pontic epistles (except for some vague, unhelpful remarks in the latter on piracy and kidnapping). The city of Aenus at the mouth of the Hebrus River and the island of Thasos, to take another kind of example, occupied commanding positions in the trade with Thrace and later with the Getae, but there is exactly one mention of slaves passing through their markets, and that a most indirect one (Antiphon 5.20): an Athenian named Herodes

Originally published in *Klio* 40 (1962), 51–59, and reprinted by permission of the editors.

returned some Thracian slaves to be ransomed, probably in the period 417–414 BC. When I say 'exactly one mention' I include not only the literary sources but also the inscriptions. In all the rich epigraphical material from Thasos there is scarcely any reference to slaves at all – and not one even remotely related to slave trade.[2] Nor does a single document from Byzantium or Ephesus illuminate the brief, but certain, evidence from Polybius (4.38.1–4) and Herodotus (7.105), respectively, about the importance of those two cities as centres of the slave trade. In general, individual epigraphical texts tend to prove no more than the fact that slaves existed or that they were sometimes freed or sold or that they sometimes revolted or ran away – points which scarcely need proof but do require elaboration, and that we do not often get.

To be sure, there is a little material about slavery among the people west and north of the Black Sea, especially the Scythians.[3] But whatever that information may be worth, it is not directly relevant to the subject of the export of people from the region for enslavement in Greece and Rome (or even in Olbia and Panticapaeum). There is no automatic correlation between the enslavement of 'barbarians' by more advanced peoples and the practice of the natives in their own society.[4] Besides, the evidence about Scythian society is not worth much. Herodotus and his predecessors really knew something, though the brief surviving reports are very opaque. By the fourth century BC, however, a Utopian myth had been created, which was fixed in that century by the historian Ephorus and repeated with little change and no new or independent information to the end of antiquity; Posidonius apparently being the transmitting agent from Greeks to Romans.[5]

II

The absence of evidence about the slave trade may prove something about the attitudes and interests of ancient writers, but it proves nothing about the existence of a slave trade or its character or scale. The argument from silence is worthless. From fifth- and fourth-century Athens alone the information is conclusive for the continuous presence there of slaves in considerable numbers from the Black Sea regions. There is the existence from 477 to 378 BC (both probable, not certain, dates) of a police-force of state-owned Scythian slaves, originally numbering 300 and later rising to perhaps 1,000.[6] Then there is the fragmentary list of slaves confiscated and sold at public auction following the trials for mutilating the herms: of the 32 slaves whose nationality can be iden-

tified, thirteen were Thracian, seven Carian, and the rest scattered –
from Cappadocia, Colchis, Scythia, Phrygia, Lydia, Syria, Illyria, Ma-
cedonia and the Peloponnese.[7] The stock use of Thratta, Davos and
Tibeios as slave names (sometimes even as synonyms for the word
'slave') in comedy and elsewhere is further evidence. Thratta is simply
the Greek feminine form of the word meaning 'Thracian'.[8] Davos is
identified by Strabo as characteristically a Dacian name, Tibeios as Paph-
lagonian, and it is noteworthy that his other examples of national slave-
names include Getas and the Phrygian names, Manes and Midas,
along with Lydos and Syros. Finally, there is Lauffer's detailed analysis
of the tombstones from the Laurium district of Attica, on the basis
of which (with other evidence) he was able to conclude that in the
Athenian silver mines, where the number of slaves may have reached
30,000 at its peak, non-Greeks were in the majority, and of these,
'most came from Asia Minor and other eastern countries, with a high
proportion from countries having their own mines, such as Thrace and
Paphlagonia'.[10]

The mere presence of Black Sea slaves in Athens implies a Black Sea
slave trade. How, we must ask, did the Athenians get the remarkable
idea near the beginning of the fifth century BC of purchasing Scythian
archers to serve as their policemen (used even to expel boisterous
citizens bodily from the assembly)? Scythians were famous archers and
were employed as mercenaries in the sixth century. But the idea of
buying them – not of hiring them – could have arisen only if Scythian
slaves were already a known phenomenon. Further, the relatively large-
scale use of slaves in the police and the mines implies a continuous,
organised trade. Mere chance – the accidents of piracy and warfare –
might maintain a general supply, but it could not guarantee that the
serious, continuous need for specialists would be satisfied on time and in
sufficient quantity. This trade, furthermore, was already in existence on
a small scale not later than the end of the seventh century BC, grew
rapidly thereafter and went on continuously – though no doubt with
fluctuations – into the sixth century of our era.

Obviously this is saying more than the Athenian material alone would
warrant. There are, in fact, a few literary texts, scattered through almost
the whole time-range of classical antiquity, which are relevant and most
suggestive once we become more conscious of the simple logic that the
presence of slaves necessarily implies a trade in slaves (when I spoke of
the silence of the sources I did not mean absolute silence but a failure to
show any interest in the slave trade as such). There are two early

references in Archilochus and Hipponax, for Thrace and Paphlagonia respectively, which though the tone leans rather to kidnapping imply at least a primitive trade.[11] Then there is the tradition, recorded by Herodotus (2.134–135), that the famous courtesan of Naucratis, Rhodopis, with whom Sappho's brother became involved, was a Thracian slave transported to Egypt by a Samian. The Thracians, Herodotus writes in another connection, sell their children for export, and Philostratus (*Life of Apollonius* 8.7.12) says the same about the Phrygians. The lexicographers explain the Greek word *halonetos* as having originated (on the model of *argyronetos*, 'bought for silver') in the fact that in the Thracian hinterland slaves could be purchased for salt.[12]

In still another context, namely, the Panionion story, Herodotus (8.105) implies that Ephesus was a slave-trade centre, and it was still performing that role 400 years later, in Varro's time.[13] Polybius suggests that Byzantium was one, too, and Strabo explicitly says that about Tanais at the mouth of the Don.[14] Polybius also writes that the Black Sea regions provided slaves in the largest number and of the best quality. We are not compelled to accept his superlatives, but that the number was large enough is clear from the repeated inclusion of Thracians, Getae, Scythians, Phrygians, Cappadocians whenever Roman or late Greek writers name the slave nationalities which fill the streets of the large cities.[15] Finally, I call attention to some relatively late references to 'Scythian' slaves – a remark by the contemporary historian Dio Cassius about the slaves of the emperor Caracalla, Julian's eulogy of his Scythian tutor, and the statement of Synesius that domestic slaves were as a rule Scythians;[16] to the important material in Ammianus Marcellinus on the large-scale slave trading which was a by-product of the flight of the Goths into Thrace in the year 376;[17] and to the evidence of Ammianus, Claudian and Procopius about the supply of eunuchs from regions east of the Black Sea.[18]

Scarcely a single passage in this list is anything more than an oblique indicator. Nor would it be difficult to throw doubt on the reliability of some of the statements or on the general veracity of individual authors. Nevertheless, I cannot see any way to escape the impression by the group of texts as a whole, ranging in time virtually from one end of the ancient world to the other. These are not mere stereotypes, repeated from one generation to the next like the fairy tales about the Scythians or Hyperboreans. On the contrary, almost every passage is unique, the authors are talking about their own society, and the cumulative effect seems to justify the generalisation about the continuous trade in Black

Sea and Danubian slaves I have already put forward. And there is some epigraphical confirmation. Perhaps one third of the slaves whose burial was marked by simple inscribed stones in Hellenistic Rhodes originated in the Black Sea region (defined broadly to include northern Asia Minor), as did roughly one fifth of the slaves with identified nationality in the Delphic manumission texts of the second century BC.[19]

These fractions are not to be taken seriously as precise statistics. However, added to the Laurium evidence for the fifth and fourth centuries, they provide sufficient confirmation of the few but continual hints in the literary sources. So far, no other comparable evidence in bulk has come to light. The nationality of a slave was a matter of considerable importance to a purchaser; this is suggested in various ways, such as the advice of the Peripatetic author of the *Oeconomica* to mix the nationalities as a security measure, both within an individual holding of slaves and within a city[20] – good advice it was, too, as the Sicilian slave revolts were to prove. In Roman law the seller of a slave was required to state the slave's nationality. The reason, says a gloss inserted in the *Digest* excerpt from Ulpian's commentary on the aedile's edict, was that some nationalities were known to make good slaves, others not.[21] The very few Roman slave-sale agreements we possess show that the law was carried out in practice.[22] Most of the epigraphical evidence, however, does not pertain to sales but to manumissions or burials, and then the nationality was a matter of no importance and was rarely given.

As a poor substitute, we must work with names, which are available in abundance. The difficulties are well known.[23] Slaves were by definition nameless. Hence in early Rome, they were called simply Marcipor or Lucipor, until they became too numerous.[24] Varro speaks as if it were always the master who assigned the name, and he gives an interesting illustration of how one might go about doing so. 'If three men each bought a slave in Ephesus', he writes 'one might take his name from that of the seller Artemidorus and call him Artemas; another from the region in which he made the purchase, hence Ion from Ionia; the third names his Ephesius from Ephesus.'[25] It is hardly necessary to add that the number of possibilities was far greater, but it is important to notice that Varro concentrates so completely on the place of purchase that he ignores altogether the slave's nationality as a basis for his name. The fact is that slaves with obvious nationality names constituted a small minority. It is a further fact that there were very few slave names as such in antiquity, that is, names not also borne by free men. Most important of all, there were no specifically slave peoples or nationalities, so that the appearance of (say) Thracian names in a group of documents is of no relevance unless the context proves, or at least creates the probability, that they refer to slaves or freedmen. A fair number of Thracian names are found in early Ptolemaic papyri, for example, but they were mercenaries in origin – free men, not slaves.[26]

Nevertheless, the scepticism which is widely shared is in my opinion a mistake. Thylander's work on the south Italian ports and Mócsy's on Pannonia have shown that name study can produce interesting results.[27] What is needed most urgently is a series of such studies, carried out systematically region by region – further advance in the analysis of ancient servitude generally, I may add, **requires** far more appreciation of regional variations. No very significant **or reliable** quantitative results can be expected, but trends and probabilities will emerge. This is especially true for the Roman imperial period, when the simple distinction between Greek and Latin names of slaves and freedmen is significant (though far from perfect) in indicating eastern or western origin; when, furthermore, after the incorporation of the Hellenistic east into the empire, most slaves with Greek names (if they were not born into slavery) came from the lower Danube, the areas north and east of the Black Sea, and the remote parts of Asia Minor.

At this point one distinction must be made between the areas north of the Black Sea and those to the south. The history of the native populations north of the Black Sea (taking 'north' very broadly again) differed essentially from that in most of the other areas in which the Greeks had settled, because of their instability. Successive waves of migration and conquest characterised this area virtually throughout Greek and Roman history. With respect to slave supply two major consequences follow. First, large-scale wars among the native peoples produced a large supply of captives for export. Secondly, frequent migration and conquest led to a great confusion in nationality, one which neither the Greeks nor the Romans were able to sort out – even if they had wished to, and under ordinary circumstances the subject was a matter of complete indifference to all but a few scholars like Posidonius or Strabo.[28] Hence general statements, like that of Synesius about the Scythian nationality of domestic slaves, are to be taken not literally but generically. By 'Scythians' the future bishop meant Goths, a not uncommon equation in the later Empire, like the identification of Goths and Getae. Before the Goths entered on the scene, 'Scythian' could mean everyone from the vast area north of the Black Sea, and there is a fair chance that such loose usage already prevailed as early as the fifth century BC. What I said earlier about the Utopian quality of ancient writing about the Scythians ties in with this suggestion.

Even now, in the imperfect state of our knowledge, I believe certain general conclusions may be attempted. From the end of the seventh century B C the countries bordering on, and west of, the Black Sea were a constant and significant source of slaves. To the end of the Christian era the southern regions and Asia generally produced more slaves than the northern, but that does not mean that the chattels coming from the latter were few or unimportant. With the *pax Romana*, the northern and north-western areas took on even greater importance than before, one which they retained to the end of the ancient world. I take Ammianus and Synesius seriously on this score. More than that, I believe that the prevailing view tends to underestimate the number of slaves in the later Roman Empire. Whatever the changes which may have occurred in the economic role of slavery or in the treatment of slaves, the numbers were still high and it is numbers which count in so far as trade in slaves is concerned.

No doubt there were fluctuations. Roman conquests in northern and western Europe may, during the period of expansion, have reduced the flow of slaves from the Black Sea areas, just as the incorporation of Asia Minor increased it. The wars among Alexander's successors, the activity of the so-called Cilician pirates in the latter half of the second century B C, and the Mithridatic wars would each have changed the regional balance for a time. Such fluctuations can only be presumed, they cannot be expressed in quantitative terms.

III

Finally I come to the trade itself, to the men like the freedman Aulos Kapreilios Timotheus, who described himself as a slave-dealer (*somatemporos*) on his funeral stele at Amphipolis, dated on stylistic grounds as not later than the first century of our era, and who had a scene engraved on the same stone showing eight slaves, chained together at the neck, being led along in a file.[29] These were the men who have left so little trace in the ancient sources, and even less in our modern literature. We overplay piracy and, besides, we leave the process half-finished. To be sure, Greek and Roman writers and epigraphical texts are as noisy about piracy as they are silent about the slave trade. The explanation is that piracy was an irresponsible, unpredictable activity – once permitted, it was indiscriminate in its victims, seizing Greeks and

Italians who fell its way as well as barbarians. When practised on too large a scale, furthermore, piracy became both symptomatic of, and a stimulus to, a general social and political breakdown, as Strabo (14.5.2) so obviously felt in his account of the Cilician pirates.

I am not suggesting that piracy (or kidnapping) was unimportant in the history of slavery, but that, first, it was not the basic way in which slaves were procured (especially not during the long periods when one major power or another succeeded in reducing such activity to very small proportions); secondly, even when it was most active piracy could not have been a complete explanation. What did the pirates do with their captives? The answer is that, when they did not ransom them (which they did often), they turned them over to professional traders, precisely as armies did with their captives. The army as a slave-supplying instrument deserves a full study by itself, for it performed that role from the beginning of the ancient world to the end – consciously and systematically, employing various agencies and devices in different periods and different circumstances. At the beginning of this chapter I mentioned Thucydides' two brief references to the Hyccara captives, numbering at least 7,500. That is one clear example. Another, immediately relevant to the Black Sea area, is the invasion of Scythia by Philip II of Macedon early in 339 B C, which, according to a tradition that probably goes back to the contemporary historian Theopompus, produced in booty 20,000 women and children (among much other wealth).[30] A third, equally relevant example, is the slaving activity of Roman officers in Thrace in 376 A D, described in detail by Ammianus.[31] The army, I suggest, was always a more significant factor in the picture than piracy.

Nor is that the whole story of slave procurement by any means. In his life of Apollonius of Tyana (8.7.12), Philostratus gives a lengthy, highly rhetorical speech that his hero was supposed to have prepared for his trial before the emperor Domitian on a charge of murdering a well-born Arcadian boy. 'Although,' he says, 'one can buy here' in Rome 'slaves from Pontus or Lydia or Phrygia – indeed, you can meet whole droves of them being conducted hither, since these, like other barbarous nations, have always been subject to foreign masters and see nothing disgraceful in slavery – the Phrygians are even accustomed to sell off their children . . . , the Greeks, on the contrary, love freedom and no Greek will ever sell a slave out of his country. That is why the kidnappers and slave-dealers never travel about in Greek areas.' Philostratus is not the most reliable ancient writer, but this particular passage, for all its rhetoric, is a general sociological statement that I see no reason to question.

It says what we could have guessed anyway from a study of slave procurement in other societies for which documentation is available, that there was a day-in, day-out operation, quite apart from wars and piracy, in which professional traders travelled to often very remote areas and purchased free children and adults (as well as captives) from the natives for export to the Greek and Roman worlds. Nor were the merchants always Greeks or Romans. The emperor Julian is reported to have rejected proposals in 362 that he campaign against the Goths on the Danubian frontier, saying that he 'sought a more worthy enemy; the Galatian merchants were good enough for the Goths, whom they offered for sale everywhere without distinction of rank.'[32] Such steps in the procurement process were far too remote for ancient writers to describe, and it is no use pretending that we will ever get any sort of picture (except by analogy from more modern experiences). But a clear hint is given by Procopius. The Abasgi, he writes (8.3.12–21), are a people living along the eastern Black Sea coast as far as the Caucasus. Power was in the hands of two chiefs, who made it a practice to seize handsome young boys, emasculate them and sell them at high prices into Roman territory. Until Justinian put a stop to the practice in the course of converting the Abasgi to Christianity, Procopius concludes, most of the eunuchs at the emperor's court, and among the Romans generally, came from this one nation.

Omitting the eunuch factor, Procopius' account can be paralleled exactly in innumerable instances in medieval and modern times all over the world.[33] No quantitative evaluation is possible, but I should rank this non-warfare, non-piracy procedure high among the ancient techniques of slave procurement – particularly so in the very regions under consideration in this paper. One must stress the role of the chieftains and the nobility, as does Procopius (and all the evidence from more modern times). This trade not only helped pay for Greek and Roman imports into native areas, but also enriched the chieftains and nobility and laid the basis for sharper social differentiation, as well as partial Hellenisation, among the Scythians and others.[34] Once procured, the new slaves were moved from inland points to the main coastal centres and from there all over the Mediterranean world.

11

TECHNICAL INNOVATION
AND ECONOMIC PROGRESS
IN THE ANCIENT WORLD

It is a commonplace that the Greeks and Romans together added little to the world's store of technical knowledge and equipment. The Neolithic and Bronze Ages between them invented or discovered, and then developed, the essential processes of agriculture, metallurgy, pottery, and textile-making. With these the Greeks and Romans built a high civilisation, full of power and intellect and beauty, but they transmitted to their successors few new inventions. The gear and the screw, the rotary mill and the water-mill, the direct screw-press, the fore-and-aft sail, glass-blowing, hollow bronze-casting, concrete, the dioptra for surveying, the torsion catapult, the water-clock and water organ, automata (mechanical toys) driven by water and wind and steam – this short list is fairly exhaustive, and it adds up to not very much for a great civilisation over fifteen hundred years.

Paradoxically, there was both more and less technical progress in the ancient world than the standard picture reveals. There was more, provided we avoid the mistake of hunting solely for great radical inventions and we also look at developments within the limits of the traditional techniques. There was less – far less – if we avoid the reverse mistake and look not merely for the appearance of an invention, but also for the extent of its employment. Food-processing offers a neat illustration. In the two centuries between 150 BC and AD 50 (in very round numbers) there was continuous improvement in the wine and oil presses used on the Roman *latifundia*. I am not referring to the screw-press, but to such advances as refinements in the shape of the millstones and their cores, by which craftsmen made presses more efficient and more manageable.[1] Somewhere in this same period the water-mill was invented, and this must rank as a radical invention permitting the replacement of muscular power, human or animal, by water power. But for the next three centuries its use was so sporadic that the total effect was very slight.[2]

Originally published in *Economic History Review*, 2nd ser., 18 (1965), 29–45, and reprinted by permission of the editors.

In agriculture there was an accumulation of empirical knowledge about plants and fertilisers. But there was no selective breeding (of plants or animals), no noticeable change in tools or techniques, whether of ploughing or exploiting the soil or harvesting or irrigating. There were repeated shifts in the uses of land, of course, but these were responses to political conditions or to changing consumer fashions (notably the insistence that status was commensurate with the whiteness of one's bread) or to rudimentary economic pressures. Neither increased productivity nor economic rationalism (in Max Weber's sense) was ever achieved in any significant measure, so far as we can tell. Someone in Gaul invented a rude ox-powered mechanical reaper which was used on the *latifundia* in the northern districts of that province, but it neither inspired landlords elsewhere in the empire to imitation nor inspired anyone to seek labour-saving devices in other branches of agriculture.[3] By contrast, an English translation of the fourth-century Latin writer Palladius, who gave a brief description of the Gallic device, was the direct stimulus for the invention of 'Ridley's stripper', which had a useful and profitable career in Australia for forty or fifty years (at least to 1885).[4]

In mining, room for invention was in a sense very constricted. The few tools needed were already developed long before the Greeks, and little improvement was possible until the invention of explosives. Where there was much to be done, however, was in the areas of prospecting, engineering, and refining, and the ancient world reached its maximum achievement very early, in the Athenian silver mines of the fifth and fourth centuries B C. The tunnelling, ventilating, and lighting in those mines, the washing, crushing, and smelting in the near-by mills and furnaces, and the utilisation of by-products were all as competent and efficient as anything to be found in the next thousand years, and better than most.[5] The geology of the Laurium district saved the Athenians from the most serious challenge, that of drainage. Others were less fortunate, notably in the western and northern provinces of the Roman empire, and once again there was a failure of effective invention. 'The cost and inefficiency of ancient drainage machinery made it difficult to mine below the ground-water line'.[6] Apart from the so-called Archimedean screw, for which there is only scattered evidence, reliance was placed either on hand bailing or on a water-wheel operated by a foot-treadle. So technically simple a device as the chain-pump with animal power is unattested.

The sheer craftsmanship of the work in the Athenian mines requires comment because it introduces a necessary distinction into the discussion.

There was a precision, a perfection of measurement, and hence an aesthetic quality, about the gallery walls and the steps – to give but two examples – which were never duplicated in antiquity. For parallels one must turn not to other mines, but to the contemporary temples and public buildings of Athens. The quality is psychological, so to speak, not technological. The artisans of fifth- and fourth-century Athens, whether free or slave, had a tradition of craftsmanship which imposed itself even in the most 'unlikely' places, such as the galleries of the silver mines. But this factor must not be confused with technical progress. Nor must increasing mastery of materials, an inevitable corollary of pride and virtuosity. I do not underestimate the significance of these qualities, or of the quality of the products which they created. Within fairly broad limits, however, limits which the pre-Greek civilisations of the eastern Mediterranean had already reached, such considerations of quality are irrelevant in an analysis of technological and economic growth. The unmatched beauty of Greek coins, after all, contributed nothing to their function as money (except to modern collectors, of course, which transfers the question to an altogether different realm of discourse).

Painted pottery is the best instance, one which takes on special significance from the fact that it is the only ancient industry whose history we can write (or will some day be able to write). The potter's wheel is a very ancient invention, and the Aegean world of the Bronze Age already knew all about the properties of clays, how to fashion a variety of pleasing shapes, how to colour and fire and produce a sheen. The heights to which the Greeks then carried this art is evident in museums all over the world. Yet these advances were all accomplished without any technical innovation, by greater mastery of the already known processes and materials, and, above all, by greater artistry. Then, in the course of the fourth century B C, the taste for fine painted pottery disappeared, almost abruptly, and at once there was a sharp decline in quality. But people continued to need pots, and rich Greeks and Romans continued to demand better pots with some sort of decoration. Moulded decorations replaced painting and therefore a new technique was introduced in the industry, the only one in its history throughout classical antiquity. That is to say, the long-familiar technique of casting in a mould was adapted from metal to clay in order to produce commodities in the new style. Experts seem to be agreed that neither the speed nor the cost of production was significantly changed as a result. A new fashion was met by the transfer of an old technique. Fourth-century Greeks were not

Neanderthal men and we need not hail this particular step as a brilliant accomplishment.

There is admittedly a danger, in pursuing this line of argument, of falling into the trap of assuming certain values are always and necessarily paramount. The idea that efficiency, increased productivity, economic rationalism and growth are good *per se* is very recent in human thinking (although it seems to take hold in a most remarkable way once it gets an effective start). *We* might consider the Pont du Gard a fantastically expensive way of bringing fresh water to a not very important provincial town in southern Gaul; the Romans in Gaul ranked fresh water and the demonstration of power higher on the value-scale than costs. That was a rational view, too, though not economic rationalism.

Granted that, the ancient world still presents us with a big question, one that is forced on us by at least two facts. The first is that the ancient world was very unambiguous about wealth. Wealth was a good thing, a necessary condition for the good life, and that was all there was to it. There was no nonsense about wealth as a trust, no subconscious guilt feelings, no death-bed restitutions of usury. The other fact, which I have already mentioned, is that, intellectually (or scientifically) speaking, there was a basis for more technical advance in production than was actually made. Why did productivity then not advance markedly, if the interest, the knowledge, and the necessary intellectual energy would seem to have been present? The question cannot be dismissed simply by pointing to alternative values, not, at least, when one of those was a very powerful desire for wealth and for large-scale consumption.

But first do we in fact know that productivity did not advance? Do we know anything about productivity at all? In a sense which can be expressed quantitatively, the answer must be that we do not. The chronic handicap of the ancient economic historian is lack of figures. Even reasonably reliable population statistics are so rare that the basic question of population growth or decline in a given area within a particular period of time can really never be answered with any assurance. But there are some population figures; there are none for production. Ancient writers never considered the matter and archaeology cannot be expected to fill this particular gap adequately. We are therefore driven to oblique approaches, to indicators rather than indexes, to arguments from attitude and inference and silence, all admittedly tricky and even suspect methods. Yet in the end I am satisfied that I have got the question right.

It will be convenient to start with the intellectual side. And again I begin with a commonplace: the ancient world was characterised by a clear, almost total, divorce between science and practice. The aim of ancient science, it has been said, was to know, not to do; to understand nature, not to tame her. The proposition is true, even if it is commonplace, and attempts to challenge it, which seem to be rather fashionable at the moment, are in my view misguided and certain to fail. Aristotle's verdict holds. At the end of the first section of the *Politics* (1258b33 ff.), he wrote as follows (in Barker's translation): 'A general account has now been given of the various forms of acquisition: to consider them minutely, and in detail, might be useful for practical purposes; but to dwell long upon them would be in poor taste. . . . There are books on these subjects by several writers . . . anyone who is interested should study these subjects with the aid of these writings.'[7] Aristotle was the greatest polymath of antiquity, a tireless researcher, and the founder of any number of new disciplines in science and philosophy. His curiosity was unbounded, but 'good taste', a moral category, interposed to put beyond the pale knowledge in its practical applications except when the application was ethical or political.

Mechanics was one of the new sciences first systematised by Aristotle and his school. In a little treatise on the subject written by an unknown disciple, the principles of the lever, wheel, balance, and wedge are explained by illustrations drawn from a significantly restricted range of instruments. The *full* list is this: the sling, the windlass, the pulley, the dentist's forceps, the nut-cracker, and the swing-beam over a well. The inference is inescapable, to me at least, that the author deliberately avoided any reference to instruments and machines used in industrial processes, and that when he could not do so altogether – in the cases of the windlass and the pulley – he made his references as abstract as possible. There is an interesting contrast here with the earlier Ionian philosophers. They were highly speculative thinkers and their concern was cosmology, a subject much more remote than mechanics. Yet they did not hesitate to draw analogies and clues from the potter's wheel, the fulling-mill, the smith's bellows, and other objects of craft and industry.[8] The Pythagoreans, too, for all their mysticism, carried their interest in waves and rhythmic impulses to very practical, and technically significant, consequences.[9] But then a change set in, and the divorce between science and philosophy on the one hand, and the productive processes on the other, can be traced in an unbroken line to the end of antiquity.

The century and a half after Aristotle marked the peak of ancient scientific achievement, and the man who towered over all the others was Archimedes, the greatest and most inventive scientist in the ancient world. And Archimedes was most praised for his refusal to contaminate his science. As Plutarch expressed it (*Marcellus* 17.3–4), he 'had so great a spirit, so profound a soul, and such a wealth of theories which gave him a name and reputation for a sort of divine, rather than human, sagacity, that he did not wish to leave behind him any treatise on these matters, but, regarding mechanical occupations and every art that ministers to needs as ignoble or vulgar, he directed his own ambition solely to those studies the beauty and subtlety of which are unadulterated by necessity.'

Archimedes' practical inventions, I hasten to add, were military and were made only under the extraordinary and irresistible stimulus of the siege of his native Syracuse by the Romans. The ancients had a passion for recording inventions and inventors. This interest goes back to the era of myth-making: Prometheus is the prime example. Eventually it became highly systematised and a considerable literature grew up on the theme, brought to its climax – as with so many other fields – by the Peripatetics. One can still read a fair example in the seventh book of Pliny's *Natural History*. 'Inventions' must be understood as broadly as possible, for the category included laws, customs, ethical beliefs, arts and crafts, as well as artifacts and processes.[10] The crucial point for us is this, that whereas in the other fields the names of individuals are the rule, in the industrial arts they are very rare: usually only the places of invention are recorded, and sometimes not even those. Writing about the screw-press for grapes. Pliny (18.317) was so precise that he dated its invention (he called it 'the Greek press') to 'within the last hundred years' and a subsequent major improvement even more narrowly to twenty-two years back. But he knew no inventor's name, though he did know who invented the diadem, the shield, music, prose, and the game of ball. Admittedly he could not attribute so recent an invention to Cecrops or Romulus, but he frequently cited conflicting claims and it is evident that in his wide, if uncritical, reading he found none at all for the screw-press. Several ancient cities laid claim to be the birth-place of Homer. Several Italian cities in the seventeenth century contested with equal vehemence (and with equal baselessness) for the honour of the invention of eye-glasses.[11] That symbolises the differences in attitude. In antiquity, 'only the tongue was inspired by the gods, never the hand'.[12] And here we have moved from the realm of pure science to that of popular taste and interest among the literate classes of society generally, and of an implicit moral judgment. It was in those circles (including men like Pliny himself) that the ownership of property rested, in other words, to whom the profits of technical improvements would have accrued in large measure, were there any. I shall have more to say about them later, but first we must look at the technicians.

Specifically, what about the writers whom Aristotle dismissed, but from whom, he conceded, one could learn all about the practical arts? He had agronomists in mind, but, rather than deal with them, I prefer to go on at once to the most critical and most advanced of all the fields and to consider Vitruvius. He was both an expert practitioner and a man of extensive and intelligent reading. In his *De architectura*, written probably in the reign of Augustus and designed as a complete textbook of the subject, Vitruvius drew on his own experience and on the far from negligible body of Hellenistic writing, and he explained scientific principles as well as the best practices. In this work we have the highest example available from antiquity of the knowledge and thinking of a man who was a do-er, not just a know-er, a man, furthermore, who was a first-class engineer as well as an architect. In sequence he dealt with the following topics: architecture in general and the qualifications of the architect, town-planning, building materials, temples, other civic buildings, domestic buildings, pavements and decorative plaster-work, water supply, geometry, mensuration, astronomy and astrology, and finally, 'machines' and siege devices.

Vitruvius was a discursive writer. He had a great deal to say, for example, about the ethics of his profession, especially in the lengthy prefaces to each of the ten books. The last one, which deals with machines, is introduced by a sermon on the carelessness of architects, a trait which could easily be remedied by universal adoption of a law of Ephesus holding the architect personally responsible for all costs exceeding twenty-five per cent above his original estimate. It is all the more significant, therefore, that in the whole work I can find only one passage which considers the achievement of greater economy of effort or greater productivity. Vitruvius recommends (5.10.1) that in public baths the hot-water room for men be placed next to the one for women, so that they can be fed from a single heat source. It will be conceded that this is not a very impressive instance. By contrast, the description of the water-mill for corn-grinding is astonishingly brief, just one short paragraph (10.5.2), and it is absolutely bare of comment, so much so that only the reader who is so minded will appreciate the implications for effort and productivity. Vitruvius gives no hint in that direction. All in all, it is correct to say that for Vitruvius the sole aim of technical advance (apart from aesthetic considerations) is the achievement of operations which are otherwise impossible, or possible only by excessive effort. Since, he writes, stage-curtains and other theatrical devices cannot be operated without machines, I thought it desirable to complete my book with a treatise on machines. He defines a machine (10.1.1) as 'a continuous material system having special fitness for the moving of weights', and discusses under that heading such a miscellany as the scaling-ladder, the multiple-pulley and windlass, the wagon and the bellows alongside the water-mill and the catapult.

Scattered in the prefaces are several stories drawn from the history of inventions. Invariably the circumstance, and therefore the explanation, is either accidental (as in the discovery of the marble quarries at Ephesus when two fighting rams chipped a bit of the hillside) or frivolous (as in Archimedes' discovery of the principle of specific gravity in response to a request for a way in which to unmask a dishonest silversmith). Neither for the past nor for the present nor for the future did Vitruvius conceive of technology as something which could be advanced by sustained, systematic effort. His outlook was altogether utilitarian. Quite the reverse of Aristotle, he discussed only practical matters and referred the reader who wished to bother with 'things which are not for use but for the purpose of our delight' (Ctesibius's automata) to the available literature (10.7.5). Yet on the matter which concerns us, Vitruvius and Aristotle were of one mind. In essence so were all the other writers on such subjects, and it is this unanimity which justifies the argument from silence.

I have considered attitudes at such length not only because of the necessity to hunt for clues there, but also because attitudes are the key to the blockage. Obviously there were material limits or hindrances to technical advance as well. Ctesibius tried to make a torsion catapult with metal springs and he also produced a compressed-air catapult, but he had to give them up as a bad job.[13] Inadequate metallurgical knowledge and lack of precision tools rendered these inventions ineffective. It may be, to take another case, that the delay in the utilisation of the screw-press can be explained by its inefficiency until a proper screw-cutter was invented. But what material conditions prevented men who could make very complicated weather-vanes from getting the idea of the wind-mill? Or from linking the lever and the wheel to make a wheel-barrow?

Above all, what about the water-mill? Potentially it was a technical revolution in itself: 'it was able', writes Forbes, 'to produce an amount of concentrated energy beyond any other power resource of Antiquity.'[14]

Its use was in the one process, corn-grinding, in which there had been a reasonably continuous history of technical advance, a process of immense importance to society, one in which the Roman state, in particular, was immediately concerned. Every 'rational' argument suggests quick and widespread adoption, yet the fact is that, though it was invented in the first century BC, it was not until the third century AD that we find evidence of much use, and not until the fifth and sixth of general use. It is also a fact that we have no evidence at all of its application to other industries until the very end of the fourth century, and then no more than one solitary and possibly suspect reference (Ausonius, *Mosella*, 362–4) to a marble-slicing machine near Trier.[15]

A common 'defence' – I choose the word deliberately because it symbolises a not infrequent false approach to the whole problem – is that use of the water-mill was checked by the absence of swift-running streams. This is no defence at all. Among a number of counter-arguments it is enough to point out that some of the best attested mills were powered from aqueducts, of which there was no shortage in the Roman empire. Even Athens had such a mill in the fifth century AD, and Athens ranks near the bottom of the world's cities when it comes to running water. But the city of Rome had none, or hardly any, until the late fourth century. In the year 39 or 40, the emperor Caligula created a bread shortage in the capital when he commandeered the mill-animals to carry his Gallic booty.[16] By then, beyond a doubt, water-mills were not only known but were functioning effectively. The *Greek Anthology* includes a short poem written about half a century before Caligula, which celebrated the new invention in these words:

> Oh stay your busy hands, ye girls that grind at the mill;
>   Let not the cock that heralds dawn disturb your sleep.
> The river nymphs are bidden by Demeter's will
>   To do your work; and on the topmost wheel they leap
> And turn the axle's winding spokes, upon whose coil
>   Concave Nisyrian's millstone's weight revolves anon.
> A golden age has come again; for free from toil
>   We learn to taste what fruits from Mother Earth are won.[17]

One cannot press a Greek poet too far, but is it altogether fanciful that unconsciously he had put his finger on the essential point? Freeing slave-girls from toil (or animals, either, if one wishes to be more precise than the poet) was not a powerful enough incentive.

It is also necessary to eliminate the argument that lack of capital was a decisive consideration. In the century following the conquest of Egypt by

Alexander the Great, the Ptolemies carried through a massive transformation, all in the interest of the royal revenue. They reclaimed great
quantities of land, improved and extended the complex irrigation system, brought in new crops and better species, introduced iron on a scale
which Rostovtzeff said was 'almost tantamount to a revolution',[18] and
made administrative and managerial changes. But everything they
achieved – and they were prepared to expend great resources – they did
by utilising the instruments and processes of the Greek world from
which they stemmed. Only the sakiyeh for raising water and the screw-
pump were genuine innovations, and their use was severely restricted.

What gives point to this picture is the fact that, simultaneously, the
Ptolemies founded and supported the Alexandrian Museum, for two
centuries the main western centre of scientific research and invention.
There Ctesibius, the greatest inventor of antiquity, was employed in
military technology when he was not exercising his ingenuity on mechanical toys. But nothing suggests that his engineering skill was ever
directed to agriculture or food-processing or manufacture. From its
inception the Royal Society, despite its aristocratic patronage, was
assigned problems of practical utility in a wide range of fields. But not the
Alexandrian Museum. Why not? Why did neither the Ptolemies nor the
Sicilian tyrants nor the Roman emperors systematically (or even spas-
modically) turn their engineers to the search for higher productivity,
at least in those sectors of the economy which produced the royal
revenues? Whatever the answer, it was not lack of capital (or lack of
authority). Funds, manpower and technical skills were made available
(and wasted) in vast and ever increasing amounts for roads, public
buildings, water supply, drainage and other amenities, but not for
production. Of course, the effort to increase productivity might have
proved unsuccessful – but it was never even attempted. I know of only
one exception: it was in the royal factories of Pergamum that parchment
was made practicable and mass-produced. This exception may not prove
the rule, but it at least proves that we are faced with a legitimate
question.

Private capital, it is true, would not have been readily available for the
promotion and utilisation of many of the possible technical innovations.
There were enough individuals who possessed the resources, but not
among the men whose interest lay in production (other than agricultural). Wherever one turns in industry and commerce, the picture is the
same and always negative: one of failure to take steps to overcome the
limits of individual cash resources. There were no proper credit instruments

– no negotiable paper, no book clearance, no credit payments. The desperate search of the 'modernisers' among economic historians of antiquity for something which they can hold up with pride against, say, fifteenth-century Toulouse or Lübeck, is sufficient proof. Barring some odd and dubious text here or there, the best they can produce is the giro system for corn payments in Hellenistic Egypt. There was money-lending in plenty, but it was concentrated on small usurious loans to peasants or consumers, and on large borrowings to enable men to meet the political or other conventional expenditures of the upper classes. Only the bottomry loan was in any sense productive, and it was in-variably restricted in amount and usurious in rate, as much an insurance measure spreading the high risks of seaborne traffic as a proper credit instrument. Similarly in the field of business organisation: there were no long-term partnerships or corporations, no brokers or agents, no guilds – again with the occasional and unimportant exception. In short, both the organisational and the operational devices were lacking for the mobilisa-tion of private capital resources.[19] The one exception points up all these negatives: the Greeks initiated and the Romans carried to a considerable pitch the associations of tax-farmers (*publicani*). Yet this simple idea was not transferred to other economic activities.

Division of labour requires special consideration in this connection. There is a passage in Xenophon's *Cyropaedia* (mid-fourth century BC) which is quoted so repeatedly and with such solemnity by modern writers that I must give it in full. The context is the superiority of the meals provided in the Persian palace with its staff of kitchen specialists. As Xenophon explains (8.2.5):

That this should be the case is not remarkable. For just as the various trades are most highly developed in large cities, in the same way the food at the palace is prepared in a far superior manner. In small towns the same man makes couches, doors, ploughs, and tables, and often he even builds houses, and still he is thankful if only he can find enough work to support himself. And it is impossible for a man of many trades to do all of them well. In large cities, however, because many make demands upon each trade, one alone is enough to support a man, and often less than one: for instance, one man makes shoes for men, another for women; there are places even where one man earns a living just by mending shoes, another by cutting them out, another just by sewing the uppers together, while there is another who performs none of these operations but assembles the parts. Of necessity he who pursues a very specialised task will do it best.

This is an important text, and I shall return to it. But it is no cause for excitement on the subject of division of labour. In the first place, Xenephon is clearly interested in specialisation of crafts rather than in division of labour. In the second place, the virtues of both are, in his mind, improvement of quality, not increase in productivity. And in general the whole 'analysis' belongs to that corpus of rudimentary 'economic' statements strewn among ancient writings which Schumpeter put in their proper place when he wrote: 'Classical scholars as well as economists . . . are prone to fall into the error of hailing as a discovery everything that suggests later developments, and of forgetting that, in economics as elsewhere, most statements of fundamental facts acquire importance only by the superstructures they are made to bear and are commonplace in the absence of such superstructures.'[20]

To be sure, it is not unthinkable that, as one scholar has argued, Xenephon's stress on quality was 'conditioned by the requirements of his comparison. The actual entrepreneur . . . would likely also have brought into calculation the increase in quantity.'[21] It is not unthinkable – but the fact is that no one has yet discovered a sentence in any Greek or Roman writer which makes such a calculation. Division of labour is not often discussed, but when it is, the interest is exclusively in craftsmanship, in quality.[22] Furthermore, everything we know about ancient production argues against extensive division of labour, or even widespread specialisation. It is enough, I think, to point first to the predominance of the *autourgos*, the man who works for and by himself, or of the small establishment with four, five, or six men, throughout ancient history; secondly to the extensive evidence of the public-works accounts recorded in inscriptions, with their incredible fragmentation of the operations, revealing the poverty of entrepreneurial resources and the low level of specialisation on the part of most workers. It is not only the opening analysis of *The Wealth of Nations* which is fifteen hundred or two thousand years ahead in the future, but the pin factory itself.

Richard Baxter said, 'If God show you a way in which you may lawfully get more than in another way (without wrong to your soul or to any other), if you refuse this, and choose the less gainful way, you cross one of the ends of your Calling, and you refuse to be God's steward.' Aristotle would have been appalled at this, although he conceded (*Politics* 1256b38 ff.) that there were men who thought wealth boundless. Old Cato, on the other hand, would have rubbed his hands in glee, adding a cynical grin at the parenthesis, 'without wrong to your soul or to any other'. But he, too, would quickly have parted company from Baxter when he came to such a sentence as, 'God hath commanded you some

way or other to labour for your daily bread.'[23] That was neither the way to
wealth nor its purpose. Cato's gods showed him a number of ways to get
more; but they were all political and parasitical, the ways of conquest and
booty and usury; labour was not one of them, not even the labour of the
entrepreneur.

Impossible as it is to lump the whole of ancient society into one
generalisation, it would not be far wrong to say that from the Homeric
world to Justinian great wealth was landed wealth, that new wealth
came from war and politics (including such by-products as tax-farming),
not from enterprise, and that whatever was available for investment
found its way into the land as quickly as it could. There was never a time,
so far as I know, when the large landholders of antiquity did not prosper
as a class. Agrarian crisis was chronic among the little men, but even in
the worst days of the third century, or the fifth, the magnates drew large
rents and profits from their estates.[24] In most periods they were absentee
urban-dwellers, who left the management and operation of their estates
either to tenants or to slaves and slave bailiffs. In either case their
psychology was that of the rentier, and hence neither their material
circumstances nor their attitudes were favourable to innovation. They
were not so stupid or so hide-bound that they could not abandon grain
production for olive and vine cultivation or pasture when circumstances
pressed them or that they could not (sometimes) tell a better landed
investment from a poorer one. But essentially their energies went into
spending their wealth, not making it, and they spent it on politics and
the good life. In this respect Cato represented a minority point of view,
that of the sumptuary legislation which repeatedly cropped up in antiquity – attempts to prevent the aristocracy from conspicuously wasting
its resources, always a failure precisely because, whatever the fate of any
given individual, the class had a continuous income which even Petronius's Trimalchio could not outrun.

Cato hated to spend money on his farms, and his *De agricultura* is filled
with minute advice about that, advice which can be summarised under
two headings. First, do not waste labour time or equipment; acquire
exactly as much of both as you need, no more and no less, and think up
ways to keep them occupied all the time. Secondly, sell, do not buy;
produce and make on the estate whatever you can to meet its consuming
needs. All this is cheese-paring; it is not economic rationalism. His
advice – to quote Schumpeter again – 'that the landowner should sell
aging slaves before they become useless and that he should show himself as hard a taskmaster as possible when inspecting his estate is no

doubt very revealing in many respects but it does not involve economic analysis'.[25] In a very literal sense, Cato was unable to determine which operation was profitable, which not, and the relative advantages of one against another.[26] Such calculations as he offers are fundamentally unintelligible, and there is his most famous omission, his failure to consider distances from the centres of consumption. Later writers – Varro and Columella – corrected him on this particular point, a matter of common sense, but they, too, if I may be permitted a very old-fashioned expression, lacked the spirit of capitalism.

The objection will be raised that I have looked in the wrong place, among the landed magnates. I accept that, though I cannot refrain from noting that the two centuries covered by Cato, Varro, and Columella were the most fertile in the invention of agricultural machinery – the Gallic reaper, the screw-press, and the water-mill – and that all three manuals seem totally ignorant of what was happening in this field. I then add that there is no other place in which to look. There were, to be sure, prosperous shippers in such centres as Cadiz, Alexandria, and Ostia, who amassed considerable wealth despite their very primitive business organisation. There were men with large investments in mining and industry; but when we scrutinise them more closely – men like the Athenian general Nicias or the Italians who exploited the Spanish mines following the Roman conquest of that peninsula – it turns out that more often than not they, too, were rentiers, obtaining their rents from slaves in mines and mills, rather than from slaves or tenants in the fields. And they were a very small minority, without influence on the shape or direction of the economy. The stress is not on 'minority' – beginnings are usually small – but on the lack of influence. Even in the Roman Empire the quantitative contribution of traders and manufacturers was tiny, their social position low, their future without interest.[27]

There is a story, repeated by a number of Roman writers, that a man – characteristically unnamed – invented unbreakable glass and demonstrated it to Tiberius in anticipation of a great reward. The emperor asked the inventor whether anyone else shared his secret, and was assured that there was no one else; whereupon his head was promptly removed, lest gold be reduced to the value of mud. I have no opinion about the truth of this story, and it is only a story. But is it not interesting that neither the elder Pliny nor Petronius nor the historian Dio Cassius was troubled by the point that the inventor turned to the emperor for a reward, instead of turning to an investor for capital with which to put his invention into production.[28] I do not doubt that he could have found the capital, but ancient writers, when they thought about the subject at all, saw little but the threat of over-production. The extremely low level of demand and its inelasticity – that is the important theme of the passage from the *Cyropaedia* which I have already quoted. In small towns there is so little demand that a man must be jack-of-all-trades, and even then he can scarcely earn a livelihood. In big cities, however, there are more people, and therefore more demand. But even in big cities, Xenophon tells us elsewhere, demand will not stand up to pressure. About 350 B C he produced a pamphlet, the *Ways and Means* it is usually called in English, in which he proposed that the Athenian state should itself become a rentier, investing in slaves to be leased out to private individuals who held concessions in the silver mines. His scheme envisaged so large an increase in mining that every citizen would eventually draw full maintenance from the rental of the state-owned slaves. He argued carefully, meeting possible objections, including the following (4.4–6): 'Of all the activities I know, this (silver mining) is the only one in which expansion arouses no envy. . . . If there are more coppersmiths, for example, copper-work becomes cheap and the coppersmiths retire. The same is true in the iron trade. . . . But an increase in the amount of the silver ore . . . brings more people into this industry.'

Here and in the *Cyropaedia* passage Xenophon thinks of manufacture only for the local market; otherwise there would be no point at all to his remarks. Xenophon was fundamentally right; it is our modern writers who are wrong when they exaggerate ancient export trade, as they often do, to enormous proportions. Export – I use the term to refer to trade out of a city or region, not merely in the narrow sense of trade with foreign nations – was economically significant only in the basic foodstuffs (corn, wine, olives), in slaves, and in luxury goods. For this statement there is ample evidence. And luxuries, though they may have been lucrative to a few merchants, were small and insignificant on the production side. Neither the potters of Athens nor the linen weavers of Tarsus, to take two examples from different periods of local trades which dominated the export market for long periods, were anything more than small crafts-men, working alone or with a handful of staff. The linen weavers, complains Dio Chrysostom (34.21–23), were respectable men, yet they were too poor to afford the 500-drachma fee required by Tarsus for the exercise of the rights of citizenship.

We are too often victims of that great curse of archaeology, the inde-structibility of pots. As R. M. Cook has observed, it is only 'because pottery survives that its industrial importance has appeared great'. In the fifth century BC Athens supplied much of the fine pottery for the whole Greek world and for the Etruscans, and the total production at any one time was the work of about 125 painters working with a still smaller number of shapers and assistants. Furthermore, the evidence is that 'a regular connection between a potter and a merchant or market was unusual'.[29] In the following century this trade died because demand disappeared, but the Athenian economy was not visibly affected, nor was its prosperity any more than Corinth's had been in the earlier age when Athens replaced it in the world market. A few craftsmen were displaced, quality dropped sharply – that is all.

The first century of the Roman Empire offers another kind of example. The fine pottery of this period was the *terra sigillata*, rather simple, well-made red ware, with moulded decorations if any. At the beginning of the period several Italian towns, including Arezzo, monopolised production (hence the name, Arretine ware). But not for long: the Augustan peace and the consequent expansion of population and urbanisation in the western provinces saw the diffusion of the manufacture of *terra sigillata* to various centres in Gaul and along the Rhine. Arezzo was knocked out of the market and quality declined. Out of this and one or two similar developments, in the manufacture of terracotta lamps, for example, Rostovtzeff and others following him have constructed a great theory about economic decentralisation, the ruin of the bourgeoisie, the end of emergent capitalism, and the seeds of the decline of the Roman Empire.[30] I mean no offence, but this theory is an anachronistic burlesque of the affluent society. All that had happened was that a few minor trades overreached the market, some hundreds of craftsmen in the western empire in a few cities were displaced by some hundreds in a few other cities, and nothing else. They were no bourgeoisie to begin with, and imperial society was both oblivious to, and unharmed by, the displacements. Not that all this is insignificant as an indicator. It reveals, first, that the minimum technology and small amounts of capital required, the wide diffusion of craft skills, and the excessive costs of transport by land, all combined to promote diffusion of manufacture when the population spread away from the Mediterranean coasts; and secondly, that production for the domestic market and inelasticity of demand were as predominant as Xenophon believed. On the larger issue David Hume saw the picture exactly, when he wrote: 'I do not remember a passage in any ancient author, where the growth of a city is ascribed to the establishment of a manufacture. The commerce, which is said to

flourish, is chiefly the exchange of those commodities, for which different soils and climates were suited.'[31]

And now I have another story, about another Roman emperor and
another unnamed inventor. This man came to Vespasian with a device
for transporting heavy columns to the Capitol at small cost. The emperor
rewarded him well but refused to use the invention, saying, 'How will it
be possible for me to feed the populace?'[32] I have never been able to
understand this story; the emperors fed the populace at Rome with
bread and circuses, not with jobs. But the oft-quoted gnomic remark
stands in sharp contrast to Arthur Young's 'Every one but an idiot knows
that the lower classes must be kept poor, or they will never be
industrious',[33] and that distinction is not hard to understand. There was
never the slightest danger in antiquity that the lower classes would be
anything but poor, and it did not much matter if some of them, notably
the citizens of the capital cities, were industrious or not. They provided
neither the products nor the profits. Those came from peasants and from
dependent labour, and their industriousness was secured by ways
which had nothing to do with wages or technology.

One constant factor throughout ancient history was the presence of a
sufficiently abundant supply of dependent labour. In the central periods
and regions, both Greek and Roman, they were chattel slaves; at other
times, they were clients, helots, debt-bondsmen, *coloni*. This is obviously
a key fact, but its implications are complex and often elusive. It is not
often that one can point to slaves and say, simply and with confidence,
'There lies the explanation for a static technology and a static economy.'
An occasional one-for-one relationship seems likely, as in the hauling of
ores or draining of water from the mines. Mechanical devices were
sometimes used for these purposes, but normally ore continued to be
brought from the mines in leather bags on the backs of slaves and water
to be removed by hand-bailing, also by slaves. On the other hand, it was
in the Spanish mines (where the exploitation shocked even contemporary writers) that the Archimedean screw was employed,[34] And it was on
the Roman *latifundia*, with their notorious *ergastula*, that most progress
was made with farm machinery. Whatever the effect of slave labour, in
this respect it was not the effect observed in the American South where
the slaves impeded progress by the destruction of fine tools and other
forms of sabotage. Columella (1.7.6–7) raised this question – alone of
ancient writers so far as I know – and curiously, he does so in the context
of corn-growing, while he urges the employment of slaves for the most
skilled jobs, such as vine-dressing. Skilled slave labour in antiquity was

as good as any: that is obvious from fine pottery, metalwork, or monumental buildings.

The crucial test came in the Roman Empire. Internal peace and the inclusion within the empire of many former centres of slave-supply reduced the flow of slaves onto the market (compensated, though to an extent which we cannot calculate, by more slave-breeding). In the later Empire, furthermore, a persistent increase in the parasitical classes – the army, the bureaucracy, and the church – created something of a man-power shortage. When we read, therefore, in Pliny's *Natural History* (18.300) in the sentence immediately following the description of the Gallic reaper, that 'the diversity of methods employed depends upon the quantity of the crops and the scarcity of labour', the implication, the consequence, ought to be self-evident. Unfortunately, the facts belie the logic. Adoption of the water-mill *does* look like another response to shortages of labour (and animals), but we have seen how slow and incomplete the response was in both instances. And otherwise there was nothing.

It is unnecessary to examine the economic history of the later Roman Empire in detail to make the point, with which no one disagrees, that neither technique nor productivity nor economic rationalism made an advance in those final centuries of antiquity. It is, necessary, however, to ask once more why, when circumstances seemed to demand progress on those lines, the only solutions to the problems of labour and production were bureaucratic pressures, greater tax exploitation, and a general debasement of the status (and perhaps the standards) of the free el-ements in the productive population. The answers, I suggest, are those I pointed to earlier. Servile and other forms of dependent labour were very profitable. Such changes as occurred in the Roman Empire in the position of the wealthy were political, not economic, and therefore *they* had no significant incentive to alter the productive arrangements. In the end, it was the military and political breakdown of the empire which drove the western aristocracy back onto their estates and to the begin-nings of a manorial system.

The interests of the state were another matter; from the second century on, the emperors were faced with continuing difficulties and crises in supplies and revenues. *They* had good reason to think of more produc-tion. That, instead, they thought of more regimentation, of a bigger bite out of the old pie, seems to me explicable largely in terms of attitudes, of thought-processes. Not even that extraordinary but anonymous man, who in the fourth century wrote a short work, *De rebus bellicis*, begging the emperor (probably Valentinian I) to adopt a number of military inventions which would save both money and manpower, had any idea that inventions might also be applied to civilian purposes. He poured out his indignation at the misery and poverty of the people, at excessive taxes, at the idleness and hoarded wealth of the aristocracy. He praised the inventiveness of the barbarians. But he had none himself outside the traditional field of military technology.[35]

The pejorative judgments of ancient writers about labour, and specifically about the labour of the artisan, and of anyone who works *for* another, are too continuous, numerous, and unanimous, too wrapped up in discussions of every aspect of ancient life, to be dismissed as empty rhetoric. In other slave-owning societies for which there is fuller documentation, these implications and their practical effects are unmistakable. Writing about the Great Trek, for example, Sir Keith Hancock said: 'The Boers very soon convinced themselves that artisans' work and slaves' work were the same thing – a conviction which struck such deep roots in their minds that their descendants in the nineteenth century left to British immigrants almost all the opportunities of skilled industrial employment in the expanding towns.'[36] Or Tocqueville, whose 1831 notebooks are filled with the theme that 'slavery is even more prejudicial to the masters than to the slaves', because, as a leading Louisville merchant said to him, 'it deprives us of the energy and spirit of enterprise that characterises the States that have no slaves'.[37] Greek and Roman slavery functioned in a different context, to be sure, both internally and externally, and comparisons must be made with caution and reserve. But this particular one seems to me to be valid and necessary.

Nothing that I have said should be taken to suggest that there was no technical or economic progress whatever in antiquity. Obviously the range and quality of products were enhanced and standards of life rose, at least for the rich. The spread of urbanisation suggests, and the quality of urban living confirms, that a larger share of the total income was available for non-productive expenditures. And there was a more or less continuous rise in population, probably through the first century after Christ. This last point is tricky. It requires qualification, and it reveals, more decisively than anything else perhaps, the low upper limit to economic expansion. Population rose in the sense that there were more Greeks in the fifth century BC than in the eighth, more Romans in the first century BC than in the fifth. In the same time-spans, however, Greeks and Romans, respectively, occupied far more territory. That is the only way a rising population could be absorbed, and to appreciate the significance of this point, we must remember that for most of the period under discussion, the terms 'Greeks' and 'Romans' are abstractions, not the labels on actual political and economic units. The so-called Greek colonisation period from about 750 to about 550 BC, for example, during which new and independent Greek states were established as far east as Trebizond on the Black Sea and as far west as Marseilles, represented no real gain to the original Greek settlements in the Aegean. They were merely the consequence of population outstripping the available means (even after allowance is made for inequitable distribution of goods).

The ancient world had only two solutions to the disequilibrium brought about by a serious increase in population. One was to reduce the population by sending it out. The other was to bring in additional means, in the form of booty and tribute from conquests. Both are stop-gaps, not solutions, and therefore proof of an incapacity to raise productivity sufficiently, or, indeed, significantly. For a relatively brief time Rome offered the illusion of an escape from this dilemma. Having acquired large, sparsely occupied areas, she proceeded to a rapid internal colonisation (in Spain and Gaul, for example). The illusion came to an end in the first century. Some historians think that there followed a stable equilibrium, Gibbon's golden age of the Antonines, but it is unnecessary to debate the question. Barbarian pressures now began to place new demands on the empire. That challenge the economy and the political organisation could not meet in the west.

PART THREE

MYCENAE AND HOMER

ZJZJZJ

12

MYCENAEAN PALACE ARCHIVES
AND ECONOMIC HISTORY

I

In June 1952 Michael Ventris made the unexpected discovery that the language of the clay tablets written in the Linear B script is Greek. The earliest Greek writing was thus pushed back more than half a millennium, to the period, roughly, 1400–1200 B C.[1] Late in 1953 Ventris published his findings in an article prepared in collaboration with John Chadwick,[2] and immediately there came a rash of articles in the press and learned journals, much of it ephemeral and too much of it misguided and misleading. Only a very few experts were in a position to judge this flow for the next three years, until Ventris and Chadwick produced their great 450-page work in 1956, with massive philological, archaeological and historical learning, thoroughly documented and illustrated; for the first time, the non-specialist could see for himself exactly what has been accomplished and what there is to be learned.[3] Part I of the book gives a history of the decipherment, a detailed analysis of the script and language, and a brief, tentative summary of findings on Mycenaean history, economy, social organisation and culture. Part II presents 300 selected texts, with translations and very detailed commentaries, occupying altogether more than half the volume. The closing section consists of a complete vocabulary, a list of all personal names, a bibliography of well over 200 items, a general index, and a table of concordances.

Although it is too soon to judge the full significance of the decipherment for the history of the period, there is every likelihood that economic

Originally published in *Economic History Review*, ser. 2, 10 (1957–58), pp. 128–41, as a review-article based on Ventris & Chadwick (1956). That book remains fundamental for all Mycenaean study and I have therefore retained the original text, making only a small number of essential corrections in matters of fact made necessary by subsequent finds. I have not attempted to bring the bibliographical references up to date, with very few exceptions; on the contrary, I have reduced the annotation by eliminating comments on ephemeral articles published in the years immediately following the decipherment of Linear B. The article is reprinted by permission of the editors of the *Economic History Review*.

history will be one of the chief beneficiaries. This review will attempt not only to assess the material in its present stage, but also to suggest, in very general and hypothetical terms, some of its broader implications for economic history, both methodological and substantive.[4] The number of known tablets is somewhat over 3,500, many of them small fragments while others have only proper names. The 300 published in the Ventris–Chadwick volume exemplify every type and include every tablet which has any individual significance. Thus far, Linear B tablets have been found only in Knossos and Chania in Crete and on the mainland in Pylos, Mycenae, and Tiryns (in the Peloponnesian peninsula) and in Thebes.[5] In length, the inscriptions vary from three or four words to a maximum of about 150, with the short ones far more common. In context they are, without exception, archival entries of one sort or another, chiefly lists and inventories stripped down to the barest minimum of words and figures. Not a single communication, agreement, administrative ruling, law, or judicial decision has been found; nothing, in other words, which can throw light on the raw postings we have; and, furthermore, nothing to show directly any connection with the outside world.

The interpretation of the texts – and, indeed, the decipherment itself – thus suffers from an almost complete lack of contextual control. Hypothetically, one could go through a considerable number of tablets reading 'Linen clothes from D.: one cloak, one tunic' (219 = KN L 594), and the like, get every single word wrong, and not know it.[6] And one can easily suggest a dozen plausible explanations of such an inventory, with no possibility of deciding among them. The script of the tablets is made up of eighty-seven syllabic signs, perhaps 250 ideograms (counting variants), numerals, and symbols of weight and volume. Taken together, the 300-odd signs are singularly inadequate for the Greek language, and the critics of the decipherment have made much of that fact. I shall return to the point in the next section. Here it is necessary to note only that the awkwardness and deficiencies of the script constitute a second major block in the progress of decipherment and interpretation.

The authors divide their documents into six categories:

1. *Lists of Personnel* (41 tablets from Pylos, 18 from Knossos, and 1 from Mycenae). Some are very brief enumerations: 'Seven corn-grinding women, ten girls, six boys' (1 = PY Aa 62). Others add the ideograms for wheat and figs together with symbols of quantity, and Ventris and Chadwick take that to mean rations. Still others, much longer, seem to catalogue men under administrative headings, specific work assignments, and the like, and even on an optimistic view little sense has so far

been made of them, with the possible exception of one group (nos. 53–60), which may, as the authors believe, record naval and military assignments of manpower made in anticipation of an attack on Pylos (and presumably the very attack which brought about its destruction).[7]

2. *Livestock and Agricultural Produce* (11 Pylos, 32 Knossos, 4 Mycenae). The livestock tablets are all brief. They reveal very large numbers of sheep, goats, and pigs (in that order), few cattle, and even fewer horses. In many, the excessive preponderance of rams over ewes and the frequency of round numbers in the totals shows that these are not flock censuses. Ventris and Chadwick suggest 'tribute imposed on his subjects by the overlord' (p. 198).[8] The produce tablets are also brief, yet sufficiently varied to suggest rations (grain, olives, figs) in some cases (to groups rather than to individuals), requisitions in others. Several quite detailed spice-lists from Mycenae have attracted particular attention, and at present they can be explained ad lib.[9]

3. *Land Ownership and Land Use* (47 Pylos, 12 Knossos). These are the most complex of all the documents, the most widely discussed, undoubtedly the most important – and the most unintelligible. A one-paragraph summary of their contents is impossible, and consideration will therefore be postponed to section III.

4. *Proportional Tribute and Ritual Offerings* (33 Pylos, 9 Knossos). Under this rather curiously worded and not altogether consistent heading, the authors include a miscellaneous assortment of texts, which they consider to be distinguished from the others by explicit indication that 'the operations are evidently of a seasonal or periodic nature' (e.g. 168 = PY Es 644: 'The year-by-year contribution of Kopreus: 84 l. wheat' and so on for 13 entries, each with a different name and amount);[10] by indication of 'assessment', 'contribution', and, if necessary, 'deficit'; or by other indications of a fixed schedule of 'tribute or offerings', sometimes religious in character (e.g. 172 = Tn 316, lines 8–10: 'PYLOS: i-je-to-que [perform a certain action?] at the [shrine] of Zeus, and bring the gifts and bring those to carry them. To Zeus: one gold bowl, one man. To Hera: one gold bowl, one woman. To Drimios the priest [?] of Zeus: one gold bowl, [lacuna]').[11]

5. *Textiles, Vessels and Furniture* (18 Pylos, 22 Knossos, 4 Mycenae). This category includes inventories of a considerable variety of goods. Most are either of the type 'From Dawo (?): . . . Three cloths of tu-na-no type measures of wool' (210 = KN Lc 526); or of the type 'One chair of spring (?) type, inlaid with kyanos (?) and silver (?) and gold on the back (?)', etc. (244 = PY Ta 714). But others suggest or explicitly indicate an operation or an occasion, and the more the detail the less the intelligibility.

6. *Metals and Military Equipment* (19 Pylos, 29 Knossos). This category is broadly comparable to the previous one, with the added interest that, from the nature of the things listed, there is considerable scope for comparison with archaeological finds, and the authors have taken full advantage and made excellent use of the opportunity.

II

The vocabulary of the tablets is remarkably restricted: apart from proper names, the total is 'no more than 630 lexical units or separate "words"'' (p. 385).[12] The significance of this fact is underscored by three additional considerations: (1) Although the texts span about 200 years and come from three relatively scattered sites, there is an altogether astonishing uniformity in language, and a less complete, but still striking, identity of content. 'Fresh finds', the authors say, 'may lead us to revise our views on this point; but at present the dialect presents an extraordinary degree of homogeneity compared with classical inscriptions as widely scattered in time and place. Not until Hellenistic times was Greece to recapture such linguistic unity' (p. 76). (2) The texts are highly formulaic, as much so in the complicated land-tenure tablets as in the simpler inventories.[13] (3) The physical survival of the tablets was accidental in a very special sense. The tablets were made of a plastic clay, written on when the clay was wet, and then dried but not baked. All the evidence (and notably the absence of dating) makes it clear that they were intended as purely temporary records. Ventris and Chadwick even suggest that they were 'pulped at intervals of a year or less' (p. 114). What survived, then, were those particular tablets which happened to be stored away at the moment when Knossos, Pylos, and Mycenae, respectively, were destroyed, and which happened to be fired during the actual destruction.

Several inferences and conclusions may be drawn. The prospect is poor that new finds will significantly enlarge the range of texts, either in substance or in language. It is extremely improbable that conflagrations in different places, at different times, should by mere coincidence have selected for survival the same types of documents out of a much more varied collection.[14]

Documentation in some form surely extended to a far greater range of activity than the existing tablets reveal. Not only is it inconceivable that there was nothing in writing regarding foreign relations (political or commercial), for example, but there is proof of further activity in the tablets themselves. The handwriting shows that at least six different scribes wrote thirty-eight of the Mycenaean texts, and that 'more than thirty were responsible for each of the Pylos and Knossos sets, in some cases a particular scribe being associated with a single kind of record' (p. 109).[15] The tablets we have are altogether insufficient, either in number or in range, to warrant so many professional scribes, and we must assume a considerable activity which has escaped the archaeologist's spade completely. It is futile to speculate about the reasons which determined the choice of materials used in documentation at this time. A survey of the practices followed in Asia Minor, Mesopotamia, and Egypt in the second millennium B C will reveal a great variety of patterns in this respect, and rarely, if at all, can we understand the choices; any more than we can adequately explain why some peoples used the most durable of all materials – stone – for a great variety of texts, whereas the rulers of Mycenae, who were great builders in stone, never recorded anything on it. The one mistake we must not make is to assume that temporary records automatically indicate relatively insignificant operations. There was neither the antiquarian interest nor the economic interest (i.e., long-range calculation or analysis) to motivate the preservation of documents once an operation was completed or a set of relationships modified. Records served current needs; habit, fashion, or the availability of raw material – not importance – determined the choice between clay, for example, and papyrus.[16] It follows then, with respect to the content of the Mycenaean tablets, that the argument from silence is more unreliable than ever, barring a few special contexts.

The peculiar circumstances of survival give us a plane surface without depth. We can learn something about Mycenaean institutions at the moment of their death, but nothing in the tablets reveals their history – not even a five-year history, let alone a five-century history. To be sure, the relative constancy and uniformity of the texts may seem to suggest that little had changed from Knossos in 1400 B C to Pylos and Mycenae in 1200. Even if that were the case, however, it is not a proper inference that similar lack of change characterised the Bronze Age ever since 2000 B C. The whole archaeological record argues against that, and so does the evidence of language and script. This is an unpleasant situation and, in this extreme form, an unusual one; but to pretend that it does not exist and to invent a history behind the tablets (largely out of etymologies and comparative philology), as is being done on all sides, is to invite the kind of revulsion which, in anthropology under analogous conditions, led many virtually to expel history from the realm of rational discourse.

It is a commonplace that, at the end of their history, institutions are often expressed in terms and forms which have lost their original meaning altogether, and which are therefore utterly misleading to the outside observer. In this context, however, that needs stressing. The severely limited vocabulary, the nearly rigid uniformity of language, the formulaic staccato of the texts, even the stylised shapes and layouts of the tablets[17] – all of these are the mark of a long scribal tradition, of a small professional class with its peculiar jargon, keeping records which no one else need read (or, in all likelihood, did read). There, I am confident, lies the key to the notorious inadequacy of the script for the Greek language. Greek poetry is inconceivable in Linear B, continuous prose is possible though unlikely, but inventories and the like would be perfectly intelligible to the initiates (much like any code).[18] But there, too, lies our greatest difficulty. A combination of ossified terms and code-like formulas makes up one continuous trap: words often mean anything but what they seem to mean, as the study of cuneiform and hieroglyphic texts has shown over and over again.[19] Before returning to the substance of the tablets, therefore, it is necessary to have a look at the present state of the decipherment.

In introducing the 630-word vocabulary, Ventris and Chadwick offer the following arithmetic: forty per cent of the words

have forms which can, allowing for historical evolution, be directly equated with Homeric or classical forms, and have corresponding meanings which fit the context of the tablets with virtual certainty . . . The remaining sixty per cent include compounds without later equivalents; spellings where the context does not allow a conclusive choice to be made between alternative identifications . . . ; and finally forms which cannot yet be explained etymologically, though their approximate meaning and function may be apparent from the context (p. 385).[20]

Semantically, however, the picture is in fact more negative than that, for the following reasons.

As the authors themselves warn in their opening chapter, 'Even where the dictionary meaning of the words on the tablets can be established with certainty (for example in a phrase like 'the smiths did not give' on 176 = PY Ma 123), there is no guarantee that we can understand the full significance of such a remark; and the actual situation or transaction which the scribe is recording can sometimes only be guessed at with the aid of very distant analogies' (p. 27).[21]

Of the forty per cent, the 'virtual certainty' of Ventris and Chadwick often turns out to be restricted to philological connection with Greek, and not to extend to the meaning in the tablets. For example, there is the important word *wo-ze*, which they define as 'works, performs, possibly "ploughs"'. The suggested alternative itself belies certainty, and on pp. 254–5 there is a lengthy discussion of the word made necessary precisely because 'its significance in this context is uncertain'. The context is land tenure, and in that context scarcely a single word can yet be given a clear sense. Thus, *da-mi-jo* is defined as 'a kind of agricultural holding, perhaps equivalent to an *onaton paro damoi*'; yet *da-mi-jo* is included in the forty per cent, *o-na-to* (defined as 'a holding, lease or purchase [?] of land') is in the sixty per cent, solely because the former seems clearly tied to the Greek *demios*; whereas the latter has no equally obvious Greek link (pp. 235–6).[22]

The way in which types of words fall into the two categories renders the forty per cent group less significant for the historian. Much of it – though by no means all – is made up of names of objects or descriptive adjectives. In the other group come virtually all the words which seem to define the character of land holdings, most occupational terms (a numerous class), and all but three of the fairly large number of 'titles' indicating social or political status.[23]

It is impossible, therefore, to express the present state of the decipherment in meaningful percentages. Progress on the linguistic side has far outstripped progress in interpretation of the contents. That is precisely what could have been predicted. Hieroglyphics and cuneiform scripts have been read for a very long time, and the texts are incomparably superior in number, variety, and length. Yet our understanding of Babylonian and Egyptian land tenure, for example, remains very imperfect.[24] The immediate question before us, then, is not a consideration of this or that detail in the Mycenaean world, but such general considerations as may legitimately be raised at this stage.

III

All the tablets were found in (or in close conjunction with) the palace ruins.[25] That is an archaeological fact of basic importance, for it leads to the hypothesis that we are here in contact with a far-reaching and elaborately organised palace economy of a broad type well attested and heavily documented all over the ancient Near East.[26] Such an economy was unknown in Greece after the fall of Mycenae, and, logically enough, equally unknown were archives and administrative texts of this character and the large, complicated palace structures with their great magazines and archive-rooms.[27] How far the Mycenaean palace economy

actually reached, whether it covered the whole of the economy or left
some areas to independent 'private' activity, is not now determinable,
but I suggest that the former is the better working hypothesis.

At least this much seems deducible from the tablets: that the palace
records embraced agriculture and pasturage; a great range of specialised
productive processes; stores of goods of a variety and number which
point well beyond the mere consumption needs of the palace narrowly
conceived (even allowing for extensive waste and conspicuous display);
and a numerous personnel hierarchically ordered from 'slaves' to the
king at the top, each stratum connected in the actual texts with either a
function (including military and religious as well as 'economic') or a
holding of land, or both. In all this activity, a number of important things
are missing. No word on any existing tablet has been read which can
confidently be taken to mean 'to buy', 'to sell', 'to lend', or 'to pay a
wage' (or the corresponding nouns).[28] Furthermore, Ventris and Chadwick note that they 'have not yet been able to identify any payment in
silver or gold for services rendered' (p. 113), and that there is no evidence
'of anything approaching currency. Every commodity is listed separately, and there is never any sign of equivalence between one unit and
another' (p. 198).[29] Taken together, these silences can, I think, legitimately constitute one exception to the general doubt I raised in section II
about arguments from silence. They reveal a massive redistributive
operation, in which all personnel and all activities, all movements of
both persons and goods, so to speak, were administratively fixed. Work
was performed, land and goods were parcelled out, payments were
made (i.e. allocations, quotas, rations) according to fixed schedules
which were frequently corrected and re-established (perhaps even
annually). Such a network of centralised activity requires records – more
precisely, records in the form, and in the minute detail, which we have
on the tablets. But it can dispense with permanent records, and even, it
would seem, with balance sheets and systematic summaries.

This is not to deny the existence of trade, but there the silence of the
texts blocks us completely. We know nothing about possible exchanges
by individuals after the chain of administrative distribution was completed. More important, we know nothing about foreign trade except
that it existed.[30] We know neither who organised it nor who carried on
the actual operations. If one must guess, I should come down on the side
of the palace, although I am unwilling to hazard any kind of guess about
the personnel or their nationality. The history of the ancient Near East
shows an unmistakable tendency for the palace (or temple) to monopo-

lise commerce whenever it could, and Mycenaean civilisation in the period of the labyrinthine palaces and the elaborate documentation has all the marks of just such a stage.[31] The absence of texts is not decisive here, no more than it is for all foreign relations.

At this point I shall digress to consider the history of one group of cuneiform tablets because it contains a number of valuable lessons for the student of Mycenaean economy. The documents concerned come chiefly from the city of Larsa and span the end of Hammurabi's reign and the first years of his successor's, and they record large-scale dealings in fish (as many as 15,000 fish in one instance). Most of the texts look simple and straightforward, and the conclusion quickly reached by Assyriologists was summed up by Heichelheim in 1938 in his standard *Ancient Economic History*: 'Numerous cuneiform documents deal with the sale and lease of property, which, with the rise of investment capital entailed the possibility of profitable investment . . . Thus fishing was drawn (though only up to a certain point) into the more advanced monetary economic patterns of the ancient Near East . . .'[32] In 1942, Koschaker drew an altogether different picture.[33] In place of large-scale buying and selling, capital, and investment, Koschaker saw a number of purely administrative operations: the fish were delivered to the palace account as obligatory payments by the fishermen, the palace then disposed of the product through an official, the *tamkarum*, though the documents do not permit us to follow the procedure after the latter took charge.

The explanation of this almost incredible divergence of views lies in the texts themselves. They look very much like ordinary sales agreements, with the words customarily translated 'buy' and 'sell', and, worse still, with 'prices' reckoned in silver, with dates of payment and occasional indications of delays in payment.[34] All this, Koschaker discovered, was a fictitious juristic cloak. The documents are not agreements or private records of any kind, but 'sheets' from the palace account books in which, for bookkeeping purposes, all the operations were recorded in fictitious, fixed 'silver' prices, as if the fish had been bought from the fishermen and sold to the *tamkarum*, whereas in reality they were moved from one to the other as part of the network of status operations within the palace economy.

Now Koschaker did not discover palace trade monopoly or an administrative palace economy. Their existence was already well known. But Koschaker's study revealed – and this, in my judgment, makes it a turning-point in economic studies of the ancient Near East – first, that this kind of economy was more prevalent than had been believed;

second, that it might lie concealed in the most unexpected places. Methodologically, it is important to stress two points in particular: (1) Hammurabi's laws turn out to be more hindrance than help in such questions, often ignoring or actually contradicting the legal practices and principles discovered in contemporary documents. (2) The key figure in the Larsa operations was the *tamkarum* (Sumerian *damgar*), who is known from a great variety of places and who appears in all the books as the Babylonian merchant par excellence. Yet now we see that, with no change in title, he was sometimes not a private trader but a member of the palace hierarchy.[35]

The extent of the legal fiction in the Larsa tablets is astounding, for an administrative operation is treated as if it were a private-law transaction, so thoroughly that a generation of experts in the law and language were completely taken in. Nor is this the only instance: the recourse to complex legal fictions was apparently a common phenomenon in the ancient Near East.[36] The reasons, I believe, escape us, but we can be certain that where such fictions are employed, the relevant institutions already have a long and complicated history behind them. By the use of fiction, the scribes of the ancient Near East, who were the jurists, adapted the law to meet new (or revived) needs while retaining the rigidity of form which is so prominent in the documents from this region.[37]

I am not leading up to the proposition that the Mycenaean tablets are full of legal fictions. We are too ignorant for such a suggestion at present, and it will probably turn out to be otherwise. But I have no doubt that a considerable history lay behind the tablets, of which we know nothing. That control over the texts is therefore lacking. And we also lack the control that comes from a variety of texts, private documents and laws to set alongside the entries in a palace archive. 'An administrative document', in Koschaker's gloomy words, 'provides only one link in a chain of proceedings, and only when complete does it reveal the administrative mechanism. Therefore one administrative document is, of itself, unyielding, its exposition a hopeless matter if other links in the chain are not available.'[38] For the Mycenaean tablets this is particularly true of the land-tenure texts, and they are the key to the whole complex of documents.

It is embarrassing to turn to these land-tenure tablets. In three years so much has been written about them, building up a fine picture of the land regime of Pylos (the only site in which a sufficient series of texts has been found), but almost none of it, in my judgment, has any reasonable warrant at this time. Everything rests on a handful of key words (plus the grain ideogram): *da-mo, ke-ke-me-na, ki-ti-me-na, ko-to-na,* and *o-na-to,* which Ventris and Chadwick render as 'village'; 'approx. communal'; '"brought into cultivation (by private initiative?)"', of land not administered by the *damos*; 'estate, plot of land'; and 'a holding, lease or purchase (?) of land', respectively.[39] Except for *ko-to-na,* not one of these meanings is contextually determined or controlled; they have all been deduced philologically. Even when the philologists reach agreement (and they have not got very far), a historian finds himself dissatisfied with the semantics – and it is meaning which is at stake. Of the five words listed, only *da-mo* is 'obvious'. The trouble is that in Homer *demos* already has three distinct meanings (none of them equivalent to 'village'), and later Greek added three or four more. Although all these meanings have a connection, the selection of the correct one makes all the difference; if, indeed, any one of them provides the proper sense of the tablets. To hit upon 'village', or 'collectivity', even as a convention, is to introduce a very precise and far-reaching interpretation through the back door, and from everything I have already said it will be clear why I cannot accept that definition.[40] *Ko-to-na* presents a difficulty of another kind. The sense of 'field, plot' can be deduced from the formulas, but its one Greek link is the rare word *ktoina,* known only from a small number of Rhodian inscriptions of the third or second century B C (i.e. a thousand years later) and from a corrupt gloss in the Alexandrian lexicographer Hesychius (probably of the fifth century A D). Just what the Rhodian *ktoina* was is by no means clear,[41] but it was surely not a 'small-scale unit of cultivation' (p. 232). The remaining three words require no examination here: the lexical situation is still worse.[42]

Nevertheless, a few facts and conclusions emerge, almost (though not quite) without reading any single word.[43] (1) Minute arrangements regarding land were an important part of the palace economy. Both the complexity and the elaborate controls of the system are evident from a number of hints, of which I shall single out, for the moment, merely the way in which the documents overlap and the very precise numbers in each entry.[44] (2) There were essential juridical distinctions in landholding. Whatever *ke-ke-me-na* and *ki-ti-me-na* mean, they are the names for two contrasting tenure categories (quite certainly not just 'cultivated' and 'uncultivated', or 'arable' and 'pasture', or anything of that character), the former 'almost invariably' linked with the *da-mo* (p. 233). And these two words, though the most common, do not exhaust the types of tenure. (3) The personnel specified in the land tablets may include the whole range of Mycenaean statuses and occupations: king to 'slave', priestess, shepherd, potter, etc. This fact, combined with the absence of any indication of rent (in 'money' or kind), suggests that much (and perhaps all) land was held with an office, status, or occupation, and that obligations to and from the centre were calculated and met by allocations and quotas of land and products (agricultural, industrial, and intellectual). We must imagine a situation in which officials, soldiers, craftsmen, herders, and farmers all held land (or worked on the land) on condition that they rendered either appropriate services or quotas of products, industrial or agricultural as the case may be. We must imagine, further, a variety of complications growing up over the centuries, so that the same individual could hold more than one estate, each under different conditions, or that different ways of allocating raw materials could exist simultaneously, or that allowance could be made for distinctions between 'slave' and 'free', and so forth. In such a system, precise numbers of things and amounts of land would have to appear in the records – and they do; but not equivalent values – and they are not found.[45]

IV

Further progress in the decipherment and interpretation of the tablets – barring the unexpected discovery of altogether different kinds of material – rests of necessity on (1) systematic, quasi-statistical investigation of words, word combinations, and formulas, on the model of cryptographic analysis; (2) complicated philological study of equations with known Greek words and forms; and (3) analogies drawn from other societies. The first two need not detain us. I have already suggested that there are grave weaknesses and dangers in trying to build on Greek words and etymologies. In any event, this is the philologist's work; the historian's comes under the third heading.[46]

Comparative analysis demands some consideration of method. The first question is: comparison with whom? Inevitably, the discovery that the language of the tablets was Greek at once directed attention to Greek sources, and particularly to the oldest, the *Iliad* and *Odyssey*. Elsewhere I have argued at length that this is an illusion, that the discontinuity between the Mycenaean world and the Greek was so great that it is fruitless to look to the latter for guidance in the former.[47] I shall not repeat my arguments here beyond the simple statement that never in the Greek world proper (that is, excluding such basically alien societies as Ptolemaic Egypt) do we find palace complexes, archives, or a palace economy like the Mycenaean. Because the Greek language survived, many Mycenaean terms lived on, too, but it is a mistake to assume that, where institutions are concerned, their meanings remained essentially unaltered in the radically different society whose embryo we see in the Homeric poems. Once that is admitted, the usefulness of Greek analogies ebbs away to a very thin trickle. [48] Other Indo-European analogies, in so far as they rest solely on philology and the discarded myth of Indo-European society, are even less useful. [49]

The alternative source of comparisons is the world which was contemporary with Mycenae – Egypt, Syria, Asia Minor, Mesopotamia – irrespective of membership in one or another language group. Mere contemporaneity, of course, is insufficient warrant for analogy, and I am using the word very loosely, to take in the whole of the second millennium B C and even some centuries outside. [50] However, in considering the administrative economy of the palace, I have tried to indicate a proper base. If I am right, then the direction of further study is self-evident. Ventris and Chadwick have made an important start. 'These contemporary records', they write, 'present the most useful and significant analogies with the Mycenaean tablets, and will often be found quoted in our commentary' (p. 106). The urgent next step is typological. The bits-and-pieces method of comparative analysis is both limited and, ultimately, misleading. [51] The world of the ancient Near East was not all of one piece. Both the material remains and the documents show great variety and considerable movement. A typology must be established, and from that working base, systematic comparative analysis will be fruitful. Out of it, I believe, the palace economy will emerge as the pivotal institution. Mycenae will probably remain on the periphery of such study, because of the nature of the documentation, but the decipherment has at least one significant contribution to make. It helps free 'Asiatic society' from its traditional links with both the 'Orient' and the inundated river-valleys. [52]

By a palace economy I understand a pattern of organisation – economic, social, political – essentially different from any which appears in the traditional western typologies. The presence of some similarities, such as slaves, for instance, or conditional tenures of land, is obvious, but their location within the total context is another matter. 'Some sort of feudal system of land tenure is certain', say Ventris and Chadwick (p. 121), and many who have written on the Mycenaean tablets share that view. But just this, in my opinion, is the stumbling-block to understanding not only Mycenae but also its contemporaries. Nowhere do the exotic feudalisms which so irritated Marc Bloch grow more luxuriantly and in less appropriate surroundings. [53] It is necessary to uproot all the weeds and to consider these social relations as something new and different. [54] That creates very great problems for the historian of the west, who lacks both the concepts and the language, and must invent them. It is a difficulty which demands disciplined boldness, and on the philological side Ventris and Chadwick have set a fine precedent.

- 13 -

HOMER AND MYCENAE:
PROPERTY AND TENURE

Until recently, it has been a received truth that the Homeric poems reflect
the Mycenaean world that came to a fairly sudden end about 1200 BC.
Not surprisingly, therefore, from the very first publication announcing
the decipherment of the Mycenaean tablets, discussion of those documents has been replete with references, parallels, analogies, arguments
and echoes from Homer.[1] The procedure has tended to be haphazard
and arbitrary in the extreme: an odd passage from the *Iliad*, the
appearance of a particular word or name in both the tablets and the
poems, and possible etymological relations are noted when they seem to
prove a point or suggest a meaning; or the absence of such identities is
invoked as evidence. But there has been no systematic consideration of
either the historical problems involved in juxtaposing the two sets of
materials, or of the methodological principles which must be applied if
the analysis is to have any validity. The purpose of this paper is to
examine both aspects of the problem, the historical and the methodological, in one field, the institutions and relationships centring about
property and tenure. I propose to consider, side by side, the extent to
which there seems to be continuity (or discontinuity) between the world
of the tablets and the society of the poems, and the extent to which
material from the poems (whether general considerations, specific passages or individual words) may properly be employed in interpreting the
Mycenaean texts (or vice versa).

I

In the search for odd bits in Homer, there is danger that the basic perspective will become altogether distorted. The archaeological record in
Greece is marked by a very sharp downward break after the destruction

Originally published in *Historia* 6 (1957), 133–59. As in the preceding chapter, I have
eliminated from the annotation comments on older publications that seem to me no longer to
merit re-publication.

of Mycenae. That is a hard fact to which we must hold tight while the argument goes on about Nestor's cup and the types of shields. It creates, of itself, the presumption that the world of the tenth and ninth centuries was very different from the world of the fifteenth, fourteenth, and thirteenth centuries. It is an equally hard fact that four centuries elapsed between 1200 and 800, twelve or thirteen generations, time enough for enormous social and political transformations.[2]

How great the changes were became apparent as soon as the first readings of the Mycenaean tablets were published. The very fact of writing is of the utmost importance; so is the loss of the art after the fall of Mycenae.[3] The poets of the *Iliad* and *Odyssey* lived in an age in which writing had returned to Greece, but the world they described did not write, and managed perfectly well nonetheless. And even the eighth and seventh centuries did not write as the society of Pylos and Mycenae wrote. For records remotely comparable to the tablets we must come down almost a thousand years, to the Athenian and Delian temple inventories; for a closer comparison, to the papyri of Egypt after Alexander the Great.

The point is not merely psychological; it is eminently practical. Illiterate peoples, even rather primitive ones, are capable of considerable feats of memory in the ordinary routines of living. They transmit their mythologies and genealogies, they sort out rather complicated kinship patterns, they know exactly where their hunting and agricultural lands are located, and what the precise status of obligations is at any moment in potlatch or bride-wealth arrangements – all without any records whatsoever. To them it would be accepted as a matter of course that Eumaeus, without consulting documents, could say to a stranger: My master is so rich that 'not twenty men together have so much wealth. I will enumerate it for you': twelve herds of cattle on the mainland, twelve of sheep, twelve of swine, and so on.[4] In the tablets, however, we have no mere enumeration of herds but a complex system of tenures, often interlocking, with a correspondingly articulated, hierarchical structure of the population and elaborate specialisation of occupation and function, with allocations of manpower and supplies, payments to men and gods, all carefully recorded (in fractions if required), catalogued and totalled. Not twenty Eumaeuses together could have kept these operations in their heads.

Neither the tenures nor the operations nor the records have left their mark on the poems. It is incredible that poets who described the construction of a swineherd's hut and the building of a raft and the mooring of a boat and the preparing of a feast could have managed to ignore so completely activities which involved everyone from the *anax* to the slaves, had such activities been part of the world they were writing about. To be sure, one does not expect to find frequent reference to the operational or administrative side of social status and power. But even in *Beowulf*, for example, which is far narrower in its range of interests – more 'princely' – than the *Iliad* (not to mention the *Odyssey*), and which is a very much shorter poem, we can learn of the practice of sending the children of noblemen to royal courts, of the recruiting of followers by gifts of treasure and land, and of the loss of land for failure to perform the services promised.[5] In the *Iliad*, despite its long autobiographical digressions, there is *not one* such note; nor is there in the *Odyssey*, which returns endlessly to the question of Odysseus' estate. I cannot believe that the indifference of the poets is a sufficient explanation for the total absence of tenurial or operational references. The authors of *Beowulf* and the *Song of Roland* and the *Nibelungenlied* were equally indifferent, but *Gefolgschaft* and vassalage and land tenures creep into their poems nonetheless.

The more plausible explanation is that the very structure of society (not merely the scale) had changed. We thus begin, before we turn to any of the details, with the fact of discontinuity, with a break between the Mycenaean world and the Homeric. Looked at whole, the documents have amply confirmed the findings of archaeology. The question is, how deep was the discontinuity?[6]

II

One of the more striking aspects of the Homeric poems is the way in which they ignore the movements of people in the period after the fall of Mycenae – not only the continuing migrations from Greece to Asia Minor and to the west, but also the migrations, conquests, settlements and resettlements which surely occurred within the orbit of the 'Greek' world. There is the account of how Tlepolemos with a large following settled in Rhodes;[7] there is the curious bit where Menelaus says he had intended to transplant Odysseus with his family and his goods and his people to Argos;[8] and there is the precise account of the movement of the Phaeacians to Scheria under Nausithous: 'And he drew a wall around the city and built houses and made temples to the gods and divided up the fields.'[9] This last is the sole reference to the division of the land in the act of settlement (as distinct from the division of an inheritance or of property seized from an individual or of booty), and it may be, as some scholars believe, not a reference to earlier times at all but a contemporary note which crept in from the practice of Greek colonists.

What we find in the poems is the Greek world after the internal movements were finished, the post-settlement period, a period of stability. Cattle raids, sometimes shading off into wars, power struggles, and frequent migrations of *individual* chieftains were common enough – but so were they in many parts of Hellas right through the archaic and classical periods. The number of stories in the poems about individuals who fled, usually because of a family dispute or to escape the consequences of a blood-feud, and who acquired positions of wealth and power abroad is, I believe, decisive. Such situations are characteristic of an archaic society in which the basic patterns of organisation and of occupation of the land have been established, and in which there has been time for the nobles and chieftains to form a network of personal alliances.

Periods of great movements of people 'customarily lead to altogether grotesque combinations of forces which can be disentangled only with difficulty.'[10] In particular, when the migrations bring peoples into areas of relatively advanced civilisation, their social structure often (probably always) undergoes extensive transformation; within a very few generations it becomes unrecognisable, so to speak. That was notably the case with the Germanic invaders of the Roman Empire, whose settlement patterns varied considerably, not only from region to region, but even more from the pre-settlement society briefly described by Tacitus to the fifth and sixth centuries.[11] Probably no other ten lines in all the world's secular literature have provoked so much writing – and so much bad writing – as the twenty-sixth chapter of Tacitus's *Germania*. Today very few responsible medievalists still hold to the nineteenth-century construct of a primeval Indo-European village community, collectively holding the land and redistributing it periodically to maintain equilibrium; a form of organisation which miraculously managed to hold on for thousands of years under the most diverse conditions and developments.[12] Unhappily, the decipherment of the Mycenaean tablets has brought about a revival of these discarded notions in a most unexpected place, in the literature on the worlds of Mycenae and Homer.

Tacitus, after all, was describing an unstable world, in which there was 'at least as much perpetual motion . . . as there was permanent settlement.'[13] We know a good deal about the social consequences of Germanic migrations, and it is most probable that the entry of Greek-speaking peoples into the Aegean early in the second millennium B C was followed by equally massive changes during the five hundred years and more which elapsed until the tablets were inscribed; and that a new situation, with a new series of changes, emerged in the course of the centuries between the fall of Mycenae and the world of the Homeric poems. The injection of the *'Markgenossenschaft'* into the literature on the tablets thus involves a double error: first it resuscitates a dubious historical picture, and then it transfers that picture from one sphere to a very different one, on the sole ground of membership in the Indo-European family of languages (buttressed by some complicated and unconvincing etymological connections of a small number of words).[14]

In the Homeric poems, the property regime, in particular, was already fully stabilised. How the original divisions and settlements were made is scarcely visible, for that had all taken place in the past and belongs to the prehistory of the society. The regime that we see in the poems was, above all, one of private ownership. I do not propose to enter into the largely sterile controversies over the applicability of words like 'private' and 'ownership' to primitive and archaic holdings.[15] It is enough to indicate that there was free, untrammelled right to dispose of all movable wealth – a right vested in a *filius familias* as well as in a *pater familias*; that the continuous circulation of wealth, chiefly by gift, was one of the major topics of the society; and thut the transmission of a man's estate by inheritance, the movables and immovables together, was taken for granted as the normal procedure upon his death. These rights might be disturbed on any given occasion, but that was always because of some defect in the sanctions, specifically in the capacity of the holder of the right to exercise it; never because the existence of such rights was questioned. Even Antinous conceded that both the estate and the kingship of Odysseus were Telemachus's 'patrimony by birth'.[16]

There are difficult problems, to be sure, but usually they centre about the family, and not about the community or an overlord. In so far as rights and claims attached to property were complicated by the fact of illegitimate birth, for example, or by the future interests of heirs, we remain within the limits of what I call 'private' property. That is to say, the choices and decisions, even when they were family matters and not purely personal and individual, were not subject to the rights and powers of some outside agency, whether a feudal overlord or a collective body. And only the latter is germane to our problem. The particular issue we must face is whether or not, in the Homeric world, land was ever held on condition, in the dual sense that retention of the holding required

fulfilment of obligations or services, and that the person (or body) from
whom one held retained a right, if only a formal veto power, to control
the disposition. It is in that area that the degree of continuity or discontinuity between the Mycenaean and Homeric worlds is to be tested.

Tenure is not to be confused with allegiance to a sovereign. The
Homeric world had its higher authorities, kingly in particular, to whom
one's wealth was subject in a variety of ways, summed up in the formula
'honour him like a god with gifts'.[17] One man could even be king over a
number of *poleis*, like Eumaeus's father.[18] The mere fact of such power,
however, does not of itself warrant the belief that feudal relations were
present. Feudal tenures constitute but one of several possible links
between lower and higher ranks. In the account of Agamemnon's offer
to Achilles of seven cities, there is not one word which suggests that the
property relations in those communities would be disturbed or altered.[19]
Instead of honouring Agamemnon with gifts, the inhabitants would in
the future honour Achilles. Nor is there a word to suggest that, in return
for the gift, Achilles would assume obligations of service to the donor.
On the contrary, it was Agamemnon who was obligated, and he was
making his amends by offering a 'free' gift.

My view is that there were no feudal, or comparably conditional,
tenures in the Homeric world, and I propose to support that view by
examining the specific texts (or situations) – remarkably few in number –
which have been adduced as evidence in the opposite direction. My
argument must of necessity be a negative one, and such an argument is
always difficult to make, especially so when the sole source at our
disposal is as slippery as the *Iliad* and *Odyssey*. The reasoning will be that
neither feudal tenure nor a village collective nor an *ager publicus* – all
phrases which have appeared in this context in the current literature on
the subject – is ever explicitly indicated; and that to imply their existence
is neither necessary nor, at times, even helpful.

The Mycenaean tablets, on the contrary, suggest that in their world
conditional tenures were the rule. A comparison between the pertinent
vocabularies of the tablets and the poems therefore provides an important link in the chain of argument, and I shall consider the terminology
first, before proceeding to individual Homeric texts.

III

Many objects and occupations have the same names in both the tablets
and the poems. For our inquiry it is not these concrete words which are

revealing, but the classificatory terminology. To express notions roughly comparable to the English 'property', 'possessions', 'wealth', 'goods', the poets had a considerable variety of words which they used more or less interchangeably: *aphenos, biotos, keimelia, kleros, kteana, ktemata, ktesis, patroïa, temenos,* and a number of other, but infrequent, words and locutions. With the single exception of *temenos,* none of these words has been read with assurance on any tablet so far. This fact need have no significance, since inventories and schedules list specific objects, not 'goods' or 'possessions' in general, so that the Mycenaean vocabulary may very well have had the words like *keimelia* or *ktemata* without their appearing on the tablets. However, it may not be entirely without significance that there are at least five words on the tablets which indicate tenure and hence have a classificatory character, and only one is Homeric, *temenos* (the other four are *kama, kekemena, kitimena,* and *kotona (ktoina)*).[20]

Then, we turn to the language of social class, further distinctions appear which prove to be critical. Both the poems and the tablets have a considerable number of words which indicate status of some kind (as distinct from craft or occupation). The most revealing are those which identify men in the higher categories, the leaders and functionaries. The two sets of words are these:[21]

anax	wanax
basileus	pa₂-si-re-u (*basileus*)
archos	damakoro
hetairos	eqeta (*hepetes*)
hegetor	korete (and porokorete)
koiranos	lawagetas
kreion	mo-ro-pa₂
medon	tereta (*telestas*)

Both *anax* and *basileus* are very frequent in the *Iliad* and *Odyssey* in the sense of 'king', 'lord', 'master'. They are often interchangeable in the poems, but not always: in the more than one hundred appearances of *basileus* there is not one in the vocative case in the masculine, or one applied to the gods, whether male or female. In the period when the poems were composed, this peculiar distinction surely did not pertain; indeed, it is most probable that *anax* had already lost its place in common usage altogether, surviving in fringe areas of the Hellenic world and otherwise only in the language of poetry and cult.[22] Wackernagel, who first perceived the Homeric linguistic pattern clearly, suggested as an explanation that *basileus* was a newer word for king, and that in direct address and in reference to the gods, there was an understandable time lag, during which the older *anax* retained its monopoly.[23] The decipherment of the Mycenaean tablets has confirmed this conjecture, but in a way which Wackernagel could not have guessed, and which leads to a different explanation of Homeric usage. In the tablets, *wanax* is clearly the ruler, but *basileus* (assuming that to be the Greek form of pa_2-*si-re-u*) is not.[24] In other words, in the period between the writing of the tablets and the Homeric poems, *basileus* climbed the social ladder until eventually it displaced *anax* completely (for reasons which I think will be found in the great social transformations that followed the destruction of Mycenae, and not merely in linguistic fashion). That process was probably completed by the late eighth century, but it was not yet complete in the poems themselves.[25]

Anax and *basileus* reveal, therefore, that even when the same classificatory word appears in both the poems and the tablets, the difference in meaning may be considerable. And apart from these two words, the two lists of social-class words are entirely unrelated.[26] This is a strange situation, for such social terminology is as a rule extremely tenacious, changing its sense when necessary and thus managing to survive even the most radical changes in government and social organisation. The peculiarity becomes even more striking when we discover that four of the Homeric words, *hegetor*, *koiranos*, *kreion* and *medon*, like *anax*, were apparently not new words, beginning their history with the poems, but archaic words with no further life outside Greek poetry.

All four words appear in both the *Iliad* and *Odyssey* and there is not the slightest distinction in the ways in which the two poets employ them. This suggests very strongly that they were already integral to the bardic formulas before the two streams separated.[27] A check of two of them, *hegetor* and *medon*, reveals, further, that whether or not they had a precise technical sense at some time, to the authors of the *Iliad* and *Odyssey* they were only vague epithets, meaning either 'leader' or simply 'soldier', 'warrior': '*Hegetores ede medontes*', usually but not always in direct discourse, is applied with complete indifference to the 'counsellors' or chieftains alone, and to the army as a whole; more often to the latter (or to no one in particular), a context in which the words really mean nothing at all.[28] With reference to *medon* in particular, the poets admit, as it were, that they had no idea what it meant. *Medon* appears alone but once, when a purely mythological figure, Phorkys, maternal grandfather of Polyphemos the Cyclops, is called *medon* of the unharvested sea'.[29]

The two separate patterns of terminology here take us beyond the point of possible coincidence or accident. When such basic words diverge so completely, we are justified in believing that the words are a significant clue to the institutions. And again it seems to me that we have signs pointing to the view that the whole structure of Mycenaean society was overturned. With the abolition of the Mycenaean tenure system and of the social classes resting on that system, came the rapid disappearance of the technical names appropriate to those classes and their various holdings and statuses. The 'leadership' words which we find preserved in the poems were either non-technical words which now received a technical dress (but only an appearance of technical significance);[30] or words actually unknown in the Mycenaean vocabulary; or a combination of both.

Words like *medon* and *hegetor*, it may be argued, are of a type which one should not expect to find in administrative texts. They are generalised words, like lord, *Führer*, *seigneur*, or *Herr*, too imprecise for such purposes as are recorded in the tablets but ideal for poetic narrative. That is surely correct, and it is very probable that Mycenaean bards were already using them regularly. However, it is not the fact that these Homeric words do not appear on the tablets which is so significant, but the reverse, the fact that six apparently important words from the tablets do not once turn up in the bardic formulae. The *Song of Roland* manages an occasional *dux*, *cuntes*, and *barun* among the repeated *reis* and *seignurs*. The *Niberlungenlied*, which interchanges *künic*, *fürst*, *reke*, *degen*, and *ritter* in truly Homeric fashion, nevertheless descends to 'unpoetic' words (and people) like *marcgrave*, *marschalc*, *scenke*, *kameraere*, and *küchenmeister*. Their occurrences are few, but they are there. In the *Iliad* and *Odyssey* there are none, and we are thus faced with an almost complete discontinuity of vocabulary with respect to tenures and social status.

There can be little hope, therefore, that either the vocabulary or the substance of the poems will provide reliable clues to a world four or five hundred years back, with a radically different kind of organisation, the two worlds being separated not only by centuries but also by a very deep breach in the tradition.

IV

Personal obligations of service, and in particular military service, run all through the poems. That these were obligations, not merely matters of friendship or good-will, is certain, but what the obligation rested on is by

no means transparent, except where kinship was the basis. The only
other bases which are ever explicitly referred to are guest-friendship and
the gift-countergift interchange, and where they exist, that is ground
enough for the strongest ties, as we are only now beginning to realise.[31]
For the rest we are reduced to the argument from silence. Not once is
tenure mentioned, even on occasions, such as Achilles' refusal to engage
in battle, when the most obvious of all threats, withdrawal of a holding
for failure to fulfil the conditions, would certainly have been
appropriate.[32] *Not once* must be underscored, for historians have been
quick to apply the word 'feudal', as in the case of Echepolos of Sicyon,
who gave Agamemnon a mare 'that he might not follow him to Ilion'.[33]
Sicyon was within Agamemnon's domain,[34] and Echepolos was bound
to go to war. It is not inconceivable that the tie which bound him was one
of vassalage, but the poet neither says so nor hints at it in any way.[35]

To take another example, when Menelaus offers to accompany Telemachus through Hellas and mid-Argos, collecting gifts among 'the cities
of men',[36] there is nothing in the poet's language essentially different
from the account of Menelaus's successful gift-collecting tour of Cyprus,
Phoenicia, Libya, and Egypt;[37] or of Odysseus' tales about his travels in
Egypt and Thesprotia.[38] No one could reasonably assert that the massive
gift-giving in Egypt and Thesprotia represented feudal dues-payments,
and I fail to see how the situation in Hellas and mid-Argos was in any
way different, other than in geographical proximity. Again it must be
recognised that feudal relationships are not inconceivable in the latter
instance; and again it must be stressed that nothing in the text says so. To
insist on filling out all these silences with feudal tenures is to commit the
methodological error of holding that when the poets fail to explain a
situation, the missing piece is usually (or always) something quite unlike
any piece for which there is positive evidence. Even a quick reading of
Beowulf or the *Song of Roland* or the *Nibelungenlied* leaves one fully aware
that *Gefolgschaft* and vassalage were key institutions, although there, too,
the details and the rules are scarely touched upon. The contrast with the
Iliad and *Odyssey* is striking; so much so that a mere comparison is almost
enough, by itself, to eliminate the possibility that the Homeric world was
a feudal one.

Two procedures characteristic of the world of the Germanic poems
appear together in a single autobiographical passage in *Beowulf*: 'I was
seven winters old when the lord of treasures, the gracious ruler of
peoples, received me from my father. King Hrethel had and kept me,
gave me wealth and food . . .' Later, Hrethel's son Hygelac 'gave me

land, a dwelling place, a glad possession. There was no need for him that he should have to seek among the Gepidae or Spear-Danes, or in the Swedish realm, a less good warrior, – to purchase him with treasure (or to obtain him at a price).'[39] Words like *thegn*, *degen*, and perhaps the Celtic *vassus* reflect (in actual usage and practice, not merely in etymology) the custom of sending the children of nobles to the court of another, whose vassals they eventually became. Among the Greeks, in contrast, there is no trace of either the practice or the terminology. The Homeric poems repeatedly call one hero another's *therapon* or *hetairos* or *keryx*, never in that context his *pais* or *teknon* or *kouros*.[40] And never is it suggested that land lay at the bottom of the relationship. The poems also record instances of warriors from abroad entering a king's service, but invariably either because they had been forced to flee from blood-vengeance or some other threat, or because they had become kinsmen (sons-in-law), not retainers.[41]

In trying to explain the Homeric failure to be sufficiently informative in the few enigmatic passages which defy easy understanding, one must not forget that most often the poets provide ample material, that the cases over which we puzzle are the exceptional cases. Alliance by kinship, marriage, and guest-friendship on the one hand, and allegiance to a king on the other, adequately explain a very large proportion of the obligations of Homeric society. Therefore the indifference of the poets in such matters – the most common explanation – seems to me less than adequate for the odd bits (though obviously possible in any given instance). Far more likely, I think, is the ignorance of the poets. They knew from their inherited formulas that there had been great rulers in Mycenae and Pylos and other 'prehistoric' centres; but they really had no idea what a great Mycenaean ruler was, or how he behaved, or on what his power rested. Just as they retained what were for them no longer real descriptions of palaces or of chariot fighting, garbled to a point of unintelligibility, and of words and expressions which they either did not understand at all or misunderstood badly, so they retained and repeated garbled and unintelligible narrative bits from a past that was lost not only institutionally, but in large part even from memory.[42]

With respect to the contents of the *Iliad* and *Odyssey*, there is a profound qualitative difference between narrative and institutions (or background). For the former, I would argue, they are essentially worthless as sources. With the one exception of the political geography of the Mycenaean world, the kernel of historical fact which may lie buried in the tales cannot usually be detected by any method of analysis, internal or comparative. For this purpose, direct external evidence is indispensable.[43] The institutions, on the other hand, are described (more often, intimated) with considerable accuracy. To take one example: the innumerable genealogies can be discarded in their entirety as annals of specific princely families in specific places; but the institutions of kinship, marriage, and dynastic alliance underlying the genealogies appear in the poems essentially as they existed at some time in the Greek world (the tenth and ninth centuries BC, I have suggested).[44]

By and large, the institutions of property and of power emerge consistently and coherently – and without a trace of conditional tenures. Here and there confusion and uncertainty creep in, as we have seen. It is impossible to *prove*, as a matter of logic, that feudal or quasi-feudal relations do not lie concealed in the exceptional passages. But it is possible to show that the feudal explanation is a not a necessary one; that either no explanation is available at all, because the poets were repeating bits which had long become meaningless, or that some alternative is as plausible and at the same time more consistent with the rest (and the bulk) of the poetic evidence.

V

In the poems, the alienation of land in any form and to any degree, other than by succession, is rarely mentioned, and I have no doubt that it was rarely carried out. Purely private alienations are, in fact, limited to a dubious reference to Odysseus' gift to his slave Eumaeus; to two probable transfers of land (by implication, not by explicit statement) to a foreign son-in-law residing in the father-in-law's country;[46] and, again by implication, to Phoenix when he fled to Peleus in Phthia.[47] The first three are irrelevant situations for our purposes, and in the fourth there is no suggestion, and scarcely a possibility, of conditional tenure.

A serious problem arises, however, with the *temenos*, commonly defined as 'a portion of the land which was not divided into *kleroi* by lot, but was set aside, held back as a gift of honour to the king or outstanding heroes'.[48] This definition is unacceptable. It fails to indicate when and with what effect the supposed division of the land 'into *kleroi* by lot' took place; above all, whether it had occurred one, two, or ten generations earlier. In the poems, the word *kleros* appears eighteen times (and twice in compounds), but not once with the faintest trace of land division by lot.[49] The definition also fails to suggest the state of the land 'set aside' during the period when, presumably, it was unoccupied; whether it was farmed, and, if so, under whose administration and with what labour force. And it fails to qualify 'gift', to consider whether the grant was conditional or permanent, whether it was the same for kings and for heroes.

Three passages (and only three) say something about the assignment of a *temenos*: by the Lycians to Bellerophon, by the Aetolians to Meleagros (a promise that was not fulfilled), and by the Trojans to Aeneas (a promise that never existed in fact, but was suggested by Achilles mockingly).[50] Six other references give various details about a *temenos*, such as its location or fruits, but do not indicate how or when it was acquired. Five of the holders are kings: Sarpedon and Glaukos jointly, the *basileus* on the shield of Achilles, Otrynteus, Alcinous of the Phaeacians, and Odysseus.[51] The sixth, a most peculiar instance, is Telemachus.[52]

The first point to be made is that it is neither obvious nor necessary, despite the lexica, that the word *temenos* have the identical meaning in all the passages.[53] In classical Greek, the word *temenos* meant 'god's land', applied equally to the Pythian race-course, the Acropolis, and a precinct of a Hero; to land set aside for a god in the initial division when a colony was founded and to land given by an individual from his personal estate, by gift, dedication, or will.[54] *Temenos* comes from *temno* (to cut), but that etymological fact no more requires every *temenos* to be cut off from some common stock of land than the root-sense of *kleros* requires every plot so labelled by Homer or Isaeus to be the product of an allotment. From Homer on, the Greeks found no difficulty in saying *kleros* when it was perfectly clear that there was no link, even the remotest, with division by lot (just as the word 'lot' is the standard term in American administrative and colloquial parlance for a piece of land); and after Homer they found no difficulty in calling every piece of land dedicated to a god a *temenos*, whether it had been 'cut off' or not. I suggest that the usual sense in Homer was equally divorced from any cutting association, and the *temenos* ordinarily meant no more than 'royal land', that is, a 'privately owned' estate which differed from all other estates solely by the fact that it belonged to a king.

This suggestion resolves what is otherwise an unanswerable puzzle, that no reference is ever made to a king's receiving a *temenos* under ordinary circumstances, at his accession; nor to the disposal of a *temenos* at his death. There are banishments and assassinations enough in the two poems, but never a word about the *temenos*, in which, if it were really a grant held only with the throne, the *demos* or *gerontes* (elders) or some other agency should have had a profound interest, when, for example, Agamemnon was murdered. In the endless talk about the fate of Odysseus' estate, no one ever mentions his *temenos*. We know Odysseus had one, because we are told it was manured. But we do not know how he obtained it, and neither the assembly nor the suitors nor Penelope, nor even Athena, shows any concern about it. When the suitors, in their more benevolent moments, reassure Telemachus that they want only the kingship and not the property of Odysseus, there is no hint that the *temenos* would go with the former and not with the latter. In fact, in one passage (though admittedly a not very reliable one) Telemachus is said to be in possession of the *temenos* which, since he was surely not king, can mean only that he was in possession of his father's estate (if it means anything at all).[55]

The only ruler who receives a *temenos* in the poems is Bellerophon in Lycia. The king 'gave him his daughter and he gave him half of all the honour of his kingship; and the Lycians set aside for him a *temenos*.'[56] Two generations later, his grandsons, Sarpedon and Glaukos, were the 'most honoured in Lycia in seats of honour and meat and full goblets, and all look upon us as gods, and we hold (*nemomestha*) a great *temenos* on the banks of the Xanthos.'[57] Here, and here only, the *temenos* seems to have special overtones and a special and direct link with receiving, and holding on to, the royal power.[58] But here we are not in the Greek world. The joint kingship, the peculiar line of descent, whereby Bellerophon's daughter's son (Sarpedon) outranks his son's son (Glaukos), and the complex later practice with respect to tombs and tombstones, all point to Lycia as standing apart in its social organisation from the Greek pattern, Homeric and post-Homeric.[59] If the poet of the *Iliad* was at all accurate in his hints about the *temenos* in Lycia, therefore, we are not warranted in transferring the Lycian institution to the Greeks, whose kings without exception are never given a *temenos* in the evidence we have.[60]

The case of heroes is something still different. Achilles merely taunted Aeneas when he asked whether the Trojans had promised him a *temenos* if he emerged victor from the single combat, and the brief passage tells us no more than that such a grant was not unthinkable in principle.[61] The Meleagros story is much more circumstantial. The *gerontes*, through the priests who were chosen to speak for them, offered Meleagros as an inducement a massive reward, his choice of acreage to be cut out (*tamesthai*) from the most fertile part of the plain of Kalydon, a *temenos* half vineyard and half arable plough-land.[62]

There is nothing in either story to suggest that the proposed land grants were conditional in the tenure sense. Indeed, it is impossible to conceive of any sensible condition. Had the gifts been made, they would surely have been free gifts in perpetuity, integral parts of the permanent holdings of Aeneas and Meleagros, to be passed on to their descendants along with the rest of their property.

Nor is there anything in either story (or in the account of the grant to Bellerophon) to suggest that the land which was offered was the property of the community. That is an assumption introduced by some scholars, solely, so far as I can discover, from the etymology of *temenos* and from a variety of comparative data, most of it irrelevant or false.[63] There were instances in later Greek history when, at the moment of settlement, provision was made to keep land in reserve for future settlers. But then it was the inferior land which was left vacant, not the most fertile.[64] *Left vacant* – whereas Meleagros had his choice from among the best cultivated land in Kalydon. Even the Spartan kings, so often called survivals from Homeric (or Mycenaean) times, were assigned estates abroad, among the *perioikoi*, not at home.[65]

I know of no text, anywhere in Greek sources, which justifies the belief in a reserve of publicly owned land kept in cultivation against the day when the community might wish to grant it, permanently or otherwise, to some individual. The practical difficulties, especially with the resources and organisation available to the Homeric world, would have been enormous. Before Meleagros made his choice, who kept the plain of Kalydon ploughed and manured and cropped; who provided and controlled the labour force; and how was the crop disposed of, in a world without a food market or public messes? (If the Homeric tale refers to public land, then the whole of the plain, it must be remembered, not merely Meleagros's *temenos*, was cultivated under public administration.) One answer which has been suggested is that 'a *temenos* cannot be conceived except as a piece of land together with the peasants who adorned it'.[66] Given the premises, that is the only possible answer – and I do not find any evidence to substantiate it. Peasants attached to the soil, like serfs, are nowhere to be seen in the poems, and there is no suggestion, either in the Meleagros story or anywhere else, that slaves were acquired by a ruler or hero as part of a grant of land.[67]

Nor was there an agency to hold and administer public land. Throughout the *Iliad* and *Odyssey* the elders serve no function other than advisory to the king, at his call and pleasure. It would be inconsistent with every other reference to the *gerontes* if somehow, with respect to public land, they had authority to act independently of the king, and even, in a sense,

as a higher power. (Illegal acts and seizure of power are not germane.) As
for the *demos*, it appears, as a body, in only two peacetime contexts in the
poems. It met in assembly, when summoned, and there its role was
purely passive. Assembly meetings served to mobilise public opinion, so
to speak, but the people neither voted nor passed judgment on matters
of policy.[68] But sometimes the *demos* did take action. All the Trojans are
cowards, Hector said to Paris at one point, 'otherwise you would have
worn a stone tunic long ago for your evil deeds'.[69] There are other
references, though none quite so picturesque, to the *demos* thus turning
upon an evildoer, in what amounts to a lynching.[70] On such occasions,
public opinion led to action, but the implication is that it was spon-
taneous, and not conducted through formal channels or representatives.
Otherwise, I cannot find a passage in which the *demos* did anything, let
alone own anything or manage anything.[71]

Two other texts remain to be considered, neither having anything to
do with a *temenos* but both sometimes adduced as evidence of collective
holding of land. The first is the simile in the *Iliad* in which the two armies
are compared to two men who contend about the boundaries, measuring
rods in their hands, in a common (*epixynos*) field, where in a narrow
space they contend for equal shares.'[72] The word *xynos* (and its compounds) appears in Homer only in the *Iliad*, and not very frequently even
there. So far as I can determine, it refers to something common among a
specified group, whose membership is directly apparent from the context. The word *koinos* continues to be used in that way (usually for an
inheritance) in classical Greek and in the inscriptions and papyri.[73]
Hence the sense of the *Iliad* passage is more likely to be 'common to the
two of them', rather than 'common to the whole community'. From the
language alone there is no warrant for Thomson's offhand rejection of
the inheritance explanation in favour of his own, that, 'with the relax-
ation of the old communal ties each holder began to plough and reap
when he pleased,' bringing about boundary disputes.[74] This view rests
on comparative materials, which are indecisive as they merely demonstrate that collective ownership of the land has existed in some places in
the world; and on ingenious and often attractive etymologies, which are
irrelevant for the Homeric meaning.[75] Against it is the fact, which I find
nearly compelling, that 'the old communal ties' are never mentioned in
the poems; and the further fact that, in one passage, we seem to have a
direct statement that settlement meant immediate division of the land
into private holdings. When he moved the Phaeacians to Scheria,
Nausithous 'divided up the fields' (*edassat' arouras*),[76] and the verb the

poet uses, *dateomai*, regularly means 'to divide into personal holdings' in the private property sense (as I am using that phrase throughout this chapter).[77]

The second text provides even less basis for the communal-land view. In the twenty-fourth book of the *Odyssey*, the hero goes to the farm which 'Laertes had himself acquired after he had toiled much'.[78] It is reasonable to assume a reference to the clearance of previously untilled land, but it seems a needless strain on the passage to read into it the further notion that the poet was trying to distinguish between privately owned and collectively owned land.[79] A straightforward reading of the lines, with no special twists or subtleties, makes perfectly good sense, with the emphasis on 'after he had toiled much', a familiar formula employed, for instance, to underscore the point that Briseis had cost Achilles great effort.[80] Then the essential meaning is that, in the post-settlement age, when raiding and inheritance and gift-giving were the ordinary modes of acquisition, Laertes had done something unusual: he had toiled to clear new land.[81]

Nothing that I have said thus far precludes the possibility that there was tillage under communal discipline on the open-field system. One of the panels on the shield of Achilles, in fact, lends itself rather easily to that interpretation.[82] If so, three errors which have been made in drawing further implications must be checked. First, the alternatives are not mutually exclusive: an open-field system can coexist with enclosures and with individual homesteads. Thus, the odd bits in Homer locating royal holdings and the repeated descriptions of them as part-orchard and part-arable should mean that those in particular lands were set apart from the open-field strips (if the latter did exist).[83] Second, 'communal' working of land never implies, as a necessary link, communal holding of land. In historical times, more often that not the former is found without the latter.[84] Third, there is no fixed evolutionary process whereby the open-field system is always the more primitive, enclosures and homesteads the later, form of organising work on the arable. Migrations and conquests were never followed by fixed settlement patterns, and it was not unknown for large private holdings to come first, followed in later generations by the creation of open fields (and sometimes of village communities), the result of complicated political, demographic, and ecological factors.[85]

Finally, nothing I have said denies the possibility that occasional grants of land were made. In the Meleagros story, the poet did not say that it was part of an *ager publicus* which was offered to the recalcitrant prince. This is an invention of modern scholars imposed upon a text which refers only to the most fertile portion of the plain of Kalydon. Why, alternatively, may we not believe that Meleagros was to choose from the best of the privately held lands, just as, according to Herodotus, the people of Apollonia made atonement to Euenios, in the generation before the Persian War, by offering him his choice of the finest *kleroi* and the finest house in the city?[86] Euenios made his selection, and the people of Apollonia compensated the owners by purchasing the properties from them.[87] In the Homeric world the procedure would have been different. There was no public treasury and there was no purchase of land. But that does not mean that there were no techniques for obtaining compensation. 'Come now,' said Alcinous to the Phaeacian nobles, 'let us each give him a great tripod and a cauldron; and we in turn shall gather among the people and be recompensed, for it is burdensome for one person to give without recompense.'[88] With that, we are again in the area of sovereignty and royal power (or community power), not of tenures and the property regime.[89]

VI

In this long negative analysis, perhaps I have overdrawn the picture by seeming to insist that there are *no* traces of communal holding and no conditional tenures in the poems. Surely it is a mistake to accept on face value the image created by the poets, that the whole Achaean world (and the Trojan with it) was essentially the same in all its parts.[90] Odysseus, Nestor, and Agamemnon differed from each other in temperament and prowess, but only as three individuals in the same community, even in the same family, might have differed. Ithaca, Pylos, and Argos differed similarly, in terrain and wealth, but not institutionally. Yet in the earliest literary and epigraphical documents other than the *Iliad* and *Odyssey*, very profound differences in social and political institutions are at once apparent. Some of these variations very probably had their roots in the period of migration and settlement that followed immediately upon the destruction of the Mycenaean civilisation; others resulted from regional differences in the tempo or direction of later social change. It may well be, therefore, that some of the odd passages in the poems which are often explained as anachronisms – Mycenaean reminiscences – are, instead, reflections of differences within the Greek world as it existed after the period of settlement.[91] And it may well be that some reflect differences within the single communities, for they were societies of considerable complexity, in which there was not necessarily a single norm of organisation to which everyone adhered with unfailing regularity.[92]

But none of this helps very much. It is the exceptional bits which are called upon to help unravel the world of the tablets, since the typical Homeric scenes are so obviously from another world. And these odd bits, unintelligible or meaningless survivals or fragmentary glimpses of genuine post-Mycenaean variations, whichever they may be, are always so elusive and uncertain in their meaning that to use them as guides to the Mycenaean world is truly a case of the blind leading the halt.

To demonstrate how different, in quality, the property and tenure regime of the tablets was from that of the poems requires no detailed analysis of the new material. A few very simple statements will suffice, which I shall put in the most general terms to escape the disputes over the precise meanings of the technical terms.

1. A significant number of the tablets, especially from Pylos, record land tenures in some fashion, either for cadastral purposes or as a record of holdings together with seed allocations.

2. All the signs suggest that the tenure situation was varied and complicated. Some land may have been held outright, while the rest was held 'of' or 'from' somebody, presumably on condition of service.

3. If *paro damo* means what it seems to mean, then a significant proportion of the land was held 'of' the *damos*.[93]

4. Among those who held land *paro damo* were men called potters, fullers, and so on, one or two priests or priestesses, and, most numerous of all, the *teoio doero* (*theou douloi*, 'servants or slaves of the god'), a mysterious group of men and women who were certainly not on a level with the ordinary *doero* (who were counted on the tablets but never named).[94]

5. Tenures and holdings could crisscross, so that a given individual could hold some land outright (at least there is no indication that he held otherwise) and another plot or plots 'from' someone else.

It seems hardly necessary to continue. On all significant points of landholding and tenure the picture is utterly different from the Homeric. That is why so much current writing is driven to etymologies, Indo-European links – and the word *temenos*, the one apparently direct connection with Homer. We have seen how difficult and unclear the word is in the poems, and now we may turn to its only certain appearance on the tablets. One Pylos tablet has on its first line the words *wanakatero temeno tosojo pema*, followed by the grain ideogram and the numeral 30; and on its second line, *rawakesijo temeno*, GRAIN, 10. The remainder of the short text, though it continues the GRAIN-numeral ending for each entry, does not repeat the word *temenos*.[95] *Temenos* is therefore a land term, connected with the *wanax* (as at times in Homer) and the *lawagetas* (unknown in Homer). More than that cannot be said at present, except by conjecture.[96]

VII

My argument can be summed up in three brief general statements.

1. What happened after the fall of Mycenaean civilisation was not merely a decline within the existing social framework but a decline and a change in character together. Then, as the new Greek society emerged from these new beginnings, it moved in a very different direction, so that the kind of world which had existed before 1200 BC never again reappeared in ancient Greece proper. In that sense, the break was complete and permanent.

2. Given the nature of the *Iliad* and *Odyssey*, it is methodologically false to consider any given word, phrase, or passage in isolation if one is studying the institutions. That holds whether one is concerned with the Homeric world alone, or with that world in comparison with any other.

3. The Homeric world was altogether post-Mycenaean, and the so-called reminiscences and survivals are rare, isolated and garbled. Hence Homer is not only not a reliable guide to the Mycenaean tablets; he is no guide at all.

MARRIAGE, SALE AND GIFT
IN THE HOMERIC WORLD

The long prevailing view of Homeric marriage has two parts: that the
base was marriage by purchase; and that new elements are visible in the
poems, foreshadowing the time when marriage by purchase would be
displaced by a formal marriage agreement, usually accompanied by a
dowry.[1] Despite the almost complete acceptance this view has gained
among jurists, it has never successfully resolved some of the more
serious difficulties presented by the texts. Its most authoritative spokesman, Paul Koschaker, in his fundamental article on the forms of marriage among the Indo-Germanic peoples, repeatedly stressed the difficulties. We do not see the bridge, he wrote, 'between marriage by
purchase, which is still demonstrable in the Homeric period, and the
later *engyesis*'. Furthermore, the state of our sources regarding the
emergence of free marriage in Greece 'is particularly unsatisfactory'.[2]

I propose to reexamine the matter in terms of two pairs of problems.

The first pair deals with sale and gift. The phrase, 'marriage by purchase', is to be understood somewhat metaphorically. In the speech of
most peoples who have (or had) the institution, the words meaning
'bride-price' are different from the usual words for 'sale-price'; and the
verbs 'buy' and 'sell' are not used for a marriage. Marriage is never
confused with the purchase of a slave woman. In the language of Homer,
a wife might be called a 'wooed bedmate', *mneste alochos*, never an *onete
alochos*, a 'purchased bedmate'. Modern jurists speak of marriage by
purchase, nevertheless, applying the test of whether or not 'the conclusion of a marriage is controlled by rules of the law of sale'.[3] What I
shall do is put side by side what we know about Homeric sale to see how
this test survives. With sale, furthermore, I shall link the institution of
gift-giving and gift-exchange.

The second pair of problems is to distinguish between matters of fact

Originally published in *Revue internationale des droits de l'antiquité*, 3rd ser., 2 (1955), 167–94,
and reprinted by permission of the editors. As in the two previous chapters, I have reduced
the annotation.

and matters of law, between practices which may have been common but not essential, and juristic practices proper; and to fix the place of marriage within the framework of Homeric society.

I

Certain relevant, and generally undisputed, facts about Homeric marriage can be summarised rapidly.

1. Apart from several references to Odysseus' giving a wife to a slave, all marriages about which we are informed occurred exclusively among the most powerful nobles and chieftains, so that it is impossible to say anything at all about the law or customs of marriage among the commoners.

2. The most frequent procedure was for a man to obtain a wife by giving her father substantial gifts, often called *hedna*.[4] This is the so-called marriage by purchase. Not only is it attested in the largest number of specific cases, but it is further underscored by the word *anaednon* used in special circumstances, such as Agamemnon's offer of a daughter to Achilles,[5] when a man could obtain a wife without giving gifts.

3. Another procedure, not uncommon, was the winning of a wife by an act of prowess or in an *agon*, a contest. Sometimes, the result was the acquisition of substantial wealth by the father, as when Melampus brought the cattle of Iphicles to Neleus,[6] so that we may think of the result as no different from the ordinary 'bride-purchase'; but in other instances no gifts are involved at all, as in the contest among the suitors to see who could wield the bow of Odysseus.[7]

4. In three instances marriage by capture is either indicated or implied. One is the marriage of Paris and Helen;[8] the second is the statement of the captive Briseis that Patroclus had promised to give her in marriage to Achilles;[9] the third is a mention in a fragment of the *Thebais* that Oeneus obtained his wife as a prize in the sack of Olenus.[10] Some jurists have dismissed the whole notion of marriage by capture as an essential misunderstanding of the juristic act of marriage.[11] But for our purposes, it is enough to note that, as a matter of fact, we have two valid marriages which are preceded by capture, whether the victim was willing or unwilling, and one that was allegedly promised.[12]

5. Several marriages involved neither bride-gifts nor an *agon* nor capture. I do not propose to consider the problematical instances of Aeolus' six sons, who were married to his six daughters,[13] and of King Alcinous of the Phaeacians, whose wife Arete may have been his sister.[14] If they reflect a historical reality at all, it is of a world still older than

Homeric society and almost totally destroyed by then. But neither Agamemnon's offer of his daughter to Achilles nor Alcinous' offer to give Nausicaa to Odysseus was anachronistic,[15] and they both included gifts to the husband instead of the reverse.

6. Altogether, clear reference to dowry – if I may use the word somewhat loosely – is made in eight instances, and there is a ninth in the *Hymn to Aphrodite*.[16]

7. With remarkably few exceptions, the marriages in the *Iliad* and *Odyssey* were between outsiders, that is to say, between a man from one community and a woman from another. This fact is to be explained by the circumstance that the characters all moved in the highest circles, in which marriage was an important instrumentality for the establishment of ties of power among chieftains and kings.

8. Finally, although it was the rule for the woman to enter the household (*oikos*) of her husband (or her husband's father), the reverse was far from unknown, whereby the husband entered the father-in-law's household and later became its head.[17]

II

Not once in either the *Iliad* or the *Odyssey* is there a sale transaction – even if we conceive 'sale' very broadly – in which we can be sure that two Greeks were involved, or two Trojans. Either one of the parties is a foreigner, usually a Phoenician or a Taphian, or the poet fails to indicate the nationality of the second party.[18] All the passages in the latter category, without exception, refer to the purchase of slaves, and the inference seems legitimate, from everything the poems tell us, that the sellers of slaves were customarily, and perhaps always, foreigners. Certainly there is no available instance in which a Greek or Trojan performed that role.

Slaves, furthermore, were virtually the only objects bought by Greeks. The two exceptions are a shipment of wine sent from Lemnos to the Achaean camp, clearly an abnormal affair, and one reference to the purchase of jewellery from Phoenician traders.[19] There is no trace of the purchase of any of the basic elements of wealth apart from slaves, neither land nor metal nor cattle nor arms nor treasure.[20] There is nothing remotely comparable to the situation envisaged by Hesiod, when the poet warns his brother in unequivocal language: Watch out, lest because of your behaviour your neighbour buy your holding and not you his.[21]

Except in the instance of the Lemnian wine freight, from which the

Achaeans in the field procured their wine supplies in return for bronze, iron, hides, cattle, and slaves – all taken as booty, I presume; the objects which the Greeks gave in return for the slaves they purchased are not specified. Instead, the poet uses vague, general words, which can be rendered only by 'substance' or 'possessions' or 'goods'.[22] A great variety of things could conceivably have come under those headings, every-thing but land, in fact. But cattle, I am sure, were not normally included, despite the fact that it was cattle which served as the standard by which exchange ratios were established.[23] 'But then Zeus son of Cronus took from Glaucus his wits, in that he exchanged golden armour with Diomedes son of Tydeus for one of bronze, the worth of a hundred cattle for the worth of nine cattle'.[24] It is significant that, apart from the Lemnian wine-freight instance, Achaeans always gave something 'worth X number of cattle' in exchange for something else, never 'X number of cattle'. Laertes purchased Eurycleia 'with some of his pos-sessions . . . and he gave the worth of twenty cattle'.[25]

Given such a rudimentary and severely limited sales pattern, the notion of a Homeric marriage by purchase seems incongruous on the face of it. For purposes of discussion, however, let us instead accept as a base Pringsheim's view of Homeric sale, which is neither so sharply drawn nor so negative. Pringsheim believes that 'in the interval between the *Iliad* and the *Odyssey* exchange is slowly transformed into sale'; that technical legal terms for buying made their appearance, though with limited application; and that sale is still restricted to certain goods and is not yet clearly separated from exchange'.[26]

Now the proposition is that marriage by purchase exists whenever 'the conclusion of a marriage is controlled by rules of the law of sale'. One immediate difficulty arises from the fact that it is exceedingly rare for a people to apply the language of sale to marriage, as Koschaker recog-nised in his last work on the subject. His answer was that it is neverthe-less proper for the legal historian, by construction, to demonstrate how in fact marriage and sale agree in their juristic structure, when that is the case.[27] But for Homeric law, if, according to Pringsheim's view, the emergence of sale only began in the period between the *Iliad* and the *Odyssey*, and did not proceed very far in the *Odyssey* either, I do not see how it is possible, even by the most skilful construction, to bring the law of marriage into conformity with a barely emergent law of sale. Propo-nents of the marriage-by-purchase view, we must remember, do not think of it as emerging in the Homeric period, but as beginning to decline. They thus imagine a situation in which a dying juristic structure was modelled after one just coming into being. That is obviously impossible.[28]

Koschaker insisted, furthermore, that by 'sale' he meant in particular the sale of real property, not the sale of slaves and movables. The latter, he argued, usually involved foreigners and hence mutual distrust, and could not have been a model for marriage law.[29] But that is precisely what we find in Homer. What rules of the law of sale could there have been in a society in which sale transactions were restricted to the acquisition by exchange of slaves and jewellery brought in by foreigners, who entered the Homeric world as rightless men, permitted to come on sufferance and to conduct their exchange at arm's length, and then required to leave immediately? There could have been nothing more than bargaining until a mutually acceptable basis of exchange was reached, followed by a simultaneous exchange of the agreed-upon objects and the departure of the foreigners.[30] Nothing short of the actual exchange itself could have been binding upon either party; and once the foreigners went away, there could have been no action of any kind for redress of error or fraud. An uncompleted sale was a nullity; a completed sale was irrevocable, regardless of conditions, terms, or consequences.

III

If sales were rare and altogether peripheral in the Homeric world, exchanges were frequent and indispensable under a great variety of circumstances – not in the form of sale but in the form of gift-exchange.[31] In essence, Homeric gift-giving was normally a bilateral action, not a unilateral one. Although it retained the outward appearance of a free, voluntary act, it came very near to being obligatory. For all practical purposes, every gift either was a return for a gift of service already received or compensation for a wrong committed, or it was intended to provoke a counter-gift, sometimes immediately and sometimes at a future date, not necessarily specified. In the second type, the giver often took a risk, as in the parting gift to a guest-friend. When the returning Odysseus first met his father, the hero was still in disguise and he told Laertes a fanciful tale about having received Odysseus as his guest-friend five years before and having given him numerous gifts. Laertes, certain that his son was dead, commented as follows: 'The countless gifts which you gave, you bestowed in vain. For if you had found that man still alive in the land of Ithaca, he would have sent you on your way well provided with gifts in return.'[32]

Gifts of wooing were precisely comparable. They were given to the girl's father with the intent of provoking a counter-gift, the girl in marriage.[33] 'For this was not the procedure of suitors in time past', was Penelope's reproach. 'Whoever wished to woo a good lady and the daughter of a rich man, and vied with one another . . . gave splendid gifts.'[34] The counter-gift was commensurate with the original gift, hence the daughter of a rich man inspired especially great gifts of wooing. But, as with the parting-gift to a guest-friend, there was always the risk that the gifts would be given in vain. The daughter of a rich man would have many suitors, competing with their gifts, and all but one would have given theirs in vain. 'He is surely most blessed of heart above all others', Odysseus said to Nausicaa, 'who shall prevail with gifts of wooing and lead you to his home'.[35] And lest any reader miss the point, one of the scholiasts carefully explained that Odysseus meant 'prevail over the suitors'.[36]

The reason for gift-giving in wooing was simply that gift-giving was a part of all important occasions. Marriage was, of course, a major occasion, and particularly so in the upper social circles in which Homeric heroes moved. There a marriage was, among other things, a political alliance; in fact, marriage and guest-friendship were the two fundamental devices for the establishment of alliances among the nobles and chieftains. And the exchange of gifts was their invariable expression of the conclusion of an alliance.

In those circles, there could be no question of compensating the father for the loss of his daughter's services. That notion is indeed to be found in many parts of the world, expressed quite openly, and it has been used to explain why a bride must be 'purchased' from her father. But there is not a word in Homer to suggest this idea, and it seems altogether inappropriate for the daughters of Homeric kings and chieftains. It was not to repay Alcinous for the loss of Nausicaa's services as laundress that the suitors for her hand were expected to vie in the magnitude of their gifts, but to attain the high standard befitting the daughter of a man of superlative status and wealth.

It has been observed that in value (as expressed in cattle) the *hedna* were many times greater than the largest given value of a purchased slave woman. But it has not been so clearly noticed that the *hedna* were immediately comparable in value with the gifts exchanged on other important occasions.[37] It was characteristic of the Homeric aristocrats that they demanded value even in the most honorific trophies, that neither cowrie shells nor laurel wreaths came within their purview. Gift objects had intrinsic value as gold and silver and cattle – that was what gave them their prestige values.[38] 'Choose a very beautiful one', is Mentes' suggestion to Telemachus regarding the latter's proferred parting-gift, 'that will bring you a worthy one in exchange'.[39] Hence the atmosphere of bidding and bargaining around the marriage gifts – Penelope's 'father and brother are now bidding her marry Eurymachus, for he outdoes all the suitors in gifts and he has greatly increased his gifts of wooing'.[40] But it is a misreading of the entire pattern of behaviour with regard to wealth to see in the bidding evidence of a sales approach.[41]

The Homeric language of gift-giving in marriage is revealing in part, and at the same time it is ambiguous and misleading. The one point which is certain is that not once does Homer employ in a marital context any of the words that appear in connection with sales, whereas from time to time he resorts to outright gift terminology.[42] The gifts of wooing are almost invariably called *hedna*.[43] The 'dowry' terminology, however, is much more varied – *hedna* is used two or three times only, and otherwise the poet employs general phraseology of giving, symbolised by the descriptive adjective, *polydoros*, that is, 'bringing many gifts' to the husband.[44]

It is the word *hedna* itself that has proved the most troublesome. Thirteen times it means the gifts from the suitor to the girl's father, and three times the word *anaednon* ('without *hedna*') indicates a marriage without such gifts.[45] In a reference to Penelope, however, which is repeated word for word a second time, *hedna* means dowry, and in another passage the related verb appears in a context which permits no decision about the sense.[46]

The fact that the same word could have two opposite meanings has been a stumbling-block to commentators ever since the ancient scholiasts.[47] If the *hedna* are understood as purchase-money, there is no satisfactory way out. Some have sought a solution by suggesting that the father gave back all or some of the purchase money as a gift to his daughter, thereby providing her with a form of security.[48] This suggestion is impossible on the evidence.[49] That the bride did receive gifts is a fact, of course. Helen, for example, gave Telemachus a fine garment for his bride to wear on her wedding-day.[50] Such a gift, however, was part of a trousseau, neither to be compared nor to be confused with the cattle and treasure given as *hedna* to the girl's father, or with the genuine dowries, such as the massive one promised by Agamemnon to Achilles.[51] The suitors, it is true, gave Penelope gifts directly after she reproached them for their failure to woo in the approved fashion;[52] but one may not generalise from this instance, because the whole point to the suitors' behaviour – if one may properly draw any conclusion from the Penelope story – was their refusal to go to Penelope's father,[53] so that there is an element of mockery in the gifts they gave her at the last moment.[54] Both the language Agamemnon used regarding his proferred dowry to Achilles and the reference to the dowry received by Priam along with his wife Laothoe leave no doubt that the rule was for the dowry to be given to the husband.[55]

Most scholars have preferred a two-stages explanation, namely, that *hedna* as dowry, the rare use, appears in the latest portions of the poems and demonstrates that the shift was already under way from bride-purchase to the classical Greek form of marriage.[56] At best, this resort to a distinction between early and late strata in the poems, a dubious one in any event, could explain a linguistic anomaly, but not the actual marriage-gift pattern. Commonly the argument becomes circular. Because *hedna* almost always means 'bride-price', the argument runs, its use for 'dowry' is a late aberration. The shift in meaning came when the dowry appeared on the scene and began to replace the bride-price. And the proof of that sequence is deduced from the use of the word *hedna*, thereby completing the circle.[57]

The essential weakness in that picture, apart from the fallacy in the very notion of marriage by purchase, is that dowry is fully attested in all sections of the poems, early as well as late. In fact, there is only one instance in the *Odyssey* of a gift from father to groom, if we exclude the Penelope passages, whereas there are five distinct dowry instances in the *Iliad*.[58] Nor is there justification for an either-or conception, either bride-price or dowry. Andromache is called Hector's *alochos polydoros* ('wife who brought many gifts'), even though he won her 'having given numerous gifts of wooing (*hedna*)'.[59] There is no ground, therefore, for holding that a basic shift in the whole marital-gift situation was taking place during the period in which the Homeric poems were being shaped, regardless of the terminology.

Curiously, there is no special word in Homer for 'dowry', neither *pherne* nor *proix*, common in later Greek, nor anything else. The occasional use of *hedna* may indicate nothing more than an attempt to fill out the gap, by a procedure which would have been absurd if *hedna* meant 'bride-price', but which is not unintelligible in gift terms. Although gift-giving went on in a great variety of situations, three particular contexts were of such special significance that an individualised terminology was developed for the respective gifts. One was the gifts of compensation for a wrong – *apoina*; a second the gifts of guest-friendship – *xeineia*; and the third the gifts of marriage – *hedna*. *Xeineia* and *hedna*, I suggest, were precisely comparable; the one meant gifts accompanying guest-friendship, the other the gifts accompanying marriage, and the same word could be used regardless of the direction in which the gifts travelled.

It seems likely that the girl herself was sometimes considered the counter-gift and that no dowry accompanied her. But the more common practice, I believe, was for an exchange of gifts, in addition to the hand of the girl. That would have been more consonant with the general gift-giving pattern of the age. Peculiar or unusual circumstances were probably present whenever no dowry was given, though we cannot expect the poet to inform us so precisely. As for gifts from the suitor, it is interesting that in the two instances in which the winning of a wife is expressly labelled *anaednon*, 'without gifts of wooing', the special conditions are clearly defined. One is Agamemnon's offer of compensation to Achilles, his daughter to wife *anaednon*, and a dowry so great 'as no one ever yet gave along with his daughter'.[60] The other is the promise of Cassandra to Othryoneus, should he succeed in his boast that he could drive off the Achaean army.[61] But again we are ill-informed on the whole, for there are not a few marriages about which nothing is said in this respect, either that there were gifts in one direction or the other, or that there were none. The historian must therefore fall back on his judgment of the pattern, and mine, as I have already indicated, is that an exchange of gift-objects was the rule, and that the exceptions stemmed from one or another peculiarity in the situation between the two male parties, the groom and the father.

IV

The next question is whether the exchange of gifts, though the approved practice and a matter of great interest to the social historian, was of essential significance juristically. In this connection we may recall the account in Herodotus of the *agon* by which Cleisthenes of Sicyon chose a husband for his daughter Agariste about 575 B C. The year-long *agon* served to guide Cleisthenes in the selection of his future son-in-law, but the act which sealed the marriage was a verbal exchange, more or less formal: *engyo – engyomai*.[62] The marriage would have been just as valid had Cleisthenes made his choice by some other method – walking in the town-square of Sicyon, for example, and designating the tenth male he encountered – provided only that the two men then exchanged the solemnities of *engyo* – *engyomai*.

On the face of it, the Homeric *hedna* were analogous to Cleisthenes' *agon* – a ritual device for mate selection. In fact, the giving of *hedna* often became an *agon*, the girl going to the most generous giver. But since valid marriages were possible – and occurred – without such preliminaries, we are forced to the conclusion that the *hedna*, for all their importance, were either irrelevant juristically or necessary only under certain conditions.[63] Two further problems then arise.

1. Were there more ways than one to conclude a juristically valid marriage? As a general proposition, Koschaker distinguished between what he called, after the Germanic terminology, *Muntehe* and *muntfreie Ehe*, that is, marriages in which the wife became subject to the husband's authority and free marriages in which the husband acquired no authority by right of marriage and in which the children usually belonged to the mother's kinship group. It was the *muntfreie Ehe*, he argued, which gave rise in various legal systems to the formless marriage resting essentially on the consent of the parties. In Homeric Greece, however, there is no trace of a marriage in which the husband does not have authority. Even in Phaeacia, where Arete the queen seems to have power far beyond that of any other women in the poems, we are told explicitly that 'on Alcinous here depend deed and word'.[64] Further, we must emphasise again that most of the Homeric marriages were between outsiders, precisely the situation in which, in other legal systems, the *muntfreie Ehe* emerged, but not here in so far as the available evidence goes. Nor have I been able to find any other combination which reveals a pattern. There were *hedna* from the groom to the father-in-law when the wife joined the father-in-law's household.[65] And there were dowries in both types of situation.[66]

2. If *hedna* were not indispensable, was there something else, some other act or ceremony which was? To this question I can find no really satisfactory answer, partly because the evidence of the poems is so fragmentary, and partly because here we move into an area in which we are face to face with what Gilbert Murray called 'Homeric expurgations'.[67] In the poems as we now have them, there was systematic expurgation of a whole complex of rites and rituals: human sacrifice, brother-sister marriage, blood covenant, and so on. Now we know that *gamos* means both 'marriage' and 'marriage-feast' in Homer, and the two senses seem so interchangeable that in several passages it is impossible to decide between them.[68] There is no evidence of sacralism connected with marriage in our texts, yet it is tempting to think that at the feast

some specific ritual action was performed – a hand rite, for instance, or a blood-covenanting rite – which was the decisive act establishing a valid marriage relationship. But there is little ground for succumbing to the temptation. One trouble is that the *gamos* apparently could be held without the presence of one of the parties, as in Menelaus' *gamos* for his daughter Hermione, who was subsequently sent off to her husband, the son of Achilles, in Thessaly.[69]

The *Odyssey* uses two different phrases here. First it is said that Menelaus was sending Hermione 'to the son of Achilles', and then, a few lines later, 'to the famous *asty* (city) of the Myrmidons'. The somewhat more common phrasing in the poems is 'to lead (or send) to (or from) the *oikos* or *doma* of so-and-so'.[70] I do not believe that this language means that a formal transfer from one household to another was accomplished by some set ritual or formal phraseology, although such a conclusion cannot be ruled out. But this emphasis on the household does point to the essence of the marriage relationship, and from there to the ultimate power of decision as to whether any given marriage was valid or not.

In classical Greece the legal validity of a marriage was a matter of public concern, for it established both the citizenship of the children and the application of the laws of inheritance. It was primarily around the legitimacy of the children that the law of marriage gravitated. This pivotal point, however, was missing in Homeric Greece, where there was no *polis*, no citizenship, no political problem of legitimacy. Who then drew the distinction, which clearly did exist, between a wife and a concubine? The answer lies in one of two directions: either this matter lay within the jurisdiction of the kinship group, or it lay within the much smaller body, the *oikos*, the household.

My choice is the latter, the *oikos*, and not the larger kinship group. Despite the prevailing view, I can find no evidence of clan authority at all in the poems outside of one clearly defined area, that of the blood-feud.[71] For our present purposes, however, it is enough to make the single point that not once in the poems is there so much as a suggestion that the selection of a husband or wife involved anybody other than the groom, his father and brothers, and the girl, her father, and brothers. The appearance even of brothers is not usual, and in any event that does not carry outside the *oikos* to a broader kinship group. Again the comparison with Africa is revealing. There the role of kin is indicated at once by the fact that frequently the marriage gifts were shared among the kinsmen, both in the giving and the receiving.[72] But never in Homer.

It has been argued that the fact that Menelaus invited his neighbours and *etai* to the wedding-feast for Hermione demonstrates the tribal character of marriage.[73] However, the attendance of the *etai* as guests is no evidence that they played any role other than that of spectators. It would be as logical to argue from this passage that the neighbours also exercised some authority, for they are bracketed with the *etai*. And finally, it is by no means so certain as it appears in the lexica that *etai* means kinsmen.[74]

To be sure, I can cite no single passage which says clearly and un-equivocally that the head of the household had the full power of deci-sion. But there are signs pointing in that direction. The repeated phrase about leading or sending a woman to a man's *doma* is one. When Athena came to Sparta to warn Telemachus that he had better return at once, 'for Penelope's father and brother are bidding her marry Eurymachus', the goddess concluded with the following generalisation: 'For you know what is the emotion in the breast of a woman, that she wishes to increase the household of him who weds her, and of her former children and of her dear husband she neither remembers once he is dead nor inquires.'[75] The supremacy of the *oikos* over all other groups and ties could hardly have been stated more sharply. That was what marriage was as an institution, above all: the introduction of a mistress into the *oikos*. A man could have 'legitimate' children by a slave woman – witness Menelaus' son Megapenthes, child of a slave, yet never called a *nothos*, a bastard, but on the contrary, *telygetos* a favourite son.[76] But no man bought a *potnia* (mistress of the household).

Perhaps we would have a better understanding of marriage law if we knew more about the significance of promises. There are four certain instances in the two poems of promises by a father to give his daughter in the future.[77] In two cases the promise was fulfilled; in the other two death intervened. Another kind of promise, that of Iphidamas to give ad-ditional *hedna* at a later date, was also blocked by death.[78] Hence we have no direct evidence from which to draw conclusions about the possible juristic significance of a promise to give in marriage and its enforce-ability. However, the whole pattern of relationships in the poems im-plies that such a promise had no great validity, especially since every instance we have was between outsiders; it could be enforced, if that word may be extended considerably, solely by personal power.[79] Per-haps the fact is worth noting, nevertheless, that a few such promises are actually recorded in the poems, as are quite a number of gifts, whereas there is not one promise in the field of sales.

Two other important aspects of the law of marriage are even further

beyond our reach for lack of evidence. The only reference to a divorce is
an implied one. In his anger over the adultery of Aphrodite, Hephaestus
said that he would demand the return of his *hedna*. Nothing more is
made of this threat in the long dramatic scene which follows, and it is
useless to seek any light there.[80] As for widowhood, the only instance
apart from captives is that of Penelope. It would require another essay as
long as this one to examine in detail the confused and contradictory
strands of the Penelope story, from which I have been unable to construct a consistent view of the status of widows.

V

The problem which Koschaker presented as still unresolved, namely, to
find the bridge between marriage by purchase and the later *engyesis*, thus
disappears. In its place we have two other problems. One is the shift
from the kind of marriage pattern I have drawn to marriage as a formal
juristic act. That shift was merely one element in a much more general
transformation, from an *oikos*-kinship world of status relations to the
polis world of transactions consummated under the rule of law. The
second is the shift from the practice of gift-giving by the prospective
husband, with or without dowry in return, to the practice of gift-giving
solely by the future father-in-law. That shift had its roots outside the
realm of law altogether. It belongs to social history, and the explanation
will depend on one's understanding of the basic social transformations
of the eighth and seventh centuries B C.[81]

NOTES
BIBLIOGRAPHICAL REFERENCES
BIBLIOGRAPHY OF M. I. FINLEY
INDEX

NOTES

EDITORS' INTRODUCTION

1 – A. Momigliano, 'The Greeks and Us', *The New York Review of Books*, 22.16 (16 October 1975), 36–8, at p. 36. The ambiguous sense of 'us' is underscored towards the end of the review.

2 – Ibid., p. 36.

3 – To the successor of which he later contributed the article on 'Slavery'; see Finley (1968d).

4 – Finley, *Studies in Land and Credit*, ix; (1951b).

5 – Finley, rev. (1966f) 289.

6 – Finley, rev. (1967b) 201.

7 – Ibid.

8 – Finley, rev. (1966f) 290.

9 – See Martin Jay, *The Dialectical Imagination. A History of the Frankfurt School and the Institute of Social Research, 1923–1950*, London, Heinemann; Boston, Little, Brown, 1973.

10 – See Finley, rev. (1935) (1941b).

11 – For an example of the debate and the superiority of the method, see M. Weber, 'Critical Studies in the Logic of the Cultural Sciences: A Critique of Eduard Meyer's Methodological Views', ch. 3.2 in *The Methodology of the Social Sciences*, trans. and ed. by E. Shils and H. A. Finch, New York, The Free Press, 1949, 113–64.

12 – See Horkheimer's foreword to the first issue of the *Zeitschrift für Sozialforschung* published in 1932.

13 – Jay, *Dialectical Imagination*, 43 and *passim*.

14 – Jay, *Dialectical Imagination*, 119, quoting from an unpublished essay of 1942. It may be suggested that Finley's strong interest in the political institutions of Athens derives from belief in a similar ideal. Certainly the distinction between 'freedom from' and 'freedom to' is fundamental to his essay on freedom in the Greek world (ch. 5).

15 – Cf. Finley, rev. (1948) 275.

16 – Finley (1934) 150 f.

17 – Finley, rev. (1935) 289.

18 – Finley, rev. (1937) 610.

19 – Ibid., 609.

20 – Finley, rev. (1941a) 127.

21 – Finley (1975) 113–14.

22 – Finley, rev. (1941b) 505.

23 – Ibid., 505–6.

24 – Finley, rev. (1977b).
25 – Finley, rev. (1941b) 507–8.
26 – Finley (1971a).
27 – Finley (1979), and his *Ancient Slavery and Modern Ideology*.
28 – Finley, rev. (1941a) 129.
29 – See e.g. Finley, revs. 1961, 1963b, 1964b–c, 1965d, 1966b, 1967b, 1968b, 1969b, 1970b, etc.
30 – Cf. Finley 1937, 1964g, 1966e, 1966f; and his eight-year stint as Chairman of the Sub-Committee on Ancient History, *JACT*, 1964–71.
31 – Finley (1977b) 140; rev. (1964g) 21 ff., and elsewhere.
32 – Cf. Finley, *The Ancient Economy*, ch. 2, and esp. p. 49.
33 – Ibid., 51.
34 – See pp. 67 ff. in ch. 4 on the same theme; both are developed in detail in ch. 2 of *The Ancient Economy*.
35 – Finley, rev. (1960b) 528.
36 – Momigliano, art. cit., 37.
37 – Finley (1975) 117.
38 – It is not our purpose in this introductory essay to review in depth all the substantive contributions that Finley has made to many different areas of ancient history. Nor do we strive to cover various aspects of his work already treated by others, e.g., P. Vidal-Naquet, 'Economie et société dans la Grèce ancienne: l'oeuvre de Moses I. Finley', *Archives européenes de sociologie* 6 (1965), 111–48, and M. De Sanctis, 'Moses I. Finley. Note per una biografia intellettuale', *Quaderni di Storia* 10 (1979), 3–37.
39 – Finley (1975) 119.
40 – Ibid., 108 and 111, with a critique of the so-called 'laws' discovered by anthropology in illustration of the futility of attempting to discover law-like behaviour in the sense of the natural sciences, especially physics.
41 – Finley (1965a) 13.
42 – Finley rev. (1965g) 253.
43 – Ibid.
44 – Finley, rev. (1960b) 527.
45 – A. Andrewes, 'Autonomy in Antiquity', *Times Literary Supplement* 74 (28 March 1975) 335.
46 – Finley, rev. (1960b) 528.
47 – Finley, rev. (1965h) 5.

1 – THE ANCIENT CITY

1 – This subject has not been properly investigated; as a beginning, see Pečirka (1973); Wightman (1975).
2 – There are important nuances distinguishing Plato and Aristotle, especially with respect to internal trade: see Finley (1970b).
3 – Berry (1972). A French inquiry managed to achieve a total of 333 variables: see Lefebvre (1970) 67.
4 – Current discussion of the *problématique* of urban culture 'is concerned in fact with the cultural system characteristic of industrial society, and, for the majority

of distinctive traits, of capitalist industrial society': Castells (1970) 1157. Cf. the opening chapter of Lefebvre (1970).

5 – Handlin (1963) 2.

6 – Thernstrom (1971).

7 – English edition of parts 1 and 3: Marx and Engels (1938) 8. The work was completed in 1846, and the fact that this part was not published in Marx's lifetime is irrelevant to my argument.

8 – The view that all pre-industrial cities, of the ancient East, classical antiquity and the Middle Ages, resemble one another closely has been projected by Sjöberg (1960) 4–5. In his pursuit of 'structural universals', Sjöberg divides societies into three types, 'folk', 'feudal' and 'industrial-urban' (p. 7), and asserts that in 'feudal' societies (among which he includes the ancient) 'relative to the total population, urban residents are few' (p. 11). From that complex of false starts there is no possible recovery.

9 – Thus, Hammond (1972) carries the identification of city with city-state so far as to exclude from his 'preliminary definition' the 'administrative center, however much built up, of a state which is organized socially and politically throughout its occupied territory without any characteristics peculiar to itself as against the rest of the state' (p. 6). Perhaps the potential reader should also be warned that Hammond begins by saying that 'the impetus of this book was the question whether the emergence of cities in Italy resulted from a natural development of the Indo-Europeans or whether it reflected Greek institutions planted in South Italy'.

10 – See, e.g., Ucko et al. (1972); Adams (1966); Wheatley (1971).

11 – See especially Martin (1975). Cf. Wycherley (1973); Homo (1951).

12 – Momigliano (1970).

13 – 'The English Manor', an introductory essay to the English translation of Fustel de Coulanges (1891) ix. The latter was first published in the *Revue des Deux Mondes* (1872) and was then reprinted in his *Questions historiques*, ed. C. Jullian (1893) part 2.

14 – On the latter, see the important inaugural lecture by Arangio-Ruiz (1914).

15 – Fustel de Coulanges (1873) 78 = (1866) 69.

16 – Lukes (1973) 58–63.

17 – Fustel de Coulanges (1873) 28 = (1866) 20.

18 – Preface to volume 1 of *L'Année sociologique* (1896/97).

19 – Introduction to Hertz (1960) 11–12.

20 – Quoted from Meek (1976) 162. Perhaps surprisingly, Sombart (1923) I, 11, 13–14, had already called attention to this passage half a century ago, and regretted the neglect of Millar's *Origin of Ranks*, 'one of the best and fullest sociologies we possess', containing the kernel of what is now known under the 'unfortunate rubric, "materialist conception of history"'.

21 – Fustel de Coulanges (1891) 1. In ch. 4 of this essay, a critique of de Laveleye (1874), Fustel demonstrated his ability to deal with ethnographic data when pressed. This chapter is actually entitled 'Of the Comparative Method'.

22 – Ashley, introduction to Fustel de Coulanges (1891) xlii-xliii.

23 – Sombart (1902) 2, 191 and 194.

24 – Ibid., 2, 191.

25 – Sombart (1916) 1, 128. The second edition was a radically rewritten, restructured and enlarged work, but the chapter on the city was not significantly altered

in substance. All subsequent editions of the original two-volume core of *Der moderne Kapitalismus* were merely photographic reprints of the second.

26 – Sombart (1902) 2, 194.

27 – Bücher had published an earlier version of his theory in an obscure journal as far back as 1876, but it received no attention until the appearance of (1893); see von Below (1901) 8.

28 – See Will (1954); Finley (1965a).

29 – The three articles are reprinted in the posthumous two-volume collection of Pirenne's works (1939) I, 1–110.

30 – Pirenne (1939) 32.

31 – Lyon (1974) 146.

32 – Pirenne (1914) 264. The English translation in the *American Historical Review* omitted much of the annotation.

33 – Lyon (1974) 199. Weber was hardly noticed in the paper, and Lyon himself manages to confuse Bücher, Weber and Marx (e.g. p. 176).

34 – Weber (1924) 7–8 (originally published in the 3rd ed. of the *Handwörterbuch der Staatswissenschaften*, 1909).

35 – von Below (1901) 33; see also his review-article of the first edition of Sombart's *Der moderne Kapitalismus* (1903).

36 – Bücher (1922) 3.

37 – Bücher (1901), enlarged and reprinted as the one-hundred page first chapter of his *Beiträge*, a completely neglected work. I have collected the main contributions to the debate under the title, *The Bücher–Meyer Controversy* (New York, Arno, 1980).

38 – Bücher (1906) 370–1 (cf. 441–4). The quotation in my text does not appear in the English translation, made from the third edition, by S. M. Wickett under the grossly misleading title *Industrial Evolution* (London and New York, 1901). My other reference, however, will be found in the latter, pp. 371–4.

39 – Sombart (1916) I, 142–3. In the first edition there is only a fleeting hint of the concept: (1902) II, 222–3.

40 – See, e.g., Weber's references to Sombart in *The Protestant Ethic*, the references in Marianne Weber (1950) and Sombart's introduction to the second edition of *Der modern Kapitalismus*.

41 – Bücher's importance for Weber is still more evident and more explicit in the second chapter of (1956), 'Soziologische Grundkategorien des Wirtschaftens'.

42 – Weber (1921) = (1956) II, 735–822 (I shall cite the latter). On the 'three layers' within the work, see Mommsen (1974) 15–17.

43 – Marianne Weber (1950) 375. The 1897 version does not refute my remarks.

44 – Heuss in the opening remarks of his centenary article (1965). His account would have been more complete, though perhaps only a little less gloomy, had he been less parochial and looked outside Germany.

45 – Weber (1956) II, 736–9.

46 – Weber (1956) II, 805–9; cf (1924) especially 139–46, 256–7.

47 – Weber (1924) 143–4.

48 – Weber (1956) II, 739.

49 – That this was Weber's own schema is shown by the most recent editors; see J. Winckelmann's introduction to Weber (1956) I, xi–xii; cf. G. Roth in his introduction to the English translation (1968) I, lxxvii, n. 87, xci–xciv.

50 – The lecture is reprinted as the first essay in Weber (1971).
51 – See Mommsen (1959); briefly in his (1974) ch. 2, with good bibliography.
52 – Marcuse (1968) ch. 3, at 201–3; cf. Habermas (1971) ch. 6.
53 – Weber (1956) II, 782.
54 – Weber (1924) 271–8.
55 – De Ste. Croix (1975a) 19–20.
56 – Weber (1956) II, 818.
57 – Finley, *The Ancient Economy*, 137.
58 – See Kocka (1966) 329–35. An excellent starting point on Marx and Weber, with good bibliography, is provided by Mommsen (1974) ch. 3.
59 – Marx (1973) 256.
60 – The texts are conveniently assembled by Welskopf (1957) ch. 10.
61 – On the centrality of capitalism in Weber's work, see Abramowski (1966).
62 – Mommsen (1974) 50–1.
63 – Marx and Engels (1976) 472.
64 – I write 'ideal types' deliberately. On important similarities in the approach of both Marx and Weber, see Ashcraft (1972).
65 – Marx (1973) 484.
66 – Weber (1924) 6.
67 – Anderson (1974) 28.
68 – I trust that it is obvious that this approach to ideal types is fundamentally different from von Below's, quoted at n. 35 above.
69 – Frederiksen (1975).
70 – For one region, see briefly Frézouls (1973).
71 – In one field, the Greek 'colonies' of southern Italy and Sicily, the persistent efforts of Lepore to introduce a proper conceptual approach should be noted: (1968a & b) (1970).
72 – See, e.g., Alford (1972); Frisch (1970).
73 – For the evidence, see Kahrstedt (1954) 132–6.
74 – Galsterer (1976) part I; see Gabba (1972).
75 – Oliva (1962) 236–42.
76 – These figures are taken from the best modern account of the city in the later empire, Liebeschuetz (1972) ch. 2.
77 – See Finley, *The Ancient Economy*, ch. 5; Jones (1974) chs. 1–2.
78 – Magie (1950) I, 81.
79 – Alföldy (1974) 43.

2 – SPARTA AND SPARTAN SOCIETY

1 – Starr (1965) 258 defined the situation succinctly: 'We are, I fear, sometimes in danger of becoming Hellenistic rumour-mongering historians.' Anyone who cares can find the whole exhausting bibliography in the footnotes in Kiechle (1963), but not one sentence to explain how so much accurate information was transmitted to Pindar, who then assembled it in a sort of Burke's *Peerage*, not to mention the *Memoirs* of Stephanus of Byzantium.
2 – Boardman (1963).
3 – Cf. Mossé (1973).
4 – The so-called Great Rhetra, if authentic, was a brief, almost gnomic, early

enactment about government, particularly about legislative procedure. No agreement exists among historians even about the date, but most place it earlier than the 'sixth-century revolution', as do I without any hesitation.

5 – On the various rites, see den Boer (1954) part 3.

6 – *Eunomia* became an ambiguous term: 'good order' slid into 'stable government' and *eunomia* became a catchword of propagandists against political change, in particular change to democracy. Herodotus was surely thinking of the primary sense. See Andrewes (1938); Ehrenberg (1965) 139–58.

7 – The fact that *homoioi* first appears as a 'technical term' in Xenophon or that Xenophon alone speaks of *hypomeiones*, 'Inferiors', does not impress me as having any significance. Spartan social terminology was filled with common nouns and participles assigned a technical meaning, such as *tresantes* (tremblers), *agathoergoi* (well-doers), *neodamodeis* (those newly enfranchised).

8 – Moretti (1959).

9 – On the whole I follow the interpretation of the *krypteia* by Jeanmaire (1939) 540–69. Aristotle, according the Plutarch, *Lycurgus* 28, tied it entirely to policing the helots, but that this is too narrow seems a legitimate inference from Xenophon's carefully veiled generalities (4.4), from the few details we have about the suppression of Cinadon's revolt, and, if it is to be trusted, from the reference to *krypteia* in Plutarch, *Cleomenes*, 28.3.

10 – Xenophon, 11.2, 13.11; cf. his *Agesilaus*, 1.26; Thucydides 4.80.5. Pierre Vidal-Naquet has reminded me that the Athenian state provided each ephebe with a shield and spear, at least in the fourth century BC (Aristotle, *Constitution of Athens*, 42.4). This comparison reinforces my preference.

11 – The main passages in Herodotus are 3.148; 5.51; 6.50; 6.72; 8.5.

12 – The inscription is reprinted in E. Schwyzer, ed., *Dialectorum Graecarum exempla . . .* , no. 12.

13 – See Aristotle, *Politics*, 1334a35–39.

14 – See Andrewes (1966).

15 – Thucydides 5.15.1 (however one prefers to heal the corrupt text), 5.34.2.

16 – De Ste. Croix (1972) 94–101.

17 – Vagts (1937) 11, 13.

18 – Isocrates 6.81; Plato *Laws*, 666E.

19 – Translated by Richmond Lattimore (University of Chicago Press, 1947).

20 – E.g. Kirsten (1941).

21 – The fragment is no. 1 in Schroeder's edition; see Will (1956) 59.

22 – Translation by Bowra (1964) 152, of fragment 189 in his edition.

23 – Jeanmaire (1939) 463–5.

BIBLIOGRAPHICAL ADDENDUM

The most substantial contributions to the study of ancient Sparta since this essay have been *Sparta and Her Social Problems*, by P. Oliva (Prague, Akademia, 1971), and the publications of Paul Cartledge, adumbrated in a programmatic article entitled 'Toward the Spartan Revolution', *Arethusa* 8 (1975), 59–84, in which he saw not only the destruction of the 'Spartan mirage' as a necessary step to the correct study of the subject, but also the introduction of a more social-scientific approach ('pre-eminently the elaboration and application of Marxist theory'). In other specialist studies, such as his study of 'Literacy in the Spartan Oligarchy', *Journal of Hellenic Studies* 98 (1978), 25–37, he has sought to analyse the impact of changed social forces on the structure and function of Spartan society as a whole – in this particular case taking issue with the general contention of Goody and Watt on the revolutionary impact of literacy *per se* on social structure. Unfortunately, not much of the new social scientific approach is readily available or obvious to the reader in his general monograph, *Sparta and Lakonia: A Regional History, 1300–362 B.C.* (London and Boston, RKP, 1979) where social institutions and relations do not receive isolated treatment (with the exception of the chapter on 'Helots and Perioikoi', 160–95, where he tends to follow the opinions of a line of thought that helots are 'essentially slaves'). On this latter problem, the most convenient recent surveys are those by J. Ducat, 'Le mépris des hilotes', *Annales (E.S.C.)* 29 (1974), 1451–64, and 'Aspects de l'hilotisme', *Ancient Society* 9 (1978), 5–46. In large part, however, he does not advance the arguments of Oliva or of Y. Garlan, 'Les esclaves grecques en temps de guerre', *Actes de colloque d'histoire* (Besançon, 1970), 29–62, esp. 40–8 on the status and functions of the helots. P. Oliva, 'Die Helotenfrage in der Geschichte Spartas' in *Die Rolle der Volksmassen in der Geschichte der vorkapitalistischen Gesellschaftsformationen*, ed. J. Hermann and I. Sellnow (Berlin, Akademie Verlag, 1975), 109–16, reinforces his earlier views on the subject. On other peripheral groups in Spartan society see T. Alfieri Tonini, 'Il problema dei *neodamodeis* nell'ambito della società spartana', *Rendiconti dell'Istituto Lombardo* 109 (1975), 305–16. On the *perioikoi* see R. T. Ridley, 'The Economic Activities of the *Perioikoi*', *Mnemosyne* 27 (1974), 281–92, and the rejoinder by G. Berthiaume, 'Citoyens spécialistes à Sparte', 29 (1976), 360–4. The problem of the influence of wealth, distribution of property and social divisions in early Sparta has been broached by A. J. Holladay, 'Spartan Austerity', *Classical Quarterly* 27 (1977), 111–26; the iconographic side of Spartan culture, including the pieces referred to by Finley, may now be seen conveniently in the well-illustrated volume by L. F. Fitzhardinge, *The Spartans* (London, Thames & Hudson, 1979). Finally, the historical events surrounding Cinadon have been reviewed by E. David, 'The Conspiracy of Cinadon', *Athenaeum* 57 (1979), 239–59, though with inadequate attention to the problems of status-conflict noted by Finley.

3 - THE ATHENIAN EMPIRE

1 – Thornton (1965) 47.

2 – E.g. Mattingly (1961) 184, 187; Erxleben (1971) 161.

3 – See Folz (1953).

4 – Will (1972) 171–3; cf. Ehrenberg (1975) 187–97.

5 – As an outstanding illustration, note how the 454 'turning-point' dominates the analysis of Nesselhauf (1933). For an incisive critique, see Will (1972) 175–6. It is anyway far from certain that the transfer of the treasury occurred as late as 454; see Pritchett (1969).

6 – Larsen (1940) 191.

7 – Schuller (1974) 3. His central thesis of 'two layers' (*Schichte*) in the structure of the later empire and his listing of continuities and discontinuities, follow from his initial confusion between the psychological notion of 'an interest in being ruled' and the realities of power.

8 – Even if one thinks, as I do not, that at the end of his life the historian came to

believe, retrospectively, that the Athenian empire had been a mistake, that would not affect my argument.

9 – Perlman (1976) 5.

10 – Wight (1952) 5. The parallel with Roman 'allies' in the third and second centuries BC comes immediately to mind.

11 – I need hardly say that I find it both irrelevant and anachronistic to play with the notions of de iure and de facto exercise of power, as does e.g. Schuller (1974) 143–8.

12 – Meiggs (1972) 215.

13 – The fullest accounts will be found in Meiggs (1972) ch. 11; Schuller (1974) 36–48, 156–63. Neither includes the Hellespontophylakes, discussed in section IV of this chapter.

14 – See Blackman (1969) 179–83.

15 – Meyer (1960) weakens an otherwise sharp-eyed analysis by his insistence that there were never more than half a dozen or so ship-contributing states, and by treating ship construction solely as a privilege granted by the Athenians.

16 – Meyer (1960) 499.

17 – The most convincing discussion of this text seems to me to be Chambers (1958).

18 – Throughout I shall ignore the temporary wartime reassessment of the tribute in 425, certainly an important indication of the strength and character of Athenian power but too much of an anomaly to be included in the analysis I am trying to make.

19 – It does not trouble me that Thucydides calls the 600 talents phoros. Xenophon surely had the same figure in mind when he gave the total Athenian public revenue at the time as 1,000 talents 'from both domestic and external sources' (Anabasis, 7.1.27).

20 – For what follows, the fullest collection and analysis of the evidence will be found in Amit (1965).

21 – See Casson (1971) 278–80.

22 – Blackman (1969) 195.

23 – Stanier (1953).

24 – Blackman (1969) 186.

25 – I see no need to spend time on Sealey's view (1966) 253, that the 'League of Delos was founded because of a dispute about booty and its purpose was to get more booty'; see Jackson (1969); Meiggs (1972) 462–4.

26 – On the ancient evidence for what follows, see Gomme's commentary on Thucydides 1.116–17.

27 – See de Ste. Croix (1972) 394–6.

28 – Thucydides 1.101.3; Plutarch, Cimon, 14.2.

29 – The list is conveniently set out in Jones (1957) 169–73. One need not accept the demographic argument in which the data are embedded.

30 – It is unnecessary for me to embark on the unresolved difficulties faced in trying to sort out colonies and cleruchies; all earlier discussions have been replaced by Gauthier (1966) and Erxleben (1975).

31 – See Finley (1976).

32 – Gauthier (1973) 163. This article is fundamental for what follows.

33 – For the texts of this block of inscriptions, now conventionally known as the 'Attic stelai', see Pritchett (1953) with full analysis in (1956).

34 – Col. II, lines 311–14; cf. II, 177. The figure is so large as to create the suspicion that there may be an error in the text.

35 – Davies (1971) 431–5, estimates Pasion's total wealth at about 60 talents.

36 – I am not persuaded by the argument of Erxleben (1975) 84–91, that the Euboean holdings, including that of Oionias, were built up through purchase of Athenian cleruchic estates on the island; or by the unsupported suggestion of de Ste. Croix (1972) 245: 'I would suppose that the Athenian state claimed the right to dispose of land confiscated from the allies . . . also by making grants *viritim* to individual Athenians, who would presumably purchase at public auction.' Such suggestions were effectively undercut in advance, in a few lines, by Gauthier (1973) 169. Nor do I understand how Erxleben, like many others, can accept as fact the statement of Andocides (3.9) that after the Peace of Nicias, Athens acquired possession of two thirds of Euboea. The whole passage is demonstrably 'one of the worst examples we have of oratorical inaccuracy and misrepresentation' (de Ste. Croix (1972) 245).

37 – On the excess of phraseology see Finley, *Studies in Land and Credit*, 75–6.

38 – Finley (1965a); *Ancient Economy*, ch. 6. On the fiction of 'commercial wars' see also de Ste. Croix (1972) 214–20.

39 – *Inscriptiones Graecae* I², 57.18–21, 34–41 (Methone); 58.10–19 (Aphytis).

40 – Grundy (1911) 77. We have no idea of the duties of the *Hellespontophylakes* apart from this reference. Xenophon, *Hellenica*, 1.1.22 and Polybius 4.44.4 say that Alcibiades introduced the first toll collection in 410, at Chrysopolis in the territory of Calchedon across the straits from Byzantium.

41 – Correctly Schuller (1974) 6–7.

42 – The best statement of this proposition is by Nesselhauf (1933) 58–68, though I shall indicate disagreement on two points.

43 – An interesting example of 'rewarding friends' has been seen in the twenty-four small cities, most of them in the Thracian and Hellespontine districts, who 'volunteered' tribute in the years from 435, by Nesselhauf (1933) 58–62, and more fully by Lepper (1962), who take these instances as proof of the doctrine that tribute payment was a necessary condition of sailing the sea. The explanation is admittedly speculative; nothing more may be involved than local manoeuvres in a period of unstable relations between Athens and Macedon: see Meiggs (1972) 249–52.

44 – Nesselhauf (1933) 64.

45 – De Ste. Croix (1972) ch. 7; see the judicious critique by Schuller (1974) 77–9.

46 – I shall not repeat my reasons for holding the coinage decree to be a political act without any commercial or financial advantage to the Athenians: see Finley (1965a) 22–4; *Ancient Economy*, 166–9.

47 – First formulated in a lecture, Hasebroek (1926), the analysis was then extended in a book, Hasebroek (1928). See Finley (1965a).

48 – See most recently Erxleben (1974); more generally, de Ste. Croix (1972) 214–20.

49 – Nesselhauf (1933) 65.

50 – I do not understand how some historians can seriously doubt that this tax was to be collected in all harbours within the Athenian sphere. At the end of the

century, the two-per-cent harbour-tax, in the Piraeus only, was farmed for 39 talents (*Andocides* 1.133–34), and no arithmetic can raise that figure to a sum, in 413 BC, that would warrant the measure, when, as there is reason to believe, the tribute in the period 418–14 BC amounted to about 900 talents a year. I should add that I am prepared to leave open the possibility of a widespread toll system in the empire even earlier, as argued by Romstedt (1914) from the still unexplained reference to a *dekate* ('tithe') in the 'Callias Decree', *Inscriptiones Graecae* I², 91.7. Romstedt's analysis is not convincing, but the possibility seems to me to deserve better than the neglect in all recent works on the empire.

51 – I shall not become involved in the discussion about the reliability of the statement by Plutarch (*Pericles* 11.4) that 60 triremes were kept at sea annually for eight months. Meiggs (1972) 427, concludes: 'However dubious the details in Plutarch, his source . . . is not likely to have invented the basic fact that routine patrols annually cruised in the Aegean.' That is surely right, and it is enough for my argument.

52 – De Ste. Croix (1975) has contested my argument on this point, but his evidence – that Rhodes occasionally paid for some offices in the late fourth century and perhaps in the Hellenistic period, and Hellenistic Iasos, too, and that Aristotle made some general remarks on the subject of pay in the *Politics* – completely misses the force of my argument.

53 – See Finley, *Ancient Economy*, 172–4; *Democracy*, 58–60. Jones (1957) 5–10 tried to falsify this proposition by pointing to the survival of pay for office after the loss of empire, and he has been gleefully quoted by scores of writers. However, it is easily demonstrated that institutions often survive long after the conditions necessary for their introduction disappeared. Trial by jury is a sufficient example.

54 – Thucydides 8.27.5, 48.4, 64.2–5. That Thucydides did not specifically endorse this particular argument of Phrynichus does not seem to me very important.

55 – I see no need to enter into the debate over the 'popularity of the Athenian empire' initiated by de Ste. Croix (1954–5); for the bibliography and a statement of his own most recent views, see de Ste. Croix (1972) 34–43.

4 – LAND AND DEBT

1 – Plato, *Republic*, 565E; *Laws*, 684D, 736C; cf. Aristotle, *Politics*, 1305a2; Isocrates, 12.259.

2 – *Inscriptiones Creticae* III, iv, 8.21–4.

3 – Homolle (1926) VII.2–6.

4 – Jones (1957) 169–73; Wagner (1914) 50–1 estimates 20,000.

5 – Sieveking (1933) 562.

6 – Quoted by Aristotle, *Constitution of Athens*, 12.4.

7 – I have refrained from speaking of mortgages primarily because the word, as it has been used throughout the history of Anglo-American law, has several connotations that render it inapplicable to ancient Greece.

8 – Land tenure shows sharp distinctions in various parts of the ancient Greek world. This chapter deals solely with Athens from 500 to 200 BC (in round numbers) unless otherwise indicated.

9 – For the full documentation see Finley, *Studies in Land and Credit*. Subsequent finds have not altered the conclusions drawn in this analysis.

10 – *Inscriptiones Graecae* II² 2726. Three different verbs appear on the *horoi*, all of which I have translated 'put up as security' because the juristic distinctions are not relevant to the question under examination. Words in brackets do not appear in the Greek original.

11 – Ehrenberg (1951) 93. The identical view will be found, for example, in Michell (1940) 85–6; Jardé (1925) 118–19; Pöhlmann (1925) I 185.

12 – Ps.-Demosthenes 42.5. De Ste. Croix (1966) argues for a much lower figure.

13 – Plato, *Alcibiades* I, 123C, and Lysias, 19.29, respectively.

14 – Demosthenes, 20.115. Plutarch, *Aristides*, 27.1, puts the size at half that figure. See Davies (1971) 51.

15 – Dionysius, *On the Orations of Lysias*, 52.

16 – Estimates of population are those of Gomme (1933).

17 – Certain complications have been ignored in this summary: a different interpretation of one or two of the texts would increase the 2,650-drachma average slightly.

18 – See Gomme (1933) 17–19.

19 – After Solon the issue seems to have reappeared but once, when the democracy was re-established following the bloody and confiscatory oligarchic government imposed on Athens by Sparta at the end of the fifth century BC. The leaders of the democratic restoration were conciliatory in all matters, including property questions, an attitude for which they were commended by Aristotle (*Constitution of Athens*, 40.3): 'In the other cities . . . the *demos*, taking power . . . brings about a redistribution of the land.'

20 – Ps.-Aristotle, *Problems*, 29.2, 950a28; cf. 29.6, 950b28.

21 – Ps.-Demosthenes, 53.12–13. Only the relationship between Apollodorus and Nicostratus is under consideration. It is therefore unnecessary to examine certain apparent contradictions and difficulties in the passage.

22 – See Ps.-Antiphon, *Tetralogy* I b 12.

23 – Ps.-Demosthenes, orat. 49. There is no suggestion of political corruption in the picture.

24 – Sieveking (1933) 561.

25 – Sieveking (1933) 561, writing in general terms, not about Greece specifically.

26 – *Inscriptiones Graecae* II² 2762. Pringsheim (1950) 163–4 offers another interpretation which would remove the credit-sale element and leave us with but one firm example.

27 – Lines 11–23 of the inscription, as reproduced in *Revue des études grecques* 63 (1950), pp. 148–9. It was sometimes the practice, still to be found in places in modern Greece, for tenants to provide their own roofs and woodwork and to take them away when they left.

28 – Kent (1948) 289–90.

29 – One need only read the Socratic parables in Xenophon, *Memorabilia* 2.7–10. There was another, money-getting strain in the Athenian world, to be sure, but our concern is solely with the wealthier landowning stratum and only with the dominant attitudes among them.

30 – That this was the situation in Athens is explicitly stated by Demosthenes, 36.6.

31 – It is necessary to reiterate that neither petty lending nor bottomry operations are under consideration. Even such activity, I may add, will show the same

characteristics summarised here, though not so rigidly. Sizable loans for manufacture, like extensive agricultural credits, were unknown. The one exception to the rule that moneylending was non-institutional is found among demes and other sub-divisions of the state, temples, and private cult bodies. Many of them made loans at interest, but the sums were almost invariably small, and, important as the activity may have been in providing funds for sacrificial animals and ceremonial banquets, there is no evidence that it contributed measurably to the economic life of the community.

32 – Nothing could be more striking than the description of the sacred chest and the public chest of second-century Delos, given by Larsen in T. Frank, ed., *An Economic Survey of Ancient Rome*, Baltimore, Johns Hopkins Press (1938) IV, 340–4.

33 – Wigmore (1896–7) 322 (stated in a discussion of late medieval Germanic law).

34 – This statement is based on the exhaustive investigation of these groups made by Poland (1909) 487 n. 10.

35 – Thornbrough *v*. Baker (1676), 1 Ch.Ca. 284. On the historic significance of this case in English law, see Turner (1931) ch. 3.

36 – H. D. Hazeltine, General Preface to Turner (1931) xlviii–xlix, lxi–lxiii.

BIBLIOGRAPHICAL ADDENDUM

In the nearly three decades since the publication of this article and the book on which it was based (1952), additional research has been published concerning specific issues discussed as well as the general problem of the fourth-century crisis. Particularly useful is J. Pečirka's, 'The Crisis of the Athenian Polis in the Fourth Century B.C.', *Eirene* 14 (1976), 5–29, which offers an up-to-date survey of the debate over the fourth-century crisis, including a review of the work done since Finley's decisive attack on the notion of the concentration of landholdings. In this survey V. N. Andreyev's studies in patterns of land tenure and loans appear prominently. A convenient English summary of these articles, which originally appeared in Russian, can be found in Andreyev, 'Some Aspects of Agrarian Conditions in Attica in the Fifth to the Third Centuries B.C.', *Eirene* 12 (1974), 5–46. Andreyev's detailed research lends support to Finley's general conclusions, which are accepted 'with some qualifications' (p. 21). Another series of Russian articles on various aspects of the fourth-century Athenian economy, including credit relations and *eranos* loans, has been published by L. M. Gluskina, who has provided a German summary with references in 'Studien zu den sozial-ökonomischen Verhältnissen im Attika im 4. Jh. v.u.Z.', *Eirene* 12 (1974), 111–38. Claude Mossé's fundamental work, both analytical and synthetic, on the subject must also be mentioned, especially her *La fin de la démocratie athénienne* (Paris, PUF, 1962; reprint: New York, Arno, 1979), some of which appeared in her *Athens in Decline, 404–86 B.C.* (London, RKP, 1973). In a general review of the whole question she revised her earlier views: 'La vie économique d'Athènes au IVe siècle: crise ou renouveau?', in *Praelectiones Patavinae*, ed. F. Sartori (Rome, Bretschneider, 1972), which has been appended to the reprint of her book.

Greek banking and credit have been treated at length by R. Bogaert, *Banques et banquiers dans les cités grecques* (Leiden, Sijthoff, 1968). Specific types of loans have been studied in detail by G. E. M. de Ste. Croix, 'Ancient Greek and Roman Maritime Loans', in *Debits, Credits, Finance and Profits: Papers presented to W. T. Baxter*, ed. H. Edey and B. S. Yamey (London, Sweet & Maxwell, 1974), and

J. Vondeling, *Eranos* (Groningen, J. B. Wolters, 1961), ch. 3 (in Dutch with an English summary). On the subject of *horoi* two articles were published soon after Finley's article was written: L. Gernet, '*Horoi*', in *Studi in onore di Ugo Enrico Paoli* (Florence, Le Monnier, 1955), 345–53, and F. Pringsheim, 'Griechische Kauf-Horoi', in *Festschrift Hans Lewald* (Basel, Helbing and Lichtenhahn, 1953), 143–60. The *horoi* which have been published since 1952 will be analysed in a study being prepared by Paul Millett.

The role of metics in Athenian commerce and moneylending has been discussed by E. Erxleben, 'Die Rolle der Bevölkerungsklassen im Aussenhandel Athens . . .', in *Hellenische Poleis*, ed. E. Ch. Welskopf, 4 vols. (Berlin, Akademie Verlag 1974), I, 460–520; cf. more generally D. Whitehead. *The Ideology of the Athenian Metic, Proceedings of the Cambridge Philological Society*, Supp. 4 (1975).

5 – FREEDOM OF THE GREEK CITIZEN

1 – Leach (1968) 74.

2 – I use the classification of Hohfeld (1920).

3 – Mill (1948) 120. For an analysis of *On Liberty* and its place in Mill's work, see Ryan (1974) ch. 5.

4 – I quote the declaration from Cranston (1973) Appendix A.

5 – For an illustration of the deployment of such empty arguments by an academic writer, see Cranston (1973), especially ch. 8.

6 – For other texts, see Larsen (1962) 230–4.

7 – On the spectrum concept, see chs. 7 and 8 in this volume.

8 – See Gomme (1933) 16–17.

9 – Loenen (1953) 5.

10 – See Lewis (1971).

11 – Xenophon, *Memorabilia*, 3.6, and Plato, *Protogoras*, 319C, are decisive on this.

12 – I have discussed aspects of Athenian leadership in *Democracy Ancient and Modern*, ch. 1.

13 – I follow Borecky (1971) on the double sense of *isonomia*.

14 – See above all Vlastos (1964), to whom I owe the word 'banner'.

15 – Translated by Frank Jones. For other texts, see Borecky (1971) 12–15.

16 – See Kelly (1966), especially ch. 3; Garnsey (1970) part 3.

17 – Thucydides 3.62.3.

18 – The analysis by Ihering (1885) 175 ff., can hardly be bettered.

19 – See the analysis by Erbse (1956), which I have followed. Dover (1968) 172–4, rejects Erbse's analysis for the traditional view that the speech was not delivered. However, he concludes that Demosthenes, 'did not judge that circulation of such a document would damage his reputation', and that is sufficient for my argument.

20 – Ruschenbusch (1957) = (1968) 362. The ancient texts are quoted there, and are all accepted at face value.

21 – Meinecke (1971); Meyer-Laurin (1965).

22 – Davies (1971) no. 9719.

23 – Weiss (1923) book 4, remains fundamental despite the correct criticism of some reviewers that throughout the book he paid insufficient attention to social and political change in Greek history; e.g. Latte (1925).

24 – See Finley (1967).

25 – See e.g. Finley, *Studies in Land and Credit*, 113–17.

26 – See now Gauthier (1974) 207–15.

27 – See Humphreys (1974).

28 – See Garlan (1972); (1974).

29 – Perhaps I should say once again that tyrannies are excluded from this discussion.

30 – The fullest account is Pritchett (1971) chs. 1–2.

31 – Much is obscure on this subject. The fullest account will be found in Amit (1965); see also above, ch. 3.

32 – That it was not always possible is obvious, and it may be that the smaller, inland agricultural *poleis* were compelled to levy direct taxes regularly, as suggested by Pleket (1972) 252. However, I must protest the sporadic attempts to elevate a tiny handful of sources, as many Hellenistic and Roman as classical, into a falsification of the generalisation in my text.

33 – Although the *metoikion* was only a drachma a month (and half that for a woman), not a great financial burden, the psychological implication is none the less for that. Cf. the comment of Lord Hailey about modern Africa under European rule: 'It might almost be said that the African begins to be recognized as a member of civilized society when he becomes subject to the payment of income tax instead of poll tax.' *An African Survey*, Oxford University Press (1957) 643.

34 – Admittedly, such narratives as we have of the struggle against, and the overthrow of, tyrants have little or nothing to say about tax grievances. I suggest that they were nevertheless an important element because, in Athens, a point is specifically made of the Pisistratid tithe (Thucydides 6.54.5; Aristotle, *Constitution of Athens*, 16.4), which we know to have been abolished as soon as the tyranny was eliminated, and because of the direct taxes among the fiscal devices in Pseudo-Aristotle, *Oeconomica*, book 2.

35 – See Adkins (1972) ch. 5.

36 – Stroud (1971).

37 – See Latte (1920).

38 – See Stroud (1974).

6 – CIVILISATION AND SLAVE LABOUR

1 – I also exclude the 'economic compulsion' of the wage-labour system.

2 – It is not a valid objection to this working definition to point out either that a slave is biologically a man none the less, or that there were usually some pressures to give him a little recognition of his humanity, such as the privilege of asylum or the *de facto* privilege of marriage.

3 – I am not considering the local helotage words here, although the Greeks themselves customarily called such people 'slaves': see the two following chapters.

4 – I have given only some examples. On the regional and dialectal variations see Kretschmer (1930). On the interchangeability of the terms in classical Athenian usage see Lauffer (1955–6), I, 1104–8; cf. Kazakevich (1956).

5 – See Aymard (1948).

6 – This statement is not invalidated by the occasional sally which a smallholder or petty craftsman might make into the labour market to do three days' harvesting

or a week's work on temple construction; or by the presence in cities like Athens of an indeterminable number of men, almost all of them unskilled, who lived on odd jobs (when they were not rowing in the fleet, or otherwise occupied by the state), those, for example, who congregated daily at *Kolonos Misthios* (on which see Fuks (1951) 171–3). Nowhere in the sources do we hear of private establishments employing a staff of hired workers as their normal operation.

7 – Scholars who argue that slavery was unimportant in agriculture systematically ignore the *Hausvaterliteratur* (traditional literature on estate and household management) and similar evidence, while trying to prove their case partly by weak arguments from silence, partly by reference to the papyri. One cannot protest strongly enough against the latter procedure, since the agricultural regime in Ptolemaic and Roman Egypt was not Greek; see Rostovtzeff (1953) I, 272–7. On Athens, see now Jameson (1977–8).

8 – Philochorus 328 F 97, quoted in Macrobius, *Saturnalia*, 1.10.22.

9 – Xenophon, *Poroi*, 4.14.

10 – Lauffer (1955–6) II, 904–16.

11 – Demosthenes 27.19; 28.12; see Finley, *Studies in Land and Credit*, 67. For another decisive text, see Xenophon, *Memorabilia*, 2.7.6.

12 – Lauffer (1955–6) II, 904–16.

13 – Jones (1957) 76–9.

14 – Starr (1958) 21–2.

15 – Stampp (1956) 29–30.

16 – See Aymard (1957).

17 – *Digest* 1.5.4.1.

18 – Buckland (1908) v.

19 – Morrow (1939) 11 and 127. Morrow effectively disproves the view that 'Plato at heart disapproved of slavery and in introducing it into the *Laws* was simply accommodating himself to his age' (pp. 129–30). Cf. Vlastos (1941) 293: 'There is not the slightest indication, either in the *Republic*, or anywhere else, that Plato means to obliterate or relax in any way' the distinction between slave and free labour.

20 – Diogenes Laertius 6.74. On the Cynics, Stoics, and Christians see Westermann (1955) 24–5, 39–40, 116–17, and 149–59.

21 – Westermann (1955) 14 n. 48.

22 – See Vernant (1965), part 4.

23 – Xenophon, *Poroi*, 4.33; cf. 6.1. The best examples of Utopian dreaming in this direction are, of course, provided by Aristophanes in *Ecclesiazusae*, 651–61 and *Plutus*, 510–26, but I refrain from discussing them because I wish to avoid the long argument about slavery in Attic comedy.

24 – This generalisation stands despite an isolated passage about the animosity aroused by Aristotle's friend Mnason (Timaeus 556 F 11 cited in Athenaeus 6.264D, 272B) which, whatever it means, cannot possibly refer to chattel slavery.

25 – See Vogt (1974) 53–7.

26 – The relevant passages in Thucydides are 4.41, 55, 80; 5.23.3; 7.26.2. The 'slave class' (*he douleia*) here meant the helots, of course. In my text, in the pages which follow immediately (on slaves in war), I also say 'slaves' to include helots, ignoring for the moment the distinction between them.

27 – Pseudo-Demosthenes 17.15. For earlier periods, cf. Herodotus 7.155 on

Syracuse and Thucydides 3.73 on Corcyra (and note that Thucydides does not return to the point or generalise about it in his final peroration on *stasis* and its evils).

28 – See Garlan (1972), (1974). Xenophon, *Poroi*, 4.42, uses the potential value of slaves as military and naval manpower as an argument in favour of his proposal to have the state buy thousands of slaves to be hired out in the mines.

29 – Stampp (1956) 132–40.

30 – Vogt (1974), ch. 3.

31 – Pseudo-Aristotle, *Oeconomica* 1344b18; cf. Plato, *Laws*, 6.777C–D; Aristotle, *Politics*, 1330a25–28.

32 – Note that Thucydides 8.40.2 makes the disproportionately large number of Chian slaves the key to their ill-treatment and their readiness to desert to the Athenians.

33 – Douglass (1855) 263–4, quoted from Stampp (1956) 89.

34 – Stampp (1956) ch. 3, 'A Troublesome Property', should be required reading on the subject.

35 – Note how Thucydides stressed the loss in anticipation (1.142.4; 6.91.7) before actually reporting it in 7.27.5.

36 – *Hellenica Oxyrhynchia* 12.4.

37 – The technical and aesthetic excellence of much work performed by slaves is, of course, visible in innumerable museums and archaeological sites. This is part of the complexity and ambiguity of the institution (discussed in section IV), which extended to the slaves themselves as well as to their masters.

38 – In the two decades since this essay was first published, some of the debate has become illuminating; see Finley, *Ancient Slavery and Modern Ideology*, ch. 1.

39 – Durkheim (1950) 28.

40 – Buckland (1908) V.

41 – 'The Greek State: Preface to an Unwritten Book', in *Early Greek Philosophy and Other Essays*, ed. M. A. Mügge, London and Edinburgh (1911) 6.

42 – Buckland (1908) 1.

43 – See Kiechle (1958) for a useful collection of materials, often vitiated by a confusion between a fact and a moralising statement, and even more by special pleading.

44 – See Rostovtzeff (1953) I, 201–8.

45 – Timaeus 566 F 11, cited in Athenaeus 6.264C; cf. 272A–B.

46 – Theopompus 115 F 122, cited in Athenaeus 6.265B–C.

47 – R. Meiggs and D. Lewis, ed., *Greek Historical Inscriptions to the End of the Fifth Century B.C.*, no. 8.

48 – It is hardly necessary to add that 'freedom' is a term which, in the Greek context, was restricted to the members of the citizen-community, always a fraction, and sometimes a minor fraction of the total male population.

BIBLIOGRAPHICAL ADDENDUM

For additional bibliography see the works cited by M. I. Finley, *Ancient Slavery and Modern Ideology* (1980).

7 – BETWEEN SLAVERY AND FREEDOM

1 – The most important sources are Sophocles, *Trachiniae*, 68–72, 248–54, 274–6 (with *scholia*); Apollodorus, 2.6.2–3; Diodorus 4.31.5–8. See further the beginning of ch. 9 below.

2 – Daube (1947) 45; cf. the important monograph of Urbach (1963).

3 – Quoted by Aristotle, *Constitution of Athens*, 12.4.

4 – Vogt (1974), ch. 3.

5 – See Thompson (1952b).

6 – Pulleyblank (1958) 204–5.

7 – See, e.g., Stevenson (1943) 175–80.

8 – Scheil (1915) 1–13; cf. Petschow (1956) 63–5.

9 – See Lotze (1959), Pippidi (1973).

10 – See Lotze (1959), (1962), and ch. 8 below.

11 – Rostovtzeff (1953) I, 320.

12 – Frankfort et al. (1948) 250.

13 – Weber (1924) 99–107.

14 – This is substantially the scheme I have formulated in ch. 8 in this volume.

BIBLIOGRAPHICAL ADDENDUM

For additional bibliography see the works cited by M. I. Finley, *Ancient Slavery and Modern Ideology* (1980).

8 – SERVILE STATUSES

1 – See Kazakevich (1958).

2 – Collinet (1937).

3 – *Inscriptiones Creticae* IV 72, together with the so-called 'second code', ibid., IV 41, cited hereafter only by number, followed by column number in Roman numerals and line number in Arabic numerals.

4 – E.g. Willetts (1955) ch. 5–6. Lotze (1959) provides the best treatment which the subject has yet received. We are in substantial agreement on the points I make at the beginning of this section (though not on others, notably with regard to the status of the helots).

5 – Lipsius (1909) 397–9.

6 – There is an apparent exception in the provision about rape of a domestic (no. 72 II 11–16), on which see Gernet (1955) 57–9; Lotze (1959) 18–19. But the exception here, I believe, was created by the desire to give special legislative protection to female domestics – a common enough problem – and not by an essential juristic status distinction.

7 – No. 41 IV 6–14; no. 72 VII 10–15, III 52, IV 23, II 2–45, respectively.

8 – No. 72 IV 31–6.

9 – On this phrasing, which is used for both free women (no. 72 II 46–7, III 18–29, 25) and unfree (III 42–3) and which should not be confused with dowry, see Wolff (1957) 166–7.

10 – For a correct interpretation of no. 72 V 25–8, see Lotze (1959) 12–14; Lipsius (1909) 394–7. The possibility remains, of course, that manumission could alter the

position, but manumission is one of the subjects not discussed by the code in any surviving provision.

11 – No. 72 II 16–33.

12 – No. 41 col. VI.

13 – *Syll.*³ 45.37–41 and *P. Hal.* 1.219–21 (see *Dikaiomata*, Berlin, 1913, 122–4), respectively.

14 – For parallels elsewhere in Greece see Wilhelm (1924).

15 – See Lemosse (1957).

16 – *Inscriptiones Graecae* VII 3172.29–34; XIV 645.154–5; and *Inscriptions de Délos* 509.27–9, respectively.

17 – *Politics*, 1272a1; cf. a18, b18. The problem of Cretan *perioikoi* is perplexing (see Lotze (1959) 8–9), but Aristotle's equation is important evidence and, for the point I am making, sufficient.

18 – *Politics*, 1329a26, 1330a29. Both 1303a8 about *perioikoi* in Argos and 1327b11 about *perioikoi* in Heraclea Pontica are ambiguous and depend for their interpretation on other writers; see Lotze (1959) 53–4, 56–8.

19 – Cf. Strabo 8.5.4 on the helots: 'The Spartans held them in a way as public slaves. . . .'

20 – Lysias 12.98; Isocrates 14.48; Diodorus 1.79.3–5.

21 – Quoted in Diogenes Laertius 5.2.55.

22 – Koschaker (1931) 38–9.

23 – See the volume in which Collinet (1937) is printed; cf. Lasker (1950) 69–71; Greenidge (1958) chs. 6–9.

24 – See e.g. Stevenson (1943) 174–81; Lasker (1950) 30–1, 57.

25 – Rostovtzeff and Welles (1931), lines 7–9, 15–16.

26 – Koschaker (1931) 20.

27 – Koschaker (1931) 49.

28 – Westermann (1945) 216; cf. (1948).

29 – *Inscriptiones Creticae* IV 58.

30 – Koschaker (1931) 39.

31 – I exclude from consideration loss of freedom by act of an external agent, through war or piracy, important as this possibility may have been in influencing ancient psychology.

32 – Among the various *poleis* there was the further distinction whether or not self-sale and sale of children were permitted to citizens: see e.g. Aelian, *Varia Historia*, 2.7, on the law at Thebes.

33 – See e.g. Paton (1951) 224–8.

34 – The fact that our sources are unable to give us a clear picture of the situation should not be allowed to detract from the significance of this point. They were at least groping for the essential when they said, in Strabo's words (8.5.4), that the helots were public slaves 'in a way' (cf. Pausanias 3.20.6). Lotze's account of the helots (1959) 38–47, for all its good features, seems to me to underestimate state power; cf., in contrast, Ehrenberg (1924) 39–41. In Rome the *servi publici populi Romani* had definite privileges generally unavailable to other slaves, though we know little about them: see Buckland (1908) 318–23. I do not imply that they were in any way comparable to the helots, except in suggesting that the public hand can weigh the balance heavily in one direction or the other.

35 – See also the closing pages of the previous chapter.

36 – It scarcely needs to be said that I reject completely any idea that we are dealing with nothing more than the remains of 'Dorian serfdom', an idea which 'postulates a kind of social petrification and an impermeability of ethnic frontiers, which are nothing but mental constructs, manifestations (often unconscious) of present-day ideologies rather than scientific hypotheses': Will (1956) 50.

9 – DEBT-BONDAGE AND SLAVERY

1 – Cf. Pollux 3.78.

2 – Earlier Aeschylus had used these words for the same affair: 'They say that Heracles was once sold, and learnt to eat slaves' bread' (*Agamemnon* 1041).

3 – Frisk (1954) evades the difficulties by ignoring the 'slave' meaning altogether.

4 – The most suggestive study we have is that of Gernet (1948–9).

5 – Omphale was originally connected with Malis and Trachis in central Greece, so that we have a completely Greek myth, shifted to Lydia probably in the sixth century BC. See, on this, Herzog-Hauser (1939) 387–8, whose institutional analysis, however, is unsatisfactory.

6 – See Mauss (1925); cf. Finley, *World of Odysseus*, index, s.v. 'gifts'.

7 – *Inscriptiones Graecae* XII suppl. 347, I, 1–5; cf. XII 8, 264.4; Pouilloux (1954) no. 7; *Bulletin de correspondance hellénique* 91 (1962) 483–90.

8 – G. Daux in *Bulletin de correspondance hellénique* 50 (1926) 217.

9 – The same text, at II 8–11, employs another procedural reference, assimilating the action and penalty for importing foreign wine to the action for watering wine.

10 – Ihering (1879) 163–76, 230–4; cf. Partsch (1909) 84–5.

11 – Larson (1935) 41. For other instances, see the index, s.v. 'robbery'. The point is made in the glossary (p. 427) that *rén* was chiefly distinguished from theft by the element of violence. On parallels in the Old Testament and post-Biblical Jewish law see Urbach (1963), especially 9–25.

12 – *Inscriptiones Creticae* IV 41, col. VI.

13 – The *legis actiones* were the old form of the Roman civil procedure and were cast in formulae characteristic of pre-literate society. Of the five formulae, I am concerned with two only: the *legis actio sacramento* and the *legis actio per manus iniectionem*. The phrase is quoted from Daube (1947) 45, who was writing about the seven-year redemption and the fifty-year jubilee of the Old Testament, but that it is equally applicable to early Rome was dramatically demonstrated in Ihering's forgotten essay (1885).

14 – See Lévy-Bruhl (1960) 298–306; for an attempt to twist see Nobrega (1959).

15 – Oppenheim (1955); cf. Yaron (1959) 160–3 and (1963).

16 – Yaron (1959).

17 – Mendelsohn (1949) 29–32.

18 – Ibid., 31–2.

19 – Ibid., 30–1.

20 – The document is now, in the final edition of the Dura texts, *P.Dura* 20, an unfortunate numeration since it was originally published by Rostovtzeff and Welles (1931) as no. 10 and it has been frequently discussed and has become widely known as such.

21 – It is likely that the two fragmentary texts, *P. Dura* 17D and 21, refer to similar transactions.

22 – See especially Schönbauer (1933), and the comments by C. B. Welles in the final edition.

23 – Lasker (1950) 114.

24 – See Leemans (1950) 64–7.

25 – David and Ebeling (1928).

26 – The widespread use of loans as a deliberate device for the creation of a compulsory agricultural labour force in modern India offers a well-known parallel. See, e.g., Thorner (1962) ch. 3. 'If we go back to the turn of the century', they write (p. 8), 'it is probable that the bulk of the agricultural labourers were unfree men, men who were in debt-bondage or some other form of servitude.' On p. 32 they produce a contract, drawn up in 1949, which bears comparison with *P.Dura* 20 despite obvious differences.

27 – Plutarch, *Solon* 13.4, 'The whole *demos* was "in debt" (*hypochreos*) to the rich', may seem to argue the other way, but *hypochreos* can mean 'under obligation to', 'dependent on', in a general sense, which would be right in my opinion, and Plutarch actually goes on at once to distinguish clearly between the *hektemoroi* and the debtors: '. . . for either they farmed land for them, paying up a sixth (*or* five-sixths) of the produce, being called *hektemoroi* or *thetes*, or else receiving necessary supplies (*or* money) against the surety of their persons, they were seized by the creditors . . .' That Plutarch had no clear image of the complexities of the situation is hardly surprising, and his confusions do not constitute evidence about seventh-century Athens.

28 – The Joseph story (Genesis 47.13–26) looks like an attempt to give an historical explanation of how Egyptian peasants came to work the land for the Pharaohs, paying a fifth part, and as such it is far from uninteresting in the present context.

29 – I do not exclude the possibility that individual *hektemoroi* may also have fallen into debt and complicated their status further, but that is quite another matter from equating all *hektemoroi* with debt-bondsmen.

30 – In this discussion we may ignore those who had fled or had been sold abroad illegally.

31 – Plutarch's '. . . they were seized by the creditors, some of them becoming slaves in Attica, others being sold abroad to foreigners' (*Solon* 13.4) is not evidence; it is merely his summary of a part of Solon's poem which I have already cited, a summary distorted by the injection of what Plutarch thought the implications were. I have not examined the view that *all* loans were secured by the person, which cannot be discussed apart from the thorny question of the alienability of land. It does not really matter for the present analysis whether or not all debts could lead to bondage or personal execution so long as many could and did.

32 – Imbert (1952).

33 – A comparable distinction is suggested by the words *katakeimenos* and *nenikamenos* in the Gortyn code, though, as I have indicated in ch. 8 the text does not permit us to carry the analysis very far. That in pre-Solonic Attica bondage followed immediately upon the loan has already been suggested by Lotze (1958), but his idea of the place of the *hektemoroi* in the picture is different from mine. Cf. Urbach (1963) 13.

34 – Imbert (1952). A striking parallel for this sense of *fides* is found in Tacitus,

Germania 24, the context being the Germanic practice of gambling oneself away, known also among Amerindians, on whom see MacLeod (1925).

35 – Varro, *De lingua latina*, 7.105. I give the text as usually emended (*debet dat* for *debebat*); other changes which have been proposed do not bear on my argument.

36 – For *obaerati* as debt-bondsmen, see also Cicero, *Republic*, 2.21.38; Caesar, *Gallic Wars*, 1.4.2, in conjunction with 6.13; as debtors, Livy 6.27.6; Tacitus, *Annals*, 6.17; Suetonius, *Caesar*, 46.

37 – Kaser (1949) 248–9.

38 – In the final edition Welles says that this is a mechanical repetition of a formula, on the ground that if the debtor had sufficient property he would not have agreed to become a debt-bondsman in the first place. That argument is based on a fundamental misconception of this sort of bondage.

39 – In the Hellenistic world, under radically different conditions, imprisonment of debtors emerged with the virtual disappearance of debt-bondage; see, briefly, Nörr (1961) 135–8 with particular reference to Matthew 18.23–34.

40 – Scheil (1915); cf. Petschow (1956) 63–5.

41 – Fürer-Haimendorf (1962) ch. 4.

42 – Cf. Ihering (1880) 155: 'Thus in the final instance one would not wish to portray the fate of the debtor in too rosy a colour, when one considers the danger, which always threatened him, that placed him totally in the hands of the creditor. And that the Romans managed such power and authority as was given the creditor with consideration and humanity is a claim which even the most zealous admirer of the Romans themselves would not risk asserting.'

43 – See particularly Bottéro (1961).

44 – For examples of the difficulties in abolition in southern Asia, see Lasker (1950) 116–17; Stevenson (1943) 175–81. The point is not the obvious one that the 'creditors' objected but that the 'debtors' were ruined by abolition decrees not backed by a programme.

45 – Mendelsohn (1949) 75.

46 – Bottéro (1961).

47 – Daube (1947) 45.

48 – Nehemiah 5; II Kings 4.1–7; Proverbs 22.7; Isaiah 50.1; Amos 2.6. For the codes, see Exodus 21.2–11; Leviticus 25.33–54; Deuteronomy 15.12–17. Urbach (1963) argues that the Biblical codes did not sanction debt-bondage but meant self-sale into slavery. However, as he himself goes on to say, this difference in interpretation is not of great significance, for 'it was in practice disregarded, especially in difficult times and during famine, or at times when the wealthy classes and the nobility proved stronger than the central authority . . . To this state of affairs Prov. xxii:7, "the rich ruleth over the poor, and the borrower is slave to the lender", bears eloquent testimony' (p. 4). Cf. the phrase quoted on p. 13, 'come and work off your debt on my premises', from an exegesis of Micah 2.2 in the Babylonian Talmud.

49 – The picture of the development after Nehemiah which I have summarised briefly is that of Urbach (1963), esp. 31–49, 87–93, who has made a convincing demonstration of the fallacy of the quite different, traditional (and essentially unintelligible) view of a rapid withering away of Jewish servitude after Nehemiah.

50 – Petschow (1956) 60–2, 150.

51 – Above at n. 40.

52 – See Mitteis (1891) 358–64.

53 – Rostovtzeff (1953) I, 320.

54 – Rostovtzeff (1953) I, 342–3; cf. Préaux (1939) 533–47. The *laoi*, it is worth stressing, were not debt-bondsmen but they could and did co-exist with debt-bondage, providing an analogy to the *hektemoroi* and debt-bondsmen of pre-Solonic Attica.

55 – See, e.g., Leemans (1950) 114–17; Bottéro (1961) 152–4; Préaux (1939) 533–47.

56 – The phrase *servire creditoribus* comes from a rescript of Diocletian and Maximian (*Justinian Code* 4.10.12), and it was precisely in their reign that the tying of *coloni* appears to have begun; see Jones (1964) II, 795–812.

57 – *Theodosian Code* 5.17.1 (Constantine) and *Justinian Code* 11.52.1 (Theodosius I), respectively.

58 – *Justinian Code* 8.16 (17).6 (AD 293).

BIBLIOGRAPHICAL ADDENDUM

Non-slave labour was the theme of the sessions on classical antiquity and the ancient Near East at the Seventh International Economic History Congress in Edinburgh in 1978. Revised versions of the papers on the Greek and Roman worlds can be found in P. Garnsey, ed., *Non-Slave Labour in the Greco-Roman World* (*Proceedings of the Cambridge Philological Society*, Suppl. 6, 1980). Many of the essays in the collection treat dependent labour and place it in the larger context of labour in the ancient world.

During the past fifteen years various aspects of dependent labour in the Greek world have received attention, especially the Solonian crisis. An excellent introduction by A. Andrewes to the historical background for Solon's reforms ('The Growth of the Athenian State') is to be published in the new edition of the *Cambridge Ancient History*, vol. III.2 (forthcoming). In this chapter Andrewes offers his own suggestion about the origins of the *hektemoroi*. The recent bibliography on Solon's reforms is too extensive to list here; much of it is critically analysed in E. Will's 'Soloniana. Notes critiques sur des hypothèses récentes', *Revue des études grecques* 82 (1969), 104 ff., which examines the evidence for the meaning of the term *hektemoroi* and Solon's actions regarding the *horoi*. A collection of the fragments of Solon's legislation is now available in E. Ruschenbusch, *Solonos Nomoi* (*Historia*, Einzelschriften 9, 1966).

As so often for other subjects, much less has been written on dependent labour outside Attica. The law of debt for the whole of Greece is considered in D. Asheri, 'Leggi greche sul problema dei debiti', *Studi classici e orientali* 18 (1969), 5–122. The Gortyn code from Crete continues to supply some of the best non-Athenian evidence. An English translation is now available: R. F. Willetts, *The Law Code of Gortyn* (Berlin, de Gruyter, 1967), in which a discussion of servile statuses can be found in the introduction. The *penestae* of Thessaly have been studied recently by I. A. Šišova, 'The Status of the Penestae', *Vestnik Drevnei Istorii* (1975), no. 3, pp. 39–57 (In Russian with an English summary); cf. J. Heurgon, 'Les pénestes étrusques chez Denys d'Halicarnasse', *Latomus* 18 (1959), 713–23. The recent bibliography on the Spartan helots is discussed in the Addendum to ch. 2 above.

With regard to the Hellenistic world, a detailed review of the subject of dependent *laoi*, including Russian research, can be found in H. Kreissig, *Wirtschaft und*

Gesellschaft im Seleukidenreich (Berlin, Akademie Verlag, 1978), pt. II; cf. P. Briant, 'Remarques sur *laoi* et esclaves ruraux en Asie Mineure hellénistique', in *Actes du Colloque 1971 sur l'esclavage* (*Annales litt. de l'Univ. de Besançon* 140, 1972), 93–133. The question of the *paramone* relationship is examined formally by A. E. Samuel in 'The Role of *Paramone* Clauses in Ancient Documents', *Journal of Juristic Papyrology* 15 (1965), 221–311; for a broader social analysis of *paramone* in the Delphic manumission inscriptions, see K. Hopkins, *Conquerors and Slaves* (Cambridge University Press, 1978), 141–58. Various aspects of dependent labour in the Hellenistic world are treated in M. A. Levi's collection of essays, *Nè liberi nè schiavi. Gruppi sociali e rapporti di lavoro nel mondo ellenistico-romano* (Milan, La Goliardica, 1976).

The institution of *nexum* in early Rome has been studied by several scholars since Finley's articles appeared. A. Watson devotes a chapter to it in his *Rome of the XII Tables* (Princeton University Press, 1975) 111 ff. The chapter supports the view taken by Finley that the debt itself produced dependence rather than default, and it supplies references to recent literature on the subject. M. W. Frederiksen, 'Caesar, Cicero and the Problem of Debt', *Journal of Roman Studies* 56 (1966), 128 ff., provides a useful study of debt in the late Republic, including remarks about dependence from failure to repay loans.

A series of very important papers on the subject of dependency in the ancient Near East can be found in E. O. Edzard, ed., *Gesellschaftsklassen im Alten Zweistromland und in den angrenzenden Gebieten* (Bayerische Akad. der Wissenschaften, Phil.-hist. Klasse, *Abhandlungen*, n.F. 75, 1972); see especially I. J. Gelb, 'From Freedom to Slavery', pp. 81–92, and I. M. Diakonoff, 'Socio-Economic Classes in Babylonia and the Babylonian Concept of Social Stratification', pp. 41–52. See also M. Heltzer, *The Rural Community in Ancient Ugarit* (Wiesbaden, Steiner, 1976), and M. Liverani, 'Communautés de village et palais royal dans la Syrie du II mill.', *Journal of the Economic and Social History of the Orient* 18 (1975), 146–64.

10 – THE SLAVE TRADE IN ANTIQUITY

1 – Herodotus 8.105. The same holds true of the even longer story in Procopius a thousand years later about the Abasgi (see below at end of chapter).

2 – Dunant and Pouilloux (1958) 35.

3 – Blavatsky (1954).

4 – This point has been overlooked by Kolossovskaya (1958) 328, when she argues that the fact that Davos and Getas are not attested as slave-names in Greece before New Comedy indicates that slavery was unknown among the Dacians themselves before the fourth century BC.

5 – The fundamental analysis of this material remains that of Rostovtzeff (1931) part I.

6 – Plassart (1913).

7 – Pritchett (1956) 276–8, supplemented by five new fragments published in *Hesperia* 30 (1961) 23–9.

8 – Aristophanes, *Acharnians*, 271–5 and *scholia*; *Peace*, 1138; *Wasps*, 826–8; *scholia* for Plato, *Laches*, 187B. Cf. the occasional vase-paintings from sixth- and fifth-century Athens signed 'Kolchian' or 'the Scythian' – those painters were surely slaves; see briefly Kretschmer (1894) 75–6.

9 – Strabo 7.13.12 (cf. Eustathius' commentary on Dionysius Periegetes, 305). For

further evidence on some of these names, see Robert (1938) 118-26, a study of some fragmentary lists of slaves from Chios, probably to be dated late in the fifth century BC. Davos was almost certainly not a Dacian name, despite Strabo, but Thracian or Danubian. There was a close kinship (extending to language) among many of these peoples west and northwest of the Black Sea, also taking in the Phrygians and Bithynians of Asia Minor.

10 – Lauffer (1955-6) 123-40.

11 – Archilochus, frag. 79 Diehl (mid-seventh century BC); Hipponax, frag. 43 Diehl (mid-sixth century). Some scholars attribute the Archilochus fragment to Hipponax too.

12 – Pollux 7.14; cf. the Suda, s.v.

13 – Varro, De lingua latina, 8.21 (see below at n. 25)

14 – Polybius 4.38.4; 4.50.2-4; Strabo 11.2.3.

15 – Strabo 7.3.12; Juvenal 11.145-8; Martial 7.80; Persius 6.75-8; Galen, De meth. med. (ed. G. Kuhn) 1.1; Philostratus, Life of Apollonius, 8.7.12 (quoted below, p. 174); Athenaeus, 1.36.20B-C.

16 – Dio Cassius 78.5.5-6.1; Julian, Misopogon 352B; Synesius, De Regno, 15. On the meaning of 'Scythian' here, see below, p. 172.

17 – Ammianus Marcellinus 31.4-6; cf. Historia Augusta, Claudius, 9.3.5, on the many Gothic slaves obtained in the fighting in Moesia under Claudius, who reigned AD 268-70.

18 – Ammianus Marcellinus 16.7; Claudian, In Eutropium 1.1-17, 47-51; Procopius 8.3.12-21.

19 – A complete list of the Rhodian texts is given by Fraser and Rönne (1957) 96-7. The distribution tables of the Delphic slaves in Westermann (1955) 33 is unsatisfactory in the way the regions are grouped.

20 – Pseudo-Aristotle, Oeconomica, 1.5.1344b18; cf. Plato, Laws 6.777C-D; Aristotle, Politics, 1330a25-8.

21 – Digest 21.1.31.21; cf. Varro, De lingua latina, 9.93: 'Therefore in buying human beings we pay more if one is better by nationality.'

22 – Fontes Iuris Romani Antejustiniani, 3: Negotia (ed. V. Arangio-Ruiz, Florence, 1943) nos. 88, 89, 132-5. How accurate these statements are is another question. Tudor (1957) expresses doubts regarding the Dacian texts (nos. 88 and 89), and, though his argument is frankly speculative, he may well be right.

23 – The best discussion is by Thylander (1952) ch. 3.

24 – Varro, De lingua latina, 8.10; Pliny, Natural History, 33.26.

25 – Varro, De lingua latina, 8.21.

26 – Heichelheim (1925) 73-4; cf. Mateescu (1923).

27 – Thylander (1952); Mócsy (1956).

28 – See Strabo 1.2.27; 7.3.2; Pliny, Natural History, 4.81. Cf. Zgusta (1955) 21-3.

29 – Published by J. Roger, Revue archéologique, 6th sér., 24 (1945) 49, no. 3; cf. Finley, Aspects of Antiquity, ch. 13.

30 – Justin 9.1-2, repeated by Orosius 3.13.1-4; see Momigliano (1933).

31 – Ammianus Marcellinus 31.4-6; cf. Themistius, Orations, 10.135D-136B.

32 – Ammianus Marcellinus 22.7.8; cf. Claudian, In Eutropium, 1.58-60, for another 'Galatian' slave dealer.

33 – See, e.g., Canot (1929); Nevinson (1906); Russell (1935).

34 – Cf. Blavatsky (1960) 103.

BIBLIOGRAPHICAL ADDENDUM
The slave trade as such has not been the object of many illuminating studies since this article was written. However, slave procurement has attracted extensive discussion, most notably by W. V. Harris, 'Towards a Study of the Roman Slave Trade', in *The Seaborne Commerce of Ancient Rome*, ed. J. H. D'Arms and E. C. Kopff (American Academy in Rome, 1980), 117–40, and E. M. Shtaerman, *Die Blütezeit der Sklavenwirtschaft in der römischen Republik* (Wiesbaden, Steiner, 1969; orig. ed.: Moscow, 1964), 36–70. Like Finley, both tend to place more emphasis on the 'normal' channels of trade than on direct procurement by warfare, even for the period of the late Republic. The first chapter of E. M. Shtaerman and M. K. Trofimova, *La schiavitù nell' Italia imperiale* (Rome, Riuniti, 1975; orig. ed.: Moscow, 1971), deals sketchily with the problem of procurement and makes no final assessment of the role of trade.

On the connection between warfare and trade, see P. Ducrey, *Le traitement des prisonniers de guerre dans la Grèce antique* (Paris, E. de Boccard, 1968), 74–92, 131–9, 255–7; W. K. Pritchett, *The Greek State at War*, vol. 1 (University of California Press, 1971), ch. 3. On the link between piracy and the slave trade, see Y. Garlan, 'Signification historique de la piraterie grecque', *Dialogues d'historie ancienne* 4 (1978), 1–16; M. H. Crawford, 'Republican Denarii in Romania: the Suppression of Piracy and the Slave-Trade', *Journal of Roman Studies* 67 (1977), 117–24; E. Maróti, 'Der Sklavenmarkt auf Delos und die Piraterie', *Helikon* 9/10 (1969/70), 24–42.

For comparative purposes there is H. Köpstein, 'Zum byzantinischen Sklavenhandel', *Wiss. Zeitschrift der Karl-Marx-Univ., Leipzig, Gesellschafts- u. Sprachwiss. Reihe* 15 (1966), 487–93. And, of course, the mass of literature on the Atlantic slave trade in modern times: see D. P. Mannix and M. Cowley, *Black Cargoes* (New York, Viking, 1962); B. Davidson, *The African Slave Trade* (Boston, Little Brown, 1961); R. Anstey, *The Atlantic Slave Trade and British Abolition, 1760–1810* (London, Macmillan, 1975), and ch. 1 in *Race and Slavery in the Western Hemisphere: Quantitative Studies*, ed. S. L. Engermann and E. D. Genovese (Princeton University Press, 1975); H. S. Klein, *The Middle Passage: Comparative Studies of the Atlantic Slave Trade* (Princeton University Press, 1978).

11 – TECHNICAL INNOVATION AND ECONOMIC PROGRESS

1 – Drachmann (1932).

2 – Moritz (1958) ch. 16; Forbes (1955) 86–95.

3 – Renard (1959); Kolendo (1960).

4 – Thompson (1952a) 80–1.

5 – Ardaillon (1897) remains basic; cf. Lauffer (1955) 1125–46.

6 – Davies (1935) 24.

7 – The relevance of this discussion of the practical writers is examined later in the chapter in a consideration of Vitruvius.

8 – Farrington (1947) 9–11. Aeschylus' Prometheus still shows this lack of 'any reservation with regard to technological skills': Vernant (1965) 193.

9 – D'Arrigo (1956) ch. 14.

10 – See Kleingünther (1933).

11 – Rosen (1956).

12 – Zilsel (1926) 22.
13 – On Ctesibius, see Drachmann (1948).
14 – Forbes (1955) 90.
15 – White (1964) 82–3; cf. the model account of Bloch (1935).
16 – Suetonius, *Caligula*, 39.1.
17 – *Anthologia Palatina* 9.418, translated by Moritz (1958) 131.
18 – Rostovtzeff (1953) I, 363.
19 – See ch. 4 above.
20 – Schumpeter (1954) 53.
21 – Rehm (1938) 153.
22 – Cf. Augustine, *City of God*, 7.4. See Vernant (1955) 208–12.
23 – *Christian Directory* (1678) I, pp. 378b and 111a, respectively, quoted from Tawney (1947) 201–02.
24 – See Jones (1964) II, ch. 20.
25 – Schumpeter (1954) 70.
26 – Mickwitz (1937).
27 – Jones (1955), cf. (1964) II, ch. 21, and especially his account (p. 841) of how 'the state, and to a lesser extent great landlords, . . . cut a considerable sector out of the market by supplying their own needs directly'.
28 – The references are Pliny, *Natural History*, 36.195; Petronius, 51; Dio Cassius 57.21.7.
29 – Cook (1960) 275, 273, respectively; cf. Cook (1959).
30 – Rostovtzeff (1957) I, 172–91; cf. Walbank (1946) 28–33.
31 – Hume (1904) 415.
32 – Suetonius, *Vespasian*, 18.
33 – *Eastern Tour* (1771) IV, 361, quoted from Tawney (1947) 224.
34 – Diodorus 5.36–8.
35 – See generally the edition of this work, with commentary, by Thompson (1952a).
36 – Hancock (1958) 332.
37 – *Journey to America*, translated by G. Lawrence, edited by J. P. Mayer (1959), p. 99.

BIBLIOGRAPHICAL ADDENDUM

At about the time this article was published, the problem of technological stagnation in antiquity was also addressed by F. Kiechle in 'Das Problem der Stagnation des technischen Fortschritts in der römischen Kaiserzeit', *Geschichte in Wissenschaft und Unterricht* 16 (1965), 89–99, and H. W. Pleket in 'Technology and Society in the Graeco-Roman World', *Acta Historiae Neerlandica* 2 (1967), 1–25 (originally published in Dutch in *Tijschrift voor Geschiedenis* 78 (1965), 1–22). Pleket independently reached conclusions very similar to Finley's in their emphasis on the mentality of the landowning class, while Kiechle argued for a greater awareness and interest in the cost of labour on the part of landowners than suggested by Finley and Pleket. Kiechle later published a full-length study, *Sklavenarbeit und technischer Fortschritt im römischen Reich* (Wiesbaden, Steiner, 1969), rejecting any direct connection between slavery and technological advance. Differing from the above on the basic premise of relative stagnation is J. Kolendo, who argues in two articles ('Le travail à bras et le progrès technique dans l'agriculture de l'Italie antique', *Acta Poloniae Historica* 18 (1968) 51 ff., and 'Avènement et propagation de la herse en Italie antique', *Archeologia* 22 (1971), 104–20), that the widespread use of the harrow in the period 100 B C to A D 100 constituted significant technological progress. In 1973 Pleket returned to the issue of technology in 'Technology in the Greco-Roman World: A General Report', *Talanta* 5 (1973), 6–47, defending his (and implicitly Finley's) position against the views of Kolendo and Kiechle. This article also provides references to relevant material published between 1965 and 1973. Sir Desmond Lee, in the same year, offered a quite different explanation for the lack of technological progress in his 'Science, Philosophy and Technology in the Greco-Roman World', *Greece and Rome*, 2nd ser., 20 (1973), 65–78, 180–93. In his view, the ancient world did not possess the requisite technical knowledge for development, which is more or less independent of social and economic conditions. This is opposed to the view, e.g., expressed by A. Burford, 'Heavy Transport in Classical Antiquity', *Economic History Review*, 2nd ser., 13 (1960), 1–18, that it was precisely the social and economic conditions that did not compel any advances in technology.

On the whole subject of ancient technological development and instrumentation, see now J. G. Landels, *Engineering in the Ancient World* (London, Chatto and Windus; University of California Press, 1978). The problem of technological invention and its relationship to the 'anti-market mentality' is investigated by L. Casson, 'Unemployment, the Building Trade, and Suetonius, *Vesp.* 18', *Bulletin of the American Society of Papyrologists* 15(1978), 43–51. New research on specific ancient technical skills has also appeared since 1965. At that time the lateen sail should have been included on the list of Greco-Roman inventions (see now L. Casson, *Ships and Seamanship in the Ancient World* (Princeton University Press, 1971), 243 ff. and 277). K. D. White has produced two volumes on Roman agricultural technology: *Agricultural Implements of the Roman World* (Cambridge University Press, 1967) and, from the same publisher, *Farm Equipment of the Roman World* (1975). On ancient mining, see P. R. Lewis and G. D. B. Jones, 'Roman Gold-mining in Northwest Spain', *Journal of Roman Studies* 60 (1970), 169–85, and J. F. Healy, *Mining and Metallurgy in the Greek and Roman World* (London, Thames and Hudson, 1978); T. Schiøler, *Roman and Islamic Water-lifting Wheels* (Odense Universitetsforlag, 1973); on energy sources, E. Maróti, 'Über die Verbreitung der Wassermühlen in Europa', *Acta Antiqua* 23 (1975), 255–80, and R. Halleux, 'Problèmes de l'énergie dans le monde ancien', *Les études classiques* 45 (1977), 46–61. And, finally, R. J. Forbes' *Studies in Ancient Technology* (Leiden, Brill) cited by Finley in the article, have now appeared in a second, revised edition (1964–71).

12 – THE MYCENAEAN PALACE ARCHIVES

1 – Linear A and B have been the conventional names for the two scripts of the area; B known from both the Greek mainland and Crete, A from Crete alone. Linear A is the older one, dating two centuries or more before 1400 B C, and most scholars will probably agree with Ventris and Chadwick (1956) 32 that 'it did not survive the introduction of Linear B at Knossos'. Linear A cannot be read, but it is certainly in some way the ancestor of linear B, and the language it conceals is almost surely not Greek.

2 – Ventris and Chadwick (1953).

3 – Ventris and Chadwick (1956).

4 – No attempt is made here to consider a number of historical matters, such as the implications of the decipherment for the general history of the Aegean area in the second millennium BC or for the history of the Greek language.

5 – Unless the context indicates otherwise, I shall use 'Mycenae' and 'Mycenaean' to include all the tablets and sites, and 'Greek' for the language and civilisation first attested in the Homeric poems. I do this partly for convenience, and partly because I believe that the Mycenaean civilisation was essentially very different from what we have always known as Greek, even though the language of the tablets is Greek. This distinction implies no ethnic or racial explanation, to which some archaeologists are prone.

6 – All transliterations of the text into Latin characters and all translations are quoted exactly as given in Ventris and Chadwick (1956), with one typographical alteration. I take no responsibility for any transliteration or translation, but objections to specific translations will be made, when it appears important to do so.

7 – This general interpretation of tablets 53–60 is attractive, despite the fallacy in the off-hand rejection of an alternative possibility: 'in all 443 men are recorded, and some numbers are obviously missing in the lacuna at the right-hand edge. These numbers make it certain that we are not here concerned with a peaceful mercantile venture, but a naval operation; and it would be unlikely that the business of trade would be thus organised by a central authority'. Later I shall suggest that there is no *a priori* justification for the final argument.

8 – Sundwall (1956) has argued that cattle, not sheep, were the most numerous of the animals, and that the Knossos tablets, at least, were 'control texts' of the palace-owned herds.

9 – I shall return to these texts briefly in section III.

10 – 84 litres is the authors' conversion of T7 which appears on the tablet, T being the symbol of dry measure. The conversion tables are explained on pp. 58–60, are admittedly tentative, and rest on a number of uncertain readings and combinations.

11 – The tablet expresses these 40 English words in 25 (partly syllabic characters, partly ideograms). This is a somewhat extreme, but not unusual, example of the code-like quality of many of the texts. The highly inflected Greek language always requires fewer words than English, and the Mycenaean scribes stripped it barer; for example, often by omitting pronouns.

12 – This figure, Ventris and Chadwick point out, 'compares unfavourably with the situation at Ugarit, where only 194 published alphabetic tablets in 1947 gave Gordon a vocabulary of some 2000 words'. Actually the figure of 630 is somewhat too negative, partly because they are nearly all 'basic' words, and partly because they are supplemented by the ideograms, which cannot appear in the vocabulary (unless duplicated in the syllabic script) since we have no idea what the actual lexical units were which the ideograms expressed, even when the meaning is fairly obvious.

13 – See especailly Bennett (1956); cf. Sundwall (1956).

14 – Although Knossos tablets were already known in the nineteenth century, the first tablets from Pylos and Mycenae were not discovered until 1939 and 1950, respectively. This long time-lag has led some archaeologists to suggest that poor

technique in past excavations explains the failure to unearth many more, and to predict a great harvest in the future. I am sceptical.

15 – Cf. Bennett (1956) 104 on the Pylos land-tenure tablets.

16 – See generally Goosens (1952).

17 – On this last see Bennett (1956) 103–9.

18 – Failure to pay sufficient attention to this point is, in my judgment, a fatal weakness in one argument of the widely publicised attack by Beattie (1956). Commenting on the orthography, which often permits the same syllable to be read in several ways, and thus leads to a large number of mathematically possible combinations in a word of three or four syllables, Beattie writes (p. 6), 'Greek cannot be written in this way; or, if it were, it could not be read. . . . In documents which purport to be a record of official accounts, this kind of spelling is, of course, particularly unsatisfactory.' Just the other way round: uncertainty whether *da-ma-te* is the word for 'wives', 'portions', or 'Demeter' (his example here) is surely possible in some contexts, but not in the land-tenure tablets where the word actually appears, because the scribes knew exactly what the subject was and no one had to read the tablets in any other context. To be sure, *we* do not know what *da-ma-te* means, but that is not the point. How many literate persons today, outside a narrow professional circle, can read a corporate balance sheet?

19 – One particularly striking cuneiform example will be given below, in section III.

20 – Although these figures are based on the first edition of Ventris and Chadwick (1956), they would not be very different today.

21 – Ironically, on this particular phrase in tablet no. 176, Ventris and Chadwick indulge in 'interpretation'. In the documents section of the volume, they render it, 'the smiths are excused payment', and in the vocabulary they give *o-u-di-do-si* still a third shading: 'they do not contribute'.

22 – Again I must say that the necessary caution shown by Ventris and Chadwick is not shared universally: 'certain' definitions of such words as *o-na-to* have appeared in astonishing number.

23 – In the last-named category, the three reasonable exceptions are *do-e-ro* (fem. *do-e-ra*) – 'slave'; *ra-wa-ke-ta* – 'leader of the people, commander (?)'; *wa-na-ka* – 'king'; and obviously neither the English 'slave' nor 'leader of the people' necessarily gives the real sense.

24 – It is not only Beattie who must be reminded of this, but also some of the more enthusiastic interpreters of the texts, who have counterattacked with an animus which has the air of protesting too much.

25 – There is no doubt of this for Knossos and Pylos, but the situation in Mycenae has been needlessly confused by Wace's calling one of the buildings 'House of the Oil Merchant', which he did largely for the reason that 'the basement yielded thirty large stirrup-jars which "had originally contained oil, for their clay is heavily impregnated with oil"' (p.217). Unfortunately, whereas Ventris and Chadwick are cognisant of the worthlessness of an identification based on such grounds, Wace's label has them turning to the possibility that some of the tablets record private activity, although all the evidence there is argues against it (see pp. 109–10, 113, 179, 225).

26 – Perhaps the best available survey is still that of Lagash, a Sumerian city at its height about 2300 BC; see Falkenstein (1954); more fully Deimel (1932), Schneider

(1920); Lambert (1953). The distinction between palace and temple need not concern us here.

27 – It is worth noting that these generalisations about the Mycenaean palace organisation do not require acceptance of any given reading in the tablets, or even of the decipherment as a whole. The palace ruins are there for everyone to see, and the archival character of the tablets had been reasonably – I should say decisively – established before 1952.

28 – I say this despite the following two texts, which I quote in English in full exactly as they are published by Ventris and Chadwick. 13 = PY Ad 691: 'At Pylos: nine sons of the supernumerary women, and of the wage-earners and casual workers.' The philological justification of this translation is extremely thin, and the whole thing is out of character with the other texts of the Ad series – and it makes little sense. 35 = KN Am 819: 'At Pharai: wages for eighteen men and eight boys: grain per month (?) 1170 l. of barley.' This could make sense, but the authors' commentary shows that it is, in fact, nothing but a pure guess and I think a wrong one.

29 – Sundwall (1956) 7–8, 10, 13–14, injects evaluation into the Knossos livestock tablets by interpreting ideogram no. 45 as a *Wertzeichen* (a 'value-sign', 'exchange receipt'). His case is weak intrinsically and draws for analogy on a conception of Homeric 'cattle money' against which I argue in ch. 14 below.

30 – The presence of gold and ivory in the archaeological finds is proof enough. Cf. the scattered evidence from Semitic loan-words given by Ventris and Chadwick (1956) 91, 135–36, 319–20. The archaeological evidence has been assembled by Kantor (1947); cf. Vercoutter (1954); Stubbings (1951).

31 – I must dissociate myself, however, from the traditional view that the Greek legends about Minos represent folk memory of a commercial empire, a view which has been vigorously combated by Starr (1955). Study of the place-names in the Knossos tablets leads Ventris and Chadwick (1956) to this conclusion: 'that the area in contact with, and probably subject to, Knossos covers virtually the whole of Crete; and that no names can be located outside the island. The isolated case of *Kuprios* applied to spices implies no more than trade. Thus there is so far no evidence to support the theory of a thalassocracy, at least at the time of the fall of Knossos' (141). For a sensible general statement on trade in this period, its proportions and its motivation, see Vercoutter (1954) ch. 1.

32 – Heichelheim (1938) 161–62.

33 – Koschaker (1942). In what follows I give a very simplified statement of a most intricate analysis.

34 – Here is proof enough, if it is needed, that the presence in the Mycenaean spice tablets (nos. 105–7, to which I made reference in section I) of the word *o-pe-ro*, translated 'deficit' by Ventris and Chadwick, is no evidence at all of 'business dealings' by a private merchant.

35 – See Leemans (1950).

36 – Perhaps the most striking instance is found in the fifteenth-century BC adoption texts from Nuzi (near Kirkuk); see Steele (1943); Lewy (1942); Purves (1945); and the interchange between Mrs Lewy and Purves in the *Journal of Near Eastern Studies* 6 (1947) 180–85. Some five hundred texts 'concern the transfer of real estate in one form or another', and yet 'there is not to be found a single example of an unequivocal sale, rent, or loan of real estate' (Steele (1943) 14–15).

Most scholars think the adoptions are a cover for sales, but Mrs Lewy argues that they are a kind of transfer of reversionary rights to the king (which, unfortunately, she dresses up in a full panoply of feudal terminology). In my layman's judgment, her arguments have not been satisfactorily refuted. Additional examples of legal fiction, especially from the Phoenician city of Ugarit, will be found in Boyer (1954). See also, with a very different emphasis, Cassin (1952).

37 – It is in providing the history behind the Larsa fiction that Leemans (1950) is so valuable for our purposes.

38 – Koschaker (1942) 180.

39 – These are the definitions in their vocabulary at the end. Minor variants will be found throughout the volume when the words come up in a text or in the discussion. One sympathises with the necessity to find English renditions, no matter how tentative, but words like 'lease' are too precise for the purpose.

40 – The medievalist, at least, will at once recognise an old friend, the Indo-European village community. I return to this in section IV.

41 – See Fraser and Bean (1954) 95–6.

42 – Despite my agnosticism about all the individual words, I agree that these texts deal with the land. There are too many echoes of relevant Greek words for mere coincidence, even if the meaning of each word eludes us, and there is the grain ideogram.

43 – It is the great merit of the first part of Bennett (1956) to have demonstrated how much can be discovered from the formulas alone, without reference to the decipherment.

44 – See Bennett (1956) 103–17.

45 – The ancient Near East is full of parallels and analogies. I shall merely point to the landholdings in Larsa of both the *tamkarum* and the fishermen; see Koschaker (1942) 135–8, 148–60. Ventris and Chadwick (1956) 123 note 'the absence of any word implying that the raising of crops was a specific occupation'. But many of the men named in the land-tenure texts have no occupation or status identification, and I suggest that where this is the case, the men were on the land (in whatever status) entirely as agriculturalists. (Why the scribe himself never appears in the tablets is a real puzzle, and I have no suggestion to offer.)

46 – There is, of course, 'common sense', the most dangerous of all tools of analysis, since it is only a cover for the author's own (modern) values and images, in the absence of, or in disregard of, evidence. When Bennett (1956) 103 says that the conclusions of his purely formal analysis of the tablets are 'then seen to correspond to the sense of the tablets as they have been interpreted through their deciphered texts', he is mistaken. His formal analysis can be made to correspond with any number of incompatible interpretations, provided only that the latter assign different meanings to different words.

47 – See ch. 13 below.

48 – Ventris and Chadwick show constant awareness of this point. Unfortunately, the magnetic pull of the language is too strong, and the restraint they themselves recommend 'in quoting from Homer *material* parallels to the subject-matter of our tablets' (1956) 107 often weakens. To call upon 'identity of climate and geography,. . . continuity of history and race' is largely irrelevant.

49 – I should not have mentioned this possibility at all, were it not for the approach of L. R. Palmer, the dominating figure in the 1950s in the study of the

Mycenaean social system. His viewpoint will be evident merely from the titles of some of his publications, e.g. (1955) and (1956). It is surely not necessary to go over this ground again. But a new source has joined Tactitus' Germans, namely, the Hittites, and it is perhaps necessary to indicate that, although at least four translations of Hittite laws have appeared in the present generation, the jurists among Hittitologists are agreed that, in the complete absence of Hittite private documents, we scarcely begin to understand the Hittite system in general, its land regime in particular, and the long history behind both. See, e.g., the opening remarks by Korošec (1939); cf. H. G. Güterbock in *Journal of the American Oriental Society*, Suppl. 17 (1954), 20–1.

50 – Contemporaneity becomes more critical in a consideration of diffusion and convergence, which I shall ignore except to note the sections in Ventris and Chadwick (1956) 53–60 on weights and measures.

51 – A check reveals that Ventris and Chadwick turned to other contemporary records chiefly for objects and descriptive items, and for that purpose the methodological problem is not so serious. Nor is it objectionable, within those limits, to go directly to the raw text collections, as they did almost exclusively. For the study of institutions, however, that is a great mistake. One must turn to the experts, who are not always the editors of the texts. They are not always infallible, either, but there is no need to become metaphysical.

52 – Mycenae also raises the question, on which too little work has been done, of social breakdown and losses of major skills and techniques – the art of writing, for one.

53 – Koschaker (1942), for example, sees no difficulty in calling the society of Larsa both feudal and *Staatssozialismus* ('state socialism'), its scribes 'nicht bloss Bürokraten, sondern Bükokratissimi' (not just bureaucrats, but bureaucrats *par excellence*). Most Orientalists talk the same way. It is therefore revealing to see what happens when a first-rate Egyptologist is brought into direct contact with historians of feudalism. In the symposium *Feudalism in History*, ed. Rushton Colbourne (Princeton, 1956). W. F. Edgerton prefaces his study of Egypt with the following (p. 120): 'It seems sure that Egyptologists who have applied the term "feudal" to certain periods of Egyptian history have not had in mind any such substantive concept of feudalism as is put forward in the *Introductory Essay* to the present volume . . . In the body of the present essay, therefore, no opinions are offered as to whether any of the institutions described are feudal; it is sought merely to show . . . what the institutions were. It may be suggested here that there were not truly feudal.'

54 – Koschaker (1942) 180 went astray when he attributed the extraordinary difficulty in grasping the Larsa pattern *solely* to the bureaucratic 'mentality' behind the texts.

BIBLIOGRAPHICAL ADDENDUM

A great deal has been written about the Mycenaean tablets and economy since this article was published. All that is offered here is a checklist of the more recent or important works. A second edition of Ventris and Chadwick's *Documents in Linear B* appeared in 1973 (Cambridge University Press), consisting of a photographic reproduction of the original and 140 pages of 'additional commentary' by Chadwick. In the past few years several books about the Mycenaean world have been published: J. T. Hooker, *Mycenaean Greece* (London and Boston, RKP, 1976), and J. Chadwick, *The Mycenaean World* (Cambridge University Press, 1976). Hooker's book is to be recommended for its caution and its extensive bibliography.

The large volume of research published about the Linear B tablets has on many issues brought scholarly consensus no nearer, which is perhaps not surprising in view of the lack of context to indicate the precise meaning of many words. Philological studies covering a wide variety of aspects of Mycenaean society and economy have been produced by L. R. Palmer, *The Interpretation of Mycenaean Greek Texts* (2. ed., Oxford University Press, 1969), and M. Lejeune, *Mémoires de philologie mycénienne*, II and III (Rome, Ateneo, 1971–2). In the latter see especially II 287–312 on the economic vocabulary of the tablets; III 135–54 on *damos* and 334–44 on *wanax* and *basileus*.

With regard to the political and social hierarchy, K. Wundsam has offered a major study: *Die politische und soziale Struktur in den mykenischen Residenzen nach den Linear B Texten* (Vienna, Notring, 1968), but it has not commanded universal assent. On the *laos* see H. van Effenterre, 'Laos, laoi et lawagetas', *Kadmos* 16 (1977), 36–55. The identity of even the *wanax* has now been called into question by J. T. Hooker, 'The *Wanax* in Linear B Texts', *Kadmos* 18 (1979), 100–11. See now also S. Deger-Jalkotzy, *E-qe-ta. Zur Rolle des Gefolgschaftswesens in der Sozialstruktur mykenischer Reiche* (Vienna, Akademie der Wissenschaften, 1978).

Finley emphasises the difficulty of coming to definitive conclusions about the land tenure tablets, and they have been the subject of much debate over the past two decades, with many uncertainties remaining. L. Deroy and M. Gerard, *Le cadastre mycénien de Pylos* (Rome, Ateneo, 1965) offered a full study of the subject. Since then articles on specific questions have appeared, including A. Heubeck, 'Myk. ke-ke-me-no', *Ziva Antika* 17 (1967), 17–21; H. van Effenterre, 'Téménos', *Revue des études grecques* 80 (1967), 17–26; and M. Lejeune, 'Le dossier sa-ra-pe-da du scribe 24 de Pylos', *Minos* 14 (1974), 60–76 and 'Analyse du dossier pylien Ea', *Minos* 15 (1974), 81–115. On the more general question of settlement patterns on the land, see J. Bintliff, ed., *Mycenaean Geography* (Cambridge Library Press, 1977), and W. A. McDonald and G. R. Rapp Jr., ed., *The Minnesota Messenia Expedition: Reconstructing a Bronze Age Regional Environment* (University of Minnesota Press, 1972). For a study of the taxation of two Pylian towns, see C. W. Shelmerdine, 'The Pylos *Ma* Tablets Reconsidered', *American Journal of Archaeology* 77 (1973), 261–75.

Some of the clearest progress in the understanding of the Mycenaean palace economies has been made in the study of sheep-raising and cloth-making on Crete. Here J. T. Killen's work is fundamental: 'The Wool Industry of Crete in the Late Bronze Age', *Annual of the British School at Athens* 59 (1964), 1–15. Some of his findings have been challenged by D. Young, 'Some Puzzles about the Minoan Woolgathering', *Kadmos* 4 (1965), 111–22; for Killen's two-part reply see: 'Minoan Woolgathering. A Reply', *Kadmos* 7 (1968), 105–23 and 8 (1969), 23–38.

As for other aspects of the economy, investigations of bronze-working have been published by G. Pugliese Carratelli, 'I bronzieri di Pilo micenea', *Studi classici e orientali* 12 (1963), 242–53, and M. Lang, 'Jn Formulas and Groups', *Hesperia* 35 (1966), 397–412. Ya. J. Lencman has written a full-scale study of slavery in early Greece: *Die Sklaverei in mykenischen und homerischen Griechenland* (Wiesbaden, Steiner, 1966). More recently, on the same subject, see P. Debord, 'Esclavage mycénien, esclavage homérique', *Revue des études grecques* 75 (1973), 225–40. On the use of non-slave, dependent labour, see now J. T. Killen, 'The Linear B Tablets and Economic History: Some Problems', *Bulletin of the Institute of Classical Studies* 26 (1979), 133 ff. For foreign trade, S. A. Immerwahr, 'Mycenaean Trade and Colonization', *Archaeology* 13 (1960), 4–13, and G. Cadogan, *Patterns in the Distribution of Mycenaean Pottery in the East Mediterranean* (Nicosia, Zavallis Press, 1973). On the trade in metals, see J. D. Muhly, 'Copper and Tin. The Distribution of Mineral Resources and the Nature of The Metal Trade in the Bronze Age', *Transactions of the Connecticut Academy of Arts and Sciences'*, 43 (1973), 155–535, with supplement in 46 (1976), 77–136; cf. H. Kuwahara, 'The Source of Mycenae's Early Wealth', *Journal of the Faculty of Letters of Komazawa University* 38 (1980), 77–133. On the significance of the absence of money, see K. Polanyi's essay, 'On the Comparative Treatment of Economic Institutions in Antiquity . . .' in *The City Invincible*, ed. C. H. Kraeling and R. McC. Adams (University of Chicago Press, 1960), 329–50.

13 – PROPERTY AND TENURE

1 – Throughout, the words 'Mycenae' and 'Mycenaean' are used broadly, covering all centres in which the tablets have been found. I make no claim to independence of judgment in the reading or philological analysis of the Mycenaean tablets.

2 – For my views of the Homeric poems as a historical source, see my *World of Odysseus* (cited throughout in the revised ed. of 1978), especially App. I; see also ch. 14 below. In the book (pp. 3–5) I have suggested that the society of the poems is to be placed in the tenth and ninth centuries B C.

3 – A few scholars insist that writing continued without a break, and that it is only an accident that no samples have been found dating later than 1200 B C. This is a particularly weak argument from silence, with nothing in its favour other than an unwillingness to believe that retrogression was possible in ancient Greece.

4 – *Odyssey* 14.96–104. Richardson (1955) seems to have overlooked the mnemonic capacity of illiterate peoples when he suggested, as a serious argument, that *Odyssey* 3.391–2 (Nestor's *tamies* 'broaches a wine in its eleventh year') 'suggests some way of recording the date of laying down'. Webster (1955), whom Richardson follows, argues (p. 11) that 'Homer has too many . . . lists of objects with numbers.' But how else could a poet convey the wealth of his heroes and the magnitude of their gift giving, except by saying 'twelve herds of goats and as many of sheep' or 'three tripods and as many cauldrons'? Such use of numbers has the same significance as the many precise statements of duration of time: they symbolise great quantity (or long duration) through their appearance of exactness; see Fränkel (1953) 2–3.

5 – *Beowulf* 2428–34, 2490–6, 2884–90, respectively. Cf. the king's promise in the *Song of Roland* 5.75–6: '*je vous donnerai de l'or et de l'argent en masse, des terres et des fiefs (fiez) tant que vous en voudrez*' (trans. by J. Bédier).

6 – Much has been made of the fact that the Mycenaean tablets were written in Greek, and that they made frequent reference (as do the poets) to slaves and tripods and the like. No one would argue that there had been total discontinuity, extending to the abolition of slavery, and therefore I cannot see the significance of such 'parallels'.

7 – *Iliad* 2.661–70.

8 – *Odyssey* 4.174–7.

9 – *Odyssey* 6.9–10. The final phrase, *kai edassat' arouras*, illustrates the danger in trying to attach precise shadings to Homeric words. *Aroura* most often refers to land under cultivation, but here it obviously means 'land which *will become* tilled land'.

10 – Schachermeyr (1955) 19.

11 – The variety in the Germanic settlement patterns is one of the main themes of the *Cambridge Economic History of Europe*, vol. 1, ed. J. H. Clapham and Eileen Power (1941), see especially chs. 1, 4 and 6.

12 – See the fundamental criticism by Bloch (1931) 63–4.

13 – R. Koebner in the *Cambridge Economic History of Europe*, 1 (1941) 13.

14 – Palmer (1956) 259 goes even further and works from the hypothesis that the 'semantic structure of different languages may be compared even when individual items are etymologically unrelated'.

15 – Williams (1956) makes very salutary reading.

16 – *Odyssey* 1.387.

17 – *Iliad* 9.155, 297.

18 – *Odyssey* 15.412–13.

19 – *Iliad* 9.149–56 = 9.291–8.

20 – Whenever I give the accepted or suggested later Greek form of a Mycenaean word, I do not imply any judgment of my own about the identification. It will be apparent that in every instance no reasonable alternative would invalidate my argument. Throughout this chapter, furthermore, I am deliberately ignoring etymological connections. The meaning of a word in a given text, whether tablet or poem, can never be discovered from its etymology. Even when the etymology is reasonably certain, it reveals only the point from which a word began its history; it cannot indicate either the direction of change, or the tempo, or the limits. The word *adelphos* (brother) provides a nice example. There is no disagreement among etymologists that it is linked with *delphus*, 'womb', and that its root-sense is 'of the same womb'. *Adelphos* appears sixteen times in the *Iliad*, four times in the *Odyssey* (all in the fourth book). When applied to Hector–Alexander, Peisistratos–Antilochos, and Zeus–Poseidon–Hades, the reference is to acknowledged brothers of the same womb; probably also for Agamemnon–Menelaus, though nowhere in the poems is there explicit evidence regarding the mother. Other uses are too general for analysis. But then we read the following in *Iliad* 13.694–5 (= 15.333–4): 'Now of these one, Medon, was the bastard son (*nothos*) of Oïleus, the godlike, and brother (*adelphos*) of Aias' (Medon is also called *nothos* in 2.727–8, where his mother is identified as Rhene). The poet of the *Iliad* was thus so unaware of the etymology that he found no difficulty in coupling *adelphos* with *nothos* to refer to two men who had the same father but different mothers.

21 – Neither list is quite complete, but the omissions do not change the picture. The one important Homeric word I have left out of this account is *therapon*, which is used so indiscriminately for anyone giving 'service', from the lowliest domestic to Patroclus (see *World of Odysseus*, 103–4), that it does not lend itself to useful analysis in the present context.

22 – In Cyprus in the fourth century BC, *basileus* was the king, *anax* the title of his sons and brothers; see *DGE* 680 (= *SGDI* 59); Aristotle, fr. 526 Rose, ap.

Harpocration, s.v. *anaktes kai anassai* (cf. Eustathius *ad Il.*13.582); Isocrates 9.72. Another instance of survival is apparently recorded in Hesychius: *bannas*: 'king among the Italiotes', 'the most important ruler *(archon)*'. The royal sense seems also to have existed in Old Phrygian; see Friedrich (1932) 125, no. 1 (= *DGE* p. 404, no. 1) and perhaps no. 6. The cult material has been assembled by Hemberg (1955).

23 – Wackernagel (1916) 209–12.

24 – There is no agreement among the experts on the status of *pa₂-si-re-u*, except that he was certainly not on a par with the *wanax*; see Ventris and Chadwick (1956) 121–2.

25 – I cannot believe that a conscious desire for archaism can adequately explain the failure of the poets to carry *basileus* all the way. Wherever they made a deliberate effort to keep an archaic flavour, as in the references to metals, that is revealed by a statistical preponderance, but never, as here, by the absolute exclusion of the later element.

26 – The word *aketoro*, which appears in Knossos VI 45, could conceivably be the genitive of *hegetor*, but that is unlikely. Metrical considerations may have had a hand in the inclusion or exclusion of a particular word, but they could not conceivably explain the whole discrepancy. Therefore, the repeated insistence on the metrical impossibility of the one word *lawagetas* is a false and misleading argument.

27 – On the vocabulary differences between the two poems, see Page (1955) 149–60.

28 – Chieftains: *Iliad* 2.79; 10.301, 533; *Odyssey* 7.136, 186; 8.97, 387, 536; 11.526. General: *Iliad* 9.17; 11.276, 587, 816; 12.376; 14.144; 16.164; 17.248; 22.378; 23.457, 573; *Odyssey* 8.11,26; 13.186, 210.

29 – *Odyssey* 1.72.

30 – The poets were able to choose freely among the various words for leader and chieftain precisely because they had no technical sense, but were merely different ways of saying 'nobleman'. This obvious fact is persistently ignored, and historians are in consequence driven to complicated explanations, which are neither necessary nor tenable. Refusal to recognise the monarchical position of Alcinous in Phaeacia is perhaps the best example. Once the possibility is accepted that *basileus* may mean 'nobleman' as well as 'king' – very much like *Häuptling* (to use the German equivalent) in fourteenth- and fifteenth-century Frisia – there is no difficulty; otherwise, the picture which is drawn simply contradicts the clear evidence of the Phaeacian section of the *Odyssey*. After all, there is never an automatic, unchanging relation between individual words and institutions; see, e.g., ch. 14 below on *hedna*.

31 – See *World of Odysseus*, index s.vv. 'Gifts', 'Guest-friendship'; ch. 14 below; part I of Gernet (1948–9); and, for interesting Latin parallels, Palmer (1956).

32 – Contrast Wiglaf's threat, in an analogous situation in *Beowulf* (2884–90): 'Now shall the receiving of treasure and gifts of swords, all joy of ownership, and comfort be wanting to your race; each man of your family will have to wander, shorn of his landed possessions, as soon as nobles far and wide hear of your flight, your despicable act' (trans. J. R. Clark Hall, rev. ed. (1950) C. L. Wrenn).

33 – *Iliad* 23.296–8.

34 – *Iliad* 2.569–77.

35 – Nor does the appearance of the word *thoe* in a comparable situation (*Iliad*

13.669) point to vassalage. If *thoe Achaion* and the only other occurrence of the word in the poems (*Odyssey* 2.192) are a clue at all, they suggest a penalty imposed by a group, not by an overlord.

36 – *Odyssey* 15.80–5.

37 – *Odyssey* 3.301–12; 4.90–9, 125–32.

38 – *Odyssey* 14.285–6, 323–6 (= 19.293–5); 19.282–7.

39 – *Beowulf* 2428–31, 2492–6.

40 – This distinction was apparently overlooked by Jeanmaire (1939) ch. 1 in his study of Homeric *compagnonnage*.

41 – Chadwick (1912) 363 had already made this point. It is also necessary to insist that the long tale told by Odysseus, beginning at 14.199, has nothing to contribute to this discussion, He married 'a wife from people with many possessions' and acquired great wealth and status as a pirate leader.

42 – See the opening pages of Jachmann (1953) though I cannot accept the *Einzeeied* (single poem) explanation which he then proposes. See further section VI of this chapter.

43 – A considerable fuss has been made over the 'nine cities of Pylos'. One group of tablets has been reasonably interpreted as revealing the names of nine localities in southwestern Peloponnesus which were somehow subordinate to Pylos (see Ventris and Chadwick (1956) 142–3), and at once some scholars pointed to *Iliad* 2.591–6 and *Odyssey* 3.5–8, where the figure 'nine' is associated with Pylos. Except for Kyparisseis, however, the names of the places are quite different in the poems and the tablets, and the Odyssean account is incompatible in every way with the information in the tablets. The recurrence of the number 'nine' may well be no more than a coincidence, for that number plays a very special role in the poems; see Germain (1954) 13–14. If, however, the *Iliad* and the *Odyssey* had in fact retained a 'memory' of an actual power relationship in Messenia, that memory was almost totally wrong. If the 'nine cities of Pylos' proved anything at all, therefore, it is the uselessness of the Homeric poems as a source of narrative history.

44 – Material objects make up still a third category. The poets' treatment of metals and armour and buildings differs markedly – in so far as their value as sources is concerned – from both their narrative and the institutional background.

45 – *Odyssey* 14.61–4.

46 – *Iliad* 14.119–24 (Tydeus in Argos); *Odyssey* 7.311–15 (Odysseus in Phaeacia).

47 – *Iliad* 9.480–4.

48 – Kurt Latte in Pauly-Wissowa-Kroll, *Realencyclopädie der classischen Altertumswissenschaft*, II.5 (1934) col. 435.

49 – This point was properly stressed by Erdmann (1942) 353. Cf. A. Dopsch, in the *Cambridge Economic History of Europe*, 1 (1941) 173, on the Visigoths: 'There was no assignment of land by lot: the term *sortes* simply means shares, and is used of divisions among the Goths themselves.'

50 – *Iliad* 6.191–5; 9.574–80; 20.391; and 20.184–6.

51 – *Iliad* 12.313–14; 18.550–60; 20.391; *Odyssey* 6.291–4; 17.297–9, respectively.

52 – *Odyssey* 11.184–5; see further n. 55 below. In addition, the *temenos* of a god is mentioned three times in the formula, 'where is your holy ground (*temenos*) and smoking altar' (*Iliad* 8.48; 23, 148; *Odyssey* 8.363), and once in a very different expression: in the Catalogue of Ships, one entry begins, 'And of those who had

Phylake and Pyrasos, Demeter's *temenos* . . .' (*Iliad* 2.695–6). We shall not be directly concerned with sacred precincts in our discussion because the texts provide no useful information.

53 – This is commonly true of land-tenure and land-measurement terminology everywhere. 'Rien de plus variable que ca vocabulaire rurale', wrote Bloch (1931) 31; cf. Bishop (1954) 30 nn. 21, 34–5.

54 – Appropriate references will be found in Liddell and Scott, s.v., and they immediately reveal the inaccuracy of the definition there given, 'a piece of land marked off from common use and dedicated to a god'.

55 – In Hades, Odysseus' mother says (*Odyssey* 11.184–5): 'No one yet holds your fine *temenos*'. Then she adds 'and he apportions the equal feasts, work that befits a man with authority', which is untrue, so that the whole passage loses much of its value as direct evidence. However, it seems to me to be a legitimate inference that the poet had no firm association, in his own mind, between *temenos* and 'land set aside', when those lines were introduced into the text. Even if one believes the whole eleventh book of the *Odyssey* to be an interpolation, that would make little difference, for the lack of any special meaning of *temenos* (other than 'royal estate') would then merely be shifted from 'Homer' to someone else who worked with the same stock of bardic formulae.

56 – *Iliad* 6.192–4.

57 – *Iliad* 12.310–13.

58 – It is a mistake, however to draw any special inference from Sarpedon's *temenos nemomestha*. Thomson (1954) 331 translates 'they have bestowed on us a *temenos*', thereby forcing an interpretation which is not in the text. By this time *nemomai* meant no more than 'have', 'possess'; see Laroche (1949) 10–11.

59 – The evidence is assembled by Bachofen (1948), I, 85–104; II, 928–45; cf. briefly Thomson (1954) 163–5. The evidence stands despite the unacceptability of the whole Bachofen position on mother-right, on which see Pembroke (1965).

60 – In particular, there is neither the word itself nor the idea in the one passage in which one would most expect to find both, *Odyssey* 6.9–10 on the founding of Scheria.

61 – Achilles' language – did Priam promise you his *time* (honour) and his *geras* (prerogative), *or* did the Trojans promise you a *temenos*? – clearly divorces the *temenos*, in this particular instance, from royal power; see Jeanmaire (1939) 74.

62 – *Iliad* 9.574–80. On this description of the *temenos*, see below n. 83.

63 – See the final paragraphs of section V.

64 – The best example is *Syll.*[3] 141 (the settlement of Kerkyra Melaina about 385 BC); see the analysis, with further documentation, in Wilhelm (1913) 3–15.

65 – It is almost impossible to discover, from modern accounts, that there is only one authority for believing in these royal holdings among the *perioikoi*, namely Xenophon, *Constitution of the Lacedaemonians*, 15.3, and even there the word *temenos* does not appear.

66 – Jeanmaire (1939) 75. Cf. Aristotle's proposal, *Politics* 1330a9–16, that public slaves work the public land set aside for cult and the needs of the *syssitia*.

67 – Achilles' lament in Hades (*Odyssey* 11.489–91) should not be offered as evidence for serfdom. 'I would rather be bound down (*eparouros*), working as a *thes* for another, by the side of a landless man, whose livelihood was not great,

than be ruler over all the perished dead' does not make sense if the sole occurrence of *eparouros* is translated 'attached to the soil'.

68 – See *World of Odysseus*, 78–82; Jeanmaire (1939) 43–58.

69 – *Iliad* 3.56–7.

70 – See *World of Odysseus*, 92–3.

71 – Again *Beowulf* supports my objection to the argument that the indifference of the poets is a sufficient explanation. The word *folc-scaru* which appears in line 73 may be obscure, but it surely means some kind of common holding. In about 27,000 lines the *Iliad* and the *Odyssey* do not once use a comparable phrase.

72 – *Iliad* 12.421–4.

73 – Cf. e.g. Lysias, 32.4; *Hesperia* 7 (1938) 9, no. 2, lines 11–24; and the material assembled by Weiss (1908).

74 – Thomson (1954) 590. This is Thomson's most recent suggestion, which he prefers to his older one that the two men 'might be representatives of two related families subdividing a holding which has been allotted to them jointly'. It is not impossible, furthermore, that *aroura* here means no more than 'potentially arable land', as in *Odyssey* 6.10 (see n. 9 above).

75 – It is worth noting that it is precisely in the similes that we can expect to find survivals of very old practices; see, on the purely linguistic side, Shipp (1972) chs. 2–3.

76 – *Odyssey* 6.9–10.

77 – See particularly *Iliad* 1.124–6; cf. *Iliad* 5.158 and *Odyssey* 14.208–9 on the division of an inheritance.

78 – *Odyssey* 24.205–7. The twenty-fourth book, like the eleventh, is held by many to be an interpolation, and the description of Laertes' farm here flatly contradicts *Odyssey* 1.189–93. Methodologically, however, it is unsound completely to ignore the *institutional* side of the passage on these grounds.

79 – Ventris and Chadwick (1956) 233 do so by underscoring the word 'acquired' (*kteatissin*). However, if the stress is to be placed on that part of the sentence, it should be on 'himself acquired' (*autos kteatissin*), emphasising acquisition by one's own efforts as against acquisition by inheritance or gift. I prefer, as my text indicates, an altogether different stress, without formal juristic overtones. Too much is made of the verb 'to acquire'. In ordinary speech, anything which comes into a man's possession was necessarily acquired somehow, by theft, discovery, gift, exchange, inheritance, labour – every possession is an acquisition.

80 – *Iliad* 1.162; 2.690. It may be, of course, that the poet chose this one among several possible formulae merely because it suited him aesthetically. If so, all discussion of emphasis is moot.

81 – Eustathius caught the point very well, but his opening remarks show a general misunderstanding of the possibilities in the world of Odysseus.

82 – *Iliad* 18.541–9; see Thomson (1954) 585–6. The difficult word *tripolos* in this passage has not found a satisfactory solution; see, besides Thomson, Pöhlmann (1895) 121–6; E. A. Armstrong, in *Classical Review* 57 (1943) 3–5. Pöhlmann correctly stressed the point that the whole passage *may*, but *need not*, reflect open fields.

83 – The *Iliad*, in particular, emphasises the two-part character of large holdings, using a number of different formulations: 6.195 (= 12.314; 20.185); 9.579–80, 14.122–3. Cf. *Odyssey* 9.108. The point, of course, is merely to make clear

concretely, by elaboration of details (as always in the poems), that these were excellent estates. It would be a mistake to read anything more in the passages.

84 – In English usage (and generally in European languages), the phrase 'common land' was restricted to non-arable. There was also 'common pasture of land' but not common holding of the arable. This is precisely the case in the fourteenth-century English poem *Piers the Ploughman*, which, curiously enough, has become a favourite parallel for the shield scene among supporters of the common-holding view of Homeric society.

85 – See, e.g., Bishop (1954) for Yorkshire; Le Lannou (1941) 113–37 for Sardinia; P. Struve, in the *Cambridge Economic History of Europe*, 1 (1941) 427–35 for Russia. Struve writes (p. 433): 'There can be no doubt that the village community with its communal ownership is the product of a comparatively late development, evolving as a result of the joint action of two forces: (1) the fiscal and administrative power of the state or of the privileged landlord over the peasant, and (2) the growth of population. Until the seventeenth century there are in Russia no signs of the village community in its modern sense.'

86 – Herodotus 9.94; cf. Erdmann (1942) 355–6.

87 – Other instances in which cities purchased real property that was then turned over to individuals are cited by Wilhelm (1913) 4–8.

88 – *Odyssey* 13.13–15; cf. 2.74–8; 22.55–9.

89 – Two other supposed hints of communal or limited tenures in the poems require notice.

(1) From time to time the attempt is made to read great sociological or juristic significance into the fact that one of the scenes on the Shield of Achilles is located on a royal *temenos*. None of these efforts needs detailed refutation after the decisive objection raised by Pöhlmann (1895) 121–6, that, taken all together, the scenes on the shield do not pretend to cover systematically the social structure or tenurial regime of Homeric society; they merely describe some activities in the life of the period. With respect to the work (and the workers), the *temenos* cannot be differentiated from the four adjoining panels, with their scenes of ploughing, vintaging, and pasturing.

(2) Palmer (1955) 12–13, suggested that the 'original meaning' of *demioergoi* was 'those who work the *damos*-land', that is, 'village land' (cf. Palmer (1954) 43–5). Although he does not say that the word had retained that meaning in the poems, the hypothesis cannot be passed over in our context. It should be noted, first, that the word *demioergos* appears only twice in the poems, once when Eumaeus asks, 'For who ever summons a stranger from abroad and brings him along, unless he be one of the *demioergoi*, a seer or healer of ills or worker in wood, or even an inspired bard'; and once when Penelope calls heralds *demioergoi* (*Odyssey* 17.382–5 and 19.135 respectively). Therefore it is wrong to call the *demioergoi* the artisan class. The only two physicians mentioned are included in the Catalogue of Ships as leaders of contingents (*Iliad* 2.729–32), and seers and heralds are found in the highest social circles. But not smiths and carpenters. The only common element that I can see is not one of class at all, but that these men, each a specialist, were available to anyone who needed their services, to the *demos* in that very broad sense. Certainly there is no hint of a past when they worked '*damos*-land' and Eumaeus's insistence on foreigners would seem to argue in an entirely different direction.

90 – The allies of the Trojans, however, must be set apart.

91 – The diversified patterns and consequences of post-Mycenaean settlement are often ignored (and not only in discussions of Homeric society); or treated, too simply and incorrectly, as a matter of survivals from the Mycenaean past or of 'race' (the Dorians against the other Greeks); see the sound arguments of Gschnitzer (1955).

92 – I have discussed this point in ch. 14 below, in connection with marriage.

93 – In the light of the complicated post-Mycenaean history of the word, it is legitimate to raise a warning against taking it for granted that *damos* means 'community' in the tablets.

94 – It may be added that thus far the tablets, unlike the poems, have revealed no word likely to mean 'wages' or 'wage-earner'.

95 – Ventris and Chadwick (1956) no. 152. *Temenos* has also been suggested as a reading following the lacuna in line 2 of Er 880 (old Er 02), but my argument is not affected.

96 – After a lengthy analysis, Palmer (1954) 50–1 concludes: 'An invading Indo-European people . . . established itself in Greece during the second millennium B C. It settled and divided the conquered lands first into three main categories: the sacred land allocated to the priest-king, the *wa na ka te ro te me no*, secondly the portion of the "folk-leader", the *ra wa ke si jo te me no*. But . . . a considerable amount of land was farmed collectively by the third estate, the *damos* on its *ke ke me na* land. Thus if we exclude the sacred land, the profane land falls into two categories, the folk-land and the feudal land. The latter was apportioned to vassals, *te re ta*, owing feudal service – *telos*.' I find it even harder to believe in the 500-year survival, essentially unchanged, of an assumed 'Indo-European' settlement plan during the Mycenaean period, with its demonstrably enormous growth in material culture and in concentration of power, than in the frequently alleged survival of 'folk-land' and the like in the post-Mycenaean world.

BIBLIOGRAPHICAL ADDENDUM

In the bibliographical suggestions for the previous chapter, studies related to the Mycenaean system of land tenure can be found. There are only a few additional items related to Homer which should be added to that list. Anna Morpurgo Davies has recently pursued the question of the differences between the Mycenaean and the later Greek worlds, with a method similar to Finley's: 'Terminology of Power and Terminology of Work in Greek and Linear B', *Actes du sixième Colloque international sur les textes mycéniens et égéens . . . 1975* (Univ. de Neuchâtel, 1979), pp. 87–108. C. Vlachos has devoted a chapter of his *Les sociétés politiques homériques* (Paris, PUF, 1974) to a discussion of Homeric and Mycenaean landholding and political structure. For another recent discussion of land tenure, see I. S. Svencickaia. 'The Interpretation of Data on Landholding in the *Iliad and Odyssey*', *Vestnik Drevnei Istorii* (1976) no. 1, 52–63 (in Russian with English summary). On the agricultural economy of Homeric Greece more generally, see W. Richter, *Die Landwirtschaft im homerischen Zeitalter* (Archaeologia Homerica, 2 H, Göttingen, Vandenhoeck and Ruprecht, 1968).

14 - HOMERIC MARRIAGE

1 - Thus, Wolff (1952) writes, 'The roots of betrothal are perhaps rightly to be sought in the prehistoric practice of bride-purchase' (p. 15). For the acceptance of this view among non-jurists, note the flat assertion of Wilamowitz (1927) 101, regarding the dowry passages in the *Odyssey*: 'The poet writes in this instance about the ancient practice of bride-purchase against the legal framework of his own time.' For full bibliographies on the supposed Homeric marriage by purchase, see Köstler (1944b) 209 n. 20; (1944a) 6 n. 2.

2 - Koschaker (1937) 86, 112.

3 - Koschaker (1937) 83-4.

4 - The word *hedna*, always used in the plural, is examined in section III.

5 - *Iliad* 9.146, 288.

6 - *Odyssey* 11.288-97; 15.225-38.

7 - *Odyssey* 21.74-9. The fact that this particular contest was a trick on Penelope's part is irrelevant for our purposes.

8 - It is well established that the relationship between Helen and Paris was a legitimate marriage in every sense; see, e.g., Erdmann (1934) 199.

9 - *Iliad* 19.297-9.

10 - *Thebais*, frag. 6, in Apollodorus, *Bibliotheca*, 1.8.4.

11 - E.g. Köstler (1944b) 207-9; Koschaker (1937) 139.

12 - Whether Patroclus' promise was made in earnest or as a joke is immaterial here.

13 - *Odyssey* 10.5-7.

14 - See Murray (1924) 125-6.

15 - *Odyssey* 7.311-15.

16 - *Iliad* 6.191-3, 251, 394; 9.147-56 (= 9.289-98); 22.51; *Odyssey* 1.277-8 (= 2.196-7); 7.311-15; *Hymn to Aphrodite*, 139-40; und the four passages which indicate that Penelope had brought a dowry, *Odyssey* 2.132-3; 4.736; 23.227-8; 24.294 (on which see Köstler (1944b) 216). The sense of *eednosaito* in *Odyssey* 2.52-4 is debatable; see below, n. 46. There is also the passage, *Odyssey* 20.341-2, in which Telemachus says that if Penelope chooses a husband willingly, 'I will ofer countless gifts'.

17 - This schematic presentation of the facts should include three more points – the promise of marriage, the nature of the marriage ceremony, and the role of the kinship group or extended family. They are considered in section IV. Something must be said here about the wooing of Penelope, which would seem to offer the best raw material for the study of Homeric marriage. It is my opinion, however, that Homeric marriage institutions can be studied only by ignoring this material in large part, first because what we have in the *Odyssey* is a confused, misunderstood, and often self-contradictory amalgam of strands in which no single institutional pattern can be rediscovered without arbitrary procedures; second, because the juristic aspects have been forced into the background by what was essentially a power struggle. 'Of course, one cannot say very much on the basis of legal assumptions; in books 19 and 21 Penelope is no longer under compulsion to name a husband, while the suitors are engaged in conflict'. I agree with this point by Wilamowitz (1927) 103 n. 1 2; see further *World of Odysseus*, 82-5 (cited throughout

in the revised ed. of 1978). I shall of course make use of individual passages pertaining to Penelope, but never as a central part of the argument.

18 – I use the word 'foreigners' instead of 'outsiders' here because I mean not merely men from another community, but men from outside the Graeco-Trojan world altogether. It should be noted that Lemnos, the source of the wine freight discussed in the next paragraph, was not a proper part of the Achaean world in the Homeric poems.

19 – *Iliad* 7.467–75 and *Odyssey* 15.415–16 (cf. 462–3), respectively. *Iliad* 18.291–2, in which Hector says to Polydamas, 'many possession have been sold and gone into Phrygia,' is unclear to me. Even if the reference is to sale, which I doubt, it again involves foreigners; see Pringsheim (1950) 93 n. 2.

20 – By 'treasure' I mean prestige goods such as gold and bronze tripods and cauldrons, which circulated so extensively among Homeric aristocrats as gifts or prizes. In *Odyssey* 1.184 Mentes, a Taphian chieftain (actually Athena in disguise), tells Telemachus that he is carrying iron to Temesa in quest of copper. This is no exception to what I have said in the text, on several grounds; it is enough to point out that both Taphos and Temesa were in every sense outside the Greek world.

21 – Hesiod, *Works and Days*, 341.

22 – The words are *biotos*, as in the long tale told by Eumaeus about the Phoenician traders who spent a year in his community and then kidnapped him as they were ready to set sail: 'having piled up in their hollow ship much substance (*bioton*)' (*Odyssey* 15.456); *onos*; and *kteana* (on which see n. 25 below).

23 – In this connection, it is worth quoting the following general statement from Quiggin (1949) 3: '. . . many objects are called "currency" which are never current. They may serve as standards of value or as a symbol of wealth . . . but they are never used in ordinary trading. They pass from hand to hand, or from group to group in important transactions and play a large part in gift-exchange and in "bride-price".' (Quiggin puts quotation-marks around 'bride-price' because, like many anthropologists, she rejects the sales implication in the phrase.)

24 – *Iliad* 6.234–6.

25 – *Odyssey* 1.430–31. This is the decisive Homeric text for excluding cattle from the *kteana* (possessions) of this formula, which also appears in three other places in the identical phrasing, *priato kteatessin eoisin* (*Odyssey* 14.115, 452; 15.483), each time with reference to the purchase of a slave.

26 – The quotations are from Pringsheim (1950) 95. On the very narrow limits within which he believes it possible to speak of a sales terminology, see especially p. 93: cf. Chantraine (1940) 11–12.

27 – Koschaker (1950) especially 211–14, 234–5. It is worth noting that in Babylonia the language of marriage and the language of sale did coincide at one important point, see pp. 215–20.

28 – In this connection it is important to note Quiggin's conclusion (1949) 7–10 that 'bride-price' and *wergeld* precede trade in the establishment of 'monetary' standards of worth.

29 – Koschaker (1950) 212–14.

30 – With reference to the Mentes passage, *Odyssey* 1.184, Pringsheim writes (1950) 92: 'barter still exists especially in the commerce with foreigners who have not accepted the Greek method of payment'. I cannot imagine what the 'Greek method of payment' was in this period, but, apart from that, the state-

ment is misleading because, as Pringsheim recognises all through his discussion, all 'commerce' was in fact trade with foreigners.

31 – See Finley, *World of Odysseus*, index, s.v. 'Gifts'; Gernet (1948–9) especially Part I, 'Debitum et obligatio'.

32 – *Odyssey* 24.283–6.

33 – The notion of 'provoking' a counter-gift, that is, of imposing an obligation on the recipient to make a return, is central to the sociology of gift-giving; see Gernet (1948–9) 26–30 on archaic Greece. Classical Greeks saw evidences all around them, though they no longer fully understood the psychology. See e.g. Thucydides 2.97.3–4 on Thrace; Xenophon, *Cyropaedia*, 8.2.7–10 on Persia; and the analysis of Mauss (1921) 388–97. Perhaps a similar misunderstanding lies behind the detailed, though admittedly second-hand, description of the auctioning of brides in Babylonia given by Herodotus 1.196. Nothing has been uncovered in Babylonian sources which substantiates his story; see Baumgartner (1950) 79–80; Ravn (1942) 89. Aristotle, *Politics*, 1268b40 speaks of 'ancient laws' (*archaioi nomoi*) by which 'the Greeks bought their wives from one another', and this bald statement is commonly quoted as proof of Homeric marriage by purchase. I doubt that Aristotle's reference is to Homer; in fact, the one Aristotelian statement I could find about marriage in Homer which is explicit (*Rhetoric* 1401b34) says that Helen married Menelaus as a matter of free choice on her part, a choice given her by her father. The context of the half-sentence in the *Politics*, which does not even mention Homer, is that of the archaic, but post-Homeric, law codes. Alternatively, we must again consider the possibility of classical Greek misunderstanding of the fine shadings of gift-giving as it operated in a more primitive world.

34 – *Odyssey* 18.275–9.

35 – *Odyssey* 6.158–9. It marks a significant departure when, in the early sixth century, Cleisthenes, tyrant of Sicyon, gave each of the unsuccessful suitors of his daughter a gift of one talent in compensation for his wasted time and effort; Herodotus 6.130.

36 – Köstler (1944a) 8 n. 4, saw that the risk factor in the *hedna* is a further argument against considering them to be a purchase-price. Other clearcut Homeric references to competitive gift-giving among suitors are *Odyssey* 15.16–18 and 16.390–2 (= 21.161–2). By far the best illustration in all the literature is the long papyrus fragment on the wooing of Helen (Hesiod, frag. 94 and 96, ed.² Rzach). Although this may be a late text – Wilamowitz dated it as not earlier than the end of the sixth century BC – both the account and the language are fully consonant with the Homeric materials. Note particularly 94.23–5 where Odysseus reveals his craftiness by refusing to take a hopeless risk; he sent no gifts 'for he knew in his heart that golden-haired Menelaus would triumph, for he was the greatest of Achaeans in possessions'.

37 – Gernet (1917) 287 draws the following conclusion from the size of the *hedna*: 'Very well, an individual does not possess one hundred cattle: it is the clan which possesses them' (cf. Gernet (1948–9) 112–14). Not only is there no evidence for this statement – thus, Eumaeus' enumeration of the possessions of Odysseus (*Odyssey* 14.98–104) is personal, not familial – but it overlooks the magnitude of gift-giving on all occasions, always personal in my judgment. That all these figures are conventional and grossly exaggerated is no doubt true, but that is not germane to the issue.

38 – See Finley, *World of Odysseus*, 120–3.

39 – *Odyssey* 1.318.

40 – *Odyssey* 15.16–18.

41 – Much has been made of the word *alphesiboia* ('cattle-bringing' to the father) as an epithet for a marriageable daughter. But the fact is that it appears exactly once in the poems, *Iliad* 18.593 (and once in the *Hymn to Aphrodite* 119). The antonym, *polydoros* ('bringing many gifts' to the husband), which is found three times (*Iliad* 6.394; 22.88; *Odyssey* 24.294; cf. *epiodoros* in *Iliad* 6.251), reveals the gift sense clearly, and it was perfectly consonant with Homeric mores for the gift potential to be underscored so explicitly. It seems significant, furthermore, that whereas in sales cattle served only as a standard, and were not exchanged except perhaps under emergency conditions, they were enshrined in the word *alphesiboia*, and they were in fact given as marriage-gifts, just as they were transferred in other gift situations. This pattern in the differentiated use of cattle is widely attested for many parts of the world among primitive peoples, most certainly, perhaps, among African tribes; see Quiggin (1949) index, s.v. 'cattle'.

42 – A study of the language of Greek gift-giving has never been undertaken. See the suggestive remarks of Benveniste (1948–9).

43 – The passages with the word *hedna* are given in n. 45. In *Iliad* 11.243, the phrase is *polla d'edoke*, for which there is an interesting parallel in *Odyssey* 8.269 (Ares' gifts of seduction to Aphrodite). *Dora* appears in *Odyssey* 18.279, where, it can be argued, the choice of words is determined by the fact that the gifts went to the woman herself, in this instance Penelope (but see below, at nn. 53–4). In *Odyssey* 15.16–18 Athena says to Telemachus that Eurymachus 'outdoes all the suitors in gifts (*doroisi*), and has greatly increased his gifts of wooing (*hedna*)'. The consensus is that *dora* and *hedna* are distinct here, the former being gifts to the bride, the latter gifts to her father; see the bibliography in Köstler (1944a) 19 n. 2. I am tempted, however, to treat them as synonyms. In Hesiod, frag. 94 and 96, we find the two words used interchangeably, without a shadow of distinction; e.g. *dora* in 94.23, 49 (or *donitai* in Wilamowitz's reconstruction); 96.1; and *hedna* in 94.39,44; 96.5. There is no objection in principle to understanding such a coupled phrase in Homer to be merely repetitive of a single idea.

44 – In the dowry passages listed in n. 16 above, *hedna* appears only in *Odyssey* 1.277–8 (= 2.196–7) and perhaps also in the verb *hednoo* of *Odyssey* 2.52–4.

45 – I have included in these figures the single usage, in *Iliad* 13.382, of *hednotai*, 'those who seek or receive *hedna*'. *Hedna* appears in *Iliad* 16.178, 190; 22.472; *Odyssey* 6.159; 8.318; 11.117, 282; 13.378; 15.18; 16.391; 19.529; 21.161; *anaednon* in *Iliad* 9.146, 288; 13.366.

46 – The Penelope passages are *Odyssey* 1.277–8 and 2.196–7. In *Odyssey* 2.52–4, Telemachus complains that the suitors 'shrink from going to the house of her father Icarius, so that he might marry off his daughter (*eednosaito thugatera*) and give her to whomsoever he chooses'. Virtually all commentators and translators take the key phrase to mean that her father 'may himself set the bride-price for his daughter'. From the context, however, 'that he may himself dower his daughter' is equally possible; see Wilamowitz (1927) 102. The virtual unanimity in favour of the other alternative merely reflects the prevalence of the marriage-by-purchase doctrine. Hesychius, s.v. *polydoros*, gives *polyednos* ('well-dowered') as a synonym, but I know of no text in which the word appears.

47 – For the scholiasts, see not only their comments on the passages listed in n. 46 above, but also on Pindar, *Olympians*, 9. 10 and *Pythians*, 3.94, where *Hednon* and *hedna*, respectively, clearly mean gifts to the groom.

48 – This view lies at the heart of the still widely cited study by Finsler (1912), who believed that in the *Odyssey*, at least, virtually all the gifts, regardless of source, were given to the bride. To establish that point, he handpicks his passages and offers arbitrary translations and generalisations.

49 – On the *hedna* given by the groom to the father, Hephaestus' remark, *Odyssey* 8.317–19, is decisive regardless of the value of the passage in other respects (see further nn. 56 and 80 below).

50 – *Odyssey* 15.125–7; cf. Athena's remarks to Nausicaa, *Odyssey* 6.26–8.

51 – On the need to distinguish between trousseau and dowry in later Greek practice, see Wolff (1944) 57–8; Gernet (1937) 396–8.

52 – *Odyssey* 18.284–303.

53 – *Odyssey* 1.276–8; 2.52–4.

54 – In another context Penelope speaks of the slave Dolius as having been given to her by her father when she married Odysseus (4.736): 'whom my father gave to me as I came here' – and this seems to be an instance of the dowry going to the daughter. But again it would be false to generalise. First, Dolius turns out to be a slave in the *oikos* generally, not Penelope's personal slave (see *Odyssey* 24, passim). Second, it is highly doubtful that a woman could in any proper sense be said to own slaves or the other basic forms of wealth.

55 – *Iliad* 9.148, 290 and 22.50–1, respectively.

56 – It is enough to cite Erdmann (1934) 218–20 and passim.

57 – The question may also be asked, why was there a specific word allegedly meaning 'bride-*purchase*' before there were any other words meaning 'buy' and 'sell'? And how can that be reconciled with the thesis that marriage by purchase is modelled after the juristic structure of sale? In general, there is an unfortunate tendency to invent categorical distinctions among closely related words used by Homer. Not only was he no professional jurist, drawing fine distinctions between one type of gift and another, but often purely metrical consideration were decisive, as in the avoidance of the word *despotes* (master), on which see Chantraine (1946–47) 222.

58 – See the references in n. 16 above.

59 – *Iliad* 6. 396 and 22.472, respectively. The fact that the two sides of the Hector-Andromache marital gift exchange are related at such a distance from each other should serve as a warning. The poet does not give a full account of any marriage, only details embedded in formulas. Therefore neither a statistical analysis nor an argument from silence is decisive or even necessarily meaningful.

60 – *Iliad* 9.146–8 (= 9.288–90). It is the size of the dowry which is unprecedented, whereas the language implies that a dowry, as such, was certainly not a subject for comment.

61 – *Iliad* 13.363–69

62 – Herodotus 6.126–30.

63 – The fact that *hedna* were not indispensable is another argument against the marriage-by-purchase doctrine; see Köstler (1944a) 20.

64 – *Odyssey* 11.346. Then there is Zeus' threat (*Iliad* 15.14–22) to whip Hera in

punishment for disobedience, coupled with his reminder to her of the time when he had hung her by the wrists, with anvils attached to her ankles.

65 – E.g. wife to husband's household: *Iliad* 16.189–90; 22.470–2; *Odyssey* 8.317; 11.281–4; 15.367; husband to father-in-law's household: *Iliad* 11.221–6 and 241–5, taken together; cf. Hesiod, frag. 94 and 96. The comparative infrequency of the latter type is nothing more than a reflection of the fact that in Homeric marriage it was normally the woman who changed households.

66 – E.g. wife to husband's household: *Iliad* 6.394; 22.49–51; husband to father-in-law's household: *Iliad* 6.191–5; *Odyssey* 7. 211–15.

67 – Murray (1924) ch. 5.

68 – E.g. *Odyssey* 6.27; 15.126.

69 – *Odyssey* 4.3–14. In general it is correct to say that there was no ceremonial occasion without feasting, as there was none without gift-giving; see Finley, *World of Odysseus*, 123–6.

70 – *Iliad* 9.146–7; 16.190; 22.471–2; *Odyssey* 6.159; 15.237–8. Cf. Penelope's phrase in *Odyssey* 21.77–8 or Alcinous' proposal in *Odyssey* 7.313–14.

71 – In this respect I am most nearly in agreement with Jeanmarie (1939), especially pp. 17–26, 97–111.

72 – See, e.g., Schapera (1940) 82–92; Fortes (1949) 272–3, and index s.v. 'Brideprice'.

73 – *Odyssey* 4.3–16

74 – I agree with Jeanmaire (1939) 105–7, that *etai* in fact refers to the members of a man's *compagnonnage*, although I am not convinced by his further identification of the word with age-classes. Even Glotz (1904) 85–93, with his well-known emphasis on the tribal character of archaic Greek society, rejected the notion that *etai* were kin.

75 – *Odyssey* 15.16–23.

76 – *Odyssey* 4.10–12. Although there was some distinction between legitimate and illegitimate children – witness the existence of the words *gnesios* and *nothos* – it was not very sharp or often very important, and the power rested with the head of the household to recognise it or not as he chose; see the summary of what little is known on the subject in Erdmann (1934) 363–8, 372–4; cf. Wolff (1952) 27–8.

77 – Agamemnon to Achilles, *Iliad* 9.144–8, 286–90; Priam to Othryoneus, *Iliad* 13.363–9; Menelaus to the son of Achilles, *Odyssey* 4.6–7; Neleus to anyone who would drive off the cattle of Iphicles, *Odyssey* 11.288–92. I have excluded from consideration Patroclus' promise to the captive Briseis, *Iliad* 9.297–9, and Odysseus' promise to his slaves, *Odyssey* 21.213–15 (cf. 14.61–4), neither of which adds anything to our understanding of the problem.

78 – *Iliad* 11.244–5; cf. Hesiod, frag. 33 (Rzach²).

79 – Cf. Erdmann (1934) 206–7; and generally Gernet (1948–9) part I.

80 – *Odyssey* 8.317–59. I am suggesting not that the return of the *hedna* may not have occurred under certain conditions, but that no conclusions may be drawn from one remark of Hephaestus, otherwise unsupported.

81. – See generally Gernet (1948–9) part I. He considers the sixth to be the key century (pp. 30–1), whereas I should emphasise the seventh.

BIBLIOGRAPHICAL ADDENDUM
For recent work on the question of land tenure see the bibliographical addenda for chapters 12 and 13 above. As for Finley's contention that 'bride-price' is an inadequate or misleading term for the property exchanges that take place in certain marriage patterns, most anthropologists now agree; see, e.g., G. Dalton, 'Bridewealth versus Brideprice', *American Anthropologist* 68 (1966), 732–8, cf. the rev. version in *Economic Anthropology and Development: Essays on Tribal and Peasant Economies* (New York and London, Basic Books, 1971), ch. 7. There has been an interesting debate on the historicity of 'Homeric society', primarily centred on the institution of marriage and the possibility of the synchronous presence of both 'dowry' and 'bridewealth' in a single historical society: see A. M. Snodgrass, 'An Historical Homeric Society?', *Journal of Hellenic Studies* 94 (1974), 114–25, and his book, *Archaic Greece: the Age of Experiment* (London, Dent, 1980). There are problems with his contention that the joint presence of the two practices is uncommon is historical societies. First, there is too heavy a reliance on G. P. Murdock's *Ethnographic Atlas* (University of Pittsburgh Press, 1967) where most of the re-corded observations already accepted the certain dichotomy between 'brideprice' and 'dowry'. In fact, J. Goody and S. J. Tambiah, *Bridewealth and Dowry* (Cambridge University Press, 1973) note that the opposition between bridewealth and dowry is quite misleading and that the ultimate recipient of 'bridewealth' as often is *not* the bride's father but the bride herself, and so they prefer to use the term 'indirect dowry' for bridewealth. One should also consult J. Goody, *Production and Reproduction: A Comparative Study of the Domestic Domain* (Cambridge University Press, 1976) for a further analysis of the relationship between exchange and devolution of property and marriage patterns. As the 'law codes' of the ancient Near East and of the later Roman Empire abundantly testify, both practices could exist simultaneously.

Two basic constributions to the understanding of 'Homeric' marriage patterns have been made by W. K. Lacey, 'Homeric *HEDNA* and Penelope's *KYRIOS*', *Journal of Hellenic Studies* 86 (1966), 55–68, and further, ch. 2 of his book, *The Family in Classical Greece* (London, Thames and Hudson, 1968), 33–50. First, he notes that there are two patterns of marriage. In the first the father or *kyrios* was approached by a number of suitors offering 'gifts' (*dora*) and promises of 'marriage presents' (*hedna*). The 'gifts' were part of the 'contest' for the hand of the bride. *Hedna* would only be accepted by the father once he had chosen his prospective son-in-law. In the second marriage-pattern the political strongman (*basileus*) accepted a son-in-law into his own *oikos* as an act of political alliance; in return the *basileus* offered the hand of his daughter along with an *oikos* or *temenos* (or both). Lacey thus estab-lished that the 'gifts of wooing' (the *dora*) were not the same as the *hedna* and secondly that *hedna* are only found in marriages of the first pattern. Second, Lacey was able to make sense of the details surrounding Penelope's prospective mar-riage by carefully separating the concepts of *hedna* and *dora*, and by relating this distinction to Penelope's ambiguous situation as a marriageable woman. As he puts it: 'Penelope's *hedna* do not . . . differ significantly from those of any other heroic personality in the Homeric poems; it is the varying interpretations of her status, and that of Telemachus, which lead to the varying proposals' (p. 66).

See further on the relationship of marriage patterns in Homer with those of the classical period at Athens, J. P. Vernant, 'Le mariage en Grèce archaïque', *Parola del Passato* 28 (1973), 51–74 = ch. 3 in *Mythe et société en Grèce ancienne* (Paris, F. Maspero, 1974), esp. 20–21 (now translated by J. Lloyd, *Myth and Society in Ancient Greece*, London, Harvester, 1979); and, most recently, E. Scheid, 'Il matrimonio omerico', *Dialoghi di Archeologia*, n.s. 1 (1979), 60–73. Finley's position seems, generally speaking, to have become the accepted 'textbook' one; see e.g. O. Murray, *Early Greece* (London, Fontana, 1980).

BIBLIOGRAPHICAL REFERENCES

Abramowski, G. (1966) *Das Geschichtsbild Max Webers*, Stuttgart, Klett.

Adams, R. McC. (1966) *The Evolution of Urban Society: Early Mesopotamia and Prehispanic Mexico*, Chicago, Aldine-Atherton (paperback ed., 1971).

Adkins, A. W. H. (1972) *Moral Values and Political Behaviour in Ancient Greece*, London, Chatto and Windus.

Alföldy, G. (1974) *Noricum*, trans. A. Birley, London, Routledge and Kegan Paul.

Alford, R. R. (1972) 'Critical Evaluation of the Principles of City Classification', in Berry (1972), ch. 11.

Amit, M. (1965) *Athens and the Sea*, Brussels, Collection Latomus no.74.

Anderson, P. (1974) *Passages from Antiquity to Feudalism*, London, New Left Books, 1974.

Andrewes, A. (1938) 'Eunomia', *Classical Quarterly* XXXII 89–102.

– (1966) 'The Government of Classical Sparta', in Badian (1966), ch. 1.

Arangio-Ruiz, V. (1914) *Le genti e la città*, Messina = *Scritti giuridici per il Centenario della Casa Editrice Jovene*, Naples, Jovene (1954), pp. 109–58.

Ardaillon, E. (1897) *Les mines du Laurion dans l'Antiquité*, Paris, Fontemoing.

Arrigo, A. d' (1956) *Natura e tecnica nel mezzogiorno*, Florence, La Nuova Italia.

Ashcraft, R. (1972) 'Marx and Weber on Liberalism as Bourgeois Ideology', *Comparative Studies in Society and History* XIV 130–68.

Aymard, A. (1948) 'L'idée de travail dans la Grèce archaïque', *Journal de Psychologie* XLI 29–45.

– (1957) 'Le partage des profits de la guerre dans les traités d'alliance antiques', *Revue historique* CCXVII 233–49.

Bachofen, J. J. (1948) *Das Mutterrecht*, 3. ed. by K. Mueli, 2 vols., Basel, Schwabe (1. ed., 1861).

Badian, E., ed. (1966) *Ancient Society and Institutions. Studies Presented to Victor Ehrenberg*, Oxford, Blackwell.

Baumgartner, W. (1950) 'Herodots babylonische und assyrische Nachrichten', *Archiv Orientálni* XVII–XVIII, no. 3, 69–106.

Beattie, A. J. (1956) 'Mr. Ventris' Decipherment of the Minoan Linear B Script', *Journal of Hellenic Studies* LXXVI 1–17.

Below, G. von, (1901), 'Ueber Theorien der wirtschaftichen Entwicklung der Völker . . .' *Historische Zeitschrift* LXXXVI 1–77.

Bennett, E. L. Jr. (1956) 'The Landholders of Pylos', *American Journal of Archaeology* LX 103–33.

Benveniste, E. (1948–49) 'Don et échange dans le vocabulaire indo-européen', *L'Année sociologique* 7–20.

Berry, B. J. L. (1972) *City Classification Handbook*, New York, Wiley.

Bishop, T. A. M. (1954) 'Assarting and the Growth of Open Fields', in *Essays in Economic History*, ed. E. M. Carus-Wilson, London, Arnold, I 26–40.

Blackman, D. (1969) 'The Athenian Navy and Allied Naval Contributions in the Pentekontaetia', *Greek, Roman and Byzantine Studies* X 179–216.

Blavatsky, V. D. (1954) 'Slavery and its Sources in the Ancient States of the North Coast of the Black Sea', *Sovetskii Archeologia* XX 31–56 (in Russian; summary in *Historia* 4 (1955) 125).

– (1960) 'Le processus du développement historique des états antiques situés au nord de la Mer Noire', in *XIe Congrès internationale des sciences historiques, Rapports*. (Stockholm), II 98–116.

Bloch, M. (1931) *Les caractères originaux de l'histoire rurale française*, Oslo, Ascheloug (trans, J. Sondheimer, University of California Press, 1966).

– (1935) 'Avènement et conquêtes du moulin à eau', *Annales d'histoire économique et sociale* VII 538–63.

Boardman, J. (1963) 'Artemis Orthia and Chronology', *Annual of the British School at Athens* LVIII 1–7.

Borecky, B. (1971) 'Die politische Isonomie', *Eirene* IX 5–24.

Bottéro, J. (1961) 'Désordre économique et annulation des dettes en Mésopotamie à l'époque paléo-babylonienne', *Journal of the Social and Economic History of the Orient* IV 113–64.

Bowra, C. M. (1955) *Homer and his Forerunners*, Edinburgh, Nelson.

– (1964) *Pindar*, Oxford, Clarendon.

Boyer, G. (1954) 'Sur quelques emplois de la fiction dans l'ancien droit oriental', *Revue internationale des droits de L'Antiquité*, 3. ser., I 73–100.

Bücher, K. (1901) 'Zur griechischen Wirtschaftsgeschichte', in *Festgabe für A. Schäffle*, Tübingen, Mohr, ch.3.

– (1906) *Die Entstehung des Volkswirtschafts*, 5. ed., Tübingen, Laupp.

– (1922) *Beiträge zur Wirtschaftsgeschichte*, Tübingen, Laupp.

Buckland, W. W. (1908) *The Roman Law of Slavery*, Cambridge University Press (reprint 1970).

Canot, T. (1929) *Memoirs of a Slave-Trader*, New York, A. and C. Boni (reprint, Théophile Conneau, *A Slaver's Log Book*, Englewood Cliffs, N.J., Prentice-Hall, 1976).

Cassin, E. (1952) 'Symboles de cession immobilière dans l'ancien droit mésopotamien', *L'Année sociologique*, 107–61.

Casson, L. (1971) *Ships and Seamanship in the Ancient World*, Princeton University Press.

Castells, M. (1970) 'Structures sociales et processus d'urbanisation: analyse comparative intersociétale', *Annales (E.S.C.)* XXV 1155–99.

Chadwick, H. N. (1912) *The Heroic Age*, Cambridge University Press.

Chambers, M. (1958) 'Four Hundred and Sixty Talents', *Classical Philology* LIII 26–32.

Chantraine, P. (1940) 'Conjugaison et histoire des verbes significant *vendre*', *Revue de philologie*, n.s. XIV 11–24.

– (1946–7) 'Les noms du mari et de la femme, du père et de la mère en grec', *Revue des études grecques* LIX/LX 219–50.

Collinet, P. (1937) 'Le colonat dans l'Empire romain', in *Recueils de la Société Jean Bodin*, II 85–122.

300   BIBLIOGRAPHICAL REFERENCES

Cook, R. M. (1959) 'Die Bedeutung der bemahlten Keramik für den griechischen Handel', *Jahrbuch der deutschen archäologischen Instituts* LXXIV 114–23.

– (1960) *Greek Painted Pottery*, London, Methuen.

Cranston, M. (1973) *What are Human Rights?*, London, Bodley Head.

Daube, D. (1947) *Studies in Biblical Law*, Cambridge University Press.

David, M. and Ebeling, E. (1928) 'Assyrische Rechtsurkunden', *Zeitschrift für vergleichende Rechtswissenschaft* XLIV 305–81.

Davies, J. K. (1971) *Athenian Propertied Families, 600–300 BC*, Oxford, Clarendon.

Davies, O. (1935) *Roman Mines in Europe*, Oxford, Clarendon (reprint: New York, Arno, 1979).

Deimel, A. (1932) *Sumerische Tempelwirtschaft zur Zeit Urukaginas und seiner Vorgänger*, Rome, Pontifical Biblical Institute.

Den Boer, W. (1954) *Laconian Studies*, Amsterdam, North-Holland Publishing Co.

De Ste. Croix, G.E.M. (1954–5) 'The Character of the Athenian Empire', *Historia*, III 1–41.

– (1966) 'The Estate of Phaenippus', in Badian (1966), 109–14.

– (1972) *The Origins of the Peloponnesian War*, London, Duckworth.

– (1975) 'Political Pay outside Athens', *Classical Quarterly* XXV 48–52.

Douglass, F. (1855) *My Bondage and My Freedom*, New York (reprint: New York, Dover, 1969).

Dover, K. J. (1968) *Lysias and the Corpus Lysiacum*, University of California Press.

Drachmann, A. G. (1932) *Ancient Oil Mills and Presses*, Copenhagen, Levin and Munksgaard.

– (1948) *Ktesibios, Philon and Heron*, Copenhagen, Munksgaard.

Dunant, D. and Pouilloux, J. (1958) *Recherches sur l'histoire et les cultes de Thasos*, vol. 2, Paris, E. de Boccard.

Durkeim, E. (1950) *The Rules of Sociological Method*, trans. from the 8. ed., Glencoe, Ill., The Free Press.

Ehrenberg, V. (1924) 'Spartiaten und Lakedaimonier', *Hermes* LIX 23–73 = (1965) 161–201.

– (1951) *The People of Aristophanes: A Sociology of Old Attic Comedy*, Harvard University Press (reprint of 3. rev. ed., New York, Schocken Books, 1962).

– (1965) *Polis und Imperium: Beiträge zur alten Geschichte*, ed. K. F. Stroheker and A. J. Graham, Zurich and Stuttgart, Artemis.

– (1975) *L'état grec*, trans. C. Picavet-Roos, Paris, Maspero.

Erbse, H. (1956) 'Über die Midiana des Demosthenes', *Hermes* LXXXIV 135–51.

Erdmann, W. (1934) *Die Ehe im alten Griechenland*, Munich, Beck (reprint: New York, Arno, 1979).

– (1942) 'Zum Eigentum bei Homer', *Zeitschrift der Savigny-Stiftung für Rechtsgeschichte (Romanistische Abteilung)* LXII 347–59.

Erxleben, E. (1969–71) 'Das Munzgesetz des delisch-attischen Seebundes', *Archiv für Papyrusforschung* XIX 91–139, XX 66–132, XXI 145–62.

– (1974) 'Die Rolle der Bevölkerungsklassen im Aussenhandel Athens im 4. Jahrhundert v. u. Z', in *Hellenische Poleis*, ed. E. C. Welskopf, Berlin, Akademie Verlag, I pp. 460–520.

– (1975) 'Die Kleruchien auf Euböa und Lesbos und die Methoden der attischen Herrschaft im 5. Jh.', *Klio* LVII 83–100.

Falkenstein, A. (1954) 'La cité-temple sumérienne', *Cahiers d'histoire mondiale* I 784–814.

Farrington, B. (1947) *Head and Hand in Ancient Greece*, London, Watts.

Finsler, G. (1912) '*Hedna*', *Hermes* XLVII 414–21.

Folz, R. (1953) *L'idée d'empire en Occident du Ve au XIVe siècle*, Paris, Aubier.

Forbes, R. J. (1955) *Studies in Ancient Technology*, 1. ed., vol. 2, Leiden, Brill.

Fortes, M. (1949) *The Web of Kinship among the Tallensi*, Oxford University Press.

Fränkel, H. (1955) *Wege und Formen frühgriechischen Denkens*, ed. F. Tietze, Munich, Beck.

Frankfort, H. et al. (1948) *Before Philosophy: The Intellectual Adventure of Ancient Man* Penguin Books (University of Chicago Press, 1946).

Fraser, P. M. and Bean, G. E. (1954) *The Rhodian Peraea and Islands*, Oxford University Press.

Fraser, P. M. and Rönne, T. (1957) *Boeotian and West Greek Tombstones*, Lund, Gleerup.

Frederiksen, M. W. (1975) Review of Finley, *The Ancient Economy*, *Journal of Roman Studies* LXV 170–1.

Frézouls E. (1973) 'Etudes et recherches sur les villes en Gaule', in Accademia nazionale dei Lincei, *Quaderno* no. 158, 153–66.

Friedrich, J., ed. (1932) *Kleinasiatische Sprachdenkmäler*, Berlin, de Gruyter.

Frisch, M. H. (1970) 'L'histoire urbaine americaine: réflexions sur les tendences récentes', *Annales (E.S.C.)* XXV 880–96.

Frisk, H. (1954–60) *Griechisches etymologisches Wörterbuch*, 2 vols., Heidelberg, Winter.

Fuks, A. (1951) '*Kolonos misthios*: Labour Exchange in Classical Athens', *Eranos* XLIX 171–3.

Fürer-Haimendorf, C. von (1962) *The Apa Tanis and their Neighbours*, London, RKP; Glencoe, Ill., The Free Press.

Fustel de Coulanges, N. D. (1866) *La cité antique* 2. ed., Paris, Hachette (trans. W. Small, 1873; reprint, John Hopkins University Press, 1980).

– (1891) 'The Origin of Property in Land', London, Sonnenschein (= 'Le probléme des òrigines de la propriété foncière', *Revue des questions historiques*, 1889).

– (1893) *Questions historiques*, ed. C. Jullian, Paris, Hachette.

Gabba, E. (1972) 'Urbanizzazione e rinovamenti urbanistici nell'Italia centro-meridionale del I. sec. a.C', *Studi classici e orientali* XXI 73–112.

Galsterer, H. (1976) *Herrschaft und Verwaltung im republikanischen Italien*, Munich, Beck.

Garlan, Y. (1972) 'Les esclaves grecques en temps de guerre', in *Actes du colloque d'histoire sociale, Besançon, 1970*, Paris, pp. 29–62.

– (1974) 'Quelques travaux récentes sur l'esclavage en temps de guerre', in *Actes du colloque sur l'esclavage, Besançon 1972*, Paris, pp. 15–28.

Garnsey, P. (1970) *Social Status and Legal Privilege in the Roman Empire*, Oxford, Clarendon.

Gauthier, P. (1966) 'Les clérouques de Lesbos et la colonisation athénienne au Ve siècle', *Revue des études grecques* LXXIX 64–88.

– (1973) 'A propos des clérouques athéniennes du Ve siècle', in M. I. Finley, ed., *Problèmes de la terre*, pp. 163–86.

– (1974) ' "Générosité" romaine et "avarice" grecque: sur l'octroi du droit de cité',
in *Mélanges . . . offerts à William Seston*, Paris, Sorbonne, pp. 207–15.

Germain, G. (1954) *Homère et la mystique de nombres*, Paris, PUF.

Gernet, L. (1917) 'Hypothèses sur le contrat primitif en Grèce', *Revue des études
grecques* XXX 249–93, 363–83.

– (1937) 'Notes de lexicologie juridique', *Annuaire de l'Institut de philologie et
d'histoire orientales et slaves* V 391–8.

– (1948–9) 'Droit et prédroit en Grèce ancienne', *L'Année sociologique*, pp. 21–119 =
Anthropologie de la Grèce antique, Paris, Maspero (1968, reprint 1976), pp. 175–
260.

– (1955) *Droit et société dans la Grèce ancienne*, Paris, Sirey (reprint: New York,
Arno, 1979).

Glotz, G. (1904) *La solidarité de la famille dans le droit criminal en Grèce*, Paris,
Fontemoing (reprint: New York, Arno, 1973).

Gomme, A. W. (1933) *The Population of Athens in the Fifth and Fourth Centuries B.C.*,
Oxford, Blackwell.

Goossens, G. (1952) 'Introduction à l'archivéconomie de l'Asie antérieure', *Revue
d'Assyriologie* XLVI 98–107.

Greenidge, C. W. W. (1958) *Slavery*, London, Allen & Unwin.

Grundy, G. B. (1911) *Thucydides and the History of his Age*, London, Murray, 1911.
(reprint: 2 vols., Oxford, Blackwell, 1948).

Gschnitzer, F. (1955) 'Stammes- und Ortsnamen im alten Griechenland', *Wiener
Studien* LXVIII 120–44.

Habermas, J. (1971) 'Technology and Science as "Ideology"', in *Toward a Rational
Society*, trans. J. J. Shapiro, London, Heinemann Educational, ch. 6.

Hammond, M. (1972) *The City in the Ancient World*, Harvard University Press.

Hancock, W. K. (1958) 'Trek', *Economic History Review*, 2nd ser., X 331–9.

Handlin, O. and Burchard, J., ed. (1963) *The Historian and the City*, Cambridge,
Mass., M.I.T. Press.

Hasebroek, J. (1926) *Die imperialistische Gedanke im Altertum*, Stuttgart, Kohlhammer.

– (1928) *Staat und Handel im alten Griechenland*, Tübingen, Mohr (trans. L. M.
Fraser and D. C. MacGregor, London, Bell, 1933).

Heichelheim, F. M. (1925) *Die auswärtige Bevölkerung im Ptolemäerreich*, *Klio* Beiheft
no. 18.

– (1938) *Wirtschaftsgeschichte des Altertums, von Päläolithikum bis zur Völkerwander-
ung der Germanen, Sklaven, und Araber*, Leiden, Sijthoff (trans.: Leiden, Sijthoff, 3
vols., 1964–70).

Hemberg, B. (1955) *Anax, Anassa und Anakes als Götternamen, unter besonderer
Berücksichtigung der attischen Kulte*, Univ. Uppsala, *Arsskrift* no. 10.

Hertz, R. (1960) *Death and the Right Hand*, trans. R. and C. Needham, London,
Cohen and West.

Herzog-Hauser, G. (1939) 'Omphale', in Pauly-Wissowa-Kroll, *Realencyclopädie
der classischen Altertumswissenschaft* 18.1, cols. 385–96.

Heuss, A. (1965) 'Max Webers Bedeutung für die Geschichte des griechisch-
römische Altertums', *Historische Zeitschrift* CCI 529–56.

Hohfeld, W. N. (1920) *Fundamental Legal Conceptions . . . and other Legal Essays*, ed.
W. W. Cook, Yale University Press.

Homo, L. (1951) *Rome impériale et l'urbanisme dans l'antiquité*, Paris, Albin Michel.

Homolle, T. (1926) 'La loi de Cadys sur le prêt à intérêt', *Bulletin de correspondance hellénique* C 3–106.

Hume, D. (1904) *Of the Populousness of Ancient Nations*, in *Essays: Moral, Political and Literary*, World's Classics Edition.

Humphreys, S. C. (1974) 'The *Nothoi* of Kynosarges', *Journal of Hellenic Studies* XCIV 88–95.

Ihering, R. von (1879) 'Das Schuldmoment im römischen Privatrecht', in *Vermischte Schriften*, Leipzig, Breitkopf & Härtel, pp. 155–240.

– (1880) *Geist des römischen Rechts*, 4. ed., Leipzig, Breitkopf & Härtel, vol. 2.1.

– (1885) 'Reich und Arm im altrömischen Civilprozess', in *Scherz und Ernst in der Jurisprudenz*, 3. ed., Leipzig, Breitkopf & Härtel, pp. 175–232.

Imbert, J. (1952) 'Fides et Nexum', in *Studi . . . Arangio-Ruiz*, Naples, Jovene, I, 339–63.

Jachmann, G. (1953) 'Das homerische Königtum', *Maia* VI 241–56.

Jackson, A. H. (1969) 'The Original Purpose of the Delian League', *Historia* VIII 12–16.

Jameson, M. H. (1977–8) 'Agriculture and Slavery in Classical Athens', *Classical Journal* LXXII 122–45.

Jardé, A. (1925) *Les céréales dans l'antiquité grecque*, I: *La production*, Paris, E. de Boccard, 1925 (reprint, 1979).

Jeanmaire, H. (1939) *Couroi et courètes: essai sur l'education spartiate et sur les rites d'adolescence dans l'antiquité hellénique*, Lille (reprint: New York, Arno, 1978).

Jones, A. H. M. (1955) 'The Economic Life of the Towns of the Roman Empire', in *Recueils de la Société Jean Bodin* VII 161–94 = Jones (1974) ch. 2.

– (1957) *Athenian Democracy*, Oxford, Blackwell.

– (1964) *The Later Roman Empire, 284–602*, 3 vols., Oxford, Blackwell: University of Oklahoma Press.

– (1974) *The Roman Economy*, ed. P. A. Brunt, Oxford, Blackwell.

Kahrstedt, U. (1954) *Das wirtschaftliche Gesicht Griechenlands in der Kaiserzeit*, Bern, Franke.

Kantor, H. J. (1947) 'The Aegean and the Orient in the Second Millennium B.C.', *American Journal of Archaeology* LI 1–103.

Kaser, M. (1949) *Das altrömische Ius*: Göttingen, Vandenhoek & Rupprecht.

Kazakevich, E. L. (1956) 'The Term *doulos* and the Concept "Slave" in Athens in the Fourth Century B.C.', *Vestnik Drevnei Istorii*, no. 3, pp. 119–36 (in Russian; see summary in *Bibliotheca Classica Orientalis* 2 (1957) 203–5).

– (1958) 'Slaves as a Form of Wealth in Fourth-Century Athens', *Vestnik Drevnei Istorii* no. 2, pp. 90–113 (in Russian).

Kelly, J. M. (1966) *Roman Litigation*, Oxford, Clarendon.

Kent, J. H. (1948) 'The Temple Estates of Delos, Rheneia and Mykonos', *Hesperia* XVII 243–338.

Kiechle, F. (1958) 'Zur Humanität in der Kriegführung der griechischen Staaten', *Historia* VII 129–56.

– (1963) *Lakonien und Sparta*, Munich, Beck.

Kirsten, E. (1941) 'Ein politisches Programm in Pindars ersten pythischen Gedicht', *Rheinisches Museum*, n.s. XC 58–71.

304 BIBLIOGRAPHICAL REFERENCES

Kleingünther, A. (1933) *Protos Heuretes. Untersuchungen zur Geschichte einer Fragestellung, Philologus* Supp. 26, no. 1.

Kocka, H. J. (1966) 'Karl Marx und Max Weber. Ein methodologischer Vergleich', *Zeitschrift für die gesamte Staatswissenschaft* CXXII 328–57.

Kolendo, J. (1960) 'La moissoneuse antique en Gaule romaine', *Annales (E.S.C.)* XV 1099–1114.

Kolossovskaya, J. K. (1958) 'Zur Geschichte des Verfalls der römischen Herrschaft in Dakien', *Bibliotheca Classica Orientalis* III 326–46 (German summary of Russian original).

Korošec, V. (1939) 'Das Eigentum an Haustieren nach dem hethitischen Gesetzbuch', in *Symbolae Paulo Koschaker dedicatae*, ed. J. Friedrich et al., Leiden, Brill, pp. 37–49.

Koschaker, P. (1937) 'Die Eheform bei den Indogermanen', *Zeitschrift für ausländisches und internationalisches Privatrecht*, Sonderheft XI 86–112.

– (1942) Zur staatlichen Wirtschaftsverwaltung in altbabylonischer Zeit, insbesondere nach Urkunden aus Larsa', *Zeitschrift für Assyriologie* XLVII 135–80.

– (1950) 'Eheschliessung und Kauf nach alten Rechten . . .' *Archiv Orientální* XVII–XVIII, no. 4, 210–96.

Köstler, R. (1944a) '*Hedna*, ein Beitrag zum homerischen Eherecht', *Anzeiger der Akad. der Wiss. in Wien, phil.-hist. Kl.* LXXXI 6–25.

– (1944b) 'Raub- und Kaufehe bei den Hellenen', *Zeitschrift der Savigny-Stiftung für Rechtsgeschichte (Romanistische Abteilung)* LXIV 206–32.

Kretschmer, E. (1930) 'Beiträge zur Wortgeographie der altgriechische Dialekte, I: Diener, Sklave', *Glotta* XVIII 71–81.

Laroche, E. (1949) *Histoire de la racine NEM- en grec ancien*, Paris, Klincksieck.

Larsen, J. A. O. (1940) 'The Constitution and Original Purpose of the Delian League', *Harvard Studies in Classical Philology* LI 175–213.

– (1962) 'Freedom and its Obstacles in Ancient Greece', *Classical Philology* LVII 230–4.

Larson, L. M., trans. (1935) *The Earliest Norwegian Laws*, Columbia University Press.

Lasker, B. (1950) *Human Bondage in Southeast Asia*, University of North Carolina Press.

Latte, K. (1920) *Heiliges Recht*, Tübingen, Mohr.

– (1925) Review of E. Weiss, *Griechisches Privatrecht*, *Gnomon* I 255–64 = *Kleine Schriften*, Munich, Beck (1968), pp. 313–22.

Lauffer, S. (1955–56) *Die Bergwerkssklaven von Laureion*, in Mainz, Akad. der Wiss. und der Literatur, geistes- und sozialwissenschaftliche Klasse, *Abhandlungen* nos. 11 and 12 respectively.

Laveleye, E. L. V., Baron de (1874) *De la propriété et ses formes primitives*, Paris, G. Baillière.

Leach, E. (1968) 'Law as a Condition of Freedom', in D. Bidney, ed., *The Concept of Freedom in Anthropology*, Paris and The Hague, Mouton, pp. 74–90.

Leemans, W. F. (1950) *The Old-Babylonian Merchant*, Leiden, Brill.

Lefebvre, H. (1970) *La revolution urbaine*, Paris, Gallimard.

Le Lannou, M. (1941) *Pâtres et paysans de la Sardaigne*, Tours, Arrault.

Lemosse, M. (1957) 'Les lois de Gortyne et la notion de codification', *Revue internationale des droits de l'Antiquité* IV 131–7.

Lepore, E. (1968a) 'Per un fenomologia storica del rapporto città-territorio in Magna Grecia', in *Atti del 7° Convegno di Studi sulla Magna Grecia*, Naples, pp. 29–66.

– (1968b) 'Napoli Greco-Romana. La vita politica e sociale', in *Storia di Napoli*, vol. 1, Naples, Società editrice Storia di Napoli, pp. 141–371.

– (1970) 'Struttura della colonizzazione focea in Occidente', *Parola del Passato* XXV 19–54.

Lepper, F. A. (1962) 'Some Rubrics in the Athenian Quota-Lists', *Journal of Hellenic Studies* LXXXII 25–55.

Lévy-Bruhl, H. (1960) *Recherches sur les actions de la loi*, Paris, Sirey.

Lewis, J. D. (1971) 'Isegoria at Athens: when did it begin?', *Historia* XX 129–40.

Lewy, H. (1942) 'The Nuzian Feudal System', *Orientalia*, n.s. XI 1–40.

Liebeschuetz, J. H. W. G. (1972) *Antioch: City and Imperial Administration in the Later Roman Empire*, Oxford, Clarendon.

Lipsius, H. (1909) *Zum Recht von Gortyns, Abhandlungen der sächs. Gesellschaft der Wissenschaft, phil.-hist. Kl.*, XXVII no. 11.

Loenen, D. (1953) *Stasis*, Amsterdam, Noord-Hollandische Uitg.

Lotze, D. (1958) *'Hektemoroi* und vorsolonisches Schuldrecht', *Philologus* CII 1–12.

– (1959) *METAXY ELEUTHERON KAI DOULON. Studien zur Rechtsstellung unfreier Landbevölkerungen in Griechenland bis zum 4. Jarhundert v. Chr.*, Berlin, Akademie Verlag (reprint: New York, Arno, 1979).

– (1962) 'Zu den *woikees* von Gortyn', *Klio* XL 32–43.

Lukes, S. (1973) *Emile Durkheim*, London, Allen Lane.

Lyons, B. (1974) *Henri Pirenne*, Ghent, E. Story-Scientia Verlag; New York, Humanities Press.

MacLeod, W. C. (1925) 'Debtor and Chattel Slavery in Aboriginal North America', *American Anthropologist* XXVII 370–80.

Magie, D. (1950) *Roman Rule in Asia Minor*, 2 vols., Princeton University Press (reprint: New York, Arno, 1975).

Marcuse, H. (1968) 'Industrialization and Capitalism in the Work of Max Weber', in *Negations*, trans. J. J. Shapiro, London, Allen Lane; Boston, Beacon, pp. 201–26.

Martin, R. (1951) *Recherches sur l'agora grecque*, Paris, E. de Boccard.

– (1975) *L'urbanisme dans la Grèce antique*, 2. ed., Paris, Picard.

Marx, K. (1973) *Grundrisse*, trans. M. Nicolaus, Penguin Books.

Marx, K. and Engels, F. (1938) *The German Ideology*, trans, R. Pascal, London, Lawrence & Wishart.

Mateescu, G. G. (1923) 'I Traci nelle epigrafi di Roma', *Ephemeris Dacoromana* I 57–290.

Mattingly, H. (1961) 'The Athenian Coinage Decree', *Historia* X 148–88.

Mauss, M. (1921) 'Une forme ancienne de contrat chez les Thraces', *Revue des études grecques* XXXIV 388–97.

– (1925) 'Essai sur le don', *L'année sociologique*, n.s. I 30–186 (trans. E. Cunnison, London, Cohen & West, 1954; paperback ed., London, RKP, 1964).

Meek, R. L. (1976) *Social Science and the Ignoble Savage*, Cambridge University Press.

Meiggs, R. (1972) *The Athenian Empire*, Oxford, Clarendon.

Meinecke, J. (1971) 'Gesetzesinterpretation und Gesetzesanwendung im attischen Zivilprozess', *Revue internationale des droits de l'Antiquité*, 3. ser., XVIII 275–360.

Mendelsohn, I. (1949) *Slavery in the Ancient Near East*, New York, Oxford University Press.

Meyer, H. D. (1960) 'Abfall und Bestrafung von Bündern im delisch-attischen Seebund', *Historische Zeitschrift* CXCI 497–509.

Meyer-Laurin, H. (1965) *Gesetz und Billigkeit im attischen Prozess*, Weimar, Böhlau.

Michell, H. (1940) *The Economics of Ancient Greece*, New York, Macmillan; Cambridge University Press.

Mickwitz, G. (1937) 'Economic Rationalism in Graeco-Roman Agriculture', *English Historical Review* LII 577–89.

Mill, J. S. (1948) *On Liberty*, World's Classics Edition.

Mitteis, L. (1891) *Reichsrecht und Volksrecht in den östlichen Provinzen des römischen Kaiserreichs*, Leipzig, Teubner.

Mócsy, A. (1956) 'Die Entwicklung der Sklavenwirtschaft in Pannonien zur Zeit des Prinzipats', *Acta Antiqua* VI 221–50.

Momigliano, A. (1933) 'Della spedizione scitica di Filippo alla spedizione scitica di Dario', *Athenaeum*, n.s. XI 336–59.

– (1970) 'La città antica di Fustel de Coulanges', *Rivista storica italiana* LXXXII 81–98 = *Essays in Ancient and Modern Historiography* (Oxford, Blackwell, 1977) ch. 19.

Mommsen, W. J. (1959) *Max Weber und die deutsche Politik 1890–1920*, Tübingen, Mohr-Siebeck.

– (1974) *The Age of Bureaucracy: Perspectives on the Political Sociology of Max Weber*, Oxford, Blackwell.

Moretti, L. (1959) 'Olympionikai, i vincitori negli antichi agoni olimpici', Accademia nazionale dei Lincei, Classe di scienze morali, *Memorie*, 8 ser., VIII 55–198.

Moritz, L. A. (1958) *Grain-Mills and Flour in Classical Antiquity*, Oxford, Clarendon (reprint: New York, Arno, 1979).

Morrow, G. R. (1939) *Plato's Law of Slavery in its Relation to Greek Law*, University of Illinois Press (reprint: New York, Arno, 1978).

Mossé, C. (1973) 'Sparte archaïque', *Parola del Passato* XXVIII 7–20.

Murray, G. (1924) *The Rise of the Greek Epic*, 3. ed., Oxford, Clarendon.

Nesselhauf, H. (1933) *Untersuchungen zur Geschichte der delisch-attischen Symmachie*, *Klio*, Beiheft 30.

Nevinson, H. W. (1906) *A Modern Slavery*, London and New York, Harper.

Nóbrega, V. L. da (1959) *'Partes Secanto'*, *Zeitschrift der Savigny-Stiftung für Rechtsgeschichte (Romanistische Abteilung)* LXXVI 499–507.

Nörr, D. (1961) 'Die Evangelien des Neuen Testaments und die sogenannte hellenistische Rechtskoine', *Zeitschrift der Savigny-Stiftung für Rechtsgeschichte (Romanistische Abteilung)* LXXVIII 92–141.

Oliva, P. (1962) *Pannonia and the Onset of the Crisis in the Roman Empire*, Prague, Academy of Science.

Oppenheim, A. L. (1955) '"Siege Documents" from Nippur', *Iraq* XVII 69–89.

Page, D. (1955) *The Homeric Odyssey*, Oxford, Clarendon.

Palmer, L. R. (1954) 'The Mycenaean Greek Texts from Pylos', *Transactions of the Philological Society*, pp. 18–53b.

- (1955) *Achaeans and Indo-Europeans*, Oxford University Press.
- (1956) 'The Concept of Social Obligation in Indo-European', in *Hommages à Max Niedermann*, Brussels, Collection Latomus no. 23, 258–69.
Partsch, J. (1909) *Griechisches Bürgschaftsrecht*, Leipzig, Teubner.
Paton, G. W. (1951) *A Text-book of Jurisprudence*, 2. ed., Oxford, Clarendon.
Pečirka, J. (1973) 'Homestead Farms in Classical and Hellenistic Athens', in M. I. Finley, ed., *Problèmes de la terre*, pp. 113–47.
Pembroke, S. (1965) 'Last of the Matriarchs: A Study in the Inscriptions of Lycia', *Journal of the Economic and Social History of the Orient* VIII 217–47.
Perlman, S. (1976) 'Panhellenism, the Polis and Imperialism', *Historia* XXV 1–30.
Petschow, H. (1956) *Neubabylonisches Pfandrecht*. Akad. der Wiss., Leipzig, phil.-hist. Klasse, *Abhandlungen*, 48 no. 1.
Pippidi, D. M. (1973) 'Le problème de la main-d'oeuvre agricole dans les colonies grecques de la mer Noire', in M. I. Finley, ed., *Problèmes de la terre*, pp. 63–82.
Pirenne, H. (1914) 'Les périodes de l'histoire sociale du capitalisme', Acad. Royale de Belgique, *Bulletin de la classe des lettres*, pp. 258–99 = *American Historical Review* XIX 493–515.
- (1939) *Les villes et les institutions urbaines*, 2 vols., Paris, Alcan.
Plassart, A. (1913) 'Les archers d'Athènes', *Revue des études grecques* XXVI 151–213.
Pleket, H. W. (1972) 'Economic History of the Ancient World and Epigraphy', *Akten des VI. Internationalen Kongresses für Griechische und Lateinische Epigraphik*, Munich, pp. 243–57.
Pöhlmann, R. (1895) *Aus Altertum und Gegenwart*, Munich, Beck (2. ed., 1911).
- (1925) *Geschichte der sozialen Frage und des Sozialismus in der antiken Welt*, 3. ed., Munich, Beck.
Poland, F. (1909) *Geschichte des griechischen Vereinswesens*, Leipzig, Teubner.
Préaux, C. (1939) *L'économie royale des Lagides*, Brussels, Fondation égyptologique (reprint: New York, Arno, 1979).
Pringsheim, F. (1950) *The Greek Law of Sale*, Weimar, Böhlau.
Pritchett, W. K. (1953–56) 'The Attic Stelai', *Hesperia* XXII 225–99, XXV 178–317.
- (1969) 'The Transfer of the Delian Treasury', *Historia* XVIII 17–21.
- (1971–79) *The Greek State at War*, 3 vols., University of California Press.
Pulleyblank, E. G. (1958) 'The Origins and Nature of Chattel Slavery in China', *Journal of the Economic and Social History of the Orient* I 185–220.
Purves, P. M. (1945) 'Commentary on Nuzi Real Property in the Light of Recent Studies', *Journal of Near Eastern Studies* IV 68–86.
Quiggin, A. H. (1949) *A Survey of Primitive Money*, London, Methuen.
Ravn, O. E. (1942) *Herodotus' Description of Babylonia*, Copenhagen, Nyt Nordisk Forlag.
Rehm, A. (1938) 'Die Rolle der Technik in der griechisch-römischen Antiken', *Archiv für Kulturgeschichte* XXVIII 135–62.
Renard, M. (1959) *Technique et agriculture en pays trévire et rémois*, Brussels, Collection Latomus no. 38.
Richardson, L. J. D. (1955) 'Further Observations on Homer and the Mycenaean Tablets', *Hermathena* LXXXVI 50–65.
Romstedt, M. (1914) *Die wirtschaftliche Organisation des athenischen Reiches*, Dissertation, Leipzig.

Rosen, E. (1956) 'The Invention of Eyeglasses', *Journal of the History of Medicine* XI 13–46, 183–218.

Rostovtzeff, M. I. (1931) *Skythien und der Bosporus*, Berlin, Schoetz.

– (1953) *The Social and Economic History of the Hellenistic World*, 3 vols., Oxford, Clarendon.

– (1957) *The Social and Economic History of the Roman Empire.* 2. ed., rev. P. M. Fraser, 2 vols., Oxford, Clarendon.

Rostovtzeff, M. I. and Welles, C. B. (1931) 'A Parchment Contract of Loan from Dura Europus on the Euphrates', *Yale Classical Studies* II 1–78.

Ruschenbusch, E. (1957) 'Dikasterion panton kyrion', *Historia* VI 257–74.

Russell, L. E. B., ed. (1935) *General Rigby, Zanzibar and the Slave Trade*, London, Allen & Unwin.

Ryan, A. (1974) *J. S. Mill*, London and Boston, RKP.

Schachermeyr, F. (1955) *Die ältesten Kulturen Griechenlands*, Stuttgart, Kohlhammer.

Schapera, I. (1940) *Married Life in an African Tribe*, Northwestern University Press.

Scheil, V. (1915) 'La libération juridique d'un fils donné en gage . . . en 558 av. J. C.', *Revue d'Assyriologie* XII 1–13.

Schneider, A. (1920) *Die sumerische Tempelstadt*, Essen (reprint: New York, Arno, 1979).

Schönbauer, E. (1933) 'Paramone, Antichrese und Hypothek, Studien zu P. Dura 10', *Zeitschrift der Savigny-Stiftung für Rechtsgeschichte (Romanistische Abteilung)* LIII 422–50.

Schuller, W. (1974) *Die Herrschaft der Athener im ersten attischen Seebund*, Berlin and New York, W. de Gruyter.

Schumpeter, J. A. (1954) *History of Economic Analysis*, ed. E. B. Schumpeter, New York, Oxford University Press.

Sealey, R. (1966) 'The Origin of the Delian League', in Badian (1966), 233–55.

Shipp, G. P. (1972) *Studies in the Language of Homer*, 2. ed., Cambridge University Press.

Sieveking, H. (1933) 'Loans, Personal', in *Encyclopaedia of the Social Sciences* IX 561–5.

Sjöberg, G. (1960) *The Preindustrial City*, Glencoe, Ill., The Free Press.

Sombart, W. (1902) *Der moderne Kapitalismus*, Leipzig, Duncker & Humblot.

– (1916) *Der modern Kapitalismus*, 2. ed., Munich and Leipzig, Duncker & Humblot.

– (1923) 'Die Anfänge der Soziologie', in M. Palyi, ed., *Hauptprobleme der Soziologie: Erinnerungsgabe für Max Weber*, Munich and Leipzig, Duncker & Humblot (reprint: New York, Arno, 1975), ch. 1.1.

Stampp, K. M. (1956) *The Peculiar Institution: Slavery in the Ante-bellum South*, New York, Knopf.

Stanier, R. S. (1953) 'The Cost of the Parthenon', *Journal of Hellenic Studies* LXXIII 68–76.

Starr, C. G. (1955) 'The Myth of the Minoan Thalassocracy', *Historia* III 282–91.

– (1958) 'An Overdose of Slavery', *Journal of Economic History* XVIII 257–72.

– (1965) 'The Credibility of Early Spartan History', *Historia* XIV 257–72.

Steele, F. R. (1943) *Nuzi Real Estate Transactions*, New Haven, American Oriental Society.

Stevenson, H. N. C. (1943) *The Economics of the Central Chin Tribes*, Bombay, Times of India Press.

Stroud, R. S. (1971) 'Theozotides and the Athenian Orphans', *Hesperia* XL 280–301.

– (1974) 'An Athenian Law on Silver Coinage', *Hesperia* XLIII 157–88.

Stubbings, F. H. (1951) *Mycenaean Pottery from the Levant*, Cambridge University Press.

Sundwall, J. (1956) *Zur Buchführung im Palast von Knossos*, Societas scientiarum fennica: *Commentationes humanarum litterarum*, no. 22.3.

Tawney, R. H. (1947) *Religion and the Rise of Capitalism*, Penguin Books (original ed., 1926).

Thernstrom, S. (1971) 'Reflections on the New Urban History', *Daedalus* 100.1, 359–75.

Thompson, E. A. (1952a) *A Roman Reformer and Inventor*, Oxford, Clarendon (reprint: New York, Arno, 1979).

– (1952b) 'Peasant Revolts in Late Roman Gaul', *Past & Present* II 11–23 = M. I. Finley, ed., *Studies in Ancient Society*, 304–20.

Thomson, G. (1954) *Studies in Ancient Greek Society*, 1: *The Prehistoric Aegean*, 2. ed., London, Lawrence & Wishart.

Thorner, D. and A. (1962) *Land and Labour in India*, Bombay and London, Asia Publishing House.

Thornton, A. P. (1965) *Doctrines of Imperialism*, New York, Wiley.

Thylander, H. (1952) *Etude sur l'épigraphie latine*, Lund, Gleerup.

Tudor, D. (1957) *Istoria sclavajului in Dacia romană*, Bucarest.

Turner, R. W. (1931) *The Equity of Redemption*, Cambridge University Press.

Ucko, P. J. et al., ed. (1972) *Man, Settlement and Urbanism*, London, Duckworth.

Urbach, E. E. (1963) 'The Laws regarding Slavery as a Source for Social History of the Period of the Second Temple, the Mishnah and the Talmud', *Annual of Jewish Studies* I 1–94 (reprint as separate vol.: New York, Arno, 1979).

Vagts, A. (1937) *A History of Militarism*, New York, Norton.

Ventris, M. and Chadwick, J. (1953) 'Evidence for Greek Dialect in the Mycenaean Archives', *Journal of Hellenic Studies* LXXIII 84–103.

– (1956) *Documents in Mycenaean Greek*, Cambridge University Press (2. ed., 1973).

Vercoutter, J. (1954) *Essai sur les relations entre Egyptiens et Préhellènes*, Paris, Adrien-Masonneuve.

Vernant, J. P. (1965) *Mythe et pensée chez les Grecs*, Paris, Maspero.

Vlastos, G. (1941) 'Slavery in Plato's Thought', *Philosophical Review* L 289–304 = M. I. Finley, ed., *Slavery in Classical Antiquity*, ch. 7.

– (1964) 'Isonomia politike', in *Isonomia*, ed. J. Mau and E. G. Schmidt, Berlin, Akademie Verlag, pp. 1–35.

Vogt, J. (1974) *Ancient Slavery and the Ideal of Man*, trans. T. Wiedemann, Oxford, Blackwell.

Wackernagel, J. (1916) *Sprachliche Untersuchungen zu Homer*, Göttingen, Vandenhoek & Ruprecht, = *Glotta* VII 161–319.

Wagner, M. (1914) *Zur Geschichte der attischen Kleruchien*, Diss. Tübingen.

Walbank, F. W. (1946) *The Decline of the Roman Empire in the West*, London, Cobbett Press.

Weber, Marianne (1950) *Max Weber. Ein Lebensbild*, Heidelberg, Schreider.

Weber, Max (1921) 'Der Stadt', *Archiv für Sozialwissenschaft und Sozialpolitik* XLVII 621–772 (trans. D. Martindale and G. Neuwirth, Glencoe, Ill., The Free Press, 1958) = Weber (1956) 735–822.

– (1924) 'Agrarverhältnisse im Altertum', in *Gesammelte Aufsätze zur Sozial- und Wirtschaftsgeschichte*, Tübingen, Mohr-Siebeck, 1–288 (trans. R. I. Frank, London, New Left Books, 1976; 1. ed., 1909).

– (1956) *Wirtschaft und Gesellschaft*, 4. ed. by J. Winckelmann, Tübingen, Mohr-Siebeck.

– (1968) *Economy and Society*, ed. G. Roth and C. Wittich, New York, Bedminster Press (paperback ed., University of California Press, 1978).

– (1971) *Gesammelte politische Schriften*, ed. J. Winckelmann, 3. ed., Tübingen, Mohr-Siebeck.

Webster, T. B. L. (1955) 'Homer and the Mycenaean Tablets', *Antiquity* XXIX 10–14.

Weiss, E. (1908) '*Communio pro diviso* und *pro indiviso* in den Papyri', *Archiv für Papyruskunde* IV 353–7.

– (1923) *Griechisches Privatrecht*, Leipzig, Teubner.

Welskopf, E. C. (1957) *Die Produktionsverhältnisse im alten Orient und der griechisch-römischen Antike*, Berlin, Akademie Verlag.

Westermann, W. L. (1945) 'Between Slavery and Freedom', *American Historical Review* L 213–27.

– (1948) 'The *Paramone* as General Service Contract', *Journal of Juristic Papyrology* XI 9–50.

– (1955) *The Slave Systems of Greek and Roman Antiquity*, Philadelphia, American Philosophical Society.

Wheatley, P. (1971) *The Pivot of the Four Quarters: A Preliminary Inquiry into the Origin and Character of the Ancient Chinese City*, Edinburgh University Press.

White, Lynn. Jr. (1964) *Medieval Technology and Social Change*, Oxford, Clarendon, paperback ed.

Wight, M. (1952) *British Colonial Constitutions, 1947*, Oxford, Clarendon.

Wightmann, E. M. (1975) 'The Pattern of Rural Settlement in Roman Gaul', in *Aufstieg und Niedergang der römischen Welt*, ed. H. Temporini and W. Haase, Berlin and New York, W. de Gruyter, vol. 2.4, 584–657.

Wigmore, J. H. (1896–7) 'The Pledge-idea: A Study in Comparative Legal Ideas, II', *Harvard Law Review* X 389–417.

Wilamowitz-Moellendorf, U. von (1927) *Die Heimkehr des Odysseus*, Berlin, Weidman

Wilhelm, A. (1913) 'Neue Beiträge zur griechischen Inschriftenkunde, III', *Sitzungsberichte der Akad. der Wiss. in Wien* 175.1, 3–15.

– (1924) 'Zu jüngsten Veröffentlichungen griechischer Inschriften', *Anzeiger der Akad. der Wiss. in Wien, phil.-hist. Kl.* LXI 93–101.

Will, E. (1954) 'Trois quarts de siècle de recherches sur l'économie grecque antique', *Annales (E.S.C.)* IX 7–22.

– (1956) *Doriens et Ioniens*, Paris, Les Belles Lettres.

– (1972) *Le monde grecque et l'orient: le Ve siècle*, Paris, PUF.

Willetts, R. F. (1955) *Aristocratic Society in Ancient Crete*, London, RKP.

Williams, G. (1956) 'The Controversy concerning the Word "Law"', in *Philosophy, Politics and Society*, ed. P. Laslett, Oxford, Blackwell, 134–56.

Wolff, H. J. (1944) 'Marriage Law and Family Organization in Ancient Athens', *Traditio* II 43–95.

– (1952) 'Die Grundlagen des griechischen Eherechts', *Tijdschrift voor Rechtsgeschiedenis* XX 1–29, 157–81.

– (1957) 'Proïx', in *Pauly-Wissowa-Kroll Realencyclopädie des klassischen Altertums* 23.1, cols. 133–70.

Wycherley, R. F. (1973) *How the Greeks Built Cities*, 2. ed., London, Macmillan.

Yaron, R. (1959) 'Redemption of Persons in the Ancient Near East', *Revue internationale des droits de l'Antiquité*, 3 ser., VI 155–76.

– (1963) 'On section II 57 (= 172) of the Hittite Laws', *Revue internationale des droits de l'Antiquité*, ser. 3, X 137–46.

Zgusta, L. (1955) *Die Personennamen griechischer Städte der nördlichen Schwarzmeerküste*, Prague.

Zilsel, E. (1926) *Die Entstehung des Geniebegriffes: Ein Beitrag zur Ideengeschichte der Antike und des Frühkapitalismus*, Tübingen, Mohr.

BIBLIOGRAPHY OF M. I. FINLEY

BOOKS AND ARTICLES

(1934) 'Mandata Principum', Tijdschrift voor Rechtsgeschiedenis XIII 150–69.

(1935) 'Emporos, Naukleros and Kapelos: Prolegomena to the Study of Athenian Trade', Classical Philology XXX 320–36.

(Studies in Land and Credit) Studies in Land and Credit in Ancient Athens, 500–200 B.C., Rutgers University Press, 1952 (reprint: New York, Arno Press, 1973)

(1953a) 'Land, Debt, and the Man of Property in Classical Athens', Political Science Quarterly LXVIII 249–68.

(1953b) 'Multiple Charges on Real Property in Athenian Law: New Evidence from an Agora Inscription', in Studi in onore di Vincenzo Arangio-Ruiz, Naples, Jovene III 473–91.

(World of Odysseus¹) The World of Odysseus, 1. ed., New York, The Viking Press, 1954.

(1954) 'The Ancient Greeks and their Nation', British Journal of Sociology V 253–64; cf. rev. version, ch. 7 in Use and Abuse of History (1975).

(1955) 'Marriage, Sale and Gift in the Homeric World', Revue internationale des droits de l'antiquité, 3e sér., II 167–94.

(World of Odysseus²) The World of Odysseus, London, Chatto & Windus, 1956.

(1957) 'Homer and Mycenae: Property and Tenure', Historia VI 133–59.

(1957–8) 'The Mycenaean Tablets and Economic History', Economic History Review, 2nd ser., X 128–41.

(The Greek Historians, ed.) The Greek Historians: the Essence of Herodotus, Thucydides, Xenophon, Polybius, New York, The Viking Press; London, Chatto & Windus, 1959.

(1959) 'Was Greek Civilization based on Slave Labour?', Historia VIII 145–64 = ch. 4 in Slavery in Classical Antiquity (1960).

(Slavery in Classical Antiquity, ed.) Slavery in Classical Antiquity: Views and Controversies, Cambridge, Heffer; New York, Barnes & Noble, 1960 (reprint with supplements to bibliography, 1968)

(1960) 'The Servile Statuses of Ancient Greece', Revue internationale des droits de l'Antiquité, 3e ser., VII 165–89.

(1961a) 'The Significance of Ancient Slavery', Acta Antiqua IX 285–6 (reply to: P. Oliva, 'Die Bedeutung der antiken Slaverei', ibid., VIII 309–19).

(1961b) The Greeks, London, BBC Publications.

(World of Odysseus³) The World of Odysseus, rev. ed., Penguin, 1962; New York, The Viking Press, 1965.

(1962a) 'The Black Sea and Danubian Regions and the Slave Trade in Antiquity', Klio XL 51–9.

(1962b) 'Athenian Demagogues', *Past & Present* XXI 3–24. = *Studies in Ancient Society* (1974) ch. 1.

(*The Ancient Greeks*) *The Ancient Greeks*, London, Chatto & Windus; Penguin; New York, The Viking Press, 1963.

(1963) 'Generalizations in Ancient History', ch. 2 in L. Gottschalk, ed., *Generalization in the Writing of History*. University of Chicago Press; cf. rev. version, ch. 3 in *Use and Abuse of History*.

(1964a) 'Between Slavery and Freedom', *Comparative Studies in Society and History* VI 233–49.

(1964b) 'The Trojan War', *Journal of Hellenic Studies* LXXXIV 1–9 (with replies by: J. L. Caskey, G. S. Kirk, and D. L. Page, pp. 9–20).

(1965a) 'Classical Greece', *Deuxième Conférence internationale d'histoire économique, Aix-en-Provence, 1962*, I: *Trade and Politics in the Ancient World*, Paris and The Hague, Mouton, pp. 11–35 (reprint: New York, Arno, 1979).

(1965b) 'Technical Innovation and Economic Progress in the Ancient World', *Economic History Review*, 2nd ser., XVIII 29–45.

(1965c) 'Myth, Memory and History', *History and Theory* IV 281–302 = ch. 1 in *Use and Abuse of History*.

(1965d) 'La servitude pour dettes', Revue historique de droit français et étranger, sér. 4, XLIII 159–84.

(*The Jewish War*, ed., abridged, and intro.) *The Jewish War and other Selections from Flavius Josephus*, trans. H. St. J. Thackeray and R. Marcus, London, New English Library, 1966.

(1966) 'The Problem of the Unity of Greek Law', in *Atti del I° Congresso Internazionale della Società Italiana di Storia del Diritto*, Florence, Olschki, pp. 129–42 = ch. 8 in *Use and Abuse of History*.

(1967) 'Utopianism, Ancient and Modern', ch. 1 in *The Critical Spirit. Essays in Honor of Herbert Marcuse*, ed. K. H. Wolff and B. Moore Jr., Boston, Beacon Press, = ch. 11 in *Use and Abuse of History*.

(*Aspects of Antiquity*[1]) *Aspects of Antiquity: Discoveries and Controversies*, London, Chatto & Windus; New York, The Viking Press, 1968; Penguin, 1972.

(*Ancient Sicily*[1]) *Ancient Sicily to the Arab Conquest*, London, Chatto & Windus; New York, The Viking Press, 1968.

(1968a) 'Sparta', ch. 6 in *Problèmes de la guerre en Grèce ancienne*, ed., J.-P. Vernant, Paris and The Hague, Mouton = ch. 10 in *Use and Abuse of History*.

(1968b) 'The Alienability of Land in Ancient Greece', *Eirene* VII 25–32 = ch. 9 in *Use and Abuse of History*.

(1968c) 'The Historical Tradition: the *Contributi* of Arnaldo Momigliano', *History and Theory* VII 355–67 = ch. 4 in *Use and Abuse of History*.

(1968d) 'Slavery', *International Encyclopedia of the Social sciences* XIV 307–13.

(*Early Greece*[1]) *Early Greece: the Bronze and Archaic Ages*, London, Chatto & Windus; New York, Norton, 1970.

(1970a) 'Metals in the Ancient World', *Journal of the Royal Society of Arts*, CXVIII 597–607.

(1970b) 'Aristotle and Economic Analysis', *Past & Present* XLVII 3–25 = ch. 2 in *Studies in Ancient Society*.

(1971a) *The Ancestral Constitution*, Inaugural Lecture, Cambridge University Press = ch. 2 in *Use and Abuse of History*.

314   BIBLIOGRAPHY OF M. I. FINLEY

(1971b) 'Archaeology and History', Daedalus C no. 1, 168–86 = ch. 5 in *Use and Abuse of History*.

(*Ancient Economy*) *The Ancient Economy*, University of California Press; London, Chatto & Windus, 1973.

(*Democracy*) *Democracy Ancient and Modern*, Rutgers University Press; London, Chatto & Windus, 1973.

(*Problèmes de la terre*, ed.) *Problèmes de la terre en Grèce ancienne*, Paris and The Hague, Mouton, 1973.

(1973) 'The Heritage of Isocrates', Edinburgh University Press, 1973 (original title: *Knowledge for What?*) = ch. 12 in *Use and Abuse of History*.

(*Studies in Ancient Society*, ed.) *Studies in Ancient Society*, London, RKP (1974).

(1974a) 'The World of Odysseus Revisited', *Proceedings of the Classical Association* LXXI 13–31 = append. 1 in *World of Odysseus*⁴.

(1974b) 'Schliemann's Troy – One Hundred Years After', *Proceedings of the British Academy* LX 393–412 = append. 2 in *World of Odysseus*⁴.

(*Use and Abuse of History*) *The Use and Abuse of History*, London, Chatto & Windus; New York, The Viking Press, 1975.

(1975) 'Anthropology and the Classics', ch. 6 in *Use and Abuse of History*.

(*The Olympic Games*, with H. W. Pleket) *The Olympic Games: The First Thousand Years*, London, Chatto & Windus; New York, The Viking Press, 1976.

(*Studies in Roman Property*, ed.) *Studies in Roman Property*, Cambridge University Press, 1976.

(1976a) 'Private Farm Tenancy in Italy before Diocletian', ch. 6 in *Studies in Roman Property*.

(1976b) 'In lieblicher Bläue', *Arion*, n.s., III 79–95.

(1976c) 'Colonies – an Attempt at a Typology', *Transactions of the Royal Historical Society*, 5 ser., XXVI 167–88.

(1976d) 'The Freedom of the Citizen in the Greek World', *Talanta* VII 1–23.

(*Aspects of Antiquity*²) *Aspects of Antiquity: Discoveries and Controversies*, 2 ed., Penguin, 1977.

(*Atlas of Classical Archaeology*, ed.) *Atlas of Classical Archaeology*, London, Chatto & Windus; New York, McGraw-Hill, 1977.

(1977a) 'The Ancient City: from Fustel de Coulanges to Max Weber and Beyond', *Comparative Studies in Society and History* XIX 305–27.

(1977b) '"Progress" in Historiography', *Daedalus* CVI, no. 3, 125–42.

(*World of Odysseus*⁴) *The World of Odysseus*, rev. ed., London, Chatto & Windus; New York, The Viking Press, 1978.

(1978a) 'The Fifth-Century Athenian Empire: A Balance Sheet', ch. 5 in P. D. A. Garnsey and C. R. Whittaker, ed., *Imperialism in the Ancient World*, Cambridge University Press.

(1978b) 'Empire in the Graeco-Roman World', *Greece and Rome* XXV 1–5 = *Review* II 55–68.

(*Ancient Sicily*²) *Ancient Sicily to the Arab Conquest*, rev. ed., London, Chatto & Windus, 1979.

(1979) 'Slavery and the Historians', *Histoire sociale – Social History* XII 247–61.

(1980) *The Idea of a Theatre: the Greek Experience*, London, British Museum Publications.

(*Ancient Slavery and Modern Ideology*) *Ancient Slavery and Modern Ideology*, London, Chatto & Windus; New York, The Viking Press, 1980.
(*Early Greece²*) *Early Greece: the Bronze and Archaic Ages*, 2. ed., London, Chatto & Windus, 1981; New York, Norton, 1982.
(*Legacy of Greece*, ed.) *The Legacy of Greece: A New Appraisal.* Oxford University Press, 1981.

SELECTED ESSAYS AND REVIEWS

(1935) Review of: *The Cambridge Ancient History*, vols. 1–10 (1923–34), *Zeitschrift für Sozialforschung* IV 289–90.
(1937) Review of E. Ciccotti, *La civiltà del mondo antico*, 2 vols. (1935), *American Historical Review* XLII 277–9.
(1939) Review of: *The Cambridge Ancient History*, vol. XI (1936), *Political Science Quarterly* LIV 609–11.
(1941a) Review of: W. Durant, *The Life of Greece* (1939), *Political Science Quarterly* LVI 127–9.
(1941b) Review of: B. Farrington, *Science and Politics in the Ancient World* (1939); M. P. Nilsson, *Greek Popular Religion* (1940); H. W. Parke, *A History of the Delphic Oracle* (1939), *Zeitschrift für Sozialforschung* IX 502–10.
(1948) Review of: H. Frankfort, *Kingship and the Gods* (1948), *Political Science Quarterly* LXIII 275–81.
(1951a) Review of: Xenophon, *L'économique*, ed. P. Chantraine (1949), *Classical Philology* XLVI 252–3.
(1951b) Review of: 'Some Problems of Greek Law: A Consideration of Pringsheim on Sale', *Seminar* IX 72–91 (review of Pringsheim (1950)).
(1957) Review of: J. Walter Jones, *The Law and Legal Theory of the Greeks* (1956), *Law Quarterly Review* LXXIII 253–6.
(1958) Review of: A. E. Boak, *Man-Power Shortage and the Fall of the Roman Empire in the West* (1955), *Journal of Roman Studies* XLVIII 156–64; cf 'Manpower and the Fall of Rome', ch. 12 in *Aspects of Antiquity*.
(1959) 'The Originality of the Greek City-State', *The Listener* LXI 289–93.
(1959–60) 'Technology in the Ancient World' (a review-article), *Economic History Review* XII 120–5.
(1960a) 'The Emperor Diocletian', *The Listener* LXIII 447–9, 474 (cf. *Aspects of Antiquity*, ch. 11).
(1960b) Review of: E. Gibbon, *The Decline and Fall of the Roman Empire*, abridged D. M. Low (1960); R. Syme, *The Roman Revolution*, paperback ed., (1960); M. Grant, *The World of Rome* (1960), *The Spectator* (7 October) 527–8.
(1961a) 'The Greeks: the Growth of the Polis', *The Listener* LXV 176–8.
(1962a) 'The Myth of Sparta', *The Listener* LXVIII 171–3.
(1962b) Review of: W. Jaeger, *Early Christianity and Greek Paideia* (1961), *New Statesman* LXIII 566–7.
(1963a) Review of: J. Vogt, *Von der Gleichwertigkeit der Geschlechter in der bürgerlichen Gesellschaft der Griechen* (1960), *Gnomon* XXXV 313–14.
(1963b) 'Crete, the Legend and the Fact', *The Listener* LXIX 493–5 (cf. 'The Rediscovery of Crete', ch. 1 in *Aspects of Antiquity*).
(1963c) Review of: J. Hawkes and L. Woolley ed., *The UNESCO History of Mankind*,

vol. 1: *Prehistory and the Beginnings of Civilization* (1963), *New Statesman* LXV 906–7.

(1963d) Review of: W. H. McNeill, *The Rise of the West* (1963), *New York Review of Books* I (17 October) 4–5.

(1964a) 'Year One', *Horizon* VI 4–17 (cf. *Aspects of Antiquity*, ch. 15).

(1964b) 'Plato in Sicily', *The Listener* LXXII 871–3 (cf. *Aspects of Antiquity*, ch. 6).

(1964c) 'Plato and Athens', *The Listener* LXXII 967–9 (cf. *Aspects of Antiquity*, ch. 6).

(1964d) 'Etruscan Things' (a review-article), *New York Review of Books* II (5 November) 17–20 (cf. *Aspects of Antiquity*, ch. 8).

(1964e) Review of: H. Rahner, S. J., *Greek Myths and Christian Beginnings*, trans. B. Batteshaw (1963), *New York Review of Books* II (5 March) 14–15 (cf. *Aspects of Antiquity*, ch. 14.1).

(1964f) Review of: M. Goguel, *The Primitive Church*, trans. H. C. Snape (1964), *New York Review of Books* III (20 August) 8–9 (cf. *Aspects of Antiquity*, ch. 14.2).

(1964g) 'The Crisis in the Classics', *The Sunday Times* (24 March) 37; enlarged version in J. H. Plumb, ed., *Crisis in the Humanities*, Penguin (1964), 11–23.

(1965a) Review of: A. French, *The Growth of the Athenian Economy* (1964), *Economic Journal* LXXV 849–51.

(1965b) 'The Silent Women of Rome', *Horizon* VII 56–64 (cf. *Aspects of Antiquity*, ch. 10).

(1965c) 'The Rediscovery of Crete', *Horizon* VII 64–75 (cf. *Aspects of Antiquity*, ch. 1).

(1965d) 'Manpower and the Fall of Rome', *The Listener* LXXIV 791–4 (cf. *Aspects of Antiquity*, ch. 12).

(1965e) Review of: R. Syme, *Sallust* (1964); F. Millar, *A Study of Cassius Dio* (1964), *New Statesman* LXIX 46–7.

(1965f) Review of: C. M. Bowra, *Pindar* (1964), *New Statesman* LXIX 575 (cf. *Aspects of Antiquity*, ch. 3).

(1965g) Review of: D. D. Kosambi, *The Culture and Civilization of Ancient India in Historical Outline* (1965), *New Statesman* LXX 252–3.

(1965h) Review of: S. Zeitlin, *Who Crucified Jesus?* 4 ed. (1964); A. N. Sherwin-White, *Roman Society and Roman Law in the New Testament* (1963), *New York Review of Books* III (28 January) 4–5 (cf. *Aspects of Antiquity*, ch. 14.3).

(1965i) Review of: E. Vermeule, *Greece in the Bronze Age* (1964); W. Taylour, *The Mycenaeans* (1964), *New York Review of Books* IV (11 March 7–8).

(1965j) Review of: A. L. Oppenheim, *Ancient Mesopotamia: Portrait of a Dead Civilization* (1964); R. Flacelière, *Daily Life in Greece at the Time of Pericles* (1965), *New York Review of Books* V (14 October) 30–2.

(1966a) 'A Few Words from the Etruscans', *Horizon* VIII 104–9 (cf. *Aspects of Antiquity*, ch. 8).

(1966b) 'Etruscans and Romans', *The Listener* LXXV 127–9 (cf. *Aspects of Antiquity*, ch. 9).

(1966c) 'The Gold Tablets of Santa Severa', *The Listener* LXXV 163–5 (cf. *Aspects of Antiquity*, ch. 9).

(1966d) Review of: Y. Yadin, *Masada: Herod's Fortress and the Zealot's Last Stand* (1966), *New Statesman* LXXII 832–3.

(1966e) Review of: A. W. Gouldner. *Enter Plato: Classical Greece and The Origins of*

Social Theory (1966); J. E. Raven, *Plato's Thought in the Making* (1966), *New York Review of Books* VII (18 August, 27–9.

(1966f) 'New Look at Ancient History for Sixth Formers', *The Times* (22 April) 9.

(1966g) 'Unfreezing the Classics', *The Times Literary Supplement* LXV 289–90.

(1967a) 'Lost, the Trojan War', *Horizon* IX 50–5 (cf. *Aspects of Antiquity*, ch. 2).

(1967b) 'Class Struggles', *The Listener* LXXVIII 201–2.

(1967c) Review of: J. Pope-Hennessy, *Sins of the Fathers, A Study of the Atlantic Slave Traders, 1441–1807* (1967), *The Listener* LXXVIII 637.

(1967d) Review of: D. B. Davis, *The Problem of Slavery in Western Culture* (1966), *New York Review of Books* VIII (26 January), 6–10.

(1967e) Review of: S. Barr, *The Mask of Jove* (1966); R. MacMullen, *Enemies of the Roman Order* (1967), *New York Review of Books* VIII (18 May) 37–9.

(1967f) Review of: C. W. Blegen and M. Rawson, *The Palace of Nestor at Pylos in Western Messenia*, vol. 1 (1967); G. E. Mylonas, *Mycenae and the Mycenaean Age* (1967), *New York Review of Books* IX (3 August) 32–4.

(1968a) 'Must the Artist Rebel? Ask the Greeks', *Horizon* X 50–5.

(1968b) 'Race Prejudice in the Ancient World', *The Listener* LXXIX 146–7.

(1968c) Review of: T. Cole, *Democritus and the Sources of Greek Anthropology* (1968); L. Edelstein, *The Idea of Progress in Classical Antiquity* (1967), *New York Review of Books* X (20 June) 36–7.

(1969a) Review of: S. Anglo, *Machiavelli* (1969), *The Listener* LXXXI 786–91.

(1969b) Review of: W. Goodman, *The Committee: The Extraordinary Career of the House Committee on Un-American Activities* (1968), *New Statesman* LXXVII 296–7.

(1969c) Review of: J. W. Mavor, *Voyage to Atlantis* (1969), *New York Review of Books* XII (22 May) 38–40.

(1970a) Review of: Aristotle, *Economique*, ed. B. A. van Groningen and A. Wartelle (1968), *Classical Review* XX 315–19.

(1970b) 'The Battle of Actium', *The Listener* LXXXIV 372–5.

(1970c) Review of: E. Badian, *Roman Imperialism in the Late Republic* (1970); F. Millar, *The Roman Empire and Its Neighbours* (1970); M. Grant, *The Climax of Rome* (1970); J. Vogt, *The Decline of Rome*, trans. J. Sondheimer (1970), *New York Review of Books* XIV (29 January) 52–4.

(1971) 'New Developments in Classical Studies', in *The Great Ideas Today*, New York, Encyclopaedia Britannica Publications, pp. 122–67.

(1972a) Introduction to Thucydides, *The Peloponnesian War*, trans. R. Warner, Penguin, pp. 9–32.

(1972b) 'The World of Greece and Rome', in D. Daiches and A. Thorlby, ed., *Literature and Western Civilization*, vol. I: *The Classical World*, London, Aldus Books, pp. 23–47.

(1972c) Review of: Connor Cruise O'Brien, *The Suspecting Glance* (1972), *The Listener* LXXXVII 723–4.

(1972d) 'The Imperial Face of Democratic Athens', *The Listener* LXXXVIII 495–7.

(1972e) Review of: D. Behrend, *Attische Pachturkunden* (1970), *Tijdschrift voor Rechtsgeschiedenis* XV 559–61.

(1974) Review of: Robin Lane Fox, *Alexander the Great* (1974), *New York Times Book Review* (28 April) 16–18.

(1975a) Review of: P. Anderson, *Passages from Antiquity to Feudalism* and *The Lineages of the Absolutist State* (1975), *The Guardian* (6 February) 14.

(1975b) Review of: J. Vogt, *Ancient Slavery and the Ideal of Man*, trans. T. Wiedemann (1975), *The Times Literary Supplement* (14 November) 1348.

(1975c) Review of: E. D. Genovese, *Roll, Jordan, Roll: The World the Slaves Made*
(1975), *The Spectator* CCXXXV 475–6.

(1975d) Review of: W. B. Stanford and J. V. Luce, *The Quest for Ulysses* (1974),
Journal of the Royal Society of Arts CXXIII 610–11.

(1976a) 'The Most Famous of All Great Historians', *The Observer Magazine* (8
February) 13–15 (on Edward Gibbon).

(1976b) 'A Peculiar Institution?', *The Times Literary Supplement* (2 July) 819–21.

(1977a) Review of: F. Millar, *The Emperor in the Roman World* (1977), *The Times*
(17 March) 22.

(1977b) 'Censorship in Classical Antiquity', *The Times Literary Supplement* (29 July)
923–5.

(1979) 'Aegean Art and the Politics of Loan Exhibitions', *New York Times* (Arts and
Leisure Section, 28 October), 1, 28.

INDEX